LAW & Advertising

CURRENT LEGAL ISSUES

FOR AGENCIES,

ADVERTISERS

AND ATTORNEYS.

[**Dean K. Fueroghne**]

THE COPY WORKSHOP
2144 N. HUDSON • CHICAGO, IL
(312) 871-1179 • FAX (312) 281-4643

For my dad—I think he would have been proud.

This publication is designed to provide accurate and authoritative information with regard to the subject matter covered. It is sold with the understanding that neither the author nor the publisher is engaged in rendering legal, accounting, or other professional service. If legal advice or other expert assistance is required, the services of a competent professional person should be sought.

From a Declaration of Principles jointly adopted by a Committee of the American Bar Association and a Committee of Publishers.

LIBRARY OF CONGRESS
Library of Congress Catalog Card Number: 95-68129

Fueroghne, Dean Keith.
Law & Advertising — Current Legal Issues for Agencies, Advertisers and Attorneys / Dean Keith Fueroghne.
p. cm.
Bibliography: p.
Includes index.
ISBN 0-9621415-8-5
1. Advertising laws—United States—Popular works. I. Title.
1995

Published by The Copy Workshop • Chicago, IL
2144 N. Hudson • Chicago 60614 • 312-871-1179

Printed in the United States of America
1 2 3 4 5 6 7 8 9 0

i

FOREWORD

Law & Advertising by Dean K. Fueroghne is an excellent compilation of the laws affecting advertising.

In one volume, Mr. Fueroghne has comprehensively brought together the major areas of legal concern in the review and preparation of advertising copy.

As an attorney who has specialized in the advertising field for 28 years, I can appreciate the effort and comprehensiveness of Mr. Fueroghne's publication.

I believe that *Law & Advertising* will act as an excellent reference tool for advertising practitioners regarding the legal framework in which they operate.

It is of course important that actual advertising copy and concerns be reviewed by an attorney experienced in these matters, as the law is constantly evolving and the interpretation of the applicable statutes, regulations and policies will depend upon the specific advertisements involved.

Any attorney practicing in this area will be more effective in solving advertising problems and advising clients when the attorney is dealing with informed laymen.

Law & Advertising will greatly assist in informing the layman about legal concerns in order to prepare more effective advertising which complies with legal requirements, and to be more efficient and effective in dealing with their attorneys on such matters.

Congratulations on a job well done.

Stephen P. Durchslag

Mr. Durchslag is a partner in the Chicago law firm of Winston & Strawn. He specializes in advertising, promotion and entertainment law.

He is a member of the American Advertising Federation (AAF) Law Committee, and the Board of the Promotional Marketing Association of America. A graduate of Harvard Law School, he is a frequent lecturer and writer on advertising and promotion matters.

PREFACE

A number of years ago while studying law at U.C.L.A., I took an advertising law class. The class was attended mostly by lawyers and professionals in advertising. The professor began by announcing that there would not be a text for the course because none existed.

That experience combined with the naivete about the implications of law that I've seen in the advertising business has led to the creation of this book. While advertising is a creative business, I have seen many agencies create more liability for themselves and their clients than awards for their ads. Most advertisers feel that advertising laws (the few that they are aware of) restrict the power of their message. Nonetheless, they need to understand these laws and their consequences.

The law has built a wall around itself with unfamiliar words and uncommon reasoning—a wall that most cannot break through. Until now there was simply no single source to provide the advertiser with ready access to information about the laws that impact the business of advertising. This book attempts to provide one source a person can use to learn about such areas of law as agency, contract, copyright, trademark, privacy and publicity rights, FTC regulations, and others.

This book is primarily addressed to all who produce, distribute, and prosper from advertising—the account executive, the art director, the copywriter, the creative director, the advertising manager—whether in the agency business or an in-house advertising department. I have tried to explain the legal principles as clearly as possible, using cases as examples to illustrate each of the points. This book is also addressed to lawyers who need a compiled resource of current advertising law.

Because of the impact of legislation, court decisions, and consumerism on the advertising field, the law should be well understood by anyone who creates and implements advertising.

While I have tried to assure that the examples used in this book are current, the case law, statutes, and regulations should not be used as authoritative unless the user researches them at the time of use to determine their validity or any changes or modifications since the date of publication. This book is intended to provide insight into the areas of law that affect advertising and to allow the reader to know when to seek specific legal advice. It is not intended to be construed as offering legal advice in any way. As with any legal problem, when in doubt, consult an attorney who specializes in that particular area.

So many people have added to this book that I must acknowledge their help. I wish to thank Lee Lefton, for his guidance, help, and encouragement in the first book I wrote on this subject, and for the time spent editing, refining, and helping me see the trees for the forest.

I also wish to acknowledge the following people who reviewed various portions of this book as it was originally written and who provided valuable insights and stories: Laurel Phillips, former attorney for Ogilvy & Mather, Los Angeles; Dan Katz, president of L.A. Ads; and Don Barshinger, creative director for Slack, Key, Barshinger, Chicago.

Many thanks to Melissa Davis, attorney, Denver, for her tireless editing efforts and advice. And many thanks to Bruce and Lorelei Bendinger for their enthusiasm, advice, and help throughout this project. To all, I hope it is justified by the result.

To everyone I've worked with over the years in this business, who have provided the stories —sometimes humorous, sometimes sad— that have helped to illustrate the book, I extend my thanks. Many I have learned from; some I have walked away from shaking my head. But all have contributed to this book— some more than they would have liked.

Dean Keith Fueroghne

INTRODUCTION

Here are some interesting trivial tidbits.

Did you know that advertising expenditures in the United States exceeded $109 billion[1] in 1987? This is more than is spent on all of public education in this country in a year. And it's a third of what the United States spends yearly on national defense. The combined expenditure on advertising for the 10 largest companies in the country is greater than the gross national product of most nations!

Did you know that a major national television commercial will be viewed by more people than the total number of people who have seen *Gone with the Wind*? The average American watches about 20,000 television commercials each year. Major manufacturers will spend a quarter of a million dollars to produce a 30-second television commercial that is designed to promote a 30-cent item.

What this trivia illustrates is that advertising is a very expensive, very pervasive, very specialized, and very institutionalized segment of our social and economic environment. But did you ever stop to ask yourself: How does advertising interact with the restrictions of society? This is one of the primary questions this book will explore.

It is generally accepted that advertising is a part of the business process. Advertising goes hand-in-hand with moving products and services from the rawest of materials to the ultimate consumer. Although it is difficult to precisely define advertising, in essence it is the catalyst that keeps a free enterprise market operating. Countries that don't have a free enterprise system don't have advertising in the commercial sense because they don't need it. A prime example of this situation is Red China. Before trade was opened up with the West, consumerism was controlled by the government. Afterwards, Western products were introduced into the Chinese culture along with something new— "advertising."

Most textbooks teach that modern advertising began in the early 1900's. Greats like William Benton, George Batton, Albert Lasker, Chester Bowles, Bruce Barton, Ernest Elmo Calkins, Leo Burnett, David Ogilvy, and others whose names you may recognize, did not create the process of advertising. What we consider to be advertising in its purest sense was around for thousands, perhaps millions, of years before the time of these industry giants.

Because it is such a powerful marketing tool, advertising draws more than its share of criticism, despite an ever increasing awareness and emphasis on social responsibility. Those advertisers who have taken a naive attitude and ignored their responsibilities have learned the pitfalls of viewing the consumer as simply a passive and unquestioning viewer of clever and creative messages.

The consumer's skeptical impression of advertising will continue to increase. Because of this, a major challenge for the advertising community is to restore the credibility of its product and to check public skepticism, lest it turn to cynicism.

The demands of advertising professionals require that they keep current on all aspects of their profession. Law is one of those areas that has a powerful effect on advertising. Therefore, the new policies dictated by regulatory agencies and the interpretations of court decisions must be well understood by advertising professionals.

As our economic system has grown over the years, it has become more complex by necessity. This complexity has forced the legal system to create an equally complex mechanism to maintain the delicate balance that exists between free enterprise and consumer protection.

On one side stand the advertiser and agency trying to display their product as favorably as possible. On the other side stands the consumer, guarded by a protective legal barrier which provides a sense of security in making purchasing decisions. The government has seen to that. Between these two constants lies a fine line. As you will see throughout the book, it is one beyond which neither side would be prudent to extend.

Throughout history, as promoters of products and advertising services have become more sophisticated and, indeed, clever, the legal system has had to keep pace. This book was written to discuss the relationship between advertiser and regulator, what brought it about, and its practical applications.

Many years ago, Calvin Coolidge said that "advertising ministers to the spiritual side of trade." While some consumers have expressed a fear of—and others have indicated a hope for—the demise of advertising, it is still integral to our market environment. Advertising provides a valuable service to the seller, the buyer, and the public and serves the spirit of trade only so long as it remains truthful and honest.

HOW TO USE THIS BOOK

As you read this book there are a few things I feel you should keep in mind. Advertising is affected by many areas of law, and each chapter of this book covers a separate area of law. The law tends to be compartmentalized. As a result, one area of law differs from another. And, therefore, the subject of each chapter differs. The regulation of each area of law varies; copyright has no effect on publicity rights, comparative advertising regulation has no effect on products liability.

You may see inconsistencies in logic from chapter to chapter. What you're actually noticing is the variations in the different areas of law. Always consider the subject of the chapter, and you'll see the law in the proper light. Also, read each chapter carefully and completely—do not skim. The subject matter is far too complex for that. I would strongly recommend reading the book straight through the first time. Many of the topics build on each other, and there is a reason that the chapters are in the order that they are. When questions arise about specific subjects, you can go back to the appropriate chapter for reference.

Another important point to consider is that you will find many examples of ads that were produced by others that violate the laws illustrated in this book. Citing such examples will not protect you if you are caught in similar violations. The fact that 20 people get away with robbery doesn't make it legal!

Finally, as you read, you will undoubtedly have questions that will be brought up by the information in this book. That's the idea—and a clue that your question might best be answered by an attorney who specializes in that area. This book cannot answer every question that arises; although it should answer many. What it <u>can</u> do is teach you the basics and give you the wisdom to know when it's time to consult an attorney.

NOTES ON CITES

In this book you will notice that each case has a citation (cite) following the name of the case. For those who have a background in law, these cites are all too familiar. But for those who do not, they represent some unknown code. Here is how to decipher the code.

Citations indicate where the specific court opinions can be found. A typical cite may look like this: *Dawn Donut Co. v. Hart's Food Stores, Inc.*, 267 F.2d 358 (2d Cir. 1959).

The name of the case appears first: *Dawn Donut Co. v. Hart's Food Stores, Inc.* The first number following, indicates the volume of the reporter: 267. The next series indicates the name of the reporter: F.2d (in this instance: Federal Reporter, second series). The next set of numbers shows the page where the case begins: 358. In parentheses is the circuit court where the case was decided and the date it was decided.

The various sources are cited by abbreviations as we saw above. The following is a list of the most common sources used in this book.

U.S.	United States Supreme Court Reports
F.	Federal Reporter (decisions by the Circuit

	Court of Appeals)
F.2d	Federal Reporter, second series
F. Supp.	Federal Supplement (decisions of the United States District Courts)
F.C.C.	Federal Communications Commission Reports
F.T.C.	Federal Trade Commission Reports
U.S.L.W.	United States Law Weekly
U.S.P.Q.	United States Patent Quarterly
A.	Atlantic Reporter
A.2d	Atlantic Reporter, second series
N.E.	North Eastern Reporter
N.E.2d	North Eastern Reporter, second series
N.W.	North Western Reporter
N.W.2d	North Western Reporter, second series
P.	Pacific Reporter
P.2d	Pacific Reporter, second series
S.E.	South Eastern Reporter
S.E.2d	South Eastern Reporter, second series
S.W.	South Western Reporter
S.W.2d	South Western Reporter, second series
S.	Southern Reporter
S.2d	Southern Reporter, second series

In addition, each state court system has its own reporters and digests where cases are recorded. While there are far too many to list here, I will give a few examples of the basic California sources. A complete list of abbreviations for all states can be found at any law library.

	California Reports (series one through three)
Cal.	California Reports (series one through three)
Cal.App.	California Appellate Reports (series one through three)

Cal.Dec.   California Decisions
Cal.Rptr.   California Reporter

ABOUT THE AUTHOR

Dean Keith Fueroghne has been an advertising professional for nearly 27 years as art director, advertising manager, creative director and president of his own agency. He is currently Vice President of Creative Services for a Los Angeles based advertising agency.

With degrees from the University of California and Edison State College, he has combined the study of law with daily involvement in advertising.

The author has also taught advertising law at the University of California at Los Angeles. He has consulted with law firms across the country on advertising law cases and has lectured and written articles on the subject.

Fueroghne has been inducted into *Who's Who in The World*, *Who's Who in America* and *Who's Who in Advertising*.

---

[1] *The Wall Street Journal*, June 8,1987, p. 10, col. 1.

CONTENTS

Contents

CHAPTER 1

THE DEVELOPMENT OF CONTROL OVER ADVERTISING

There's a sucker born every minute.
— P. T. Barnum

W. C. Crosby was an astute businessman. He understood all too well the power of advertising. Crosby had a knack for practicing the subtle art of persuasion. He knew how to pique a person's interest by using the right words: how to light a fire in the prospect, how to promote, how to sell—abilities that any great ad man must possess. He lived during the early 1900s, when he eloquently described his profession as "a business, like all business," which "takes rise from the conditions of life about it and adapts itself as does social life. And . . . plays an invariable chord in the human make-up . . . according to the times and circumstances."

His was not a name that would go down in the history books as one of the great advertising giants. He would, however, be remembered as a craftsman of the art of persuasion. W. C. Crosby was a con man, and one of the best. He kept company at the turn-of-the-century with such notables as Willie "The Sleepy Kid" Loftus, Jimmy McViccor, Charley (changed to Henry in the movie *The Sting*) Gondorf, "The Crying Kid," "Hungry Joe" Lewis, George Pole, and "Big Joe" Turley.

The con man's migration to America was a natural occurrence. One frontier opened itself up to another. Long before the Civil War, the con man could be found in the Gold Rush shanty towns of California, riding the paddle wheelers down the

Mississippi to New Orleans, drifting through high society in the East, and riding the first rails to the West.

W. C. Crosby and the others brought with them the skills of the great European harbinger, Richard Town, who had so incurred the wrath of his victims that on May 23, 1712, in London, he was hanged. His open-air execution was viewed by a cheering throng of spectators. "My friends, this is my birthday," Town stated coolly. "I see you have come to help me honor it. . . . my compliments, and thank you for coming to my adventure."

THE POSTAL FRAUD LAWS —THE FIRST FORM OF ADVERTISING REGULATION

In 1872, stringent postal fraud laws were passed in order to wage a relentless war against the con man who was perpetrating his grandiose schemes through the mail. While these laws were needed, they did not do away with the con man overnight. Unfortunately, passage of these laws was only a small step toward stemming the tide of mail fraud. Even in the early 1900s, American con men still ran rampant among a gullible public—a public that responded to advertisements for mining rights, real estate, securities, inventions, cure-alls and medicines of all types.

The bulk of advertising during that time was carried through the newspaper—the only media readily available to the masses. All that was required on the con man's part was the up-front capital to purchase relatively inexpensive newspaper space and postage stamps. Despite teeth-gritting indignation, the victims were virtually helpless against the guile of the con man. In fact, the Post Office estimated that in 1911 alone, con men netted $77 million from duped investors in mail-order schemes.

Peddlers placed advertisements offering nostrums and medicines guaranteed to cure anything. A man named Perkins sold through the mails two shiny rods he called "Metallic Tractors." These were to be passed over the ailing victim to redirect his "electrical" current and cure him of any disease. Perkins believed his own swindle so well that when he contracted yellow fever, he refused medical attention believing his "Metallic Tractors" would heal him. For three days the rods were passed over Perkins; then, as you might expect, he died.

The Essence Of Life

A newspaper ad appeared in the *Connecticut Courant* in October 1834:

●●●●●●●●●●●●●●●●●●●●●
MOORE'S ESSENCE OF LIFE
A safe and efficient remedy for whooping cough
Sold by appointment at the sign of
the Good Samaritan.
●●●●●●●●●●●●●

The Essence of Life was nothing more than colored water. Many bogus doctors and pharmacists offered products that would cure almost any ailment known to man. Turlington's Original Balsam, for example, promised to remedy 51 deadly diseases. In another instance, Dr. Spear offered his magic Balsam of Life through newspaper advertisements. It was claimed that the product would cure consumption (tuberculosis) overnight. The con man who offered Brandreth's Pills placed advertisements in newspapers for years which read:

●●●●●●●●●●●●●●●●●●●●●
Remember in all cases of disease
no matter whether
it be cold or cough, whether it be asthma or
consumption, whether it be rheumatism or pleurisy,
whether it be typhus fever and ague, or bilious fever,
cramp or whooping cough or measles, whether it be
scarlet fever or small pox, Brandreth's Pills will
surely do more than all the medicines of the drug stores
for your restoration to health.
●●●●●●●●●●●●●●●●●●●●

A Portrait Of The President

When the mail-order fraud reached its peak, the perpetrators seemed to take a perverse pleasure not only in the fraud itself, but in pouring salt into their victims' wounds. They often exhibited the sort of "I dare you" attitude that challenged the victims to protest. The following classic nose-thumber appeared in over 200 newspapers in 1882—the year after President Garfield's assassination caused immense national grief:

● ● ● ● ● ● ● ● ● ● ● ●
I HAVE SECURED
the authorized steel engravings of the late
President Garfield, executed by the United States Government,
approved by the President of the United States, by Congress,
and by every member of the President's family as the most
faithful of all the portraits of the President. It was
executed by the Government's most expert steel engravers,
and I will send a copy from the original plate, in full
colors approved by the Government,
postpaid, for one dollar each.
● ● ● ● ● ● ● ● ● ● ● ● ● ● ● ● ● ●

To each person sending in the required $1, the con man mailed the promised engraving of President Garfield—a 5-cent U.S. postage stamp.

Some 15 years later an offer appeared in newspapers promising a way to eliminate annoying moths:

● ●
DO THE MOTHS BOTHER YOU?
If so, send us fifty cents in stamps, and we will furnish
a recipe CERTAIN SURE to drive the pests from
furs or rugs or any other old things.
● ●

A few weeks later the consumer received the foolproof recipe, as advertised. The reply read as follows:

● ●
Dear Madam: Dampen the article in question in
kerosene thoroughly (to soak it is even better)
and add one lighted match.
If the moths do not disappear, your money
will be cheerfully refunded.
Yours truly, The Buncomb Company
● ●

Indeed, it was the era of the con man—of getting wealthy off the gullibility of the consumer. Some got very wealthy. In 1927 (his last year of operation) a con man named Hugh B. Monjar brought in a cool $7,666,631 before being sent to a federal prison for mail fraud.

In the late 1800s and early 1900s the exploits of the con man were the main form of deceptive advertising. This is without a doubt where consumers learned distrust for all advertising—a skepticism many consumers have to this day.

Times, however, have changed. No longer can the advertiser rampantly seek out the weaknesses in consumers and exploit them as did early con men. The consumer now has stiffer advertising controls on his side. These controls have brought heavy restrictions for today's advertiser, who has to deal with the problem of being heard in our over-communicated society. Yet, the advertiser must be very careful about how he gets the consumer's attention. The myriad issues the advertiser must consider today are far more serious than they were in earlier days before regulation.

With the advent of the Federal Trade Commission (FTC) in 1914, a force of regulation against taking unfair advantage of the consumer began. Over the years since its inception, the consumer has gained substantial protection.

THE CREATION OF THE FEDERAL TRADE COMMISSION

The FTC was conceived by Congress in 1914 to enforce the country's faltering antitrust laws. Ironically, the first two cases it heard involved false advertising.[1] The only intent of the FTC at that time was to preserve fair competition between businesses by preventing restraint of trade—that is, such acts as creating a monopoly, which reduce or eliminate competition. Although this concerned only how businesses dealt with each other, in essence, the Federal Trade Commission Act protected consumers because it protected sellers against each other. This was an indirect consumer benefit at best.

Since its establishment, the scope of the FTC has been enlarged with the adoption of the Wheeler-Lea Amendments[2] in 1938. These brought direct protection for the consumer by modifying the authority of the FTC. The commission was originally authorized to regulate "unfair methods of competition in commerce." The Wheeler-Lea Amendments, however, added to this definition the phrase ". . . and unfair or deceptive acts or practices in commerce," thus expanding the act's coverage to consumers, as well as to competitors. The emphasis shifted to protecting the consumer against injury. This has been extended even further with the enactment of the FTC Improvement Act in 1975. We'll examine this act in more detail in Chapter 2 and 3.

In 1962, President John F. Kennedy gave a special message to the Congress on the importance of protecting the consumer interest.[3] He stated that every person, as a consumer, had four rights: To be informed; to be safe; to have a choice; and, to be heard. And, he promoted legislation to protect these rights.

This sparked the modern consumer movement. Since that time, major new legislation and amendments to prior regulation have been enacted. The FTC and the courts have dramatically increased their efforts to protect the consumer and to place him on equal ground with the advertiser.

The Long Arm Of The FTC

The FTC, as a federal organization, is assigned the task of policing advertising on a national level under Section 5 of the act. As a result, Section 5 only covers advertising that promotes products involving interstate commerce—transactions between one state and another. The advertiser must realize, however, that he is not safe from the FTC if his products are sold only in his own state. Courts are broadly interpreting the act to also bring intrastate activities within the authority of the FTC. This means that if any part or ingredient of the product was manufactured or purchased out of state, the courts consider interstate commerce to be involved; therefore, the product falls within the control of the federal act.

The FTC's influence reaches into state activities in another way. Most states have laws that carry the same implications as the federal act. These are known as "Little FTC Acts" and Uniform Deceptive Acts and Practices Acts (UDAP), and are discussed in Chapter 3. In fact, many of these state statutes direct the state courts to be guided by FTC decisions. California, for example, controls false and deceptive advertising under Section 17500 of the California Civil Code.

Disclosure Of Information

An obvious element in creating advertising is determining what to say in an ad. The advertiser must determine which of all the facts and points about a product should be featured in the limited space of an ad. Generally, regulation of advertising addresses the availability of information and how it is presented. Enough information should be made available to the consumer for him to make a valid purchasing decision—one in which he gets everything he bargained for, without surprise or deception.

In recent years, legislation has required that accurate information be disclosed in many areas of the marketplace, including the durability of light bulbs, octane ratings for gasoline, mileage-per-gallon statistics for new automobiles, and care labeling of all textile wearing apparel. The list continues to grow (See Chapter 3 for specific information on these regulated products and industries.)

The way in which the advertiser provides information and the relevance of that information are areas that must be carefully considered. Because of the competitive nature of the market system in the United States, every advertiser tries to show his product in the best possible light. As everyone in advertising knows, a good ad demonstrates the product's strengths while playing down its weaknesses. But when the strengths are distorted or when significant weaknesses are either played down or ignored altogether, a deception is created.

While it may be required, information disclosure creates certain problems simply by the nature of the marketplace. Well-established manufacturers may tend to avoid disclosing too much product information in their advertising for fear of opening opportunities for new competitors to enter or expand their market. An example of this situation is found in the history of the gasoline industry. Gasoline manufacturers attempted to avoid disclosing gasoline octane formulation because this would have highlighted the fact that ratings of high-priced brands were substantially the same as those of low-priced, unadvertised brands. Since the survival of the small independent manufacturers depended largely on their ability to maintain a cost advantage, they could not have easily undertaken expensive advertising campaigns to inform consumers about comparative octane ratings.

In other product areas, information disclosure may create an industrywide disadvantage for all sellers. Resistance in the past to an intensive advertising campaign promoting the smoking of low tar and nicotine cigarettes as a way to reduce health hazards would have obviously played up the fact that smoking any cigarette creates health problems. There was a reluctance to do this because total cigarette sales would suffer as a result.

Even after scientific evidence proved that smoking is harmful, advertisers of both low and high tar cigarettes played down negative comparison claims to avoid negative reactions toward other brands in their product lines. In fact, aggressive marketing of low tar, low nicotine brands has only recently occurred as a result of increased health issues and government pressure.

In December of 1970, cigarette manufacturers responded to threatened action by the government by voluntarily including the government test results for tar and nicotine contents in their advertisements. Soon after, television advertising of cigarettes was ended. Now there is talk of a federal statutory ban on all cigarette advertising. We'll discuss cigarette, as well as alcohol, advertising and related issues in detail in Chapter 13.

Another problem in gathering and disclosing accurate product information is the extreme expense, especially in certain industries. For example, technical data such as chemical formulas for over-the-counter drugs probably have no meaning to the average consumer. Yet the cost of providing this information could, for many manufacturers, be prohibitive.

UNFAIRNESS VIOLATIONS

In contrast to straight deception, the FTC has developed a category of unfairness violations. Unfairness takes into account whether a practice, which is not considered unlawful, offends public policy as established by statute, common law, or otherwise. A practice is also considered unfair if it is immoral, unethical, oppressive, or unscrupulous, or causes substantial injury to consumers, competitors, or other business people. This gives the FTC room to maneuver. It allows the commission to pursue activities that it couldn't under the principle of straight deception.

As the FTC has expanded the unfairness concept, it has determined that there are certain types of advertisements that can be considered nondeceptive, yet still be unfair. These include claims made without prior substantiation, claims which exploit vulnerable groups like children and the elderly, and where the advertiser fails to provide consumers with certain information about competing products. We will discuss unfairness issues in more detail in Chapter 2.

CRIME AND PUNISHMENT—
DECEPTIVE ADVERTISING

The most significant developments in recent federal regulation of advertising involve sanctions for deceptive claims. Previously, the standard remedy for deceptive advertising was a cease-and-desist order. This consisted of an order to stop the action and not continue with the deceptive practice. Today, however, violation of the commission's cease-and-desist order can be quite expensive.

The original cease-and-desist order proved to be grossly inadequate. Advertisers, as well as their advertising agencies, routinely violated the law and went virtually unpunished, or more accurately, unnoticed. Advertisers were taking a calculated risk that the chance of being detected and ultimately prosecuted was extremely small, given the limited resources of the FTC and the tremendous amount of advertising that the commission was required to review.

However, recent efforts by the FTC have focused on eliminating the gap in enforcement of sanctions for deceptive advertising violations. One development involves corrective advertising orders. These direct the guilty advertiser to spend a specific percentage of its future advertising budget to inform the public as to the false claim that was originally made. The reasoning behind corrective advertising was that it provided a way of dissipating the effects of a previously misleading advertisement since the original ad that misled could not be removed or discounted from the minds of the consumer. Yet, it could be counteracted (or at least neutralized) if the original deceiver was required to disclose information to "properly" inform the consumer. It was hoped that this corrective ad would offset the original inaccurate impression.

In 1975 the Commission proceeded against Warner-Lambert and the advertising of its product Listerine mouth wash.[4] Listerine's advertising had claimed that the product could prevent colds because it killed germs associated with colds. This was an unsubstantiated claim, which left an inaccurate message with the consumer. This case was the first in which the Commission imposed the remedy of corrective advertising.

Sanctions

The price advertisers must pay under this sanction can be quite severe if they are found to have used misleading or deceptive advertising. For example, in 1971 the manufacturer of Ocean Spray Cranberry Juice Cocktail was required to devote 25 percent of the company's advertising budget for one year to informing the public of a previous deception.[5] The makers of Profile bread were required to expend 25 percent of their advertising budget for one year toward advertisements stating: "Profile bread will not engender weight loss," contrary to the claims of its previous advertising.[6]

"Enterprise liability" is probably the most powerful area where the FTC can sanction an entire industry. This is a relatively new concept, but one that has given broad power to the conventional cease-and-desist order. When a cease-and-desist order is filed against a particular advertiser to prohibit a deceptive practice, it applies industrywide. All other advertisers and their agencies are bound by the same order. One advertiser cannot sidestep the responsibility for a practice found to be deceptive simply by avoiding getting caught. This is the FTC's version of the shotgun effect. It gives the widest coverage from a single shot.

These sanctions are typical of the nature, extent, and

impact of the Commission's punitive efforts and of what these efforts bring to bear against deceptive advertising and those who create it. Today, false, misleading, deceptive, or unfair practices carry much greater penalties for the would-be lawbreaker.

COMPARATIVE ADVERTISING

Other considerations for the advertiser lie in the area of comparative advertising. One form of this occurs when manufacturers go head-to-head to challenge each others' claims. Specific comparative advertising of products, if inaccurate, tends to open up the challenger to the possibility of a disparagement suit or FTC intervention based on deceptive advertising practices.

Most advertisers resist this form of advertising since a manufacturer who brings a competitor's claim to the attention of the public may be looked upon negatively by the consumer. In other words: "People who live in glass houses shouldn't throw stones." The reputation of an overly aggressive advertiser may be diminished in the eyes of the consumer by exposing another company. Thus, most manufacturers tend to spend their advertising budget on the positive features of their own products.

Comparative advertising regulation stems basically from the Lanham Trademark Act of 1946,[7] Section 43(a). This Act allows a remedy for people or companies "likely to be damaged" by "false descriptions or representations" regarding comparisons of products or services. In other words, when Company X publishes an advertisement that compares its product to Company Y's product, and that ad proves to be untrue, Company X can be held liable.

Comparative advertising litigation concerns situations where a company implied a superiority of its own or an inferiority of the competitor's product. A good example of this can be found in *Smith* v. *Chanel, Inc.*[8] In this case, the perfume manufacturer Smith claimed in an advertisement that its version of Chanel perfume was "equal to the original." That claim was found by the court to be false, and under the Lanham Act, Smith was held liable.

In situations where the comparative ad claim does not fall under the federal Lanham Act, remedies are available under state law as well. False statements of this nature may well be actionable under laws against unfair competition or under tort remedies of disparagement or libel. We will discuss the Lanham Act and its relation to advertising claims more thoroughly in Chapter 8.

COUNTERADVERTISING
TO CHANGE PUBLIC OPINION

In recent years, we have seen another form of advertising take hold. It is a more useful and beneficial form, designed to offset public opinion about a specific product or industry. One example is Tampax's advertising campaign designed to counter the ill-effects it experienced because of the toxic shock syndrome scare. Another was Bristol Myers' advertising campaign attempting to offset fears about product safety after a series of tamperings and resultant poisonings had frightened consumers away from purchasing Tylenol.

INDUSTRY SELF-REGULATION

Consumer abuse or exploitation from false, misleading, or deceptive advertising doesn't necessarily have to be controlled by the government alone. Deceptive advertising may also be controlled by the advertising industry through self-regulation. We look at these issues in more depth in later chapters.

Self-regulation of advertising can be accomplished through a number of avenues. The various industry trade associations have established codes of conduct or ethics. Within the advertising industry such agencies as the American Association of Advertising Agencies, the Printing Industry Association, the American Society of Magazine Photographers, the American Advertising Federation, the Graphic Artists Guild, the Screen Actors Guild, and the American Federation of Television and Radio Artists have specific conduct requirements for their members.

In addition, the National Advertising Division/National Advertising Review Board (NAD/NARB) is the major advertising self-regulation body in the United States. The NAD/NARB inquires into complaints, evaluates them on their merits, and negotiates agreements. The board can also establish an arbitration panel to handle appeals. Lastly, the NAD/NARB can refer what it considers to be unlawful advertising to government agencies for action.

Media Regulation

The television networks also have rules about what they will and will not accept for commercials. Network clearance departments set standards that commercials must meet in order to be aired. These departments pass judgment on TV commercials, and will be discussed in more detail in Chapter 12.

In his well-known book on the ad agency business, *From Those Wonderful Folks Who Gave You Pearl Harbor*, (Simon and Schuster, 1970), Jerry Della Femina says this about censorship (now referred to as "network clearance"): "One of the biggest problems that all agencies have is the headache of censorship. There is simply no reason for it. Censorship, any kind of censorship, is pure whim and fancy. It's one guy's idea of what is right for him. It's based on everything arbitrary. There are no rules, no standards, no laws."

In many instances, censorship can get out of control. An example is the time the Ted Bates agency produced a TV commercial for a toy company. The spot showed a little boy playing with the toy machine gun. The scene was shot on a mound of dirt with the kid blasting away at whomever it was we were blasting away at in the late 60's—Vietcong maybe.

"This commercial is not acceptable," said the network censor. The agency was sure that the rejection had something to do with the portrayal of war and violence with children. Not so. "Well, it's obvious that the mound of dirt is part of the game," said the censor. "The kid will obviously think that it's part of the game since it's on the screen for the entire commercial, and the kid spends his time on the top of the mound of dirt." The network, fearing that kids would expect to get a mound of dirt with the toy machine gun, would approve the spot only if it ran with a line of copy on the screen telling kids that the mound of dirt was not included. When the agency tried to explain that a child wouldn't actually believe that the dirt came with the gun, the censor replied, "It's not the five-year-olds we're worried about. It's the one-and two-year-olds who might be swayed." The irony was that the network censor wasn't concerned with the five-year-old who might be deceived, but rather about younger children who couldn't read anyway.

The smaller independent stations also tend to follow the lead of the networks. If the networks won't clear the spot, then the local stations probably won't run it either.

We in the U.S. are not the only one's who have to deal with media censorship. In the early 1970s the French agency Dupuy-Compton Advertising produced a television commercial for Levi-Strauss, to appear on French television. The commercial depicted a sad group of Boy Scouts all in grey uniforms, who were transformed into a bright new group dressed in Levi's. This happy group then undressed, scattering Levi's everywhere, and ran bare-bottoms-beaming down to a river to bathe in the cool sparkling water.

When the completed film was presented to RFP (Regie Francaise Publicitaire) for clearance, it was refused outright.

"No problem!" said Jed Falby, the agency's transplanted American director. "We have lots of other shots of Levi's on bushes and on the grass—we can cut around the nude bathing scenes."

The group at RFP looked at Falby as though he was mad.

"We aren't concerned about the nude bathing, Jed. Don't

you realize you can't make fun of the Boy Scouts?!"

Falby had to re-shoot the whole opening to change the Boy Scouts to college boys in school uniforms.

Print media has its codes as well. Some years ago, I produced an ad for vitamins. The ad was to run in a series of health and fitness magazines. One of these rejected the ad because they had limits as to the levels of each ingredient, e.g., if a multivitamin contained 500 mg. of vitamin C, the maximum that could be claimed was 300 mg., even if the product contained a higher level. We had to produce a special ad for that magazine showing lower levels of the vitamins.

While these self-regulation efforts don't have the force of law behind them, they have become an increasingly effective method of checks and balances. And they are gaining in power. It's only when these efforts get overly aggressive and arbitrary that they lose credibility. Yet, these are issues with which the advertiser must deal.

DAVID VERSUS GOLIATH—CONSUMER ACTION

It is also possible for consumer interests to be protected directly by the consumers themselves. The consumer can sue an advertiser directly, although this rarely occurs. The rare consumer suit against an advertiser typifies a larger pattern in our legal system—one where consumers find themselves powerless to take advantage of their legitimate legal rights. Most people simply cannot afford the often prohibitive expense of a lawsuit, especially when battling the virtually unlimited resources of a major company.

In most cases, the deceptive practice involved a purchase of such small cost that it makes no practical sense to consider retaining an attorney to pursue the matter through the courts, other than for reasons of principle. Although fighting for a principle can be rewarding, it can also be very expensive.

The extent of consumer injury from a deceptive

advertisement is difficult to prove, and the extent of the damage even more so. Unlike the FTC—who doesn't need to show that damage actually occurred (only a likelihood to deceive), the individual consumer has different burdens of proof in order to win an award. This adds to the complication and expense of a court battle.

As an alternative, class-action suits have become nearly impossible to pursue because federal court decisions do not allow individuals to combine separate claims in order to satisfy the minimum $10,000 damage amount required to file a lawsuit in federal court. While a few states have rejected the federal approach (notably California), opportunities for consumers to pursue class actions in state courts vary. What this all boils down to is that even when consumers are aware that their rights have been violated— and that retribution is available on their behalf—they are often frustrated by the obstacles that lie in their path.

Consumer protection organizations are a major force for advertisers to contend with in today's environment. As these organizations grow in strength, so does their power to effect change. The group Mothers Against Drunk Driving (MADD), for example, has had a tremendous impact on alcohol advertising practices.

ADVERTISING'S ROLE IN PRODUCTS LIABILITY

There is another area of real concern to advertisers. Consumers are recovering substantial damages in products liability litigation. These are actions to recover damages when a defective product causes injury. For example, a can of beans is intended to be edible. If a consumer buys the product and gets food poisoning, products liability is involved, and the consumer can sue for damages. Advertising has begun to play a large role in these lawsuits since product advertising can considerably influence liability. The problem occurs when the image created in advertising may not be substantiated by the product's actual performance. Courts assume that a product will perform as claimed. So does the consumer. When it doesn't and damage results, the advertising may be instrumental in showing the advertiser's failure to "live up to" the product's claim.

Products liability is an area where the FTC can become involved under false advertising violations, and the consumer can receive punitive damage awards in private lawsuits. The many areas of law that fall under "products liability" create an arsenal for the consumer who has been damaged from use of the product. As you can well imagine, cases of this nature can be a tremendous financial burden on an advertiser and its agency. Chapter 4 is devoted exclusively to the subject of products liability and its relation to advertising.

OTHER AREAS OF LAW THAT AFFECT ADVERTISING

Up to this point we have only mentioned how the FTC and the courts have played a major role in the regulation of advertising by prohibiting deception, misrepresentation, and unfairness. While Section 5 of the Federal Trade Commission Act accounts for the majority of legal activity concerning advertising, there are other areas of law that impact the advertiser.

There are many different areas of law beyond those of misleading and deceptive advertising including issues of copyright and trademark, the rights to privacy and publicity of individuals, and specific problems of advertising concerning warranties, guarantees and contests. We explore these areas later in the book.

The client/agency relationship is another area of concern to the advertiser. A client/agency relationship is one where an individual or company makes use of the services of another to accomplish things that could not be accomplished alone. When such a relationship is created—whether intentionally or implied by the law—it involves a well-developed area of law. The law defines the rights and liabilities of the parties, their relation to each other, and their relation to third parties. Therefore, we have seen an increasing number of court actions in which the advertising agency is brought in with the miscreant advertiser and held jointly liable. In most cases, each party is liable for the actions of the other. This subject will be discussed in Chapter 11.

---

[1] *FTC* v. *Circle Cilk*, 1 F.T.C. 13 (1916) and *FTC* v. *Abbott*, 1 F.T.C. 16 (1916).

[2] 52 Stat. 11.

[3] 88th Cong., 1st Sess., pt. 1, at 465 (1963).

[4] *Warner-Lambert Co.*, (1973-1976 Transfer Binder) Trade Reg. Rep. (CCH) & 21, 066 (F.T.C. 1975), appeal docketed, No. 76-1138 (D.C. Cir., filed Feb. 13,1976).

[5] *Ocean Spray Cranberry, Inc.*, 80 F.T.C. 975 (1971).

[6] *ITT Continental Baking Co.*, 79 F.T.C. 248 (1971).

[7] 15 USC, Section 1125a.

[8] *Smith* v. *Chanel, Inc.*, 402 F.2d 562 (9th Cir. 1968).

CHAPTER 2

AN OVERVIEW OF THE FEDERAL TRADE COMMISSION'S ROLE IN ADVERTISING REGULATION

Big brother is watching.
—*George Orwell*

In 1946, Frederic Wakeman wrote a novel about the exploits of an advertising agency and an arrogant client named Evan Evans. Since then, *The Hucksters* has become the public image of the advertising profession. In the movie adaptation, Clark Gable plays the part of the advertising account executive caught in a struggle of right and wrong with the ne'er-do-well soap king played by Sidney Greenstreet. As these two battle, symbols of good conscience and selfish motives dominate the screen. "Advertising," exclaimed the soap tycoon, "is nothing more than pompous ranting," which he relishes when accomplished with the poorest of taste.

George Washington Hill, the real-life Evan Evans and owner of the American Tobacco Company, was well-known for his exaggerated advertising claims. When "creating" his own preference test statistics, Hill said, "I know the great preference for Lucky Strike is a fact, but the public won't believe it. Anyway, two-to-one has a better ring to it."

The Hucksters was written in an era when the advertiser took many liberties in selling his merchandise. For almost fifty years however, moviegoers have overlooked the fact that Wakeman's book was a work of fiction. The book convinced the public that advertising flourished—with the consumer falling victim to the guile of the advertiser—in a sea of broken promises that were never intended to be kept. Unfortunately, this feeling has prevailed. Today, the type of blatant deception demonstrated in *The Hucksters* is rigidly policed, primarily through the efforts of the Federal Trade Commission, which has successfully raised the standard of conduct of the advertising industry.

THE FEDERAL TRADE COMMISSION

As most advertising people already know, the Federal Trade Commission (FTC) has the greatest control over advertising and the way it is used. Yet, few understand the extent of the FTC's involvement. The formation of the FTC was an outgrowth of the Sherman Act, an antitrust law that prohibited conspiracies in restraint of trade and the formation of monopolies. The original mandate from Congress (under Section 5 of the Federal Trade Commission Act) was simple and straightforward: to prevent "unfair or deceptive acts or practices . . . [and] . . . unfair methods of competition."

In January 1914, President Wilson addressed Congress calling for the creation of a Federal Trade Commission saying:

The business men of the country desire something more than that the menace of legal process in these matters be made explicit and intelligible. They desire advice, the definite guidance and information which can be supplied by an administrative body, an interstate trade commission.

Constructive legislation, when successful, is always the embodiment of convincing experience, and of mature public opinion which finally springs out of that experience . . . . It is not recent or hasty opinion.

The opinion of the country . . . would not wish to see it [the commission] empowered to make terms with monopoly or in any sort to assume control of business, as if the Government made itself responsible. It demands such a commission only as an indispensable instrument of information and publicity, as a clearing house of the facts by which both the public mind and the managers of great business undertakings should be guided, and as an instrumentality for doing justice to business where the processes of the courts are inadequate to adjust the remedy to wrong in a way that will meet all the equities and circumstances of the case.

In an early move, the Seventh Circuit of Appeals in 1919, stated its definition of the FTC's role in *Sears, Roebuck & Co.* v. *FTC*,[1] saying:

The commissioners, representing the government as parens patriae, are to exercise their common sense, as informed by their knowledge of the general idea of unfair trade at common law, and stop all those trade practices that have a capacity or tendency to injure competitors directly or through deception of purchasers, quite irrespective of whether the specific practices in question have yet been denounced in common-law cases.

The commission, as part of its scope, has the task of preserving a variety of marketplace options for consumers. Its efforts against deception help ensure that consumers will not make choices on the basis of misleading information. The ban on unfair practices also broadens the FTC's scope by protecting consumers from practices that are "exploitative or inequitable. . . morally objectionable, [or] seriously detrimental to consumers or others."[2]

As we discussed earlier, Section 5 of the act, which was once considered only a tool against unfair methods of competition between businesses, was expanded in 1938 with the Wheeler-Lea

Amendments to cover unfair and deceptive acts against individuals as well. While the rationale to abolish unfair methods of competition grew from the need to protect competitors from each other, the reasoning against unfair and deceptive acts and practices evolved out of the desire to protect the consumer from the advertiser.

While the Wheeler-Lea Amendments specifically gave the FTC jurisdiction in the consumer protection area, the commission continued its fight against unfair trade practices and monopolistic power. At times these divergent roles were in conflict.

Reasoning Behind The FTC Act And The Wheeler-Lea Amendments

Here, we will examine the different stages that the FTC has gone through in its development and the reasoning behind these developments.

The FTC Act

First, look at this excerpt from the Senate Committee on Interstate Commerce Report, 1914, supporting the enactment of a trade commission bill.

> The committee gave careful consideration to the question as to whether it would attempt to define the many and variable unfair practices which prevail in commerce and to forbid their continuance or whether it would, by a general declaration condemning unfair practices, leave it to the Commission to determine what practices were unfair. It concluded that the latter course would be the better, for the reason, as stated by one of the representatives of the Illinois Manufacturers' Association, that there were too many unfair practices to define, and after writing 20 of them into the law, it would be quite possible to invent others.

As we have seen, the original intent was to prohibit unfair trade practices as they existed between businesses.

The Wheeler-Lea Amendments

Now, look at this excerpt from Senator Burton Wheeler in debate on the Wheeler-Lea Amendments, 1938.[3]

> The Commission spent most of its time and most of its money allotted to it by the Congress, in running down the question of whether or not one man has lost some money by reason of unfair trade practices on the part of another. After all, Congress is not interested in whether John Smith lost some money as the result of the advertising complained of, but the question is whether or not the general public has been deceived or injured by reason of it. We are here to legislate with respect to that question.

This, then, also prohibited deceptive acts in commerce, thereby bringing consumer deception into the picture, and allowing the FTC to act on that as well.

The 1975 FTC Improvement Act

Essentially, the FTC Improvement Act[4] of 1975, modified section 5 of the FTC Act in one major way. It added the phrase "or affecting" to the existing phrase "in commerce." Now, as we'll see in the next section, the phrase reads "in *or affecting* commerce." This gives the FTC wider latitude in determining the existence of deception.

Key Sections Of The FTC Act

At this point, it may be valuable to look at the specifics of current key sections of the FTC Act.

Section 5. (a) (1) Unfair methods of competition in **or**

affecting commerce, <u>and unfair or deceptive acts or practices in</u> **or
affecting** <u>commerce</u> are hereby declared unlawful. (Underline
added with Wheeler-Lea Amendments; bold added with 1975
FTC Improvement Act.)

Section 5. (b) Whenever the Commission shall have reason
to believe that any such person, partnership, or corporation has
been or is using any unfair method of competition or unfair or
deceptive act or practice in **or affecting** commerce, and if it shall
appear to the Commission that a proceeding by it in respect
thereof *would be of interest to the public*, it shall issue and serve
upon such person, partnership, or corporation a complaint stating
its charges. (Italic shows concern for a public interest; bold added
with 1975 FTC Improvement Act.)

Section 12. (a) It shall be unlawful for any person,
partnership, or corporation to disseminate, or cause to be
disseminated, any false advertisement.

(b) The dissemination or the causing to be disseminated of
any false advertisement within the provisions of subsection (a) of
this section shall be an unfair or deceptive act or practice in **or
affecting** commerce within the meaning of section 5. (Section 12
added with Wheeler-Lea Amendments; bold added with 1975
FTC Improvement Act.)

Key Events In The History Of The FTC

The following list includes a history of events that have
played an important role in the evolution of the Federal Trade
Commission, many of which we will look at in this chapter.

1887   Interstate Commerce Commission created
1890   Sherman Antitrust Act passed
1903   Bureau of Corporations created
1914   Federal Trade Commission Act passed
       Clayton Antitrust Act passed
1918   Webb-Pomerone Act passed
1919   *FTC v. Sears, Roebuck & Company*

1920 *FTC v. Gratz*
1921 Packers and Stockyard Act passed
1922 *FTC v. Winsted Hosiery*
1929 *FTC v. Klesner*
1931 *FTC v. Raladam*
1934 *FTC v. Keppel & Brothers, Inc.*
1935 *Humphrey's Executor v. United States*
1936 Robinson-Patman Act passed
1938 Wheeler-Lea Amendments passed,
     amending the 1914 FTC Act
1939 Wool Products Labeling Act passed
1949 Hoover Commission Report
1950 Celler-Kefauver Antimerger Act passed
     Oleomargarine Act passed
1951 Fur Products Labeling Act passed
1952 McGuire Act passed
1953 Flammable Fabrics Act passed
1958 Textile and Fiber Products Act passed
1975 FTC Improvement Act passed
1984 *In the Matter of Cliffdale Associates*

We see in this chapter how the FTC's activities have greatly expanded the definition of "unfair" and "deceptive." This chapter concentrates on the concepts that the commission and the courts have developed. In this chapter we also cover the guidelines that the FTC uses to determine if a violation exists. The next chapter will examine specific concerns and types of violations under the Federal Trade Commission Act.

THE FTC'S REGULATION OF ADVERTISING

Because the FTC's goal is to protect the consumer from false claims, deception, and misrepresentation, the level of control it exerts over advertising has increased in recent years. The commission has gained increased authority and effectiveness for two reasons: first, through the cases it has heard and decided; and second, through the courts affirming the commission's decisions. In fact, courts have upheld the majority of the commission's decisions. For a specific discussion, see Chapter 3, Exhibit: 3-2.

An advertiser must understand how the FTC views an ad. Overall, what deceptive qualities does it look for? What qualifies as a deceptive ad? Or an unfair one? How does the advertiser know if the ad he creates will be acceptable in the eyes of the commission? This chapter addresses each of these questions in depth.

As mentioned, the FTC follows certain guidelines where advertising claims are alleged to be unfair or deceptive (see Chapter 3, Exhibit: 3-1). It first examines the advertisement to interpret all the information contained in it to determine if the ad is deceptive, or under current interpretation, if it is *likely* to deceive. The commission also looks at the net impression of the advertisement—the overall impression that the ad projects to the consumer. The commission views the materiality of all the representations in the advertisement and particularly the claims that are alleged to be false. The FTC also determines if the claims are simply sales exaggerations or puff.

The recent case, *In the Matter of Cliffdale Associates, Inc.*,[5] (which we will examine later in this chapter), establishes the commission's current stance on deception. Exhibit 2-1, includes a copy of a letter from then FTC Chairman James C. Miller, III to the Committee on Energy and Commerce. This letter, written in October, 1983, attempts to explain the commission's current position and interpretation of deception.

Now we'll examine each of the components of deception in more detail.

DECEPTIVENESS OF AN ADVERTISEMENT

From 1914 until 1984, "tendency or capacity" to deceive was the FTC's benchmark. One early case that dealt with this concept of "tendency or capacity" to deceive was *FTC* v. *Raladam Co.*[6] In that case the United States Supreme Court decided the issue of whether a cease-and-desist order by the commission (issued after a hearing in 1935) should stand. The case involved Raladam's product, Marmola. Marmola was a preparation for weight-reduction and was advertised as such. The company made claims in its advertisements that were misleading and deceptive. The statements concerned the product's qualities as a remedy for obesity.

Raladam did not argue whether the statements were deceptive (they had been caught before in 1929 as well). Its argument was that no proof was offered to show that injury occurred. However, the court held that no actual injury need be proven, only a tendency to deceive. The court felt that it was impossible to determine whether any injury occurred, or would occur in the future, because of Raladam's false claims. In fact, one of the principles of the act was "to prevent potential injury by stopping unfair methods of competition in their incipiency."

There's an interesting side note from the history of the con man's role in early advertising. A man named Edward Hayes, a con man extraordinaire, marketed a product for years called Man Medicine. Hayes claimed his product would bestow the purchaser "once more with gusto, the joyful satisfaction, the pulse and throb of physical pleasure, the keen sense of man sensation." Man Medicine was merely a laxative that Hayes used to bilk millions of dollars from a susceptible male market.

Hayes was caught and brought to trial by the Postmaster General for fraud. He was found guilty in April 1914, fined $5,000, and had to promise never to get involved with such wild schemes again. Only months later, Hayes was back out in the market advertising a new miracle product—a foolproof cure for obesity. The product was called Marmola, the same product which, with its new owner Raladam, was taken to court in 1929 and later in 1935.

Then in 1984, the case of *In the Matter of Cliffdale Associates, Inc.,* caused a change in the FTC's stance on deception. Today, the FTC uses a new standard to determine the existence of deception. "Tendency or capacity" to deceive has been replaced by "likely" to deceive. Since *Cliffdale*, the FTC takes a very close look at an advertisement to determine if a false representation or omission is "likely" to deceive a substantial number of consumers. As it was before 1984, actual deception is not necessary under the FTC act to constitute a violation.

In 1979 alone, Cliffdale Associates sold $692,998 in one of its products called the Ball-Matic Gas Saver Valve. The valve, what is commonly called an air-bleed device, was intended to be installed on an automobile engine to admit additional air into the engine to lean the air-fuel mixture, and thereby improve gas mileage. Ads promoted the sale of the Ball-Matic through mail order. Typical of these ads is the following:

● ●
GET UP TO 4 EXTRA MILES PER GALLON
— 100 EXTRA MILES BETWEEN FILL-UPS —
SAVE UP TO $200 A YEAR ON GAS.
GUARANTEED SAVINGS!
We firmly believe the Ball-Matic to be one of the best investments you can make to save money this year. The exact saving you will receive may vary significantly depending on the kind of car you drive, the condition of your engine, weather, your driving habits and the amount of driving you do; however we guarantee that you MUST SAVE AT LEAST FIVE TIMES the amount you paid for your BALL-MATIC in the first year or you may return it for a full refund.
CONTROLLED TESTS CONFIRM BIG DOLLAR SAVING!
In the Spring of 1978, we arranged for a local Shell Service Station to conduct a controlled, supervised, test using seven different cars owned and driven by non-professional drivers. Each car was fitted with a locked gas cap and the keys kept in the

possession of the testers.

After establishing base mileage consumption data for the various cars, the BALL-MATIC was installed and miles-per-gallon figures were re-checked. Every single car in the test showed meaningful improvement.

IMPROVEMENT RANGE ...8% to 40%!

Yes, you can actually get up to 70...80...90...even 100 extra miles from every single tankful. No matter how old or rundown your car may be...no matter how many gallons of gasoline it now devours each week.

READ THE RESULTS FOR YOURSELF!

"The BALL-MATIC (gas saver) that I purchased has proven itself. I drive a 1970 Oldsmobile, now I get tour miles more per gallon."

C.T. –Orange, California

"I want to express my thanks for the BALL-MATIC. Since it has been installed in my car, my gas mileage has not been under 18 miles per gallon. This is an increase of 5.5 miles per gallon."

Rev. R.N. –Claremont, California

● ●

Ads like the one above were typical. Cliffdale's ads guaranteed an increase in gas mileage of 8% to 40% or more with the Ball-Matic. Part of the convincing nature of these ads were the claimed scientific tests and the consumer endorsement letters— all of which turned out to be false and clearly deceptive.

When this case went to court, it was proven that no valid scientific tests had been performed on the valve. The endorsements used in the ads were deceptive since all but one letter was written by someone connected with the company. In addition, the Ball-Matic was proven to not provide any measurable increase in gas mileage when tested by a series of credible university facilities.

The commission, stated that it:

. . . will find an act or practice deceptive if, first, there is a representation, omission, or practice that,

second, <u>is likely to mislead consumers acting
reasonably under the circumstances</u>, and third, the
representation, omission, or practice is material.
These elements articulate the factors actually used in
most earlier Commission cases identifying whether
or not an act or practice was deceptive, even though
the language used in those cases was often couched
in such terms as 'a tendency and capacity to
deceive.' (Emphasis added).

The requirement that an act or practice be
'<u>likely to mislead</u>,' for example, reflects the long
established principle that the Commission need not
find actual deception to hold that a violation of
Section 5 has occurred. (Emphasis added).

The commission went on to expand on another new
reference; a "reasonably acting consumer." They said that:

The requirement that an act or practice be
considered from the perspective of a '<u>consumer
acting reasonably in the circumstances</u>' is not new.
Virtually all representations, even those that are true,
can be misunderstood by some consumers. The
Commission has long recognized that the law
should not be applied in such a way as to find that
honest representations are deceptive simply because
they are misunderstood by a few. . . [A]n
advertisement would not be considered deceptive
merely because it could be 'unreasonably
misunderstood by an insignificant and
unrepresentative segment of the class of persons to
whom the representation is addressed.'(Emphasis
added).

Now, the FTC has changed its requirement that a mere

possibility of deception could occur, to a probability that deception will result from the claim. The new definition requires a higher degree of proof than the previous one. In essence, it provides less protection for the consumer than did the earlier "capacity or tendency" standard.

The change in the FTC's position on deception as a result of the *Cliffdale* case has been well articulated in the case's dissenting opinion of Commissioner Pertschuk.

> Under the guise of making the law more 'clear and understandable,' the [FTC] has actually raised the evidentiary threshold for deception cases. [We] have found it necessary to improve on language long understood by the courts and previous commissioners, by substituting the word 'likely' for 'tendency or capacity.' 'Likely to mislead,' they insist, expresses more clearly the notion that actual deception need not be found! . . .the word 'likely' suggests that some particular degree of likelihood of actual deception must be found. Therefore, it may create the impression, intentionally or not, that the burden of proof is higher than it has always been under the traditional 'tendency or capacity' standard.

Commissioner Bailey also dissented in part to the *Cliffdale* decision, and stated:

> The [FTC's] first criterion for deception is that there be a claim, omission or practice that is 'likely to mislead' consumers. It is true that the courts have occasionally used this or similar phrasing, such as 'the likelihood or propensity' of deception, interchangeable with tendency or capacity.
> Here, however, the majority makes

unmistakable its intent to exchange the phrase
tendency or capacity for the term likely, with only
the brief explanation that it is meant to convey an
understanding that 'actual' deception need not be
shown. As that was never in doubt, it does not
explain the use of the term 'likely' generally.

A standard Webster's definition of likely, 'having
a high probability of occurring or being true,'
suggests, however, that the purposeful substitution
of this term for tendency or capacity may well be
intended to raise, or may be construed so as to raise,
the burden of proof the Commission must meet in
demonstrating that deception has occurred.

The commissioner concluded by saying: "Thus, use of the
term 'likely' here may be fairly perceived to be at least a partial
retreat from the Commission's traditional position that it may on
the basis of its own expertise determine what representations a
seller has made to the public."

THE MATERIALITY REQUIREMENT

To reach the conclusion that an ad is deceptive, the
questionable representation (or omission) must also be a material
one. A claim is material if it is likely to affect the consumer's choice
of a product and his conduct in purchasing that product. In other
words, it is material if it is important to the consumer in making
his purchasing decision. Another way to understand this concept
is in terms of injury to the consumer. Finding that a claim is
material is finding that injury is likely, and injury exists if the
consumer would have chosen differently had there been no
deception. The consumer would be injured because he would be
purchasing something other than what he thought he was
purchasing. Thus, likelihood of injury and materiality are different
sides of the same coin.

Let's utilize an example of this concept. In most of the cases throughout this chapter and the next, we will see deceptions that are material. The Rapid Shave case (which we will examine later in this chapter), where a television commercial demonstrates that the shave cream can shave sandpaper (when in reality it cannot), is a perfect example of a material deception. This ability is central to what the product is purchased for—its ability to shave sandpaper must mean that it is great for a beard. The consumer would probably be swayed to purchase the product after seeing this demonstration. Thus, the demonstration created a material deception. This case will be discussed in more detail later in this chapter.

Another example of a material deception occurred in 1990. Volvo ran into major legal trouble over a television commercial which it aired to dramatically demonstrate the structural strength of its automobile. A 13,000 pound "monster truck" called "Bear Foot" was shown rolling over a line-up of cars. All of the cars shown were crushed under the weight of the truck except the Volvo station wagon.

Later it was discovered that additional steel supports had been welded into the Volvo to reinforce it against the monster truck's weight. The other cars, on the other hand, were weakened by having their roof supports cut with a saw to aid them in collapsing.

As part of an out-of-court settlement, Volvo agreed to pull the commercial off the air and replace it with corrective ads. Volvo was also required to run newspaper ads apologizing to consumers for the deceptive advertising.

Scali, McCabe, Sloves in New York, Volvo's advertising agency for twenty-four years, and the creator of the commercial, resigned the $40 million account.

To look at the other side, when can a deception not be material? Some years ago I produced a television commercial for a resort community in Palm Springs, California. In the commercial a craftsman was shown carving a silver sign that was the logo of the community. This was done to develop a theme of pride and detail of the craftsmanship that went into the development of the community itself. In reality the craftsman was not carving the actual sign, but only chiseling silver wax from the sign. This was deceptive but not material. Why? Because the consumer would not purchase a home at this resort based on the carving of the sign. It had nothing to do with his decision to buy the product.

The commission feels that certain types of claims are unquestionably material in nature. Such claims include express claims; implied claims as intended by the advertiser; claims relating to health, safety, and other similar areas of concern to the consumer; claims that relate to the main characteristics of the product or service; claims establishing the purpose, efficiency, cost, durability, performance, warranty or quality of a product; and statements regarding findings by a governmental agency concerning the product.

The *Cliffdale* case created much controversy in addition to new views on the three elements of deception; one of those being the materiality requirement. Commissioner Pertschuk, concurring in part and dissenting in part in the *Cliffdale* case, took exception with the new definition of materiality:

> The third element of deception is materiality. As the Supreme Court has explained, Section 5 prohibits the misrepresentation of 'any fact which would constitute a material factor in a purchaser's decision whether to buy.' Heretofore, any fact that is important to consumers has been considered material, regardless of whether consumer choices would actually turn on that fact. As the Commission has previously said, '[t]he fact that consumers were not harmed because they would have purchased the product anyway . . . is not relevant.' The Commission has not required a showing of reliance

or injury to establish deception.

The majority opinion in this case [Cliffdale], however, suggests somewhat ambiguously that a misrepresentation is not material unless it is 'likely to affect' consumers' conduct and '[c]onsumers thus are likely to suffer injury.' Similarly, the October 14, 1983, Policy Statement on Deception states: 'a finding of materiality is also a finding that injury is likely to exist.... Injury exists if consumers would have chosen differently but for the deception."

If the majority commissioners intend to require proof of actual or likely reliance on the misrepresentations of respondents in future cases, they have changed the meaning of materiality and made it more difficult to establish violations of Section 5.

Commissioner Bailey also dissented in part to *Cliffdale* by saying:

The Commission has long held that a challenged act or practice must be misleading in a material respect in order to be found deceptive. Just when all appears to be going well, however, the opinion . . . introduces a series of new concepts which appear to qualify standard principles of materiality in a restrictive fashion. At one point the opinion seems to equate materiality with the actual effects of claims or practices on consumer conduct, and the Policy Statement expressly states that 'injury and materiality are different names for the same concept' and that deception will be found where an act or practice 'misleads . . . to the consumer's detriment.' (Detriment is, of course, legally defined as injury.) The Policy Statement also notes that injury exists if consumers would have chosen differently 'but for' the misleading act or practice, suggesting that reliance and causation are elements of materiality.

The commissioner went on to say:
> Conclusions that injury and materiality are synonymous, that causation and reliance must be shown, or even that the likelihood of consumer detriment must be demonstrated in every case do not square with these accepted understandings of materiality.
>
> I have no quarrel with the conclusions reached in this case, but analyzing it by applying these new elements is a wholly unnecessary exercise which demonstrates, I fear, the serious evidentiary difficulties and the exercise of even greater analytical gymnastics that will be necessary in future, more complicated Commission cases.

It appears that the *Cliffdale* case has stirred up much dust which will not soon settle..

THE EVOLUTION OF THE "REASONABLE MAN" STANDARD

Although the standard has gone through much change from the "reasonable man" to the "ignorant man" and back, the FTC has decided, for now, on the reasonable man standard. Yet, today the level has been raised to a stricter scale since the opinion in the *Cliffdale* case.

The reasonable man standard was first mentioned in 1837.[7] He is a man of average prudence and ordinary sense, who uses ordinary care and skill.

To understand why the FTC has changed its stance over the

years regarding the reasonable man standard, it is helpful to look at the way the standard evolved. Soon after the Wheeler-Lea Amendments to the Federal Trade Commission Act were passed in 1938, the reasonable man standard began to be replaced with a new ideology: the ignorant man standard. This new standard was based largely on a case concerning an encyclopedia company that had used many false statements in a sales campaign. These were not simply innocent misrepresentations, but rather blatant untruths intended to deceive potential buyers.

However, some or all of these falsehoods could have been detected by consumers.

The case was *Federal Trade Commission* v. *Standard Education Society*.[8] In selling their *Standard Reference Work* and *New Standard Encyclopedia*, the company representative convinced the prospects that they had been selected because of their prestige and stature in the community from a small list of well connected, representative people in various areas. Allegedly, the company was presenting them with an "artcraft deluxe edition" of the encyclopedia free of charge. As the scheme developed the representative would state that "they [were] giving away a set of books . . . free as an advertising plan . . . that the prospect [had] been specially selected, and that the only return desired for the gift [was] permission to use the name of the prospect for advertising purposes."

The prospects were told that they would only have to pay for the loose leaf extension service, which was $69.50. This, the prospects were told, was "a reduced price and that the regular price of the books and the extension service is $150, sometimes even as high as $200." These statements were false and were part of the scheme. In fact, the $69.50 price was the regular price for both the encyclopedia and the loose leaf extension. Clearly, it was the practice of Standard Education Society to mislead customers into believing that they were being given a free encyclopedia, and that they only were to pay for the extension service. The record in

this case is filled with testimony from people in 10 states that
confirmed this.

What is interesting here is that the Circuit Court of Appeals
for the Second Circuit (the lower court heard the case before the
U.S. Supreme Court) had decided they could not seriously
entertain the notion "that a man who is buying a set of books and
a 10 year extension service, will be fatuous enough to be misled by
the mere statement that the first are given away, and that he is
paying only for the second."[9] Here the court felt that no reasonable
man would believe the claim that he was getting one item for free
if he paid for the other. The U.S. Supreme Court, however, felt—as
did the FTC originally—that the lower court was wrong; an
ignorant man could believe the claim.

To illustrate that point, Justice Black in the majority
opinion authored by him in 1937 wrote:

> The fact that a false statement may be obviously
> false to those who are trained and experienced does
> not damage its character, nor take away its power to
> deceive others less experienced. There is no duty
> resting upon a citizen to suspect the honesty of
> those with whom he transacts business. Laws are
> made to protect the trusting as well as the
> suspicious. The best element of business has long
> since decided that honesty should govern
> competitive enterprises, and that the rule of caveat
> emptor should not be relied upon to reward fraud
> and deception.

This case could have been interpreted in several ways, and
it was by the appeals court. However, it was interpreted by the
U.S. Supreme Court as having abolished the reasonable man
standard altogether. In fact, it firmly entrenched the ignorant man
standard, which would continue for some time.

The Ignorant Man Standard

During the decade that followed, the ignorant man standard flourished, as was illustrated in *Gelb* v. *FTC*.[10] The case concerned an advertising claim that, among other things, a shampooing and coloring preparation known as Progressive Clairol and Instant Clairol permanently colored hair. One of the questions in this case dealt with the standard of perception of the consumer—specifically, whether an order should be upheld that would enjoin Clairol from "representing that the effect produced upon the color of the hair by the use of said preparation is permanent."

Looking at the advertisements for Clairol literally, it is obvious that the preparation permanently colors hair to which it is applied. But the commission found (and this would seem obvious) that the preparation has no effect on new hair as it grows in. Hence the commission concluded that the claim of the preparation "permanently" coloring hair was misleading. It seems absurd that any user of the preparation could be so simple-minded as to suppose that hair not yet grown out would be colored as well. (One witness was found who, after some prodding, finally testified "that you would think 'permanent' means you would never need to bother having it dyed again," although the witness knew better.) Yet the commission construed the advertisement as representing that it would do just that. Therefore, it ruled that the claim was false and deceptive.

The court, in this appeal from the earlier FTC ruling, validated the commission's earlier decision. Both the court and the commission reasoned that Section 5 of the act was designed for the protection of the trusting, as well as the suspicious. The result of this case was that evidence of deception, regardless of how unintended or unreasonable, was sufficient for a finding of deceptive advertising, even if only a single person were deceived, and even if that person was incompetent or a fool. The status quo at the time was that, "People have a right to assume that fraudulent

advertising traps will not be laid to ensnare them."[11] Yet it appears
that the concept was taken to its extreme.

Back To The Reasonable Man Standard

Beginning in 1963 and modified in 1984, the FTC has
moved back in the direction of a reasonable man standard of
perception. The commission withdrew from the concept that
deception of a single consumer, no matter how foolish or
imperceptive, constitutes a deceptive practice.

True, the commission's responsibility is to prevent
deception of the gullible and credulous, as well as the cautious and
knowledgeable. This principle, however, loses its credibility if it is
pushed to an absurd extreme as it was with the ignorant man
standard. An advertiser cannot be held liable for every
misconception, however outlandish. His representations cannot be
subject to interpretation by the foolish or feeble-minded—the
"ignorant man." Some people, because of ignorance or
incomprehension, may be misled by even a scrupulously honest
claim.

Perhaps a few misguided souls believe that all Danish
pastry is made in Denmark. Is it deceptive to call a bakery item
"Danish pastry" if it is made in California? Of course not! Under
the reasonable man standard, an ad claim does not become false
and deceptive merely because it will be misunderstood by an
insignificant and nonrepresentative segment of people within the
market the ad addresses.

In 1973 the commission presented its opinion, *In the Matter
of Coca-Cola Company*.[12] In this case the commission dealt with an
issue involving the Coca-Cola Company's marketing of a drink
called Hi-C. It had been advertised as "the sensible drink . .. made
with fresh fruit . . . [and] . . . being high in Vitamin C, . . . [and
that children] . . . can drink as much . . . . as they like." Television
commercials and some package labels showed oranges and other
fruits, from which the juices are used to make Hi-C.

The complaint in this case stated that these advertisements compared Hi-C with natural citrus juices by implication. Therefore it was deceptive.

The commission maintained that Hi-C advertisements implicitly compared Hi-C with natural citrus juices and with orange juice in particular. It was alleged that consumers would likely take the advertisement to mean that Hi-C was made from fresh orange juice and was equal to, or better than, actual fresh orange juice in nutritional value.

Here the advertising representations were "not reasonably likely to have communicated" characteristics of Hi-C which were contrary to fact. It is possible to agree that the statements were "not reasonably likely" to deceive based purely on the facts. However, the statement of Commissioner Jones (dissenting) brings into play the standard of perception model:

> The commission's opinion ignores or perhaps reverses the standard model of the consumer as "the ignorant, the unthinking and the credulous" consumer which the commission has been commanded to use in determining whether a particular act is unfair or deceptive. Instead, without any evidence in the record to support it, the commission implicitly adopts a new consumer model as its standard for interpreting whether a claim is likely to deceive.

> This standard is actually one portraying the consumer as discriminating, sophisticated, and highly knowledgeable as well as skeptical and unbelieving. This consumer knows that fruit drinks are not the same as citrus juices despite what Hi-C ads said.

The commission has toughened its stance on the reasonable man standard as it exists today. The commission announced, through its 1984 *Cliffdale* decision, that only consumers "acting reasonably in the circumstances" were protected by the government. This new standard runs parallel with the "reasonableness" standard used in tort law negligence. Because of this, if the consumer is negligent in his behavior as a consumer, the FTC won't protect him.

It would appear then, that today the percentage of consumers affected would be required to be greater than with the earlier reasonable man standard. Perhaps we should call this the "prudent man standard." The main difference here is that in the past, the reasonable man standard was based on "a <u>reasonable person</u> in the situation," whereas now the issue involves "a consumer <u>acting reasonably</u>." (Emphasis added).

In the *Cliffdale* case, much concern had been raised regarding the new direction that the commission had taken. Commissioner Pertschuk, concurring in part and dissenting in part to the *Cliffdale* decision, said that "[t]he new deception analysis has a more serious effect that is clearly not unintentional. That is, to withdraw the protection of Section 5 from consumers who do not act 'reasonably'."

The Commissioner went on to say that:

> The sad fact is that a small segment of our society makes its livelihood preying upon consumers who are very trusting and unsophisticated. Others specialize in weakening the defenses of especially vulnerable, but normally cautious, consumers. Through skillful exploitation of such common desires as the wish to get rich quick or to provide some measure of security for one's old age, professional con men can prompt conduct that many of their victims will readily admit —in hindsight—is patently unreasonable.
>
> Of course, what strikes me as 'unreasonable' consumer behavior may not seem so to other

commissioners. The very subjective nature of the 'reasonable consumer' standard is cause for concern. How can consumer conduct be measured for reasonableness? I know of no test for it, and I am fearful of the *ad hoc* determinations that will be made in the future.

Also concurring in part and dissenting in part to *Cliffdale* was Commissioner Bailey. She had trouble with the new distinction as well.

Commissioner Bailey said: "The second requirement is that an act or practice be likely to mislead consumers 'acting reasonably under the circumstances.' Of the three newly introduced elements, I believe this is on its face the most divorced from prior precedent and also the most likely to produce troubling results."

She went on to explain that:

A claim or practice must deceive a 'substantial number' of consumers in order to trigger a finding of deception . . . Thus, while the Commission has indicated that it will not subject sellers to every interpretation made by an 'insubstantial and unrepresentative segment' of the seller's audience, it has at the same time faithfully adhered to the enduring proposition that consumers are entitled to take commercial representations at face value and need not mistrust them. I believe the imposition of a 'reasonable consumer' test as an element of the legal standard for deception may seriously jeopardize this guiding principle of deception law, which has permitted and encouraged the Commission to spread its protective mantle over the uninformed and credulous, those with understandable but often unreasonable hopes, those with limited reasoning

abilities, such as children, and even 'average'
consumers whose guard may be down or who may
behave somewhat carelessly in the face of deceptive
conduct.

Clearly, this element of deception will, no doubt, see much
activity and debate in the future.

SUSCEPTIBILITY OF THE AUDIENCE

In determining the consumer's interpretation, the guide is
the susceptibility of the audience to which the advertisement is
directed. The level of susceptibility is flexible and is adjusted to the
norm of the intended audience. It is different for children than for
adults. It is also different for the elderly or terminally ill than for
the healthy young adult. This often falls into the area of
"unfairness" claims, which we will discuss later in this chapter.

In the case *In the Matter of Doris Savitch*,[13] the commission
measured the susceptibility of an audience to which the ad was
directed. Personal Drug Co., owned by Doris Savitch and Leo
Savitch, manufactured and advertised products under the names
Quick-Kaps and *D-Lay Capsules*. Quick-Kaps were advertised as
medication that would relieve a woman's overdue period.

• • • • • • • • • • • • • •

PERIOD DELAYED?

(Overdue)

Don't Risk Disaster

Don't Worry

At last—it CAN BE SOLD, a new, extra effective, Doctor approved
formula— "Quick-Kaps" capsules may relieve you of your biggest
worry—when due to minor functional menstrual delay or
borderline anemia. Scientifically prepared by registered
Pharmacists, "Quick-Kaps" capsules contain only medically
recognized drugs, having no harmful after effects—Complete

supply—packed in a confidential box only $5.00. Send no money and we will mail C.O.D. plus small postal and C.O.D. charges or send $5.00 cash and we will rush AIR MAIL.

"Just the thing to have on hand."

● ●

The implication here is strong: Relief from delayed menstruation due to pregnancy will be achieved by using Quick-Kaps. The advertisements also represented that its use would provide relief from delayed menstruation due to "minor functional disorders and borderline anemia." The first problem here is with the causes of delayed menstruation. The biggest cause is pregnancy. A more infrequent cause is iron deficiency anemia. Borderline anemia is not a cause of delayed menstruation other than in those rare cases when it is due to iron deficiency anemia.

Some of the phrases used in the advertisement are significant—for example, "Don't Worry"—"Don't Risk Disaster"— "May relieve you of your biggest worry"—"Medically recognized drugs having no harmful after effects"—"At last—it CAN BE SOLD, a new, extra effective, Doctor approved formula." The above-quoted phrase would seem to imply that, either because of a change in the law or recent medical discoveries, a new preparation was now being put on the market. This was not the case, and the ad was held to violate the FTC Act.

The commission felt that it was a commonly known fact that selling preparations or devices that would induce an abortion was prohibited by law. People looking for such a product would not expect to find it advertised as obviously and openly as products that were not prohibited. This advertisement seems to invite reading between the lines. It is reminiscent of bootlegging days when a knowing wink to a buyer implied that the "cold tea" being sold was in fact illegal liquor. Obviously, the implication about a product is as important as the literal truth of each sentence or picture. "The ultimate impression upon the mind of the reader (or viewer) arises not only from what is said, but also from what is reasonably implied."[14] We explore more on this area of interpretation of an ad later in this chapter.

The *Doris Savitch* case illustrates the susceptibility of an audience to which an advertisement is directed. It is reasonable to say that a woman would worry about delayed menstruation and could believe that this was caused by pregnancy. If she wanted to alleviate that situation, the advertisement for Quick-Kaps might be interpreted as promising that relief (an abortion). In any event, the commission stated in its conclusion to the case: ". . . the mental condition of such a person is an element to be considered in arriving at which construction might reasonably be put upon the advertisement."

Ads Directed At A Specific Audience

Let's take another situation. Suppose that an advertisement appeared in a medical journal. The ad was not deceptive to a physician. Yet it fell into the hands of a layman who was actually deceived. Under these circumstances would the advertisement be deceptive even though a different person was actually deceived?

That was the situation in *Belmont Laboratories, Inc. v. FTC.*[15] Obviously false claims regarding the curing potential of Mazon, a soap and ointment, had been made. In medical pamphlets addressed to doctors and nurses, Mazon claimed to permanently eliminate specific ailments.

● ● ● ● ● ● ● ● ● ● ● ● ● ● ● ● ● ● ● ●

Mazon—an ethical preparation
compounded under the personal
supervision of its originator—is the original treatment of its
character for:

Eczema	Ring worm
Psoriasis	Athlete's foot
Head scalds	Barber's itch
Ivy poison	Other skin disorders

The colloidal nature of the base of Mazon and its strong

penetrating characteristics, together with its healing and soothing
ingredients, afford quick and permanent elimination of Eczema
and other skin disorders. No other treatment for permanent cure
has ever been discovered. Some of the best-known skin specialists
in the city are using it exclusively and praise it highly.
● ●

The claims found in the example were medically untrue.
A major problem was with the claim that the product
"permanently eliminated" certain diseases. The copy tends to
convey that by an external application of an ointment, internal
disorders can be cured. It fails to recognize the need to apply
internal remedies to diseases caused by internal problems.

Many of the diseases listed (eczema, psoriasis, etc.) are
caused by internal disturbances. The application of an external
remedy can do little more than alleviate the exterior symptoms.
The ad also creates an impression of newness. One may have a
vision of thousands of doctors and druggists working diligently at
hundreds of hospitals and laboratories to develop the new medical
wonder—Mazon. This was certainly not the case.

These advertisements were found in pamphlets, which
were circulated to the medical profession, and in a medical
journal. Leaflets were also included inside the packages. The court
said: "physicians and readers of professional journals are too smart
to be deceived and that lay purchasers buy blind because the
leaflet is inside the carton containing the ointment. We think that
one position is untrue legally and the other factually."

In other words, the advertisements were blatantly untrue.
Doctors and nurses would know that, but the consumer would
not. The consumer would buy the product blindly because the
leaflet was inside the package.

The benchmark of this concept is: who is deceived? If a
person of low intellect is deceived by an advertisement for a Rolls
Royce, does this demonstrate a likelihood to deceive? The test for
deception (or rather deceptiveness) is rooted in the market at

which the advertisement is directed. However, if the advertisement reaches another market, the perception of that reader or viewer will be considered. Based on that reasoning, Belmont Laboratories lost.

THE ISSUE OF NET IMPRESSION

Whether an advertisement is deceptive must not be determined by viewing isolated parts of the advertisement (this has been alluded to earlier), but rather it should be based on the net impression of the entire ad. The net impression of the ad is the understanding that the reader walks away with after coming into contact with the advertisement. Keep in mind the reader will be determined by the current reasonable man standard, as we have discussed earlier.

Directly on this issue are statements by FTC Commissioner Mary L. Azcuenaga during a speech to the American Advertising Federation, National Government Affairs Conference, in Washington, D.C., on March 8, 1994. She addressed the relationship between claims made in a headline and claims or qualifications made in the text of the ad.

Azcuenaga pointed out that, "it would not be good policy to condone advertisements that make strong false or misleading claims in a headline, only to disclaim them in what is referred to as 'mouse print.'" She went on to say: "In evaluating the impact of the headline, the Commission will consider the 'net impression' created by the advertisement. The meaning of the advertisement should be construed in the context of the advertisement as a whole, not by individual elements of the ad taken out of context."

One very well-established case that demonstrated the principle of "net impression" is *Zenith Radio Corp.* v. *FTC*.[16] In this case, the commission alleged two primary issues in a series of advertisements for Zenith radios to determine if they were deceptive. The first involved Zenith's assertion regarding the capacity of its radio to receive foreign broadcasts. The second assertion involved the number of tubes contained in its radio sets.

These claims were found to be deceptive. A typical advertisement read as follows:

● ●

Europe is talking to you every night
in English. Are you listening?
With Zenith, the short wave radio that gives
you Europe direct, you can hear all the leaders,
all the daily news broadcasts.
You need not depend on re-broadcasts which bring
you only a small part.
Europe, South America, or the Orient every day
guaranteed or your money back on all short wave Zeniths.
1940 Zenith, the guaranteed short wave radio.

● ●

In truth, atmospheric conditions existed that made it impossible to receive satisfactory reception of foreign broadcasts. The Zenith radios were incapable of satisfactory reception of foreign broadcasts every day and under all conditions. The commission reasoned that the effect of the claims was to induce consumers to believe that radio reception problems would be completely overcome by using the Zenith radio. This is a good example of how deception was possible due to the consumers' lack of knowledge about the technical limitations of radio reception.

The second issue concerned the number of tubes contained in the radio. The ads listed different models available with the following tubes:

● ●

6-Tube Superheterodyne Table Model
8-Tube Superheterodyne with Wavemagnet Aerial
10-Tube Superheterodyne with Rotor Wavemagnet Aerial
11-Tube Superheterodyne with Rotor Wavemagnet Aerial

● ●

The commission defined "tubes" as devices that perform "the primary function of detecting, amplifying, or receiving radio signals." However, some of the tubes contained in the Zenith radio, and which were included in the advertised tube count, had nothing to do with receiving radio signals. They were, in fact, used for tuning and converting alternating current into direct current, and therefore the commission determined that they did not qualify under its definition. The commission, after concluding that a large portion of purchasers believed that a radio was better and more powerful because of the number of tubes it contained, ruled against Zenith.

The point in the Zenith case was that while the statements about the number of tubes contained in the sets were accurate, viewed as a whole the ad was deceptive. The consumer couldn't determine the relevance of the number of tubes, other than "the more tubes, the better the set." As for the first issue in the case, reception capability, the consumer would believe that reception problems would be overcome with the Zenith set. The net impression created by the ad was, therefore, a deceptive one.

DISTORTION OF FACTS

Let's take a look at another situation. In *Lorillard Co.* v. *FTC*,[17] isolated segments of an article taken from *Reader's Digest* were used in an advertisement for Old Gold cigarettes. Lorillard attempted to use the argument that the ads merely stated what had been stated in that article. By examining the advertisements however, the court determined that the meaning of the *Reader's Digest* article had been distorted. In essence, it amounted to the "use of the truth in such a way as to cause the reader to believe the exact opposite of what was intended by the writer of the article."

By comparing the advertisement with the article, we see where the problem lies. The article, referring to results of independent laboratory tests of the leading brands of cigarettes, actually said:

• •

The laboratory's general conclusion will be
sad news for the advertising copywriters, but good news
for the smoker, who need no longer worry as to which
cigarette can most effectively nail down his coffin.
For one nail is just about as good as another.
The differences between brands are, practically speaking,
small, and no single brand is so superior to its competitors
as to justify its selection on the ground that it is less harmful.
How small the variations are may be seen from
the data tabulated on page 7.

• • • • • • • • • • • • • • • • • • • •

That table showed the insignificance of the difference in the
tar and nicotine content of the various brands. While the tests did
show that Old Golds contained less nicotine, tars, and resins than
the others, the difference was so small as to be entirely
insignificant to the smoker. Yet the company advertised this
difference as if it had been awarded a commendation for public
health, rather than a slap in the face by *Reader's Digest*. Now that
we know this, here's an example of one Old Gold advertisement:

• • • • • • • • • • • • • • •

OLD GOLDS FOUND
LOWEST IN NICOTINE
OLD GOLDS FOUND
LOWEST IN THROAT-IRRITATING
TARS AND RESINS

See Impartial Test by *Reader's Digest*
July Issue.
See How Your Brand Compares with Old Gold.
Reader's Digest assigned a scientific testing laboratory to find
out about cigarettes. They tested seven leading cigarettes
and *Reader's Digest* published the results.
The cigarette whose smoke was lowest in nicotine

was Old Gold. The cigarette with the least throat-irritating
tars and resins was Old Gold.
On both these major counts Old Gold was best among
all seven cigarettes tested.
Get July *Reader's Digest.* Turn to page 5.
See what this highly respected magazine reports.
You'll say, "From now on, my cigarette is Old Gold!"
Light one?
Note the mild, interesting flavor. Easier on the throat?
Sure. And more smoking pleasure? Yes. It's the new Old Gold
—finer yet, since "something new has been added."

• •

Almost anyone reading the ad would get an entirely
different impression from the actual facts. A person would think
that Old Golds were less irritating and less harmful than the other
leading brands, all because of the *Reader's Digest* research. Few, in
fact, would have bothered to look up the article. As we have seen,
the truth was exactly the opposite. In this case, the court
concluded by saying:

> In determining whether or not advertising is
> false or misleading . . . regard must be had, not to
> fine spun distinctions and arguments that may be
> made in excuse but to the effect which it might
> reasonably be expected to have upon the general
> public. The important criterion is the net impression
> which the advertisement is likely to make upon the
> general populace.

The Use Of Visual Distortion

In addition to the blatant deception we saw in the Volvo
case discussed earlier, the use of mock-ups (a model built to depict
an actual situation) has also been an area of concern, particularly
where television is employed.

A problem exists here since television, as well as other media, has certain limitations in the area of reproduction. As we'll see, the deception issue arises when these limitations are overcome in a way that portrays the product as something it isn't.

In television commercials aired in late 1959, Colgate-Palmolive Company promoted its product Rapid Shave in the following manner.

The spot opens showing a football being kicked and the ball zooming toward the camera. The scene then cuts to a football player whose face is hidden behind a mask of sandpaper.

Voice-over:
"Who is the man behind the sandpaper mask?"
The football player removes the mask revealing a heavy growth of beard. The player rubs his face.

Voice-over:
"It's triple-threat man, Frank Gifford—backfield sensation of the New York Giants . . . a man with a problem just like yours . . ."
Camera cuts to sandpaper mask and a hand brings a can of Rapid Shave into the frame in front of the sandpaper:

Voice-over:
"A beard as tough as sandpaper . . . a beard that needs . . . PALMOLIVE RAPID SHAVE . . . super-moisturized for the fastest, smoothest shaves possible."
Type is superimposed on screen, "Super Moisturized Fastest, Smoothest Shaves."
Hand presses the top of the Rapid Shave can to dispense a small amount of the lather into the other hand.

Voice-over:
"To prove RAPID SHAVE's super-moisturizing power, we put it right from the can . . ."
The lather is spread in one continuous motion onto the surface of

the sandpaper. The first hand brings a razor into view and shaves a clean path through the lather and the gritty sandpaper.

Voice-over:
". . .onto this tough, dry sandpaper. It was apply . . . soak . . . and off in a stroke."

The picture then cuts to Frank Gifford lathering his face.

Voice-over:
"And super-moisturizing PALMOLIVE RAPID SHAVE can do the same for you."

In a split-screen, on one side a hand applies Rapid Shave to sandpaper. On the other side a hand applies Rapid Shave to Frank Gifford's face. As Gifford makes a razor stroke down his face, a hand does the same to the sandpaper.

Voice-over:
"In this sandpaper test . . . or on your sandpaper beard, you just apply RAPID SHAVE . . . then . . . take your razor . . . and shave clean with a fast, smooth stroke."

Gifford then strokes his clean-shaven face with a look of satisfaction. Screen cuts to a picture of cans of Rapid Shave surrounded by the words Super-Moisturizing and Fastest, Smoothest Shaves.

Voice-over:
"Try RAPID SHAVE . . . or cooling, soothing RAPID SHAVE MENTHOL . . . both super-moisturized . . . for the fastest, smoothest shaves possible. They both outshave the tube . . .outshave the brush."

Musical tune ends spot with the lyrics: "RAPID SHAVE outshaves them all. Use RAPID SHAVE in the morning."

In an attempt to demonstrate the shaving power of its shave cream, the Colgate-Palmolive Company showed the moistening and shaving of a piece of sandpaper, or so the viewer would think. The commercial purported to shave tough, dry sandpaper to demonstrate the moistening power of the cream, and it was blatantly demonstrated that way. However, the sandpaper turned out to be a sheet of plexiglass sprinkled with a layer of sand. The viewers were tricked into believing that they had actually seen the sandpaper test and they had been asked to make their purchasing decisions based on the test they had seen. In the case, *Federal Trade Commission v. Colgate-Palmolive Co.*,[18] the commission dealt directly with the issue of mock-ups in television. This case addressed a number of important sides to the mock-up issue. The court reasoned that "without this visible proof of Rapid Shave's claimed moisturizing ability, some viewers might not have been persuaded to buy the product."

Initially, it was determined that real sandpaper could be shaved if moistened for a sufficient length of time (in fact a very long time). However, it could not be shaved in the actual length of time used in the commercial, as the demonstration implied. They also found that, through the inadequacies of television, real sandpaper would appear to be only colored paper when photographed by the television camera. The advertiser attempted to use this as an excuse to justify the mock-up technique. It didn't work.

In a similar case, *In the Matter of Campbell Soup Co.*,[19] the commission looked at advertisements that showed a bowl of Campbell's soup. To all appearances, the soup had been prepared according to the directions on the can and was shown in a "ready to eat" situation. By viewing the ad the consumer saw an abundance of carrots, peas, potatoes, and onions present in a bowl of Campbell's soup.

The commission stated the reality of the advertisement:

In truth and in fact, in many of the . . . advertisements, which purport to demonstrate or offer evidence of the quantity and abundance of solid ingredients in a can of Campbell soup, [the advertiser has] placed, or caused to be placed in the aforesaid bowl . . . a number of clear glass marbles which prevent the solid ingredients from sinking to the bottom, thereby giving the soup the appearance of containing more solid ingredients than it actually contains, which fact is not disclosed. The aforesaid demonstration exaggerates, misrepresents, and is not evidence of, the quantity or abundance of solid ingredients in a can of Campbell soup; therefore, the aforesaid advertisements are false, misleading, and deceptive.

Campbell Soup Co. had placed marbles in the bottom of a bowl of soup that was shown in an advertisement. This caused the solids in the soup to stay at the surface. Here again the respondent claimed that the limitations of the medium necessitated the use of this mock-up to portray the actual viscosity of the product. The commission didn't agree with that reasoning and ordered Campbell to stop using the ads. This case was settled by consent order; Campbell agreed to the commission's determination and consented to abide by it.

As seen in the above examples, the reality of an advertisement's net impression must be considered carefully.

THE ISSUE OF UNFAIRNESS

We touched on this earlier in Chapter 1. We should revisit the concept here. While it is rare that the FTC will attack a claim under the unfairness theory, the advertiser must understand its implications. Notable cases include: *FTC v. Sperry & Hutchinson Co.*;[20] *In the Matter of Pfizer, Inc.*;[21] *In the Matter of I.T.T. Continental*;[22] and, *In the Matter of International Harvester Co.*[23]

This area permits the commission to expand on the strict limits of deception to correct a variety of injustices including immoral, unethical, oppressive or unscrupulous conduct. The commission treats deception and unfairness as separate issues.

Deception focuses on "likely" injury, while unfairness requires a showing that someone was actually harmed and could not have avoided the harm. A good example might involve a situation of coaxing a child to nag their parent into purchasing a product.

An ad can be nondeceptive yet still unfair. Generally, this situation would fall into one of the following areas:

- Claims that are advertised without prior substantiation;
- Claims which tend to exploit such vulnerable groups as children and the elderly; and
- Instances in which the advertiser fails to provide consumers with necessary information about competing products with which to make valid choices.

THE ISSUE OF PUFFING

Puffing is an area of advertising where the law allows the advertiser to make certain exaggerated statements or opinions about his product. Ivan Preston in his book, *The Great American Blow-Up: Puffery in Advertising and Selling*, defined puffing as the use of advertising that praises with "subjective opinions, superlatives, or exaggerations, vaguely and generally, stating no specific facts." Such statements as "Coke is the real thing" and "Sleeping on a Sealy is like sleeping on a cloud" are perfect examples of puff. A certain degree of puffing has always been allowed in advertising. Yet, the tolerance for this practice is limited due to the inherent gray area in its use.

The use of puffing in advertising has generally been acceptable to both the FTC and courts, based on certain rationale. Courts have reasoned that consumers do not rely on expressions of opinion by advertisers about their products. Also, the FTC recognizes that certain statements of general praise are not likely to be relied on by consumers under its "capacity to deceive" standard. Lastly, certain forms of superlative praise are permissible simply because there is no way to establish that they are false.

LEGAL INTERPRETATION OF PUFFERY

If the puff takes the form of a pure statement of opinion, and if the law prohibits only false factual statements, then it may be impossible for courts to prove that a false representation was made. While exaggerations, superlatives, and unsupported opinions in advertising have been tolerated, it is also clear that the extent of puffing has been reduced over the years. This is because of the increased desire of the FTC and courts to recognize that false factual representations can arise by implication, as we have discussed. This occurs in the use of some forms of puffing.

The commission investigated a situation of puffing in the case of *In The Matter of Better Living, Inc.*[24] Better Living, Inc. was in the business of selling and distributing aluminum storm doors, storm windows, and aluminum awnings. They had published advertisements and sales literature that made many blatantly false statements. The company made two claims that illustrate puffing. The first was the statement, "WORLD'S LOWEST PRICES." The second was "Better Living, Inc., 'Beauty Prize' storm windows and doors. Acclaimed from Coast to Coast First Prize Winners for Beauty. Choice of Famous Home Stylists."

As to the claim that the products were offered at the world's lowest prices, the company's advertising agent claimed that "for several weeks prior to the publication of the advertisements, a check was made of local competitive prices and that the prices [thereafter] advertised were slightly lower than their competitors'." The advertising agent admitted that there was no real factual basis to support the claim and, in fact, stated that the claim was typical puffing.

At this point the commission expressed its definition of puffing saying:

> Puffing . . . is a term frequently used to denote exaggerations reasonable to be expected of a seller as to the degree of quality of his product, the truth or falsity of which cannot be precisely determined. In

contrast, . . . the representation as to "the world's lowest price" is a statement of objective actuality, the truth or falsity of which is not variable and can be ascertained with factual precision. This representation cannot, therefore, properly be termed puffing. It is either true, or it is false; and, accordingly, such a determination must be made.

The other statement made by Better Living, Inc. related to the awards it had won in certain beauty contests. Despite the advertising claim, the advertising agent admitted that "these storm windows were never awarded a beauty prize of any kind." To this, Better Living added that such a statement was mere subjective puffing, which is acceptable in advertising. The commission disagreed and held that such claims would mislead consumers. The statement was one of fact, which could be proven or—in this case, disproved.

The commission continued to develop this concept with the decision in *In The Matter of Dannon Milk Prods., Inc.*[25] Here, Dannon had made claims about its product, Dannon Yogurt. Specifically, Dannon claimed in advertisements, brochures, pamphlets, and radio broadcasts that "Dannon is known as nature's perfect food that science made better." Dannon argued that the perfect food claim was mere puffing. However, the commission reasoned that because of the present day emphasis on dieting, health, and nutrition, to make the claim that a food is perfect far exceeds puffing or exaggeration of qualities. It is a misrepresentation of a material fact.

The Federal Trade Commission is not authorized to foreclose expression of honest opinion. The same opinion, however, may not be utilized to mislead or deceive the public or to harm a competitor. Because the dividing line between permissible puffery and implied deception is vague and because false implications of fact can be easily found, there is an increasing risk of liability from using puffery in advertising. The continued rise in consumerism has affected when puffery will be regarded as appropriate. A claim considered as opinion and puffery years ago could now be considered a deception.

Therefore, advertisers must be very careful in using hyperbole in their advertisements. The test is whether the average consumer will recognize or perceive the hyperbole for what it is or be deceived by it. Advertiser be warned: the puffing rule is not a license to lie. Terms like "best," "perfect," "prime," "exceptional," "original," "comparable in quality," "wonderful," and so on have been dealt with by the commission and the courts and do not qualify as puff. It should be obvious that puffing can cross over into deception very easily.

EXHIBIT: 2-1

FEDERAL TRADE COMMISSION
WASHINGTON, D.C. 20580
October 14, 1983

The Honorable John D. Dingell
Chairman
Committee on Energy and Commerce
U.S. House of Representatives
Washington, D.C. 20515

Dear Mr. Chairman:

This letter responds to the Committee's inquiry regarding the Commission's enforcement policy against deceptive acts or practices. We also hope this letter will provide guidance to the public.

Section 5 of the FTC Act declares unfair or deceptive acts or practices unlawful. Section 12 specifically prohibits false ads likely to induce the purchase of food, drugs, devices or cosmetics. Section 15 defines a false ad for purposes of Section 12 as one which is "misleading in a material respect." Numerous Commission and judicial decisions have defined and elaborated on the phrase "deceptive acts or practices" under both Sections 5 and 12. Nowhere, however, is there a single definitive statement of the Commission's view of its authority. The Commission believes that such a statement would be useful to the public, as well as the Committee in its continuing review of our jurisdiction.

We have therefore reviewed the decided cases to synthesize the most important principles of general applicability. We have attempted to provide a concrete indication of the manner in which the commission will enforce its deception mandate. In so doing, we intend to address the concerns that have been raised about the meaning of deception, and thereby attempt to provide a greater sense of certainty as to how the concept will be applied.

I. SUMMARY

Certain elements undergird all deception cases. First, there must be a representation, omission, or practice that is likely to mislead the consumer. Practices that have been found misleading or deceptive in specific cases include false oral or written representations, misleading price claims, sales of hazardous or systematically defective products or services without adequate disclosures, failure to disclose information regarding pyramid sales, use of bait and switch techniques, failure to perform promised services, and failure to meet warranty obligations.

Second, we examine the practice from the perspective of a consumer acting reasonably in the circumstances. If the representation or practice affects or is directed primarily to a particular group, the Commission examines reasonableness from the perspective of that group.

Third, the representation, omission, or practice must be a "material" one. The basic question is whether the act or practice is likely to affect the Consumer's conduct or decision with regard to a product or service. If so, the practice is material, and consumer injury is likely, because consumers are likely to have chosen differently but for the deception. In many instances, materiality, and hence injury, can be presumed from the nature of the practice. In other instances, evidence of materiality may be necessary.

Thus, the Commission will find deception if there is a representation, omission or practice that is likely to mislead the consumer acting reasonably in the circumstances, to the consumer's detriment. We discuss each of these elements below.

II. THERE MUST BE A REPRESENTATION, OMISSION, OR PRACTICE THAT IS LIKELY TO MISLEAD THE CONSUMER.

Most deception involves written or oral misrepresentations, or omissions of material information. Deception may also occur in other forms of conduct associated with a sales transaction. The entire advertisement, transaction or course of dealing will be considered. The issue is whether the act or practice is likely to mislead, rather than whether it causes actual deception.

Of course, the Commission must find that a representation, omission, or practice occurred. In cases of express claims, the representation itself establishes the meaning. In cases of implied claims, the Commission will often be able to determine meaning through an examination of the representation itself, including an evaluation of such factors as the entire document, the juxtaposition of various phrases in the document, the nature of the claim, and the nature of the transaction. In other situations, the Commission will require extrinsic evidence that reasonable consumers reach the implied claims. In all instances, the Commission will carefully consider any extrinsic evidence that is introduced.

Some cases involve omission of material information, the disclosure of which is necessary to prevent the claim, practice, or sale from being misleading. Information may be omitted from written or oral representations or from the commercial transaction.

In some circumstances, the Commission can presume that consumers are likely to reach false beliefs about the product or service because of an omission. At other times, however, the Commission may require evidence on consumers' expectations.

Marketing and point-of-sales practices that are likely to mislead consumers are also deceptive. For instance, in bait and switch cases, a violation occurs when the offer to sell the product is not a bona fide offer. The Commission has also found deception where a sales representative misrepresented the purpose of the initial contact with customers. When a product is sold, there is an implied representation that the product is fit for the purposes for which it is sold. When it is not, deception occurs. There may be a concern about the way a product or service is marketed, such as where inaccurate or incomplete information is provided. A failure to perform services promised under a warranty or by contract can also be deceptive.

III. THE ACT OR PRACTICE MUST BE CONSIDERED FROM THE PERSPECTIVE OF THE REASONABLE CONSUMER

The Commission believes that to be deceptive the representation, omission or practice must be likely to mislead reasonable consumers under the circumstances. The test is whether the consumer's interpretation or reaction is reasonable. When representations or sales practices are targeted to a specific audience, the Commission determines the effect of the practice on a reasonable member of that group. In evaluating a particular practice, the Commission considers the totality of the practice in determining how reasonable consumers are likely to respond.

A company is not liable for every interpretation or action by a consumer. In an advertising context, this principle has been well-stated:

> An advertiser cannot be charged with liability
> with respect to every conceivable misconception,

however outlandish, to which his representations
might be subject among the foolish or feeble-
minded. Some people, because of ignorance or
incomprehension, may be misled by even a
scrupulously honest claim. Perhaps a few misguided
souls believe, for example, that all "Danish pastry" is
made in Denmark. Is it therefore an actionable
deception to advertise "Danish pastry" when it is
made in this country? Of course not. A
representation does not become "false and
deceptive" merely because it will be unreasonably
misunderstood by an insignificant and
unrepresentative segment of the class of persons to
whom the representation is addressed. *Heinz W.
Kirchner.*[26]

To be considered reasonable, the interpretation or reaction
does not have to be the only one. When a seller's representation
conveys more than one meaning to reasonable consumers, one of
which is false, the seller is liable for the misleading interpretation.
An interpretation will be presumed reasonable if it is the one the
respondent intended to convey.

The Commission has used this standard in its past
decisions. ". . . The test applied by the Commission is whether the
interpretation is reasonable in light of the claim." In the Listerine
case, the Commission evaluated the claim from the perspective of
the "average listener." In a case involving the sale of encyclopedias,
the Commission observed "[i]n determining the meaning of an
advertisement, a piece of promotional material or a sales
presentation, the important criterion is the net impression that it is
likely to make on the general populace." The decisions in *American
Home Products*, *Bristol Myers*, and *Sterling Drug* are replete with
references to reasonable consumer interpretations. In a land sales
case, the Commission evaluated the oral statements and written

representations "in light of the sophistication and understanding of the persons to whom they were directed." Omission cases are no different: the Commission examines the failure to disclose in light of expectations and understandings of the typical buyer regarding the claims made.

When representations or sales practices are targeted to a specific audience, such as children, the elderly, or the terminally ill, the Commission determines the effect of the practice on a reasonable member of that group. For instance, if a company markets a cure to the terminally ill, the practice will be evaluated from the perspective of how it affects the ordinary member of that group. Thus, terminally ill consumers might be particularly susceptible to exaggerated cure claims. By the same token, a practice or representation directed to a well-educated group, such as a prescription drug advertisement to doctors, would be judged in light of the knowledge and sophistication of that group.

As it has in the past, the Commission will evaluate the entire advertisement, transaction, or course of dealing in determining how reasonable consumers are likely to respond. Thus, in advertising the Commission will examine "the entire mosaic, rather than each title separately." As explained by a Court of Appeals in a recent case:

> The Commission's right to scrutinize the visual and aural imagery of advertisements follows from the principle that the Commission looks to the impression made by the advertisements as a whole. Without this mode of examination, the Commission would have limited recourse against crafty advertisers whose deceptive messages were conveyed by means other than, or in addition to, spoken words. *American Home Products.*[27]

Commission cases reveal specific guidelines. Depending on the circumstances, accurate information in the text may not remedy a false headline because reasonable consumers may glance only at the headline. Written disclosure or fine print may be insufficient to correct a misleading representation. Other practices of the company may direct consumers' attention away from the qualifying disclosures. Oral statements, label disclosures or point-of-sale material will not necessarily correct a deceptive representation or omission. Thus, when the first contact between a seller and a buyer occurs through a deceptive practice, the law may be violated even if the truth is subsequently made known to the purchaser. *Pro forma* statements or disclaimers may not cure otherwise deceptive messages or practices.

Qualifying disclosures must be legible and understandable. In evaluating such disclosures, the Commission recognizes that in many circumstances, reasonable consumers do not read the entirety of an ad or are directed away from the importance of the qualifying phrase by the acts or statements of the seller. Disclosures that conform to the Commission's Statement of Enforcement Policy regarding clear and conspicuous disclosures, which applies to television advertising, are generally adequate.[28] Less elaborate disclosures may also suffice.

Certain practices, however, are unlikely to deceive consumers acting reasonably. Thus, the Commission generally will not bring advertising cases based on subjective claims (taste, feel, appearance, smell) or on correctly stated opinion claims if consumers understand the source and limitations of the opinion. Claims phrased as opinions are actionable, however, if they are not honestly held, if they misrepresent the qualifications of the holder or the basis of his opinion or if the recipient reasonably interprets them as implied statements of fact.

The Commission generally will not pursue cases involving obviously exaggerated or puffing representations, i.e., those that the ordinary consumers do not take seriously. Some exaggerated claims, however, may be taken seriously by consumers and are actionable. For instance, in rejecting a respondent's argument that use of the words "electronic miracle" to describe a television antenna was puffery, the Commission stated:

> Although not insensitive to respondent's concern that the term miracle is commonly used in situations short of changing water into wine, we must conclude that the use of "electronic miracle" in the context of respondent's grossly exaggerated claims would lead consumers to give added credence to the overall suggestion that this device is superior to other types of antennae. *Jay Norris*.[29]

Finally, as a matter of policy, when consumers can easily evaluate the product or service, it is inexpensive, and it is frequently purchased, the Commission will examine the practice closely before issuing a complaint based on deception. There is little incentive for sellers to misrepresent (either by an explicit false statement or a deliberate false implied statement in these circumstances since they normally would seek to encourage repeat purchases. Where, as here, market incentives place strong constraints on the likelihood of deception, the Commission will examine a practice closely before proceeding.

In sum, the Commission will consider many factors in determining the reaction of the ordinary consumer to a claim or practice. As would any trier of fact, the Commission will evaluate the totality of the ad or the practice and ask questions such as: How clear is the representation? How conspicuous is any qualifying information? How important is the omitted information? Do other sources for the omitted information exist? How familiar is the public with the product or service?

IV. THE REPRESENTATION, OMISSION OR PRACTICE MUST BE MATERIAL

The third element of deception is materiality. That is, a representation, omission or practice must be a material one for deception to occur. A "material" misrepresentation or practice is one which is likely to affect a consumer's choice of or conduct regarding a product. In other words, it is information that is important to consumers. If inaccurate or omitted information is material, injury is likely.

The Commission considers certain categories of information presumptively material. First, the Commission presumes that express claims are material. As the Supreme Court stated recently, "[i]n the absence of factors that would distort the decision to advertise, we may assume that the willingness of a business to promote its products reflects a belief that consumers are interested in the advertising." Where the seller knew, or should have known, that an ordinary consumer would need omitted information to evaluate the product or service, or that the claim was false, materiality will be presumed because the manufacturer intended the information or omission to have an effect. Similarly, when evidence exists that a seller intended to make an implied claim, the Commission will infer materiality.

The Commission also considers claims or omissions material if they significantly involve health, safety, or other areas with which the reasonable consumer would be concerned. Depending on the facts, information pertaining to the central characteristics of the product or service will be presumed material. Information has been found material where it concerns the purpose, safety, efficacy, or cost of the product or service. Information is also likely to be material if it concerns durability, performance, warranties or quality. Information pertaining to a finding by another agency regarding the product may also he material.

Where the Commission cannot find materiality based on the above analysis, the Commission may require evidence that the claim or omission is likely to be considered important by consumers. This evidence can be the fact that the product or service with the feature represented costs more than an otherwise comparable product without the feature, a reliable survey of consumers, or credible testimony.

A finding of materiality is also a finding that injury is likely to exist because of the representation, omission, sales practice, or marketing technique. Injury to consumers can take many forms. Injury exists if Consumers would have chosen differently but for the deception. If different choices are likely, the claim is material, and injury is likely as well. Thus, injury and materiality are different names for the same concept.

V. CONCLUSION

The Commission will find an act or practice deceptive if there is a misrepresentation, omission, or other practice, that misleads the consumer acting reasonably in the circumstances, to the consumer's detriment. The Commission will not generally require extrinsic evidence concerning the representations understood by reasonable consumers or the materiality of a challenged claim, but in some instances extrinsic evidence will be necessary.

The Commission intends to enforce the FTC Act vigorously. We will investigate, and prosecute where appropriate, acts or practices that are deceptive. We hope this letter will help provide you and the public with a greater sense of certainty concerning how the Commission will exercise its jurisdiction over deception. Please do not hesitate to call if we can be of any further assistance.

By direction of the Commission, Commissioners Pertschuk and Bailey dissenting, with separate statements attached and with separate response to the Committee's request for a legal analysis to follow.

/s/James C. Miller III
Chairman

[1] *Sears, Roebuck & Co. v. FTC*, 258 F. 307 (7th Cir. 1919).

[2] 29 Fed. Reg. 8324, 8355 (July 2,1964).

[3] (Harris and Milkis, 1989).

[4] P.L. 93-637, 88 Stat. 2183.

[5] *In the Matter of Cliffdale Associates, Inc.*, 103 F.T.C. 110 (1984).

[6] *FTC v. Raladam Co.*, 316 U.S. 149, 62 S.Ct. 966, 86 L.Ed. 1336 (1942).

[7] *Vaughan v. Menlowe*, 3 Bing. N.C. 468, 132 Eng. Rep. 490 (1837).

[8] *Federal Trade Commission v. Standard Education Society*, 302 U.S. 112, 58 S.Ct. 113,
82 L.Ed. 141 (1937).

[9] *Standard Education Society v. FTC*, 86 F.2d 692 (2d. Cir. 1936).

[10] *Gelb v. FTC*, 144 F.2d 580 (2d Cir. 1944).

[11] *Donaldson v. Read Magazine, Inc.*, 333 U.S. 178, 68 S.Ct. 591, 92 L.Ed. 628 (1948).

[12] *In the Matter of Coca-Cola Company*, F.T.C. Docket No. 8839.

[13] *In the Matter of Doris Savitch*, 50 F.T.C. 828 (1954), affirmed per curiam, 218 F.2d
817 (7th Cir. 1955).

[14] *Aronberg, trading as Positive Products Company v. FTC*, 132 F.2d 165
(7th Cir. 1943).

[15] *Belmont Laboratories, Inc. v. FTC*, 103 F. 2d 538, (3rd Cir. 1939).

[16] *Zenith Radio Corp. v. FTC*, 143 F.2d 29 (7th Cir. 1944).

[17] *Lorillard Co. v. FTC*, 186 F.2d 52 (4th Cir. 1950).

[18] *Federal Trade Commission v. Colgate-Palmolive Co.*, 380 U.S. 374, 85 S.Ct. 1035,
13 L.Ed. 2d 904 (1965).

[19] *In the Matter of Campbell Soup Co.*, 77 F.T.C. 664 (1970).

[20] *FTC v. Sperry & Hutchinson Co.*, 405 U.S. 233, 92 S.Ct. 898,
31 L.Ed. 2d 170 (1972).

[21] *In the Matter of Pfizer, Inc.*, 81 F.T.C. 23 (1972).

[22] *In the Matter of I.T.T. Continental*, 90 F.T.C. 181 (1977).

[23] *In the Matter of International Harvester Co.*, 104 F.T.C. 949 (1984).

[24] In *The Matter of Better Living, Inc.*, 54 F.T.C. 648 (1957),
aff'd 259 F.2d 271 (1958).

[25] In *The Matter of Dannon Milk Prods., Inc.*, 61 F.T.C. 840 (1962).

[26] *Heinz W. Kirchner*, 63 F.T.C. 1282, 1290 (1963).

[27] *American Home Products*, 695 F.2d 681 (3d Cir. 1982).

[28] CCH Trade Regulation Reporter, ¶7569.09 (Oct. 21, 1970).

[29] *Jay Norris*, 91 F.T.C. 751, 847 n.20 (1978), affd. 598 F.2d 1244 (2d Cir.),
cert. denied, 444 U.S. 980 (1979).

CHAPTER 3

SPECIFIC AREAS OF CONCERN UNDER THE FEDERAL TRADE COMMISSION ACT

Welcome back my friends to the show that never ends.
—*Keith Emerson*

In the previous chapter we discussed the scope of the jurisdiction of the Federal Trade Commission. The theory and reasoning the commission uses in its review of advertising was analyzed. In this chapter specific issue claims and language usage in advertising that can cause trouble are addressed.

We look at the types of advertising claims that the advertiser deals with almost every day, in almost every ad. We review examples of untruthful ads, and explore problems with pricing, labeling and endorsements. Also, we discuss the uses and pitfalls of using qualified language and ads containing claims that a product is unique or will perform in a certain way. Such other problem areas as deception by implication or inference, use of technical language, vagueness, and deceptive truth are also presented. Parallel state laws and FTC industry guidelines are additionally addressed. First, let's examine the most obvious type of deceptive ad, one that is strictly untrue.

UNTRUTH AND DECEPTION

This may seem to be contradictory, but an untrue claim is not, in and of itself, deceptive. The nature of the untruth must be explored to determine if it is deceptive. In simpler terms, there are claims that are factually untrue, but at the same time are certainly not deceptive.

Fantasy Claims

This type of claim is called fantasy advertising. While the claim, "Coke adds life" is clearly untrue, it is not deceptive because an ordinary consumer would not believe such a blatant claim. As we have seen in Chapter 2, these types of claims are not considered deceptive if we look to the reasonable man standard, that is, the perception of any ordinary, reasonable consumer. While fantasy claims are very similar to puffery, they are more than subjective opinion. They are blatant absurdities.

Claims That Are Considered Untrue

Literal untruths in any other form are almost always deceptive. Samples of some of the most blatant in advertising run the gamut. For example, Alix Cohn, a junk dealer, was sued by the state of Connecticut for advertising his second-hand merchandise as being antique. The merchandise was certainly not "antique" in the true sense of the word.[1] In another case, a product designed to repair aluminum cookware, called So-Luminum, was advertised as being able to withstand a direct flame of 2,000 degrees. The company's claim was absolutely untrue.[2] Advertisements were created that gave the impression that goods were made of leather when they were not. Duraleather— a material used in cars, suitcases, and upholstery—contained no leather but was painted and embossed with a grain to look like leather.[3] In another example, a product called Sebrone claimed to permanently eliminate dandruff due to new discoveries of scientific research. In fact, the product only temporarily removed dandruff scales.[4]

In one case, Murry Space Shoes circulated reprints of a news article as an advertisement. The article claimed that the manufacturer's shoe would "cure many bodily ailments . . . corrects foot deformities (and cures) . . . corns, fallen arches, and bunions." Murry Space Shoes had no corrective or therapeutic value whatsoever and could not cure anything.[5]

To further illustrate untrue claims, let's take a more detailed look at two such cases where claims were considered to be plainly untrue. The first, *United States* v. *Hindman*,[6] involved the manufacturer of military uniforms. Seymour Hindman had been promoting his uniforms as custom-made and custom-tailored. In fact, the uniforms were all mass produced. Hindman argued that the term custom-tailored did not mean that the uniform was made individually to fit, but that it was given "particularly fine stitching or other tailoring finish." The court felt that the average consumer would not agree with such a definition, but rather would believe that the uniform was made to order. Therefore, it was untrue that Hindman's uniforms were custom-made.

The second case, *Prima Products* v. *Federal Trade Commission*,[7] involved the advertising of certain qualities of a masonry sealer called Aquella. The manufacturer, Prima Products, promoted to the public a waterproofing paint used mainly on brick walls. One of the claims that Aquella made was that it was "easy to apply . . . almost as simple as whitewashing." In fact, the application was somewhat more complex, including numerous washings and repeated applications. The court ruled that Aquella was not "easy to apply," as it was advertised.

USING QUALIFYING LANGUAGE TO OVERCOME DECEPTION

Another area of concern is the use of a deceptive statement made in an advertisement with the advertiser trying to offset the deception by clarifying it elsewhere with other language, the proverbial "small print." The practice of clarifying a deceptive—or possibly deceptive—claim with other language is sound policy for the advertiser. However, if the potentially deceptive statement is more noticeable than the qualification, either intentionally or unintentionally, then the statement will still be considered by the

FTC to be false and deceptive.

The idea here is that the qualifying statement (often called a disclaimer) must relieve any misrepresentation made by the other statement. If this is effectively accomplished, deception has probably not occurred. But remember, this works only if the qualifying statement is made with the same weight and conspicuousness. But where the qualifying statement is made in an inconspicuous manner (compared to the qualified statement), then it has been held that deception probably exists.

Double Eagle Lubricants manufactured a motor oil that was re-refined from previously used oil. The oil was displayed in the standard one-quart can, the type found in any auto parts store. The trade name of the product was printed on the front of the can. On the side of the can was printed a statement that the oil was re-refined.

The cans were intended for display with the fronts showing, stacked side-by-side on the shelf. The front of the can faced the prospective customer to attract his attention. By placing the clarifying statements on the side of the can, the customer would conceivably pick up the can and purchase it based on the face label. For there to be a clear and conspicuous disclosure, the clarifying statement should have appeared on the front panel of the can.

The case, *Double Eagle Lubricants, Inc. v. FTC*,[8] discussed this situation and the court found that the labeling practice was deceptive. We will see more on labeling requirements later in this chapter. True, Double Eagle had made a disclosure about the product, but not with enough weight to avoid a misinformed purchase. What was interesting in this case was that Double Eagle brought in witnesses who testified that the labeling did not deceive them. Yet the court, in deciding against Double Eagle, said: "Evidence of [actual] deception is not necessary where the exhibits themselves sufficiently demonstrate their capacity to deceive." Remember, the test is now "likely" to deceive.

The court went on to say:

If the commission can find deception without
evidence that the public was deceived, we believe
that it can make the same finding on the basis of its
visual examination of exhibits even though
numerous members of the public have testified that
they were not deceived.

As we discussed in Chapter 2, actual deception is not
required, only a likelihood of deception need be shown to satisfy
the requirement of the FTC act.

Visibility Of A Qualifying Statement

In *Giant Food, Inc.* v. *FTC*,[9] the qualifying statement was not
placed close to the statement that it was supposed to clarify. This
case dealt with the small print in an ad. Giant Food, Inc., a large
eastern retail chain, advertised its products through the
newspapers, printing its sale price along with what it referred to as
a regular price. The regular price was derived from a
manufacturer's suggested price list and was not indicative of prices
that the merchandise was ever actually sold at in the area.

A typical ad, which ran in three Washington, D.C. area
newspapers, read as follows:

• •
Proctor Steam & Dry Iron #10010
Regular Price $15.95
Sale Price $8.47
• • • • • • • • • • •

Giant Food used the phrase "Regular Price" in a way that
led the consumer to believe that it had sold the product at that
price "in the recent, regular course of its business." That was
untrue. Giant Food argued that its advertising was not deceptive

because a disclaimer in small print ran at the bottom of the ad. The disclaimer was worded in a rather lengthy and confusing manner. The witnesses who testified at the trial said that they would not normally read the disclaimer, or that they would have been more confused if they had read it. The court said, "That the disclaimer might engender confusion appears to us . . . to be an understatement."

Giant Food also used the phrase "Manufacturer's List Price," which represented to the consumer the price at which the product was usually and customarily sold at retail. In fact, the manufacturer's list was substantially in excess of the usual and customary retail price. The way to look at this is if you state a "regular price" in an ad, the product must have actually been sold by you, at that price, generally within the previous 30 days. Specific pricing terms and their uses are discussed later in this chapter.

PRIOR KNOWLEDGE OF A FALSE STATEMENT

What happens when the consumer knows that an advertisement is false? Simply because the consumer knows that a claim is false does not relieve its being deceptive.

In *Heavenly Creations, Inc.* v. *FTC*,[10] knowledge of false statements was at issue. Although this case involved dealers, rather than consumers, the practice was still deceptive. Heavenly Creations sold a variety of products to distributors, jobbers, salesmen, and retailers. These products were then resold to consumers. The problem here was with the pricing of the manufacturer's product to the dealers.

Dealers knew that Heavenly Creations had a practice of pre-ticketing goods at inflated prices. Heavenly, as a defense, tried to prove that there was a custom of fictitious pricing within the retail trade. However, the court maintained that "A practice does not cease to be . . . unfair because the falsity of the . . .

representation has become so well-known to the trade that dealers . . . are no longer deceived."

CLAIMS OF UNIQUENESS

A claim of uniqueness about a product or service is another area of concern under Section 5 of the FTC Act. It is deceptive to state that a product has extraordinary features or is unique, if it is not. But what is considered to be a claim of uniqueness? Again, it's based on the average reasonable consumer of that type of product.

Fedders Corporation manufactured air conditioners and, in the mid-1970s, advertised them as being unique due to their having "reserve cooling power." This was a claim that could not be substantiated. In *Fedders Corp. v. FTC*,[11] they even admitted that the statement "reserve cooling power" was "intended to imply an unusual ability to produce cold air under extreme conditions of heat and humidity." The false claim that Fedders air conditioners possessed "reserve cooling power" implied to the consumer that some feature of the cooling, circulation, or dehumidifying systems in the air conditioner allowed them to outperform other brands in extreme temperature situations. In reality, Fedders air conditioners had no real technical advantage over its competitors' equipment.

The court ordered Fedders to cease and desist from making claims that its air conditioners were unique in any material respect, unless it was a fact which could be proven. In the commission's order, it prohibited Fedders from:

Making, directly or indirectly, any statement or representation in any advertising or sales promotional material as to the air cooling, dehumidification, or circulation characteristics, capacity or capabilities of any air conditioner, unless at the time of such representation [they] have a reasonable basis for such statement or representation, which shall consist of competent scientific, engineering or other similar objective

material or industry-wide standards based on such
material.

PERFORMANCE CLAIMS

There are specific problems inherent in performance
claims. These are claims that a product will do what the ad says it
will do. The Fedders case we just looked at was a good example of
this. In fact, uniqueness is a claim of performance.

Substantiation Of Performance Claims

In *Sears, Roebuck and Co.* v. *FTC*,[12] the claim that "our
dishwasher cleans dishes so well that they do not have to be pre-
rinsed" was an example of an absolute performance claim. If the
claim were made that "our dishwasher cleans better than theirs," it
would be considered as a relative or comparative performance
claim. Sears, Roebuck & Co. is the largest retailer of general
merchandise in the United States. In the early 1970's Sears devised
a program to increase the sales of its "Lady Kenmore" dishwasher.
Sears did not reengineer or redesign the product. Instead it
attempted to change the image of—or reposition—the product.
The objective was expressed by Sears advertising agency as seeking
to: "transform the consumer image [of the Lady Kenmore] from a
price brand to a superior product at a reasonable price. Eventually,
the brand should move from market leadership to market
dominance as the market share increases."

Sears produced ads claiming that the Lady Kenmore
"completely eliminated" the need for prescraping and prerinsing.
Sears labeled the machine as the "Freedom Maker." In various
media over a four-year period, and at a cost of over $8 million,
Sears advertising for the Lady Kenmore claimed:

● ● ● ● ● ● ● ● ● ● ● ● ● ● ● ●
SEARS LADY KENMORE
THE DO-IT-ITSELF DISHWASHER

No scraping. No rinsing. Lady Kenmore has 6 powerful
hot water jets for the bottom rack,
surging hot water with enough force to
scrub every dish, pot and pan really clean.
Even baked-on food comes off.
And the dishes on top get as clean as those on the bottom.
With a Kenmore you'll never have to scrape or rinse again.
Even dishes crusty with leftover food.
Kenmore's 14 powerful hot water jets scour every dish clean
. . . with no scraping or rinsing.
It's great! You'll like the way it makes pre-rinsing
and soaking of heavily soiled dishes, pots and pans
a thing of the past.
Gets even the messiest baking dishes and roasting pans
spotlessly clean . . . without pre-rinsing!
Wouldn't the woman in your life love a Kenmore Dishwasher
for Mother's Day?
A Kenmore Dishwasher from Sears means no more dishpan hands,
she'll never have to touch dishwater again!
Egg, lipstick, peanut butter, jelly, even spaghetti sauce
come right off with no pre-rinsing.

● ●

As a result of the Lady Kenmore campaign, unit sales rose
more than 300 percent from 35,029 units in 1971 to 105,570
units in 1973. Sears total dishwasher sales rose from $73.47
million to $94.5 million during that period.

Now let's look at the reality of the case. Sears "no scraping,
no pre-rinsing" claim was simply not true, and it had no
reasonable basis upon which to make the claim. In fact, the
instruction manual, which customers could only get after their
purchase, contradicted the claim. The manual specifically
instructed the owner to presoak or lightly scour certain dishes.

What the commission ordered Sears to do is worth noting.
In addition to a cease-and-desist order, Sears was ordered to

maintain written records "in connection with the advertising, offering for sale, sale, or distribution of dishwashers or other major home appliances." The records required included:

1. All materials that were relied upon in making any claim or representation in advertising . . . concerning the performance characteristics of any Sears . . . dishwashers or other major home appliances; and

2. All test reports, studies, surveys, or demonstrations . . . that contradict, qualify, or call into question any claim or representation in advertising . . . on behalf of . . . Sears, Roebuck & Co.'s dishwashers or other major home appliances . . . for a period of three years.

Requirements Of Substantiation

We've seen that if you make a claim in an ad, you must be able to substantiate it. That brings up a valid question. What type of substantiation is acceptable? The courts have decided that the proof to support a claim must have a reasonable basis. In other words, the proof can't be contrived, out of context, or based on distorted facts or statistics. This was discussed in *FTC v. Pharmtech Research, Inc.*[13]

In July 1983, the following television commercial aired for a product manufactured by Pharmtech Research called Daily Greens:

●●●●●●●●●●●●●●●

The following message
concerns a revolutionary new concept in diet and nutrition.
According to this report, commissioned by the
National Cancer Institute, a combination of cruciferous and
carotene rich vegetables, has been proven to help our bodies build
certain important biological defenses.
Of course, to get the most benefit from any vegetable,
you should eat them raw. But that's difficult to do everyday.

So I'd like to introduce you to Daily Greens. Daily Greens
are not just another vitamin pill.
They're natural, fresh, cruciferous and carotene-rich vegetables,
dehydrated and compressed, to give you the important
nutritional supplements that could be so vital to your future
health. So, if you're not getting enough raw vegetables, everyday,
rely on Daily Greens—to help
your body defend itself.

• • • • • • • • • • • • • • • • •

Other advertisements ran in magazines, on the radio, and on television. While each ad varied somewhat, they all claimed that by taking Daily Greens the consumer would reduce the risk of certain cancers. The claim was also made that using Daily Greens would contribute to building certain biological defenses.

The advertisements didn't claim that the use of Daily Greens would prevent cancer. Yet the problem stemmed from the fact that Pharmtech relied solely on a report published by the National Academy of Sciences entitled *Diet, Nutrition, and Cancer.* The report itself states: "These recommendations apply only to foods as sources of nutrients—not to dietary supplements of individual nutrients." The report also warned "that the removal of water which occurs during dehydration may alter the protective effect of nutrients and other compounds."

Pharmtech's ads represented that the use of Daily Greens was connected to a reduction in the risk of cancer. The Daily Greens ads were deceptive for two reasons. First, they misstated the findings of the report—that the use of supplements reduces the risk of cancer or the building of biological defenses. Second, they fail to disclose some important material facts that the report's findings did not apply to processed supplements, but only whole foods. In other words, the report was taken and used out of context. The advertisement's substantiation did not have a reasonable basis.

DECEPTION BY IMPLICATION OR INFERENCE

In ads that contain deception by implication or inference, there is no specific untruth, yet for various reasons the advertisement's net impression is not one of truthfulness. In 1884 Mark Twain wrote *The Adventures of Huckleberry Finn*. In Chapter 1 Huck describes the way Twain had written about him earlier in *The Adventures of Tom Sawyer*. In Huck's honest opinion he said about Twain: " . . . he told the truth, mainly. There was things which he stretched, but mainly he told the truth."

An ad can cause the same effect. Some mainly tell the truth while some are stretched quite a bit. But an ad is not a work of fiction. At least, it's not supposed to be. It's a commercial message that has to create an impression of truthfulness. And it has to live up to that impression. An important point is that an advertiser should not try to hide behind the excuse that there was no intention to deceive. A claim of an innocent deception is no defense. The ad speaks for itself.

Innuendo That Creates Deception

Obvious misrepresentations are one thing. But deception through innuendo is much more subtle. The makers of Hollywood brand bread created the impression that its product was a low calorie food. Specifically, the Hollywood bread advertisements claimed that its product was lower in calories than ordinary bread and, that by using Hollywood in a normal diet, the user would lose weight or prevent a weight gain.

The ads for Hollywood bread showed a picture of a beautiful movie star in a sleek full-length pose. The ads also showed a picture of the product. The copy read:

• • • • • • • • • • • • • • • • • • •
When a woman's Panther Slim,
she's vital as well as slender.
A good figure is more than luck when a lady

watches her weight the famous Hollywood Way.
Hollywood Bread is high in protein, vitamins
and minerals, yet has only 46 calories per 18 gram slice.
Choice of Golden Light or
Nut-like Dark Hollywood.

● ● ● ● ● ● ● ● ● ● ● ● ● ● ● ● ● ●

The court in *National Bakers Serv., Inc.* v. *FTC*,[14] found that the average consumer had no perception of the average caloric content or gram weight of a slice of bread. It also felt that the claim "only 46 calories per 18 gram slice" was intended to, and did, convey the impression that Hollywood bread had fewer calories than other breads. The claim also implied that by eating the same amount of Hollywood bread as other breads, the consumer could lose weight.

In reality, there is no significant difference in the caloric content of Hollywood bread and other commercial white breads. Both contain about 276 calories per 100 grams. However, other breads are sliced into twenty 23-gram slices while Hollywood is sliced into twenty-five 18-gram slices. The only reason that Hollywood bread contains fewer calories per slice is that it is sliced thinner.

The ad was technically true in that there were no incorrect facts. Yet, innuendo created an impression that was not altogether truthful. Hollywood bread had no fewer calories than other commercial breads, and, in fact, its only usefulness in a diet came from the fact that its thinner slices meant the consumer would consume smaller individual portions and therefore fewer calories.

Implication That Creates Deception

Another area of concern under Section 5 of the act is deception by inference or implication. Between 1967 and 1968, Firestone Tire Company ran ads which claimed:

● ● ● ● ● ● ● ● ● ● ● ● ● ● ● ● ● ● ●

THE SAFE TIRE. FIRESTONE.
When you buy a Firestone tire
—no matter how much or how little you pay—
you get a safe tire.
Firestone tires are custom-built one by one
by skilled craftsmen.
And they're personally inspected for an extra margin of safety.
If these tires don't pass all of the exacting
Firestone inspections, they don't get out.
Every new Firestone design goes through rugged tests
of safety and strength far exceeding any driving
condition you'll ever encounter.
We prove them in our test lab,
on our test track,
and in rigorous day-to-day driving conditions.
All Firestone tires meet or exceed the new
federal government testing requirements.
(They have for some time.)
Firestone. The Safe Tire.
At 60,000 Firestone Safe Tire Centers
At no more cost than ordinary tires.

● ●

Firestone, in *Firestone Tire & Rubber Co.* v. *FTC*,[15] admitted that it was technologically impossible to assure that a tire was free of defects. By implying an unqualified assertion of safety, they created a deceptive ad. While Firestone made no explicit claim about the safety of its tires under all driving and road conditions, it did imply a claim. The court said: "[Firestone's] advertisement asserts flatly that the Firestone tire is 'The Safe Tire' and describes the exacting, rugged tests . . . which the tires are put through to assure this safety. [Firestone's] advertisement gives no indication that there is any limit to the safety of this tire." As a result of this case Firestone was required to disclose clearly and conspicuously, in close proximity to any safety claim, that "the safety of any tire is affected by conditions of use, such as inflation pressure, vehicle weight, wear, and other operating conditions."

THE USE OF TECHNICAL LANGUAGE AND VAGUENESS

Deception can be accomplished through the use of technical language the consumer is not likely to understand, or by making vague or ambiguous statements. Technical language or complicated verbiage cannot be expected to be understood by the average consumer.

Use Of A Foreign Language

About 1840 Edouard Pinaud opened a business in Paris, France, to manufacture perfumes. His goods, as well as his name, became very well known. Monsieur Pinaud for many years built a reputation for the quality of his products. After Pinaud's death in 1868, the Koltz Company took over the Pinaud line.

From 1891 to 1895 a Mr. Hecht worked for Koltz. After leaving, Hecht began manufacturing, in the United States, his own line of toilet preparations. Hecht's bottles, contents, stoppers, and labels were all made in the United States. The labels, however, were printed in French. The labels contained the sentence:

• • • • • • • • • • • • • • •
Preparee par M. Hecht,
Dernierement avec Parfumerie Ed. Pinaud, Paris.
• •

Roughly translated the line means "Prepared by Mr. Hecht, formerly with perfumer Ed. Pinaud, Paris." The court in *Koltz* v. *Hecht*,[16] stated that using foreign words, although literally true, can be considered deceptive. Hecht admitted at the trial that it was, in fact, his intent to mislead the public into believing that his domestic perfume was made in France, therefore trading on the reputation of French perfume and the name of Ed. Pinaud. While it was true that nowhere on the bottle was it stated that the product was foreign made, Hecht ingeniously conveyed that impression through his labeling, especially if the purchaser was not fluent in French.

Deception By Implying A Technical Term

Let's look at another example. The following ad ran in trade magazines (directed toward mattress manufacturers) by a manufacturer of mattress cloth:

● ●
STERITIZED FABRIC has a proven sales idea,
proven in shoes, proven in clothes, proven in hats.
The sales appeal of a STERITIZED FABRIC has been proven
in many other fields.—
We are not guessing when we say that what has been done
in the shoe, the hat, and the dress industries
can also be done in the mattress industry.
In the Nation's Greatest Stores,
other merchandise has shown sales jumps by using the same
Germ-Repellent Method.
STERITIZED FABRIC—Repellent to Bacteria. Repellent to Water.
STERITIZED mattress ticking avoids
perspiration, stains, and odor.
STERITIZED FABRIC is absolutely noninjurious.
STERITIZED FABRIC Repels Germs,
Helps protect all the family against spread of infection,
is positively nonirritating, guards against odors.
STERITIZED Mattress Fabric . . .
Tested under standards stated in Circular 198,
U.S. Department of Agriculture,

made by Blumenthal Print Works, New Orleans, U.S.A.
Blumenthal Print Works, Converters of Cotton Cloth.
● ●

In *In the Matter of Blumenthal*,[17] the use of the word
"Steritized" created a problem for the advertiser because the buyer
perceived the word to say "sterilized." This was a natural
assumption. Why was this a problem if the fabric lived up to the
claims? Well, there's the rub. It didn't. The steritized fabric didn't
do any of the things that the ad claimed it could. It was not sterile,
sanitary, antiseptic, odorless, bacteriostatic, or bacteria-, germ-, or
water-repellent. It would not prevent perspiration odors, wear
longer, or guard against the spread of infection. People would
believe that, by some new sterilizing process, the Blumenthal
fabric could have all of the claimed qualities. Blumenthal simply
made up a name for its product, which bore an amazing
resemblance to another word.

Deception Through Technical Language

In *Chrysler Corp.* v. *FTC*,[18] we see an example of confusing
technical language. During the 1973-74 energy crisis, Chrysler ran
ads for their Dodge Darts. A typical ad promoted the fuel
efficiency of Chrysler cars and ran as follows:

● ● ● ● ● ● ● ● ● ● ● ●
THE SMALL CAR
VS.
THE SMALL CAR
You can buy a Chevrolet Nova OR
you can buy a small car that can beat
it on gas mileage*....
● ● ● ● ●
The answer is a small car at your
Chrysler-Plymouth and Dodge dealers....
● ● ● ● ●

See all the Darts at your
Dodge/Dodge Trucks dealer.
See the Dusters and Valiants at your
Chrysler-Plymouth dealer.
●●●●●●●●●●●●●●●●●●

The asterisk in the ad referred to a disclaimer which read:
"Gas mileage figures based on October 1973 *Popular Science*
magazine. Tests performed by *Popular Science* for its report were
conducted on '73 vehicles with figures adjusted by *Popular Science*
for 1974 model changes and the results of EPA tests."

That was one of a series of ads, all with the same message.
The *Popular Science* tests referred to in the ad showed that the
Plymouth Valiant and Dodge Dart equipped with 6-cylinder
engines got better gas mileage than a Chevrolet Nova equipped
with either a 6-cylinder or a V-8 engine. The same report also
showed that Valiants and Darts equipped with V-8 engines got
worse mileage results than Novas equipped with V-8s or 6-
cylinder engines. In essence, the ads claimed that, based on the
magazine report, all Chrysler small cars got better gas mileage than
all Chevrolet Novas. In reality, however, the report covered only
those cars equipped with 6-cylinder engines. But that was not
stated clearly in the ad.

DECEPTIVE TRUTH

Up to this point, we have dealt with deceptive untruths.
But what about deceptive truth? There is a common element to all
of the cases involving statements of deceptive, literal truth. That is,
there is always some element missing, or a conclusion is inferable
that is short of the truth.

In *Donaldson v. Read Magazine, Inc.*,[19] the U.S. Supreme
Court discussed ads that, as a whole, may be misleading even
though every sentence taken separately is literally true. This may
occur when things are omitted or when ads are composed in

such a way that they mislead.

Donaldson, who was the Postmaster General, sued *Read Magazine* based on its puzzle contests. Donaldson sued because he felt that *Read's* contest was "a scheme . . . for obtaining money through the mails by means of false and fraudulent pretenses, representations, and promises."[20]

In 1945 *Read Magazine* advertised its *Facts Magazine* Hall of Fame Puzzle Contest. Customers were led to believe that they would be eligible to win prizes by paying a $3 fee. In reality they would have to pay up to $42. Customers were also led to believe that the contest was a puzzle contest. It was not. The puzzles were so easy to solve that most people would solve all of them. The prizes were awarded, if the truth be known, based on a tie-breaking letter-essay contest.

Read Magazine argued that it had explained all of these facts in its ads. The ads contained wording that specified that the first $3 puzzles might result in a tie. This would require a second and third series of $3 puzzles. Ultimately, if no winner appeared, one would be selected based on essays on "The Puzzle I Found Most Interesting and Educational in This Contest."

There were sentences in *Read's* advertisements which, taken alone, would have conveyed to a deliberate reader all of these details of the contest. But they were not sentences standing alone. They were small and inconspicuous bits of lengthy descriptions. *Read's* ads were very long, and its form letters to contestants were even more lengthy.

In bold one inch type their ads barked:

● ●
$10,000 FIRST PRIZE PUZZLE CONTEST
● ●

Pictures of sample puzzles covered the page. The ads left little doubt that the contest presented an opportunity to win large prizes (remember, this was 1947) by solving the puzzles. In the lower left corner of the ad appeared the "Official Rules of the Contest." There were 10 rules. Somewhere near the middle of the ninth rule appeared the only reference to the possible need for essay letters as a means of tie-breaking. While all of the information was in the ad, and no claims were made that were not factual, the ad was still deceptive. Granted there is a fine line here, but there is still a line.

This case is used to illustrate the principles of deceptive truth. Regulations that specifically control the advertising of contests and sweepstakes are explained in Chapter 9.

INDUSTRY GUIDES AND TRADE PRACTICE RULES FOR SPECIFIC PRODUCT AND SERVICE ADVERTISING

In addition to the general laws we've examined up to this point, there are also heavy regulations regarding some specific product and industry areas. These include types of products like jewelry, auto parts, and furniture, to mention a few. There are also areas which include pricing and credit advertising, which are important for advertisers to understand.

Specific information for the advertiser in the form of "guides" is available from the FTC, and the various agencies listed below. I would urge the advertiser or agency to get a copy of the appropriate guides. Familiarize yourself with the requirements of that particular area, and you'll help avoid problems.

While most of these areas are covered by the FTC (under the auspices of policing deceptive and misleading advertising claims), other government agencies may be involved as well. Check with the appropriate group for information on the legalities of that specific trade or industry. The federal agencies are listed in the phone book under U.S. Government. In addition to the federal agencies listed, check with the applicable state government in the states where you advertise for specific local regulation information.

Here is a general reference list of the federal agencies that have an impact on advertising and marketing activities and the common products that each govern.

Federal Trade Commission

Light bulbs
Binoculars
Radios
Sewing machines
Amplifiers
Appliances
Consumer products
Foods
Drugs
Cosmetics
Medical devices
Wool, fur, and textile products
Cigarettes

Food and Drug Administration

Food
Drugs
Nonalcoholic beverages
Cosmetics
Medical devices
Biological products
Hearing aids
Radiation emitting devices (microwaves)

Department of Housing and Urban Development

Real estate
Land
Mobile homes

Apartments

Department of Transportation

Motor vehicles
Tires
Boats

Department of the Treasury

Imported goods
Alcoholic beverages
Tobacco products

Department of Agriculture

Meat products
Poultry products
Eggs and egg products
Fruits
Vegetables
Seeds

Department of Commerce

Seafood
Fire detection devices
Fire extinguishing devices
Consumer products
Fruits
Vegetables

Consumer Product Safety Commission

Consumer products
Flammable fabrics
Poisons
Hazardous materials
Bicycles
Toys

Refrigerators

Department of Energy

Dishwashers
Refrigerators and freezers
Washers and dryers
Water heaters
Air conditioners
Heating devices
Televisions
Stereos
Furnaces
Ovens and ranges and microwaves

Environmental Protection Agency

Motor vehicles
Engines
Fuels and fuel additives
Noise emitting devices
Insecticides and pesticides
Poisons
Insect and rodent traps and repellents

FTC INDUSTRY GUIDES

The Federal Trade Commission has created a series of
guides, rules, and regulations pertaining to the advertising,
labeling and disclosure requirements of these products and
services. While these FTC "Industry Guides" generally deal with
misrepresentations and deceptions in advertising, they also
provide information on other issues important to the advertiser.
If you advertise in any of these areas, you should get a copy of the
specific guide. They generally prohibit claims in advertising or
labeling that are likely to mislead or deceive consumers about the
materials, quality, or features of the products. Listed below are

the FTC's guides (footnoted with the guide's location in the Code of Federal Regulations) and the product areas they cover.

- Guides for the Metallic Watch Bank Industry[21]
- Guides for the Rebuilt, Reconditioned, and Other Used Automobile Parts Industry[22]
- Guides for the Mirror Industry[23]
- Guides for the Hosiery Industry[24]
- Guides for the Jewelry Industry[25]
- Guides for the Luggage and Related Products Industry[26]
- Tire Advertising and Labeling Guides[27]
- Guides for Advertising Shell Homes[28]
- Guides for Shoe Content Labeling and Advertising[29]
- Guides for Advertising Radiation Monitoring Instruments[30]
- Guides Against Deceptive Labeling and Advertising of Adhesive Compositions[31]
- Guides for Avoiding Deceptive Use of the Word "Mill" in the Textile Industry[32]
- Guides for the Decorative Wall Paneling Industry[33]
- Guides for the Watch Industry[34]
- Guides for the Ladies' Handbag Industry[35]
- Guides for the Household Furniture Industry[36]
- Guides for Labeling, Advertising, and Sale of Wigs and Other Hairpieces[37]
- Guides for the Feather and Down Products Industry[38]
- Guides Concerning Use of Endorsements and Testimonials in Advertising[39]
- Guides for Sleeping Bags[40]
- Guides for Dry Cell Batteries[41]
- Guides for Table Cloths and Related Products[42]
- Guides for Waist Belts[43]
- Guides for Light Bulbs[44]
- Guides for Radio Transistors[45]
- Guides for Extension Ladders[46]
- Guides for Sewing Machines[47]

Certain guides also require that other information be included in ads, such as the country of origin. As examples, the advertising regulations for jewelry, household furniture, appliances, televisions sets, audio equipment, fur products, wool products, and textiles are outlined below. These will give you an idea of the type of items covered in the FTC's guides.

Jewelry Guides

The FTC's *Guides for the Jewelry Industry* prohibit all forms of advertisement that mislead or deceive consumers about the type, quality, metallic content, size, weight, cut, and color of jewelry products.

The jewelry guides make it an "unfair trade practice to misrepresent [or withhold] the place of origin, production or manufacture" of any jewelry item (or major components). It is also illegal to misrepresent the guides' specific advertising requirements for gold, silver, precious and semiprecious stones, as well as the use of quality designations such as "carat," and "sterling."

For example, it is illegal to use the word "gold" (or its abbreviation), to describe any product "not composed throughout of fine (24 karat) gold."

Household Furniture Guides

The FTC's *Guides for the Household Furniture Industry*, cover the advertising of "[a]rticles of utility, convenience or decoration which are suitable for use as furniture in a house, apartment, or other dwelling place." Other related products, including mattresses, metal cots, cedar chests, musical instruments, radio and television sets, as well as lamps, clocks, rugs, draperies, appliances, and fixtures are covered by other guides.

The household furniture guides prohibit any misrepresentation or failure to disclose any material facts that would likely mislead or deceive consumers and, therefore, influence their purchase decision. "This includes situations where deception may result from the appearance alone, which in the absence of affirmative disclosures, could have the capacity and tendency or effect of misleading or deceiving." For example, using veneers or simulated materials without disclosure is an unfair trade practice in violation of the FTC Act.

If an advertiser makes representations regarding test results or performance characteristics of fabrics, they must be prepared to submit substantiating data that existed prior to making the claims. Because of this, it is wise to keep documentation for three years after a representation is made. The FTC can demand to review the proof within that three-year period.

If furniture is made in the United States, it should not be advertised by terms that suggest a foreign origin, such as "Danish" or "French." Unless, that is, the fact that the furniture was made in the U.S. is clearly and conspicuously disclosed in the ad. The ad should contain a disclaimer, such as "made in the U.S.A." or "manufactured by Acme Co, New York, NY, U.S.A."

It is also illegal to represent, either directly or implicitly, that the advertiser is also the manufacturer or owns or controls the factory where the products were made if this is not true.

Appliances And Electronic Goods Guides

It would be wise to obtain and review *Rules for Using Energy Costs and Consumption Information Used in Labeling and Advertising for Consumer Appliances Under the Energy Policy and Conservation Act.*[48]

It is a violation of the FTC Act for an ad to represent the energy consumption of certain consumer appliances or the cost of energy consumed unless the product has been properly tested and the claim accurately portrays the results of the testing. This applies to refrigerators, refrigerator-freezers, dishwashers, water heaters, room air conditioners, clothes washers and dryers, and furnaces.

In order to comply with the guides, ads, brochures and catalogs for appliances and electronic products must include the

following information:
- The capacity of the model;
- Energy efficiency ratings for room air conditioners and furnaces;
- Estimated annual energy costs or energy efficiency ratings (as of the date of publication); and
- A clear and conspicuous statement that "Important energy information is available. Turn to page(s) 000." Or, "See your dealer for details."

Television Set Guides

A major concern when advertising televisions sets involves the size of the viewable area of the picture tube. It is illegal to state the picture size of a television set unless it is "the actual size of the viewable picture area [as] measured on a single plane basis."[49]

If the stated size is other than the actual horizontal measurement of the set's picture area, the size designation must be accompanied by a clear and conspicuous clarification, "in close connection and conjunction therewith." A footnote or other disclosure does not work. For example, making reference to a "19 inch diagonal picture tube" is acceptable, but "21 inch set" is not.

Home Entertainment Products Guides

When stating the power output ratings for amplifiers used in radios, record and tape players, compact disc players, and component audio amplifiers, certain performance characteristics of the power amplification equipment must be made. If the ad doesn't include the required ratings, it is an unfair or deceptive ad. It is advisable to refer to the appropriate guide for details.

One exception to the above rule is if the ad "clearly and conspicuously disclose[s] a manufacturer's rated power output and that rated output does not exceed two . . . watts (per channel or total)."

Textile Fiber Products Guides

Textile fiber products are governed by the Textile Fiber Products Identification Act (the "Textile Identification Act").[50] This governs the advertising of textile fiber products when a reference to the fiber content is made or the ad includes a "fiber trademark," (identification of a particular fiber). The ad will be considered deceptive if it does not identify any constituent fiber content of the product. Let's look at an illustration. If a garment is made of 100% cotton, this can be stated. However, if it is only 60% cotton, the actual content of the other fibers must be listed: 60% cotton, 40% rayon.

Ads must include a clear and visible statement of the product's origin. A clarification that the product was made in the U.S.A., was imported, or both must be made in all advertising and labeling as well.

The requirements of the Textile Identification Act and its regulations do not apply to products regulated by the Wool Products Labeling Act of 1939.

Wool Products Guides

The Wool Products Labeling Act of 1939,[51] (the "Wool Act") relates to the labeling of fabrics composed of wool.

When a wool product is advertised, a statement of origin must be made which makes a clear and conspicuous statement that the product was either made in the U.S.A., imported, or both. And, this statement must be consistent with the labeling on the actual product.

The Wool Act does not make any requirements for advertising other than those stated above. However, the FTC looks closely at advertising that violates the principles of the Wool Act and creates a deceptive or misleading claim.

Linings, paddings, stiffening, trimmings, facings (except where express or implied representations of fiber content are commonly made), or other products whose fiber content is customarily stated or whose fiber content is insignificant, do not fall under the Wool Act.

Fur Products Guides

Advertising for furs and fur products must be in line with the Fur Products Labeling Act (the "Fur Act").[52] This act prohibits deceptive advertising, and specifically governs misrepresentation of pricing.

A statement of the country of origin is required in an ad for imported furs and fur products. If the ad shows a group of fur products made in more than one country, a statement such as: "Fur products labeled to show country of origin," is acceptable. This does not apply, however, to catalogue, mail-order, or other types of advertising where the purchaser cannot inspect the product and label before buying. In this case, a clear origin reference must be made.

ADVERTISING PRICE ISSUES

The Use Of The Word "Free"

Probably the single word that has caused the most anguish for advertisers is "free." Just plug the word "free" into an ad and you're asking for trouble. It is important for the advertiser to understand how the word "free" can be used and what bargain must be lived up to when it is. Indeed the guidelines in this area are quite clear-cut. The simplest form of free offer is a gift or sample truly given without any strings attached. The operative word here is any. The word "free" means the consumer pays nothing and is required to do nothing.

Often an advertisement offers a free sample that will be sent to the consumer for paying a small amount to cover mailing and handling. This is acceptable only if the amount requested is no more than the actual cost to the advertiser of the handling and mailing. But if the consumer must pay more than the actual cost, the offer is improper.

Mark Twain once said, "Few things are harder to put up with than the annoyance of a good example." So here is one. It involves a major furniture retailer by whom I was once employed. The company found out what can happen when the word "free" is used too loosely.

These folks had been running advertisements for appliances. In these ads a simple, direct statement was made: "FREE DELIVERY." Things were going along fine, for many years in fact, until one day we got a call from a distraught older woman. She had not received satisfaction from our local store, so she called our general offices. She had purchased a new refrigerator at a competitor's store and wanted us to pick it up and deliver it to her home. After all, our ad did say "free delivery" and she wanted her refrigerator delivered—free.

The more we argued with her, the worse it got. We finally passed her off as a trouble-maker out to get a free ride, no pun intended. Sometime later we were contacted by the FTC, and they wanted some answers. Unfortunately the ones we gave them weren't the right ones. The statement had to be lived up to— literally—or be changed.

From that day on the ads read: "FREE DELIVERY INCLUDED." You had to buy our merchandise to get us to deliver it free of charge. Granted, the average consumer understands that we will only deliver our own merchandise. But the problem went beyond that because "free delivery" is a deceptive claim. The delivery is not actually free. The consumer has to do something— usually buy the merchandise. In basic contract law this action is called consideration. In this case delivery is not free; it is included in the price of the merchandise. You don't pay extra to receive it, but the point is, you do pay for it because it's built into the price.

A Free Offer Must Contain No Consideration

As we have just seen, consideration is the legal term for payment. But payment can be in forms other than the commonly used version, money. Consideration can be any action that induces someone into a contract. It can be a price, or an action, or a motive, or a forbearance (an agreement not to do something). *Black's Law Dictionary* defines consideration as: "Some right, interest, profit, or benefit accruing to one party, or some forbearance, detriment, loss, or responsibility, given, suffered, or undertaken by the other." In other words, an item is not free if it is given with some other consideration.

Along the same lines, *FTC* v. *The Book of the Month Club*,[53] dealt with the use of the word "free." In this case the Book-of-the-Month Club had published advertisements that read:

• • • •
FREE
TO NEW MEMBERS OF THE
BOOK-OF-THE-MONTH CLUB
• •

The "free" was another book. At the bottom of the ad was a coupon that the consumer filled out and sent in. This constituted a contract with the new member. The coupon stated that the consumer would receive the designated book free of charge, and that that person agreed to purchase at least four books a year from the club. However, in the court's opinion, there was no free book. If the member failed to buy the four other books within the year's time, the club would demand payment for the "free" book. The book was not a gift. It was not free.

In deciding this case the court looked at the definition developed by the FTC on January 14, 1948.[54] The definition read as follows:

The use of the word free or words of similar
import, in advertising to designate or describe

merchandise . . . that is not in truth and in fact a gift or gratuity or is not given to the recipient thereof without requiring the purchase of other merchandise or requiring the performance of some other service . . . is considered by the commission to be a violation of the Federal Trade Commission Act.

"Free With Purchase" Offers

An offer of one item for "free" with the purchase of another item indicates to the consumer that they are paying nothing for the "free" item and not more than the regular price for the other item. The term "regular price" is taken to mean the price at which the advertiser has actively sold the same product, in the same market area. This must have occurred within a recent span of time and for a reasonably substantial period, (usually thirty days).

The rationale is, a purchaser has a right to believe that the merchant will not directly and immediately recover, in whole or in part, the cost of the free merchandise or service by marking up the price of the article which must be purchased, by substituting inferior merchandise or services.

When creating a free offer, it is important to prevent the likelihood that the consumer might misunderstand the terms of the offer. To accomplish that, the FTC wants free offers to "set forth clearly and conspicuously at the outset of the offer" all limitations and conditions.

There are a few considerations for the timing and repetition of offers, as well. A "free" offer should not be advertised for more than six months in any twelve-month period. No more than three identical offers in the same area should be made in any twelve-month period, and at least 30 days should elapse before another such offer is promoted in the same area.

For another example of how not to use the word "free," let's look at *FTC v. Mary Carter Paint Co.*[55] Here, Mary Carter Paint had a practice of advertising that for every can of paint purchased the buyer would get a free can of equal quality. However, Mary Carter Paint Co. did not have a history of selling single cans of paint. In fact, it only sold two can sets. The company claimed in its advertising that the usual and customary retail price of each single can of paint was $6.98. This was actually the price needed to cover the cost of two cans of paint. What Mary Carter did, in essence, was double the retail price of its paint, sell the cans in twin sets, and then offer one of the cans as "free." Mary Carter's practice was deceptive and violated the FTC Act.

On February 8, 1968, an American Army officer firing on Ben Tre, Vietnam, said, "It became necessary to destroy the town in order to save it." It's not what you call it, it's what it is that counts.

Comparative Pricing And "Sale" Terminology

Advertisements that make price or value comparisons or that offer "sale" merchandise fall under the FTC's guides.

Pricing guides cover only "the most frequently employed forms of bargain advertising."[56] Yet "variations which appear from time to time . . . are . . . controlled by the same general principles." When advertising any bargain offer, the guides amplify the point that "advertisers should make certain that the bargain offer is genuine and truthful."

Advertising Price Reductions

A company may advertise that an item is being offered at a reduced price, if the former price "is the actual, bona fide price at which the article was offered to the public on a regular basis for a reasonably substantial period of time." But beware: the FTC has not defined a "reasonably substantial period of time."

One illegal tactic is to state an unusually high price to give a misleading impression of an actual saving and later reducing it to a "sale" price. To avoid this, it's important that the former price listed in the ad is not a fictitious one. Even if it's accompanied by terms like "regularly," "usually," or "formerly," make sure that the former price is not a false one.

The guides state that a "former price is not necessarily fictitious merely because no sales at the advertised price were made." Yet, be very careful that the former price is one that was "openly and actively offered, for a reasonably substantial period of time, in the recent, regular course of business, honestly and in good faith—and, of course, not for the purpose of establishing a fictitious higher price on which a deceptive comparison might be based." If substantial sales were not actually made at the former price, the advertiser "should scrupulously avoid any implication" that the former price is a "selling price" (for example, with language such as "Formerly sold at $000") as opposed to an "asking price."

What if the former price or the amount or percentage of the price reduction is not disclosed? When an ad simply states "sale" the amount of the reduction cannot be so insignificant as to be meaningless. The issue here is whether the price difference is large enough that the consumer, if he knew the difference, would believe that he was getting a genuine bargain or saving. That should be your guide.

Using Phrases Like "Formerly," "Originally," "Regularly," And "Usually"

Using phrases like "formerly," "originally," "regularly," and "usually" in relation to an advertised sale will project a certain impression to the consumer. Because of this, it is important that these terms are used properly, so as not to mislead the consumer.

"Originally," is defined as the advertiser's own original customary price offered in the recent, regular course of business. A price no higher than the first price used in the current selling season. If the original price is not the most recent price, it should be made clear along with any intermediate price reductions. One way to overcome this is to make a statement such as, "40% Off

Original Prices (intermediate markdowns taken)," or, "Originally $299, Formerly $185, Now $149."

Terms like "formerly," "reduced," "Was $80, Now $60" or "$80 radio $60," convey to the consumer that this was the last, most recent previous price for the same article. As always, truth is the benchmark.

Using the term "regularly" means the last previous price. Using "regularly" also implies that the item will later return to that regular presale price. This needs to be the truth.

"Usually" is taken to mean the current or last previous price. This term may also mean the advertiser's own customary price for the same article or the usual customary price for the same article in the area. Therefore, it is wise for the ad to clearly disclose the basis used for the comparison.

Value Comparisons

It's a common practice for one company to advertise the same goods at prices lower than the competition in the area in which both companies do business. This is acceptable if the advertised higher price is based upon fact (not fictitious or misleading) and the advertiser is reasonably certain that the claimed competitor's price does not appreciably exceed the price at which substantial sales of the item are being made by typical sellers in the same area.

It is acceptable to show comparisons of prices charged by others in the same market for comparable goods, if such goods are of essentially similar quality and are obtainable in the area. It must be clear in the ad that a comparison is being made. However, as with comparisons of the same merchandise, the advertiser must be certain that the advertised price of comparable or competing goods does not exceed that at which it is being sold by other retail outlets in the area.

Advertising Manufacturer's Suggested Retail Or List Prices

Another common practice involves advertising price reductions based on a "manufacturer's list price" or "suggested retail price." This won't cause a problem if the listed price is the amount at which substantial (not isolated or insignificant) sales are made in the area in which the advertiser does business.

This general rule applies to national companies, regional manufacturers, mail-order and catalog distributors who deal directly with the public, or a local retailer. In other words, any company, any advertiser.

The key here is to determine whether the manufacturer's list price is actually the price regularly charged by other outlets in the area. This must be done before advertising the list price comparison. If the business operates on a large regional or national basis, they may advertise a suggested list price if the main retail outlets in a significant number of representative areas are selling the product at that price. To sum up, the retailer who engages in advertising a list price must act honestly and in good faith, and not with the intention of establishing a basis for a deceptive comparison in any trade area.

Bargain Offers Requiring The Purchase Of Other Merchandise

Ads that offer a bargain if another item is purchased by the consumer, must clearly state all of the terms and conditions of the offer. For example, by using language such as "Free," "2-For-1 Sale," "Half Price Sale," or "Buy One-Get One Free." This must be done clearly in the ad and not in an attempt to mislead the consumer. Refer back to the *FTC* v. *Mary Carter Paint Co.* case that we discussed earlier in this chapter.

As stated in the *Mary Carter* case, a deception that violates the FTC Act would occur "[w]here the seller, in making such an offer, increases his regular price of the article required to be bought, or decreases the quantity and quality of that article, or otherwise attaches strings (other than the basic condition that the article be purchased)."

Introductory Sales

An introductory or "advance" sale may be promoted when the advertiser expects in good faith to increase the price at a later date. There is no requirement that the price in fact be raised later, but the intent must be made in good faith. It would be deceptive to advertise an introductory sale, while intending to keep the price at that level later.

"Cents-Off" And Other Savings Offers

Advertising that makes "cents-off" or other price representations may be required to comply with the Fair Packaging and Labeling Act and the FTC's regulations under the Fair Packaging Act,[57] or with regulations under the federal Food, Drug and Cosmetic Act.[58] The regulations under the two statutes require similar disclosures in advertisements and impose similar conditions. Let's take a closer look.

"Cents-Off" Promotions

A "cents-off representation" is any printed matter consisting of the words "cents-off" or similar words placed on any ad, label or packaging stating or implying that a consumer commodity is being sold at a price below the "customary retail sale price."

"Cents-off" representations are prohibited unless the labeled item has, recently and during regular business within the area, been sold at an ordinary and customary price and, is currently sold at a reduction from the ordinary price in an amount at least equal to the "cents-off" amount that is shown on the package or label.

The "cents-off" claim must be marked as a savings from the retailer's regular price, such as, "Price Marked is 00¢ Off the

Regular Price." The regular price must be clearly and conspicuously displayed on the package or label, or on a sign, placard or shelf-marker along with the display.

Within any twelve-month period, "cents-off" promotions for the same size item in the same trade area must not be initiated more than three times, extended more than six months, or exceed fifty-percent of the item's total sales volume. At least thirty days must have passed between each promotion. Invoices or other records should be maintained for at least one year following the twelve month period in which the promotion occurred.

A "cents-off" representation cannot be made where it is known or should be known that it will be used to deceive, e.g., where the retailer charges a price which does not fully pass on to the consumers the represented price reduction or fails to post the regular price, as required.

Introductory "Cents-Off" Offers

"Cents-off" representations made in connection with introductory offers are prohibited unless:
- The item is new, introduced into a new area for the first time, or has been substantially changed;
- The offer is clearly and conspicuously qualified as an "Introductory Offer;" and
- The offer does not continue within the area for more than six months.

At the time the introductory offer is made, the advertiser must intend in good faith to offer the item, alone, at the anticipated ordinary and customary price for a reasonably substantial period of time after the introductory promotion ends.

The term "economy size" or similar words should not be used unless the advertiser simultaneously offers the same brand of that commodity in at least one other size or form, and only if one size of the item is labeled "economy size." The item labeled "economy size" must be sold at a price-per-unit of weight or other measure which is substantially reduced, i.e., at least five percent.

THE FEDERAL FOOD, DRUG, AND COSMETIC ACT

The Federal Food, Drug, and Cosmetic Act also regulates "cents-off" and other savings claims used on labeling for food, drug, cosmetic products or devices.

"Cents-off" representations may be made for an item if it has been openly and actively sold in the recent and regular course of business in the market area for at least thirty days, and if the selling price, "has been reduced by at least the savings differential represented on the package or labeling."

Sponsors of "cents-off" promotions, as well as persons involved at all other levels such as wholesalers and jobbers, must keep records of all promotions within any twelve-month period. These must be kept for at least twelve months after the end of the year in which the promotion occurs to document that the retailer has passed the represented savings on to the purchaser, should the FTC ask. And they just might.

Other savings offers, such as "two-for-one" or "one-cent" sales, which appear on the label or labeling of food, drug, or cosmetic items or devices "shall include all material facts relative to the offer and shall in no way be misleading."

BAIT-AND-SWITCH ADVERTISING

Bait-and-switch advertising is stringently prohibited. The FTC has defined bait-and-switch advertising as:

An alluring but insincere offer to sell a product or service which the advertiser in truth does not intend or want to sell. Its purpose is to switch consumers from buying the advertised merchandise, in order to sell something else, usually at a higher price or on a basis more advantageous to the advertiser. The primary aim of a bait advertisement is to obtain leads as to persons interested in buying merchandise of the type so advertised.

Remember, showing actual sales of the advertised items doesn't necessarily prove that a bait-and-switch scheme did not exist. The commission has determined that, on occasion, an actual sale is a "mere incidental by-product of the fundamental plan and is intended to provide an aura of legitimacy to the overall operation." Therefore, the FTC advises, "[n]o advertisement containing an offer to sell a product should be published when the offer is not a <u>bona fide</u> effort to sell the advertised product."

The ad must not create a false impression of the product or any of its characteristics, such as grade, make, color, availability, or otherwise misrepresent the product so that, "on disclosure of the true facts, the purchaser may be switched from the advertised product to another."

To determine whether the advertiser has created a bait-and-switch scheme, the FTC examines each of the following criteria:

- Refusal to demonstrate or sell the product as offered;
- Disparagement of the product as advertised, or features such as the guarantee or credit terms;
- Failure to meet reasonable demands for the advertised product unless the ad "clearly and adequately" discloses that "supply is limited" or item is "available only at designated outlets;"
- Refusal to accept orders for the advertised item, for delivery within a reasonable period;
- Showing an item that is "defective, unusable or impractical" for its advertised purpose; or
- Use of a sales program or compensation method that is designed to prevent, discourage, or penalize employees from selling the advertised product.

Attempts by a company to "unsell" merchandise or to sell other merchandise instead, is also prohibited. The FTC will consider that a sale was not made in good faith, but rather was a scam to sell other merchandise if it finds:

- Acceptance of a deposit for an advertised product and then switching the buyer to a more expensive item;
- Failure to deliver an advertised product within a reasonable time, or failing to offer a refund;
- Disparagement of the advertised product or any characteristic connected with it; or
- Delivery of the product in a condition that is defective, unusable, or impractical for its advertised purpose.

MAIL ORDER MERCHANDISE

The FTC's Mail Order Merchandise rule ("Mail Order Rule") controls advertising of all merchandise that is purchased by cash or credit through the mail. However, the Mail Order Rule doesn't cover orders made on a C.O.D. basis. This rule also excludes mail order items purchased by telephone and charged to a credit card.

The federal Mail Order Rule overrides any state law, municipal ordinance, or other local regulation that does not provide equal or greater rights to the buyer.

The Mail Order Rule states that it is "an unfair or deceptive act and practice" for a seller "[t]o solicit any order for the sale of merchandise to be ordered by the buyer through the mails unless, at the time of the solicitation, the seller has a reasonable basis to expect he will be able to ship [the] ordered merchandise to the buyer." The order must be shipped within the time specified in the ad or, if no date is specified, within thirty days after receipt of the order from the buyer.

What happens if the seller can't ship the ordered items before the thirty-day period or by the specified shipping date? Then the company must (without the consumer demanding) offer the buyer the option to either agree to a delay in shipping the item or cancel the order and receive a prompt refund.

CREDIT ADVERTISING

The federal Truth-in-Lending Act,[59] controls all advertising of consumer credit. That means credit offered to a consumer "primarily for personal, family, or household purposes." Anyone who advertises consumer credit in any form, must comply with the act's consumer credit regulation, also known as "Regulation Z."[60]

The FTC oversees and enforces Regulation Z as it applies to retailers, real estate developers, consumer finance companies, nonbank credit-card issuers, and all creditors not regulated by other agencies.

It would be advisable for anyone offering credit in an advertisement to get a copy of Regulation Z, and study its terms.

Definition Of Consumer Credit

The Truth-in-Lending Act defines two forms of consumer credit: "open-end" and "closed-end."

Open-end consumer credit generally includes credit cards and revolving charge accounts. It is extended in one of the following situations where:
- The creditor reasonably anticipates repeat transactions;
- The creditor may impose a finance charge from time-to-time on any outstanding balance; or
- The amount of credit that may be extended to the consumer during the term of the plan (up to the limit set by the creditor) is generally based upon how any outstanding balance has been repaid.

"Closed-end" credit covers any other form of consumer credit.

Terms That Trigger Disclosure

The Truth-in-Lending Act includes a list of certain "triggering" terms. If any of these terms are used in an advertisement, the act requires certain additional disclosures to be made.

Triggering terms for open-end credit include any reference to one of the following:

- The circumstances when a finance charge will be imposed and an explanation of how it will be determined;
- A statement of when the finance charge begins to accrue, including any "free ride" period;
- The periodic rate used to calculate the finance charge, the range of balances to which it applies, and the annual percentage rate;
- The method used to determine the balance on which the finance charge is computed;
- The method used to determine the amount of the finance charge, including a description of how any finance charge (other than periodic rate) will be determined;
- Any amount, other than a finance charge, that may be imposed, or an explanation of how the charge is determined. Examples include application fees charged to credit applicants, late and delinquent payment amounts, and annual or periodic charges;
- If the creditor has or will acquire any security interest in the property purchased under the plan, or in any other property; or
- A statement outlining the consumer's rights and the creditor's responsibilities.

If any triggering terms are used in an advertisement, it must also clearly and conspicuously explain each of the following points:

- Any minimum, fixed, transaction, activity, or similar charge that may be imposed;
- Any periodic rate that may be applied, shown as an annual percentage rate; and
- Any membership or participation fee that may be imposed.

Triggering terms for closed-end credit include any reference to one of the following:
- The amount or percentage of any down-payment;
- The number of payments or period of repayment;
- The amount of any payment; or
- The amount of any finance charge.

If any closed-end triggering terms are used in an advertisement, it must also clearly and conspicuously explain all of the following points:
- The amount or percentage of any down-payment;
- The terms of repayment; and
- The "annual percentage rate," using that term, and the details, if the rate may be increased.

In the case of a brochure, insert, catalog or other multi-page advertisement only one set of disclosures is required if a table or schedule fully explains each type of credit. If there is a triggering term anywhere in this type of promotional material, there must also be a reference to the page on which the table or schedule is located.

CONSUMER LEASING

In addition to the above, the Truth-in-Lending Act requires certain disclosures in ads promoting consumer lease transactions.[61] The consumer leasing disclosure provisions of the Truth-in-Lending Act are implemented by "Regulation M."[62]

A "consumer lease" is "a contract in the form of a bailment or lease for the use of personal property by a natural person primarily for personal, family, or household purposes, for a period of time exceeding four months, for a total contractual obligation not exceeding $25,000, whether or not the lessee has the option to purchase or otherwise become the owner of the property at the expiration of the lease." Excluded from this section are leases that otherwise fall under the definition of a credit sale and therefore are controlled under Regulation Z.

As with consumer credit advertising under Regulation Z, certain triggering terms used in an ad for a consumer lease require that disclosures be made. In an ad for a consumer lease, triggering terms include any reference to the following:

- Statements as to the amount of any payment;
- The number of required payments; or
- Any or no down-payment, or other payment, is required upon entering into the lease.

Ads that include any triggering terms listed above must also clearly and conspicuously state all of the following:

- That the transaction advertised is a lease;
- The total amount of any required payment such as a security deposit or capitalized cost-reduction required at the execution of the lease, or that no such payments are required;
- The number, amounts, due dates, or periods of scheduled payments, and the total of such payments under the lease;
- If the lessee has the option to purchase the leased property and at what price and in what time. A statement of the method of determining such price is acceptable; and
- The amount (or method to determine it) of any liabilities the lease imposes upon the lessee at the end of the lease. Also required is a statement that the lessee shall be liable for the difference, if any, between the estimated value of the property and its actual value at the end of the lease.

As in the case of consumer credit examined earlier, a catalog, brochure, or multi-page ad used to promote a consumer lease requires only one set of clear disclosures for the triggering terms. If a triggering term appears on other pages, a clear reference must be made to where the table or schedule begins.

In the case of point-of-sale tags (for items that include triggering terms) there must be a clear and conspicuous reference to where a table or schedule of the additional terms can be found.

FTC GUIDES REGARDING THE USE OF ENDORSEMENTS AND TESTIMONIALS IN ADVERTISING

The FTC monitors testimonials and endorsements as part of its enforcement of the Federal Trade Commission Act.

In its *Guides Concerning Use of Endorsements and Testimonials in Advertising*,[63] the FTC defines an endorsement as:

> Any advertising message (including verbal statements, demonstrations, or depiction's of the name, signature, likeness or other identifying personal characteristics of an individual or the name or seal of an organization) which message consumers are likely to believe reflects the opinions, beliefs, findings, or experience of a party other than the sponsoring advertiser.

The guides provide many examples of the type of representations the FTC considers to be endorsements or testimonials. As an example, a film critic's excerpted statements regarding a specific film, which were put into an ad would be considered an endorsement. This is because the consumer would readily believe that the statement is the critic's view rather than the view of the advertiser. Let's take another example: a television commercial for baseball bats showing a well-known professional ball-player hitting balls would qualify as an endorsement, even if the professional makes no actual statement in the commercial.

On the other hand, an advertisement for a pain reliever using a long-standing spokesperson as the announcer would not be considered an endorsement by the spokesperson. The reasoning here is that the audience would recognize the announcer as a representative of the drug company and not a neutral and unbiased expert.

Note— An endorsement or testimonial can be created by any person; it does not need to be a celebrity. The FTC looks at any endorsement or testimonial regardless of who makes it. The fame (if any) of the person making the claim only affects how closely the FTC's magnifying glass is held to the issue.

FTC Principles

In order to be acceptable under the FTC's guidelines, testimonials and endorsements must accurately portray the honest beliefs and experiences of the endorser. Further, the endorser cannot make any representation that the advertiser could not directly make on its own. This means that the endorser cannot make any representation that would be deceptive or unsubstantiated even if it is his own belief.

We looked at the *Cliffdale* case in Chapter 2. We'll revisit it here. In *In the Matter of Cliffdale Assocs., Inc.*,[64] the FTC issued a complaint alleging Cliffdale, a mail-order company, with misrepresenting the value and performance qualities of an automobile engine part called the "Ball-Matic Gas Saver Valve." The advertisements stated that the Ball-Matic was "the most significant automotive breakthrough in the last 10 years," that "every car needs one," and that car owners could "save up to 20 percent and more" in gasoline costs.

Several of these advertisements included consumer "test results" showing gasoline savings of 8 to 40 percent. Some ads included testimonials by consumers reporting gasoline savings of two to six miles per gallon. These claims were highlighted in a heavy-bordered box in the ad asking readers to "read the results for yourself."

It's of little surprise that the FTC ruled the Ball-Matic ads to be false and deceptive. After reviewing the substantiation provided by Cliffdale and the results of tests conducted by the FTC, they found that "even under conditions most likely to produce benefits from the Ball-Matic," the fuel savings did not even approach those claimed in the alleged consumer test or testimonials.

This points out that the advertiser is required to possess a reasonable basis for claims contained in testimonials, even if the testimonials reflect the honestly held views of the testifier. The commission rejected Cliffdale's argument that the testimonials, in and of themselves, validated the claims. The FTC stated that "consumer tests and testimonials . . . are not a recognized way of testing fuel economy." As the FTC stated, "irrespective of the veracity of the individual consumer testimonials, [the] use of the testimonials to make underlying claims that were false and deceptive was, itself, deceptive."

Cliffdale made substantial use of consumer endorsements to make performance claims about it's product. About this, the commission said:

> The clear impression created was that the quotes came from actual, current users of the Ball-Matic. For example, several advertisements quote phrases such as 'Now I get four miles more per gallon,' and, 'Now that I have installed your unit . . .' Further, . . . the wording conveyed a sense that the testimonials were given voluntarily: 'It gives me great pleasure to express to you my satisfaction,' and 'Just a short note to inform you of the performance of your Ball-Matic.'

These claims were false, and the testimonials were not what they appeared to be.

In another case, *In re Cooga Mooga, Inc.*,[65] the FTC ordered the manufacturer of a topical acne medication to prohibit celebrity Pat Boone from representing (as it had in the ads) that all of his daughters used the medication with favorable results, unless those statements were true. The FTC reasoned that since not all of Boone's daughters used the acne medication, the statements were materially false and misleading.

If a person states in an ad that she uses a certain product, the advertiser may run the advertisement only if it knows that the endorser actually uses the product. In addition, an expert or celebrity can serve as an endorser only during the time when the endorser "continues to subscribe to the views presented."

CONSUMER ENDORSEMENTS

Requirement That Endorsements Must Be Typical

The FTC will examine an ad that represents a consumer's experience regarding a material attribute of the product. Further, the consumer claim must be representative of what an ordinary consumer will experience when using the product. Therefore, an advertiser should not employ endorsements in an ad unless it can adequately verify that the endorser's experience is representative of what will generally be achieved by others.

The *Cliffdale* case discussed above illustrates this requirement well. In this case, the advertiser stated that the claimed experiences were typical because the consumers (endorsers) represented a variety of locations, makes of cars, and occupations. In addition, the ads claimed "over 100,000 in use."

The commission, however, presumes that viewers will accept consumer testimonials as representative experiences, unless there is a clear disclaimer to the contrary. The scientific record in *Cliffdale* revealed the typical fuel economy improvement was, in the very best case, half that claimed in the consumer endorsements. The commission said: "We have already found that no competent scientific test supports respondents' performance claims." Therefore, the FTC ruled that the testimonials were deceptive since, "even if the individual experiences were accurate, they cannot be typical experiences . . . ."

Use Of Disclaimers

The guides make it clear that, unless the endorser's experience is typical of what other consumers may generally expect to realize with the advertised product in actual use conditions, the advertiser must disclose the performance that would generally be found in similar circumstances or in the limited applicability of the endorser's experience. In other words, clarify the facts.

The FTC guides warn that "[t]he mere disclosure that 'not all consumers will get this result' is insufficient because it can imply that while all consumers cannot expect the advertised results, a substantial number can expect them." The FTC provides no general rule concerning how specific the disclaimer must be, so it would be wise to err on the safe side.

Advertisements for LaSalle Correspondence School (owned by Macmillan, Inc.) offered numerous testimonials of graduates reporting stunning careers and salary advances. Some ads did, in fact, imply that the testimonials were "exceptional cases" of "more successful graduates." However, the FTC found in *In re Macmillan, Inc.*[66] that the advertisements promoted an image that similar success could be readily expected by the reader. The commission, therefore, required all unrepresentative testimonials to be accompanied by the specific disclaimer: "This testimonial does not reflect the typical and ordinary experience of LaSalle students," in typeface that is as large as the testimonial itself.

Use Of Actual Consumers

Clearly, the advertiser should use actual consumers if it implies in an advertisement that the endorser is an actual consumer. To do otherwise would violate Section 5 of the FTC Act by creating a false and deceptive impression that is likely to mislead consumers.

Use Of Consumer Endorsements In Drug Ads

The manufacturer of a drug product should not use a lay person's endorsement in its ads unless: (a) the advertiser possesses comprehensive scientific substantiation to prove the validity of its claims, and (b) the claims do not violate any FDA regulation regarding the drug or device.

Going back to an earlier case *In re Cooga Mooga, Inc.,*[67] the FTC ordered the advertiser of acne medication to possess reliable information, tests, or studies that substantiated any results claimed in its consumer testimonials. Cooga Mooga, through the. endorsement by Pat Boone, had falsely represented that its product penetrated the pores of the skin and cured acne. Nevertheless, the FTC permitted Cooga Mooga to rely solely on the personal experiences of the endorsers when the product or service was not related to health and safety and "where the evaluation of such products or services, for purposes of any endorsement, requires no professional expertise and such products or services can be reasonably evaluated through lay use."

In *American Home Prods. Corp.* v. *Johnson & Johnson,*[68] the court upheld American Home Product's (AHP) television advertisements in which an actor depicted as "a typical Anacin user" stated: "My headache's gone, and Anacin didn't upset my stomach."

The defendant had alleged that such statements falsely implied that "Anacin," an aspirin product, caused less stomach upset than ibuprofen or acetaminophen. The court rejected McNeil's (manufacturer of Tylenol and a subsidiary of Johnson & Johnson) claims, stating that the only message the "Anacin" advertisement "literally communicates is that one user got pain relief without stomach upset."

The court further stated that while aspirin-based products are the most likely over-the-counter (OTC) analgesics to produce gastric discomfort, AHP's commercial made no implied claim that "Anacin" caused less stomach discomfort than non-aspirin pain relievers. The court reasoned that "Anacin's 'no stomach upset' advertising is within the acceptable and expectable limits of commercial puffery and is therefore unlikely to mislead consumers."

Endorsements By Experts

When using an expert to endorse a product or service, the expert must actually evaluate the product or service he or she is endorsing. It cannot be a blind claim where the endorser has not actually used and evaluated the product. Further, the evaluation must be "as extensive as someone with the same degree of expertise would normally need to conduct in order to support the conclusions presented in the endorsement."

Any endorsement made in the ad must be clearly supported by the endorser's actual evaluation. It also must be relevant to his area of expertise. This, however, does not prevent an expert from expressing a personal opinion about a product as long as it involves matters outside his area of expertise. But, as always, this situation (as an opinion) must be clear in the ad.

Another area where problems can arise involves comparisons of products. In cases where a endorsement is used, the expert endorser relying upon his expertise must have concluded that the endorsed product and the competitor's product are essentially equal. If the ad creates the impression that the endorsed product is superior to the competitor's product, it must be clear that it is the expert (not the advertiser) that concluded the product is superior to the competitor's product. An expert may not be used in an ad to falsely imply that he is endorsing a product.

When an endorsement is made by an organization that is claimed as an expert it must be based upon recognized experts within the organization, or by documented standards (that are suitable for evaluating the products) previously in existence within the organization. We'll look more into endorsements by organizations later in this chapter.

What Is Required To Be Considered An Expert

If an ad claims or implies that the person giving the endorsement is an expert, the endorser must actually possess qualifications as an expert in that area. Dan Mar Products manufactured and advertised a product called the G.R. Valve. This was an automotive retrofit device advertised as a product to improve fuel economy. NASA astronaut Leroy Gordon Cooper gave endorsements, as an expert, in ads for the G.R. Valve. In large part Cooper's credibility came from his fame as an astronaut and the implied scientific knowledge that went with that position.

In the case *In re Cooper*,[69] the FTC held that NASA astronaut Leroy Gordon Cooper was not qualified to represent himself as an expert with respect to fuel saving devices for automobiles. The commission held that "Gordon Cooper does not have the education, training, and knowledge to qualify him as an expert in the field of automotive engineering."

The commission reasoned that the ad falsely represented, either directly or by implication, that Gordon Cooper was a qualified expert in the field of automotive engineering. In fact, he was not.

Product Efficacy Claims

Dr. Bricklin, a professor of clinical psychology, had developed the basic "rotation" diet principles that were the basis for a weight reduction program marketed by Buckingham Productions, Inc. He also served as director of the company. In addition, Dr. Bricklin personally participated in the promotion of the diet by appearing in print ads as an expert endorser.

The FTC initiated an action in June 1985, against Dr. Barry Bricklin, an expert endorser, as well as against Buckingham and others, claiming that ads for the so-called "rotation" diet plan made false and deceptive claims about typical weight losses achieved, ease of dieting, permanence of results, and the energizing, hunger-inhibiting and fat-burning properties of the wafers and tablets used in the diet.

The FTC in *In re Bricklin*,[70] alleged that by virtue of his expert endorsements, Dr. Bricklin claimed he had a "reasonable

basis" for his representations. Yet, no such basis existed.
A "reasonable basis" would consist of testing of the product and programs involved, which would support the conclusions presented in the endorsement. This is the standard required by the FTC in its guides.

The FTC prohibited Bricklin from representing in ads that consumers can lose weight without disclosing that weight loss depends on an overall reduction in caloric intake, and that a comparable weight loss can be obtained from any weight-control program. That is, unless these claims can be supported by a competent, reliable survey or other scientific evidence that substantiates the representation.

Implied Endorsements

"I want a pain reliever I can really trust," said the young lady. "When I sprained my ankle and went to the hospital, they gave me Tylenol. I learned that Tylenol is the pain reliever hospitals use most. Hospitals trust Tylenol. Last year, hospitals dispensed ten times as much Tylenol as the next four brands combined. If hospitals trust Tylenol, shouldn't your choice be Tylenol?" American Home Products (AHP), makers of Anacin, challenged the above ad for Tylenol.

The court in *American Home Prods. Corp.* v. *Johnson & Johnson*,[71] examined the assertion that the advertisement presented an implied expert endorsement. If you'll recall, we looked at another element of this case earlier.

AHP objected to the advertisement on the basis that it gave the false impression that hospitals use more "Tylenol" than other analgesics because "Tylenol" is a superior pain reliever. According to AHP, the real motivation in dispensing more "Tylenol" was that McNeil (a subsidiary of Johnson & Johnson) supplied "Tylenol" to them at extremely low prices.

The court reasoned that the Tylenol ad was not false or unfair, because hospitals would, in fact, not use "Tylenol" if it were ineffective or unsafe. The court said; "At worst, the statement is a half-truth, in that it omits to mention that hospitals choose Tylenol for the additional reason that it costs less than competitive analgesics."

In its counterclaim, McNeil complained of an AHP ad that used a similar marketing tactic. In response to McNeil's "hospitals trust" advertisements, AHP conducted a campaign in which it mailed free samples of "Anacin-3" to 250,000 doctors with attached postage prepaid postcards, which when returned entitled doctors to additional free samples. AHP then surveyed a sample of the 108,000 doctors who returned the cards and computed a percentage from the sample of those who responded that they had recommended "Anacin-3." AHP then multiplied the percentage by the 108,000 total responses to arrive at its advertising claim that 70,000 doctors recommended Anacin-3. McNeil complained that this advertisement falsely implied that most doctors recommend "Anacin-3" when 70,000 doctors represented only about ten percent of the doctors in the United States.

The court rejected McNeil's argument. Assuming that AHP's extrapolation was reliable, it held that AHP could say that "70,000 doctors recommend Anacin-3" whether or not most laymen understood the percentage of doctors that figure represented.

In addition, the court noted that the more problematic issue was that "the 70,000 doctors did not spontaneously recommend Anacin-3 [but v]ery likely, all that most of them did was to pass on to patients free samples which AHP had furnished them." It concluded that AHP had, in effect, carried "McNeil's scheme to its logical extreme" by reducing the price of "Anacin-3" to zero. The court accordingly held that AHP's campaign was not false or "unacceptably misleading" since 70,000 doctors impliedly recommended "Anacin-3."

OTHER CONSIDERATIONS ABOUT ENDORSEMENTS AND TESTIMONIALS

Endorsements By Organizations

An organization's endorsement must fairly reflect the collective view of the group. This is because consumers view endorsements by organizations as a collective judgment, free from the sort of subjective influences inherent in an individual's judgment.

In the case *In re Biopractic Group, Inc.*,[72] the commission ordered the manufacturer of a treatment for arthritis and musculoskeletal ailments called "Ice Therapy" to stop representing that the treatment had been endorsed by various medical organizations and athletic groups. Biopractic's advertisement stated that "[d]octors, medical pain centers, physical therapists, health clinics, professional athletic teams, U.S. and Russian Olympic Track Teams Praise Ice Therapy." The commission alleged that no such medical or athletic organizations had given Biopractic the endorsements and found the ad to be false and misleading.

In another case, *In re Estee Corp.*,[73] the FTC ordered the maker of a fructose-sweetened food product to stop representing that its products had been recommended by the FDA or the American Diabetes Association when no such endorsements had been made. And in *In re Bristol-Myers Co.*,[74] the FTC ordered a drug manufacturer to stop representing in its ads that doctors recommended "Bufferin" more than any other pain reliever, without a reasonable basis for the claim.

In *In re Emergency Devices, Inc.*,[75] the commission ordered the manufacturer of a gas mask to stop ads containing an approval by any municipal, state, or federal agency when such an endorsement was not true. The ads had included statements such as "[t]ested and approved! In the U.S. and Canada, the mask has undergone vigorous testing by fire officials" and "[t]he filtering system was evaluated by an independent chemical testing lab, approved by OSHA and the California State Health Department." This was not true.

Disclosure Of Business Connection

Any connection between the endorser and the advertiser, which cannot reasonably be recognized by the audience, that might materially affect the credibility of the endorsement must be fully disclosed.

Consumers expect an advertiser to pay an expert or a well known personality for an endorsement, but they do not expect such a payment for a non-celebrity endorsement. Therefore, if an advertiser is paying a non-celebrity for an endorsement, the compensation must be conspicuously disclosed in the advertisement.

The FTC reiterated its position concerning the disclosure of business connections in *In the Matter of Cliffdale Assocs., Inc.*,[76] a case which we looked at earlier. The FTC held that Cliffdale implied that the consumer endorsements in its advertising were "freely given by individuals who were unrelated to the marketers of the Ball-Matic" on the basis of specific language in the testimonials such as, "It gives me great pleasure to express to you my satisfaction" and "Just a short note to inform you of the performance of your Ball-Matic." In fact, many testimonials were solicited by Cliffdale employees from business associates.

As the commission states in their guidelines, when a connection exists between the endorser and the advertiser that might affect the weight and credibility of the endorsement, the connection must be disclosed. The FTC found the connection between the endorsers and Cliffdale to be material because potential purchasers would have difficulty evaluating the Ball-Matic on their own and would therefore be apt to rely heavily on endorsements of other users. The FTC also reasoned that the language used by the endorsers specifically implied that their testimonials had been unsolicited.

In another case we have looked at already, *In re Cooga Mooga, Inc.*, Pat Boone also had a financial interest in the advertised product, Acne-Statin. In fact, Boone had the majority control of the company. The commission maintained that "...if a material connection exists between the endorser and the advertiser or its advertising agency, such connection must be disclosed in the advertisement(s) which contain the endorsement." The commission went on to further explain that: "A 'material connection' shall mean, . . . any financial interest in the sale of the product or service which is the subject of the endorsement or any familial connection between the endorser and the advertiser or its advertising agency."

However, the FTC guides do not require the disclosure that a testimonial is solicited.

LABELING

A number of labeling laws affect a wide variety of products. As an example, various provisions of the federal Food, Drug, and Cosmetic Act regulate labeling for those products. These regulations are administered by the Food and Drug Administration (FDA). Other examples include wool products (regulated by the Wool Products Labeling Act of 1939), textile products (regulated by the Textile Fiber Products Identification Act), and fur products (regulated by the Fur Products Labeling Act). These various acts outlaw mislabeling, which is often referred to as "misbranding" and are administered by the Federal Trade Commission.

THE RELATIONSHIP BETWEEN THE FDA AND THE FTC CONCERNING LABELING

As a general rule, the Food and Drug Administration (FDA) maintains jurisdiction for labeling of food, drug and cosmetic products, while the FTC has jurisdiction over the truth or falsity (and likelihood of deception) of any advertising used in relation to these products.

In the absence of an express agreement between the two agencies to the contrary, the FTC will exercise primary jurisdiction over all matters regulating the truth or falsity of advertising of food, drugs (with the exception of prescription drugs), devices and cosmetics.

The Food And Drug Administration

The FDA controls labeling under the federal Food, Drug, and Cosmetic Act (FDC Act),[77] and the Fair Packaging and Labeling Act (FPL Act).[78] Both acts apply to foods and drugs for humans, as well as animals, cosmetics and medical devices. In addition, many states have similar laws modeled after the FDC Act. Among other things, this act is designed to insure that labeling and packaging is truthful, non-deceptive and informative. On the other hand, the FPL Act controls the location and contents of information on packages and labels.

Basically, the FDC Act forbids distribution within or importation into the United States of products that are adulterated or "misbranded." In this context, "misbranding" includes statements, designs, or pictures on labels that create a false or misleading impression. It also covers failure to display required information in labeling.

The FDC Act contains detailed definitions of "misbranding." For example, the FDC Act states that a product is "misbranded" if its label is false or misleading in any manner. As an example, use of testimonials constitute misbranding if the impression given is that the drug is effective for a particular condition when it isn't, or hasn't been proven effective for that condition.

The FDC Act defines "labeling" as all labels and other written, printed, or graphic matter accompanying the product. You should be aware that the FDA, and the courts, will interpret "accompanying" in very broad terms. Therefore, "labeling" may also include items that help identify the article, its uses, and give directions, even if it is not actually included with the product. Under this definition the FDA can proceed against a false or misleading food or drug ad. If the FDA believes a threat to the public health may exist in such an ad, they can attempt to link the ad with the product to give the agency the authority to act.

In 1981, then FDA Commissioner, Dr. Arthur Hull Hayes, Jr., stated in a speech to the American Advertising Federation Conference that:

> The line between advertising and labeling sometimes is very thin. In certain cases, advertising may become labeling when it accompanies a product. For example, tear sheets from newspapers or magazines, when they are placed on the counter next to the product, are labeling. Catalogues may be labeling, as may brochures used to promote a product. Courts have held that written, printed or graphic promotional material accompanying a product is labeling, regardless of the nature of the material, or the manner in which it became associated with or accompanies the article.

Dr. Hayes also provided three examples of situations where the FDA might take action against an ad:

- A drug or medical device product is legally misbranded if its advertising contains conditions, purposes or uses for which the labeling does not bear adequate directions for use;
- A drug or product may not be promoted, in either its labeling or advertising, with any representation or suggestion that approval by FDA is in effect; or
- A drug or medical device is illegally misbranded if its advertising is false or misleading in any way.

Ads For Prescription Drugs

It is important to understand that prescription drug ads are treated differently than ads for over-the-counter (OTC) drugs. As we have just seen, OTC drug advertising is regulated by the FTC; prescription drug ads are regulated by the FDA because prescription drug ads are typically directed toward doctors and the medical community, rather than the general public.

Prescription drug ads must show the drug's established name in type at least half as large as that used for the trade name, the drug's quantitative formula as it is required on the drug label, and a true and non-misleading summary of adverse side effects, contraindications, and the effectiveness of the drug. The specific regulations state the requirements in detail, provide for so-called "reminder ads" to the health profession, and require ads to provide price information to consumers. Running prescription drug ads that do not comply with the regulations is considered misbranding under the FDC Act.

Labeling And Its Relationship To The Lanham Act

Recently, competitors have brought others into court in advertising cases. That trend is the result of Section 43(a) of the Lanham Trademark Act,[79] which we look at in detail in Chapter 8. While most of the cases to date have arisen as a result of problems with advertising, this statute applies to labeling. In fact, the statute specifically provides:

> Any person who shall affix, apply, or annex, or use in connection with any goods or services, or any container or containers for goods, a false designation of origin, or any false description or representation, including words or symbols tending falsely to describe or represent the same, and shall cause such goods or services to enter into commerce, and any person who shall with knowledge of the falsity of

such designation of origin or description or
representation cause or procure the same to be
transported or used in commerce or deliver the
same to any carrier to be transported or used, shall
be liable to a civil action by any person doing
business in the locality falsely indicated as that of
origin or in the region in which said locality is
situated, or by any person who believes that he is or
is likely to be damaged by the use of any such false
description or representation.

Keeping this in mind, what if you wanted to make
reference to a competitor's trademark on your own product label?
You can, if your label reference is truthful, according to a decision
in *C. D. Searle & Co.* v. *Hudson Pharmaceutical Corp.*[80]

The case was brought under Section 43(a) of the Lanham
Act and involved a vegetable laxative marketed and sold by two
competitive pharmaceutical firms. Since 1934 Searle marketed a
laxative product containing psyllium hydrophilic mucilloid using
the registered trademark METAMUCIL. In 1964 Hudson
Pharmaceutical Corp. marketed a laxative containing the same
psyllium hydrophilic mucilloid, under the registered trademark
name REGACILIUM.

Hudson had developed a comparative advertising
campaign that ran for many years, not only in trade publications
but also in point-of-purchase materials. Since 1972, Hudson had
included in its comparative ads the claim that REGACILIUM is
"Equivalent to METAMUCIL."

Until 1980, both of these companies' competitive products
were packaged very differently. In that year, however, Hudson
changed its product's packaging to resemble the METAMUCIL
packaging. In addition to the ads, Hudson's new package label
contained the statement Hudson had long used in trade catalogs
and point-of-purchase advertising: "Equivalent to METAMUCIL."

The new packaging with its comparative statement brought on the lawsuit. Searle sued Hudson to halt any mention of METAMUCIL on the REGACILIUM container. The court held that Hudson could not make further reference to METAMUCIL on the REGACILIUM container, stating:

> Unless the defendant's container is changed such that 'METAMUCIL' appears in type no larger than the word 'Equivalent' and in green letters on the white background. Defendant shall place an asterisk next to the METAMUCIL mark and shall state adjacent to said mark the statement 'a product of G.D. Searle, not a Hudson product'.

It was "proper for Hudson, on its REGACILIUM container, to truthfully characterize REGACILIUM as 'Equivalent to METAMUCIL.'" The court said: "Whether one is entitled to refer to a competitor's trademark depends not on where the reference appears, but on whether the reference is truthful."

STATE LAW PARALLELS TO THE FTC ACT

In addition to the federal regulations under Section 5 of the FTC Act just discussed, there are also state statutes and regulations. You should research and understand the unfair and deceptive acts and practices ("UDAP") statutes that exist in the states where you plan to advertise.

In the past twenty-five years, most states have developed some type of consumer protection law. Many of these statutes parallel the Federal Trade Commission Act and are appropriately called "Little FTC Acts" or "Mini FTC Acts." However, unlike the FTC Act many of these statutes afford consumers the right to bring a civil action for damages. There are four types of UDAP statutes which we will discuss in the following sections:

- Unfair trade practice and consumer protection laws;
- Uniform consumer sales practices acts;

- Uniform deceptive trade practices acts; and
- Consumer fraud acts.

Unfair Trade Practice And Consumer Protection Laws

This type of UDAP statute follows a form drafted by the Federal Trade Commission in association with the Committee on Suggested State Legislation of the Council of State Governments. There are three versions of this model that are used in various states:

- Pure "Little FTC Acts" specifically outlawing unfair methods of competition and unfair or deceptive acts or practices. These have been adopted in fourteen states: Connecticut, Florida, Hawaii, Illinois, Louisiana, Maine, Massachusetts, Montana, Nebraska, North Carolina, South Carolina, Vermont, Washington and West Virginia;
- Acts prohibiting certain specific practices, in addition to any other practice that is essentially unfair or deceptive. These are found in ten states: Alabama, Alaska, Georgia, Idaho, Maryland, Mississippi, New Hampshire, Pennsylvania, Rhode Island and Tennessee; and
- Acts prohibiting false, misleading, or deceptive practices. These statutes are found in Kentucky and Texas.

Uniform Consumer Sales Practices Acts

Developed by the American Bar Association and the National Conference on Uniform State Laws, this act applies only to consumer transactions and makes deceptive and unconscionable practices illegal. This act has been adopted by Kansas, Ohio and Utah.

Uniform Deceptive Trade Practices Acts

This type of act gives businesses the right to take action

against a competitor that uses deceptive techniques to attract customers. In addition, the act has also been applied to consumer cases. Twelve states have adopted this act in different forms: Colorado, Delaware, Georgia, Hawaii, Illinois, Maine, Minnesota, Nebraska, New Mexico, Ohio, Oklahoma and Oregon.

Consumer Fraud Acts

The Consumer Fraud Acts forbid misrepresentation, fraud, deception, and unfair or unconscionable acts. States that currently employ such acts include: Arizona, Arkansas, Delaware, Indiana, Iowa, Michigan, Missouri, Nevada, New Jersey, New York, North Dakota, South Dakota, Virginia, Wyoming and the District of Columbia.

Remedies Available Under State Laws

UDAP statutes offer a wide range of remedies, including actual damages, multiple damages, injunction, rescission of contract, and recovery of attorney's fees.

In the previous sections we looked at the way the FTC Act is enforced by the FTC. However, enforcement under the UDAP statutes is not as straightforward. While these statutes are frequently enforced by the state's attorney general or other government authority, consumers and businesses can generally make use of these statutes through private actions as well. Most states allow such actions to be brought, with the exception of Arkansas, Iowa, Nevada, and North Dakota.

Class actions are yet another powerful enforcement tool. In certain states, special UDAP provisions expand on the state's basic class-action statute. One case brought under such an expanded statute is *Miner v. Gillette*.[81] In that case, the Illinois Supreme Court ruled that an Illinois consumer could bring a class action under the Illinois UDAP statute on behalf of both resident and nonresident class members.

Another important enforcement power is injunctive relief.

Some UDAP statutes specifically allow injunctions, while others allow "appropriate" or "other" relief.

A FEW FINAL WORDS ON THE SUBJECT

Having now studied the various problem areas involving the Federal Trade Commission Act and the state unfair and deceptive acts and practices statutes, the advertiser should be better equipped to avoid creating a deceptive ad. Advertisers and their agencies, with this knowledge in mind, must carefully and objectively evaluate their advertising to avoid trouble.

You should study the following document, reproduced in full in Exhibit 3-1, which was created in 1975 by the Federal Trade Commission. It contains a series of questions that the Commission uses to investigate advertising cases. In 1981, FTC Chairman, James C. Miller, III, stated that this protocol would be a key document during his tenure. Also in Exhibit 3-2 is a list of cases and staff analysis submitted by the FTC to a House Subcommittee on Commerce, Transportation and Tourism, in 1982. These are key examples of cases that show how the FTC's decisions have stood up on further examination by the FTC staff and the courts.

EXHIBIT 3-1:

Federal Trade Commission Policy Planning Protocol For Deceptive and Unsubstantiated Claims

These questions [which follow] are not cumulative. The answer to less than all of them may indicate the need for action. Moreover, answers to certain of these questions will frequently not be available at all, or may not be available except at considerable cost and delay. Answers to these questions therefore should not be required where obtaining the answers would be unduly burdensome or speculative, or where the answers to other of the questions indicate that the action proposed is a particularly good one, or, of course, where the answers could be obtained only by compulsory process and the action which the Commission is being asked to take is to authorize such process.

A. Consumer Interpretations of the Claim

1. List the main interpretations that consumers may place on the claim recommended for challenge, including those that might render the claim true/substantiated as well as those that might render the claim false/unsubstantiated.

2. Indicate which of these interpretations would be alleged to be implications of the claim for purposes of substantiation or litigation. For each interpretation so indicated, state the reasons, if any, for believing that the claim so interpreted would be false/unsubstantiated.

B. Scale of the Deception or Lack of Substantiation

3. What is known about the relative proportions of consumers adhering to each of the interpretations listed above in response to Question 1?

4. What was the approximate advertising budget for the claim during the past year or during any other period of time that

would reflect the number of consumers actually exposed to the claim? Is there more direct information on the number of consumers exposed to the claim?

C. Materiality

5. If consumers do interpret the claim in the ways that would be alleged to be implications, what reasons are there for supposing that these interpretations would influence purchase decisions?

6. During the past year, approximately how many consumers purchased the product [refers to the particular brand] about which the claim was made?

7. Approximately what price did they pay?

8. Estimate, if possible, the proportion of consumers who would have purchased the product only at some price lower than they did pay, if at all, were they informed that the interpretations identified in response to Question 2 were false.

9. Estimate, if possible, what the advertised product would be worth to the consumers identified by Question 8 if they knew that the product did not have the positive (or unique) attributes suggested by the claim. If the claim can cause consumers to disregard some negative attribute, such as a risk to health and safety, to their possible physical or economic injury, so specify. If so, estimate, if possible, the annual number of such injuries attributable to the claim.

D. Adequacy of Corrective Market Forces

10. If the product to which the claim relates is a low ticket item, can consumers ordinarily determine prior to purchase whether the claim, as interpreted, is true or invest a small amount in purchase and then by experience with the product determine whether or not the claim is true? Does the claim relate to a credence quality, that is, a quality of the product that consumers ordinarily cannot evaluate during normal use of the product

without acquiring costly information from some source other than their own evaluative faculties?

    11. Is the product to which the claim relates one that a consumer would typically purchase frequently? Have product sales increased or decreased substantially since the claim was made?

    12. Are there sources of information about the subject matter of the claim in addition to the claim itself? If so, are they likely to be recalled by consumers when they purchase or use the product? Are they likely to be used by consumers who are not aggressive, effective shoppers? If not, why not?

E. Effect on the Flow of Truthful Information

    13. Will the standard of truth/substantiation that would be applied to the claim under the recommendation to initiate proceedings make it extremely difficult as a practical matter to make the type of claim? Is this result reasonable?

    14. What are the consequences to consumers of an erroneous determination by the Commission that the claim is false/unsubstantiated? What are the consequences to consumers of an erroneous determination by the Commission that the claim is true/substantiated?

F. Deterrence

    15. Is there a possibility of getting significant relief with broad product or claim coverage? What relief is possible? Why would it be significant?

    16. Do the facts of the matter recommended present an opportunity to elaborate a rule of law that would be applicable to claims or advertisers other than those that would be directly challenged by the recommended action? If so, describe this rule of law as you would wish the advertising community to understand it. If this rule of law would be a significant precedent, explain why.

    17. Does the claim violate a Guide or is it inconsistent with relevant principles embodied in a Guide?

18. Is the fact of a violation so evident to other industry members that, if we do not act, our credibility and deterrence might be adversely affected?

19. Is there any aspect of the advertisement—e.g., the nature of the advertiser, the product, the theme, the volume of the advertising, the memorableness of the ad, the blatancy of the violation—which indicates that an enforcement action would have substantial impact on the advertising community?

20. What, if anything, do we know about the role advertising plays (as against other promotional techniques and other sources of information) in the decision to purchase the product?

21. What is the aggregate dollar volume spent on advertising by the advertiser to be joined in the recommended action?

22. What is the aggregate volume of sales of the advertised product and of products of the same type?

G. Law Enforcement Efficiency

23. Has another agency taken action or does another agency have expertise with respect to the claim or its subject matter? Are there reasons why the Commission should defer? What is the position of this other agency? If coordination is planned, what form would it take?

24. How difficult would it be to litigate a case challenging the claim? Would the theory of the proceeding recommended place the Commission in a position of resolving issues that are better left to other modes of resolution, for instance, debate among scientists? If so, explain? Is there a substantial possibility of whole or partial summary judgment?

25. Can the problem seen in the ad be handled by way of a rule? Are the violations widespread? Should they be handled by way of a rule?

H. Additional Considerations

26. What is the ratio of the advertiser's advertising expense to sales revenues? How, if at all, is this ratio relevant to the public interest in proceeding as recommended?

27. Does the claim specially affect a vulnerable group?

28. Does the advertising use deception or unfairness to offend important values or to exploit legitimate concerns of a substantial segment of the population, whether or not there is direct injury to person or pocketbook, e.g, minority hiring or environmental protection?

29. Are there additional considerations not elicited by previous questions that would affect the public interest in proceeding?

EXHIBIT 3-2:

LIST OF CASES AND STAFF ANALYSIS AS SUBMITTED BY FTC CHAIRMAN JAMES C. MILLER, III, TO HOUSE SUBCOMMITTEE ON COMMERCE, TRANSPORTATION AND TOURISM, ON APRIL 1, 1982

Claims On Which The Commission Prevailed

In the Matter of Kroger Co.,
98 F.T.C. 639 (1981)

Kroger's advertising described the results of its "Price Patrol," in which homemakers surveyed prices of 100 to 150 items at local supermarkets. The Commission conceded "that the evidence does not dispute Kroger's basic argument that its prices were frequently below or equal to those of its competitors." Nevertheless, based on its own expertise, without any other evidence of the ad's meaning, the Commission held that the ads were deceptive because they implicitly represented that the surveys were "methodologically sound" and "statistically projectable."

Commissioner Patricia Bailey dissented on the meaning of the ads. She noted that Kroger made a point of emphasizing the informality of the surveys. She wrote, "the notion that these surveys were 'methodologically sound' and therefore 'prove' an overall 'projection' of lower prices is simply, in my view, an artificial construct imposed by the majority [of the Commissioners] on the ads in question." On the merits of bringing this case, she wrote, "I fear that the majority opinion will chill the development of useful comparative price advertising, especially among retail grocers, which is extremely useful to the public, particularly in times of high inflation."

In the Matter of Block Drug Company,
90 F.T.C. 893 (1977)

The FTC challenged claims that Poli-Grip would help denture wearers eat problem foods, such as apples, without discomfort or embarrassment. This product is cheap, frequently purchased, and easy for consumers to evaluate for themselves. When these three facts are present, the FTC is not needed to police the marketplace, because advertisers cannot make enough money from deception to recoup their investment in the advertising.

In the Matter of Ford Motor Co.,
87 F.T.C. 756 (1976)

The headline of the challenged ad claimed that "All 5 Ford Motor Co. small cars got over 26 mpg." The ads stated that mileage varies according to maintenance, equipment, total weight, driving habits, and so forth, and added that no two drivers, or even cars, are exactly alike. Despite these disclaimers, the Commission found an implied claim that the average driver would get the advertised mileage. The Commission found this claim based solely on its own expertise, and without considering a survey conducted by Ford.

In the Matter of Levitz Furniture Corporation,
88 F.T.C. 263 (1976)

A discount furniture store ran ads that claimed "New Reduced Prices," and "Levitz Furniture actually lowers prices." The Commission alleged that the ads claimed consumers would save from Levitz's regular price. As former Commissioner Pitofsky wrote in criticizing the Commission for bringing these fictitious pricing cases, "as long as consumers are accurately informed of the offering price, they can make sensible decisions, and the transactions may still be at prices lower than could be obtained at most other outlets in the marketing area."

In the Matter of Nagle, Spillman & Bergman,
88 F.T.C. 244 (1976) and
In the Matter of Morton-Norwich Products,
86 F.T.C. 299 (1975)

In these cases, the Commission challenged claims for two salt substitutes. Both companies claimed that their products, substituting potassium chloride for sodium chloride, were appropriate for those who wanted to decrease their salt intake. None of the ads mentioned potassium. Nonetheless, the Commission found that the ads were deceptive because they failed to mention that the product should not be used by those on a potassium-restricted diet. In Nagle, the Commission also challenged a claim that the product "tastes like salt." Not only is this claim inherently subjective, but because the product is cheap and frequently purchased, consumers can easily evaluate whether it tastes like salt.

In the Matter of General Motors Corp.,
85 F.T.C. 27 (1975)

GM advertised that *Road and Track* magazine found the Vega to be the best handling passenger car ever built in the U.S. The Commission interpreted GM's claim to mean that Vega really is the best handling car. Because the Commission apparently felt that *Road and Track* magazine was not adequate substantiation, GM could not substantiate the broader claim the Commission inferred from the ad. The result of the order in this case is that consumers are deprived of learning through advertising valuable opinion information from reputable publications.

In the Matter of Spiegel, Inc.,
82 F.T.C. 20 (1973), 494 F.2d 59 (7th Cir. 1974),
cert denied 419 U.S. 896 (1974)

In its advertising circulars, Spiegel offered products on 30 days "free trial" or at a "percentage off." These offers were subject to the customer meeting credit qualifications, a requirement mentioned only in small print and stated in the Spiegel catalogue. Spiegel required the customer to submit credit-related data with the order. The Commission, over the dissent of Commissioner Miles Kirkpatrick, concluded that the ads created the impression that the offer was unconditional when actually it depended on the customer's credit rating. When the appellate court upheld the Commission, Judge Pell, in dissent, wrote that the Commission had found "a detriment to the public interest in the situation of deadbeats being deceived into thinking they are going to receive a free trial of, or discount on, merchandise which they could not realistically purchase on either a cash or a deferred basis."

In the Matter of Brite Mfg. Co.,
65 F.T.C. 1067 (1964), 347 F.2d 477
(D.C. Cir. 1965)

Brite involved watch bands that were imported largely from Japan, and so marked on the back. Based on its own expertise, the Commission found that there was a preference among Americans for domestic watches and that it was deceptive to fail to disclose the foreign origin of the watches prior to sale.

In the Matter of Dannon Milk Products, Inc.,
61 F.T.C. 840 (1962)

Dannon's advertising described yogurt as "Nature's perfect food that science made better." Although Dannon argued that this was mere puffing, the Commission found that the claim that a food is perfect "concerns nutrition," and is therefore a factual claim. The Commission challenged this claim because a person could not subsist on a diet of yogurt alone.

In the Matter of Mohawk Ref. Co.,
54 F.T.C. 1071(1958), 263 F.2d 818
(3d Cir. 1959), see also
In the Matter of Kerron,
54 F.T.C. 1035 (1958), 265 F.2d 246
(10th Cir. 1959)

The point-of-merchandise materials and labels did not make any claims alleged to be false, but they failed to disclose that the oil being sold was refined from previously used oil rather than virgin crude oil. Although the evidence showed that re-refined oil was as satisfactory for lubrication as virgin crude oil, the Commission held that the failure to disclose that the oil was re-refined was deceptive.

In the Matter of Liggett & Myers Tobacco Co.,
55 F.T.C. 354 (1958)

In this case, a cigarette company claimed that its product had a taste that was "always milder." The hearing examiner dismissed this charge as mere puffing and said that there was no public interest in litigating the case. The Commission reversed and found that in the context of the ad, the "milder" claim suggested that it was less irritating in a physical sense, and, not just milder to taste or smell. Under either interpretation, consumers can determine for themselves whether this cigarette is milder.

In the Matter of Gelb,
33 F.T.C. 1450 (1941), aff'd as modified,
144 F.2d 580 (2d Cir. 1944)

The Commission sued a manufacturer that claimed its hair coloring product was permanent because it was feared that some consumers might believe it would color hair that had not yet grown out. The Court of Appeals noted that "it seems scarcely possible that any user of the preparation could be so credulous as to suppose that hair not yet grown out would be so colored."

Nonetheless, it upheld the Commission's order.

In the Matter of Sebrone Co.,
34 F.T.C. 1126 (1942), aff'd 135 F.2d 676
(7th Cir. 1943)

A deodorant that claimed to "kill strongest odors" was challenged as false by the Commission because it only masked, and did not destroy, odors. Deodorants are an inexpensive, frequently purchased product, and consumers can easily determine for themselves whether they are satisfied with the product.

Claims On Which The Commission Lost On Appeal

The courts have often stated that the meaning of an ad is a matter for the discretion of the Commission. As former commissioner Pitofsky wrote, "this modest-sounding rule is a principal reason that the Commission has managed to prevail in the appellate courts in the overwhelming majority of its advertising decisions that have been appealed." 90 Harvard Law Review 661 (1977) at 667-78.

The following cases provide a sign that the courts are no longer deferring to the Commission completely. Yet, it is not clear that the courts will impose a significant check regarding deception.

In the Matter of Standard Oil Co.
of California,
84 F.T.C. 1401 (1974), modified 577 F.2d 653
(9th Cir. 1978)

This case involved claims that a gasoline additive, F-310, would reduce air pollution. The Commission interpreted a visual demonstration, featuring black smoke from a car's exhaust without F-310 added, then clear exhaust after F-310 was used, as a claim that the additive would "cause the disappearance of virtually 100 percent of exhaust emission pollutants." The Court of Appeals reversed this finding, stating "we do not think that any television viewer would have a level of credulity so primitive that he could expect to breathe fresh air if he stuck his head into a bag inflated by exhaust, no matter how clean it looked."

In the Matter of Trans World Accounts, Inc., 90 F.T.C. 350 (1977), modified, 94 F.T.C. 141, further modified, 94 F.T.C. 1051, aff'd in part and remanded in part 594 F.2d 212 (9th Cir. 1979)

This case involved letters sent by a debt collection agency urging immediate payment and stating failure to comply may result in immediate commencement of litigation by our client. The Commission found that the letters were deceptive because they threatened imminent legal action when no such action was contemplated. Commissioner Collier dissented, writing that "may" means legal action is possible, not probable. He noted, "[t]he majority's decision effectively regulates the word 'may' out of respondents' vocabulary." The Court upheld the finding of liability, but reversed the Commission's restrictions on the use of the word "may."

Claims In Which The Commission Disagreed With The Staff

In these cases, the Commission issued a complaint that was later rejected either by an administrative law judge, or by the Commission itself on appeal. Although the staff ultimately did not prevail, the mere fact that the Commission thought there was reason to issue a complaint illustrates the current problems with the deception standard.

In the Matter of California Milk Producers Advisory Board,
94 F.T.C. 429 (1979)

The complaint challenged an advertising slogan that "every body needs milk." The Commission, in issuing the complaint, interpreted the claim to mean that milk is essential for all individuals, even those who are allergic to milk, and that it is beneficial in large and unlimited quantities. The administrative law judge agreed with the interpretation of the ads, but concluded that since less than one percent of the population was allergic to milk, there was no public interest in proceeding.

In the Matter of Jay Norris, Corp.,
91 F.T.C. 751 (1978), aff'd as modified
598 F.2d 1244 (2d Cir. 1979)

The Commission challenged the claim that nylon socks were "guaranteed to wear forever in normal use." The complaint alleged that these claims meant that the socks were literally indestructible and would last forever. The administrative law judge dismissed this allegation. He held that the ad claimed that the socks would last a long time, and that if they wore out, Jay Norris would replace them. This portion of the decision was not appealed to the Commission.

In the Matter of Bristol-Myers Co.,
85 F.T.C. 688 (1975)

The complaint in this case challenged advertisements that depicted Dry Ban as clear and dry when it was applied in contrast to another leading brand, that was oily and sticky. The complaint interpreted these ads to mean that Dry Ban was "a dry spray that is not wet when applied to the body." On appeal from the initial decision, the Commission concluded that the ads claimed only that the product was drier than other brands. The Commission dismissed the complaint. As Commissioner Mayo Thompson noted in his concurring opinion, "[i]f the American consumer has no more serious problem than the possibility of being deceived as to the relative 'dryness' of his underarm deodorant, he is in much better shape than I had been led to suppose at the time I joined this agency."

In the Matter of Firestone Tire and Rubber Co.,
81 F.T.C. 398, aff'd 481 F.2d 246 (6th Cir. 1973)

The Commission's complaint alleged, among other things, that the tire name "Safety Champion" implied that these tires were safer than all other tires. A consumer survey conducted by the company showed that only 1.4% would perceive the claim alleged in this complaint. Nonetheless, the Administrative Law Judge enjoined the use of the term because he interpreted it as representing that the tires were free from defects and safe under all conditions of use. The Commission reversed the prohibition against the use of the term, finding that "Safety Champion" does imply that these tires were safer than all other tires.

[1] *State v. Cohn*, 24 Conn. Supp. 188, 188 A.2d 878 (1962).

[2] *In the Matter of Perfect Mfg. Co.*, 43 F.T.C. 238 (1946).

[3] *Masland Duraleather Co. v. FTC*, 34 F.2d 733, 2 U.S.P.Q. 442 (3d Cir. 1929).

[4] *Sebrone Co. v. FTC*, 135 F.2d 676 (7th Cir. 1913).

[5] *Murray Space Shoe Corp. v. FTC*, 304 F.2d 270 (2d Cir. 1962).

[6] *United States v. Hindman*, 179 F.Supp. 926 (1960).

[7] *Prima Products v. Federal Trade Commission*, 209 F.2d 405 (1954).

[8] *Double Eagle Lubricants, Inc. v. FTC*, 360 F.2d 268 (10th Cir. 1965).

[9] *Giant Food, Inc. v. FTC*, 322 F.2d 977 (D.C. Circuit 1963), *cert. dismissed*, 376 U.S. 976, 84 S.Ct. 1121, 12 L.Ed. 2d 82 (1964).

[10] *Heavenly Creations, Inc. v. FTC*, 339 F.2d 7 (2d Cir. 1964).

[11] *Fedders Corp. v. FTC*, 529 F.2d 1398 (2d Cir. 1976),

[12] *Sears, Roebuck and Co. v. FTC*, 676 F.2d 385 (9th Cir. 1982),

[13] *F.T.C. v. Pharmtech Research, Inc.*, 576 F. Supp. 294 (D.D.C. 1983).

[14] *National Bakers Serv., Inc. v. FTC*, 329 F.2d 365 (7th Cir. 1964).

[15] *Firestone Tire & Rubber Co. v. FTC*, 481 F.2d 246 (6th Cir. 1973).

[16] *Koltz v. Hecht*, 73 F. 822 (2d Cir. 1896).

[17] *In the Matter of Blumenthal*, 43 F.T.C. 158 (1946).

[18] *Chrysler Corp. v. FTC*, 561 F.2d 357 (D.C. Cir. 1977).

[19] *Donaldson v. Read Magazine, Inc.*, 333 U.S. 178, 68 S.Ct. 591, 92 L.Ed. 628 (1948).

[20] 39 U.S.C. 259, 732.

[21] 16 C.F.R. pt. 19.

[22] 16 C.F.R. pt. 20.

[23] 16 C.F.R. pt. 21.

[24] 16 C.F.R. pt. 22.

[25] 16 C.F.R. pt. 23.

[26] 16 C.F.R. pt. 24.

[27] 16 C.F.R. pt. 228.

[28] 16 C.F.R. pt. 230.

[29] 16 C.F.R. pt. 231.

[30] 16 C.F.R. pt. 232.

[31] 16 C.F.R. pt. 235.

[32] 16 C.F.R. pt. 236.

[33] 16 C.F.R. pt. 243.

[34] 16 C.F.R. pt. 245.

[35] 16 C.F.R. pt. 247.

[36] 16 C.F.R. pt. 250.

[37] 16 C.F.R. pt. 252.

[38] 16 C.F.R. pt. 253.

[39] 16 C.F.R. pt. 255.

[40] 16 C.F.R. pt. 400.

[41] 16 C.F.R. pt. 403.

[42] 16 C.F.R. pt. 405.

[43] 16 C.F.R. pt. 152.

[44] 16 C.F.R. pt. 153.

[45] 16 C.F.R. pt. 154.

[46] 16 C.F.R. pt. 155.

[47] 16 C.F.R. pt. l56.

[48] 16 C.F.R. § 305.4(d), pt. 305.

[49] 16 C.F.R. § 410.1.

[50] 15 U.S.C. § 70.

[51] 15 U.S.C. § 68.

[52] 15 U.S.C. §§ 69-69j.

[53] *FTC v. The Book of the Month Club*, 202 F.2d 486 (2nd Cir. 1953).

[54] Federal Register, January 14, 1948, Administrative interpretations with reference to the use of the word *free* and words of similar import under certain conditions to describe merchandise.

[55] *FTC v. Mary Carter Paint Co.*, 382 U.S. 46, 86 S.Ct. 219, 15 L.Ed. 2d 128 (1965).

[56] 16 C.F.R. § 233.5.

[57] 15 U.S.C. §§ 1451-1461 (1982); 16 C.F.R. §§ 502.100-.102 (1987).

[58] 16 C.F.R. § 1.35.

[59] 15 U.S.C. §§ 1601-1614,1661-1665a (1987).

[60] 12 C.F.R. pt. 226 (1987).

[61] 15 U.S.C. §§ 1667-1667e (1982).

[62] 12 C.F.R. pt. 213. (1987).

[63] 16 C.F.R. § 255.0(a) (1987).

[64] *In the Matter of Cliffdale Assocs., Inc.*, 103 F.T.C. 110 (1984).

[65] *In re Cooga Mooga, Inc.*, 92 F.T.C. 310 (1978).

[66] *In re Macmillan, Inc.*, 96 F.T.C. 208 (1980).

[67] *In re Cooga Mooga, Inc.*, 92 F.T.C. 310 (1978).

[68] *American Home Prods. Corp. v. Johnson & Johnson*, 654 F. Supp. 568 (S.D.N.Y. 1987).

[69] *In re Cooper*, 94 F.T.C. 674 (1979).

[70] *In re Bricklin*, 106 F.T.C. 115 (1985).

[71] *American Home Prods. Corp. v. Johnson & Johnson*, 654 F. Supp. 568 (S.D.N.Y. 1987).

[72] *In re Biopractic Group, Inc.*, 104 F.T.C. 845 (1984).

[73] *In re Estee Corp.*, 102 F.T.C. 1804 (1983).

[74] *In re Bristol-Myers Co.*, 102 F.T.C. 21 (1983), *aff'd*, 738 F.2d 554 (2d Cir. 1984), cert. denied, 469 U.S. 1189, 105 S.Ct. 960, 83 L.Ed. 2d. 966 (1985).

[75] *In re Emergency Devices, Inc.*, 102 F.T.C. 1713 (1983).

[76] *In the Matter of Cliffdale Assocs., Inc.*, 103 F.T.C. 110 (1984).

[77] Food, Drug, and Cosmetic Act, 15 U.S.C. §§ 301-392.

[78] Fair Packaging and Labeling Act, 15 U.S.C. §§1451-1461.

[79] 15 U.S.C. § 1125(a).

[80] *C. D. Searle & Co. v. Hudson Pharmaceutical Corp.*, 715 F.2d 837 (3rd Cir. 1983).

[81] *Miner v. Gillette.*, 871 F.2d 7, 428 N.E.2d 478 (1981), *cert. dismissed*, 51 U.S.L.W. 5013 (12-6-82).

CHAPTER 4

PRODUCTS LIABILITY AND ADVERTISING

It's such a perfectly imperfect human thing.
—*Charles Bragg*

"This is a stickup. Open the safe." Startled, John Klages turned toward the voice from the other side of the registration counter. Klages worked as a night clerk at Conley's Motel in Hampton Township, Pennsylvania. It was about 1:30 a.m. on an otherwise quiet March morning, and two armed men stood across the counter. Klages indicated that he didn't have the combination to the safe. In an instant, one of the robbers pointed a gun at him and fired.

The gun, fortunately, was only a starter pistol, and Klages suffered only minor injuries.

The day after the robbery attempt, Klages decided that he needed something to protect himself from future holdups. After reading some literature, a fellow employee, Bob McVay, suggested that they investigate mace as a weapon. McVay gathered four brochures from Markl Supply Company. The manufacturer of one of the mace weapons was General Ordnance Equipment Corporation. Klages selected the MKII model because it was easy to conceal yet, he felt assured, had the stopping power he needed.

The literature claimed that the product:

● ●
Rapidly vaporizes on face of assailant effecting
instantaneous incapacitation . . .
It will instantly stop and subdue entire groups . . .
Instantly stops assailants in their tracks . . .

An attacker is subdued—instantly, for a period
of 15 to 20 minutes . . .
Time magazine stated the chemical mace is
"for police the first, if not the final,
answer to a nationwide need . . ."
A weapon that disables as effectively as a gun . . .
and yet does no permanent injury.
The effectiveness is the result of a unique
incapacitation formulation (patent pending)
projected in a shotgun-like pattern of heavy liquid droplets
that, upon contact with the face, cause extreme tearing,
and a stunned, winded condition, often accompanied
by dizziness and apathy.

● ● ● ● ● ● ● ● ● ● ● ● ● ● ● ●

McVay and Klages read the brochure and, after discussing it with their boss, purchased an MKII mace weapon from Markl Supply.

About 1:40 a.m. on the morning of September 22, 1968, two men entered the motel office where Klages was again on duty. The two men requested a room. Klages handed them a registration form and turned to reach for the room key. One of the men announced that it was a holdup, pulled out a gun, and demanded that Klages open the safe.

Klages moved behind the cash register where the mace was kept and, using the register as a shield, squirted the mace directly into the robber's face. Klages quickly ducked behind the counter. Unfortunately, the robber followed and shot him in the head—this time with a real gun, with real bullets. He survived the attack, but the bullet wound left Klages blind in his right eye.

Klages sued General Ordnance for damages. On March 4, 1974, a jury trial began in *Klages* v. *General Ordnance Equipment Corp.*[1] When it was over, the jury ruled in favor of Klages, awarding him $42,000.

This case is an example of products liability. Granted, the

advertising did not cause the injury. However, the advertising was the machinery that created the image in the mind of the consumer—an image that the product would perform in a certain way.

Here's how it works. The manufacturer made a product for a specific purpose. The consumer purchased the product for that purpose. When the product failed to live up to it, the manufacturer was liable for the injury that resulted.

A manufacturer, through its advertising, implies that its product is safe for—and will perform—its intended use. The manufacturer makes a promise or representation about his product. In the Klages case the manufacturer sold a product designed solely as a device to deter would-be assailants. Its sole use was to protect the purchasers from harm under extremely dangerous conditions. Klages bought the product with these specific purposes in mind. The product failed to live up to its promise, and the injury that resulted made the manufacturer liable.

PRODUCTS LIABILITY AND ITS EFFECT ON ADVERTISING

Products liability is an area of law that deals with a product's failure to perform whatever function for which it was sold. In this chapter we explore the connection between a company's advertising and products liability lawsuits.

The manufacturer's advertising or promotion may be a direct reason to bring suit or it may become evidence during a suit; evidence that can establish what the consumer expected from the product. The advertising may demonstrate the manufacturer's inability to live up to the representations made in the advertisement.

In the eyes of the law, a manufacturer is liable for any deficiency in its product. The point here is that in products liability lawsuits the plaintiff must prove that the advertising somehow lulled him into a false sense of security about the product's safety or capability enough to induce him into its purchase or use. This was the situation with Mr. Klages.

Theories of Products Liability

To assess the role advertising plays in products liability litigation, we should understand that there are a number of legal theories under which a products liability lawsuit can be brought. Those theories are briefly described below with specific illustrative cases, which you'll find discussed later in the chapter.

Negligence exists when there is a failure to exercise reasonable care to protect others against high risks. A manufacturer may be negligent for an act (such as poor quality control) or for a failure to act (such as not testing the product). See *Baxter* v. *Ford Motor Co.* on page 160.

Deceit occurs when there is intent to mislead regarding the existence or nonexistence of a material fact, the consumer relies on the misleading information and damages result. A good example is *Bahlman* v. *Hudson Motor Car Co.* on page 166.

Fraudulent concealment covers situations in which the manufacturer withholds information when he has a duty to speak. A case in point is *Hasson* v. *Ford Motor Co.* on page 173.

Negligent misrepresentation allows the consumer to bring suit when the manufacturer's statements become misrepresentations that he should have known were untrue or inaccurate. Again, this deals with the duty of reasonable care. See *Leichtamer* v. *American Motors Corp.* on page 170.

Strict liability holds the manufacturer liable for a consumer's physical injury resulting from a misrepresentation about the product. In these cases the consumer does not need to prove that the misrepresentation was made negligently or fraudulently. An example is *Procter & Gamble Mfg. Co.* v. *Superior Court.* on page 162.

Express warranty occurs when any specific warranty that

becomes a part of the purchase. Any act, representation, affirmation of fact, or promise made by the manufacturer about the product becomes a part of the bargain.[2] This creates an express warranty that the product will live up to the act, representation, and so on. See *Greenman* v. *Yuba Power Prods., Inc.* on page 163.

   Implied warranty exists by operation of law. Simply stated, it is implied in the sale of the product. One such warranty is for merchantability,[3] which means that the product is fit for the purpose for which it was sold. There is also a warranty of fitness for a particular purpose.[4] Two good examples are *Ford Motor Co.* v. *Lonon* on page 165 and *Filler* v. *Rayex Corp.* on page 168.

   Strict tort liability occurs when the product is defective and that defect causes injury or damage. It is not necessary to prove that the manufacturer or seller was negligent.[5] A good example is *Greenman* v. *Yuba Power Prods., Inc.* on page 163.

   These theories form the basis for all of the cases in this chapter. In one form or another, all products liability litigation stems from these areas of law.

Placing Liability On Advertising Claims

   In *Rogers* v. *Toni Home Permanent Co,*[6] Ms. Rogers purchased a Toni Home Permanent set marked "Very Gentle." She bought the product because of the manufacturer's claims in its advertising and on its packaging. After following the directions supplied with the kit, Rogers' hair became "cotton-like . . . and . . . gummy." Her hair would not dry, and when the curlers supplied with the kit were removed, her hair fell out, leaving only one-half inch of hair remaining.

   This case is important because it was the first time the court made an effort to change how a manufacturer's liability was viewed. Originally, a consumer could sue only the seller of a product for breach of warranty. It was considered that a contract did not exist between the ultimate consumer and the manufacturer, and therefore no warranty existed. The only contract was between the consumer and the store where the item was purchased. The manufacturer could not be sued directly, except in cases of negligence.

Because of the *Rogers* case, the courts have taken the position that the consumer can sue the manufacturer directly for breach of warranty actions (otherwise known as products liability). The court said:

> Today, many manufacturers of merchandise, including the defendant herein, make extensive use of newspapers, periodicals, signboards, radio, and television to advertise their products. The worth, quality, and benefits of these products are described in glowing terms and in considerable detail, and the appeal is almost universally directed to the ultimate consumer. Many of these manufactured articles are shipped out in sealed containers by the manufacturer, and the retailers who dispense them to the ultimate consumers are but conduits or outlets through which the manufacturer distributes his goods. The consuming public ordinarily relies exclusively on the representations of the manufacturer in his advertisements. What sensible or sound reason then exists as to why, when the goods purchased by the ultimate consumer on the strength of the advertisements aimed squarely at him do not possess their described qualities and goodness and cause him harm, he should not be permitted to move against the manufacturer to recoup his loss. In our minds no good or valid reason exists for denying him that right. Surely under modern merchandising practices the manufacturer owes a very real obligation toward those who consume or use his products. The warranties made by the manufacturer in his

advertisements and by the labels on his products are inducements to the ultimate consumers, and the manufacturer ought to be held to strict accountability to any consumer who buys the product in reliance on such representations and later suffers injury because the product proves to be defective.

Basically, products liability cases involve the performance that the consumer can reasonably expect from a product and also any resulting injury because of a consumer's reliance.

Products liability is not an area in which a manufacturer can be sued because of an advertising claim. However, products liability cases can be made using the advertising as proof of what the consumer expected from the product. Since advertising imparts an image, that image can become a large part of what the consumer expects when he or she purchases the product. If it fails, the advertising can be brought in to substantiate what the consumer expected. And, it can also confirm that the manufacturer is liable for any injury that resulted.

Now let's take a closer look at some cases that involve products liability issues and advertising.

THE SHATTERPROOF GLASS CASE

In one case, the literature about an automobile claimed that the windshield of the car was shatterproof. The case was *Baxter* v. *Ford Motor Co.*[7] During the month of May 1930, Mr. Baxter purchased a Model A Ford town sedan from St. John Motors, an authorized Ford dealer. Baxter had read and relied on statements made in Ford's promotional literature; statements that the windshield was made of glass that would not break or shatter. Baxter recovered damages because on October 12, 1930, while he was driving the car, a flying rock shattered the windshield of his car, causing small pieces of glass to destroy his left eye. The literature that Baxter read contained the following:

• •

Triplex Shatterproof Glass Windshield

All of the new Ford cars have a Triplex shatterproof glass
windshield—so made that it will not fly or shatter under the
hardest impact. This is an important safety factor because
it eliminates the dangers of flying glass—
the cause of most of the injuries in automobile accidents.
In these days of crowded, heavy traffic, the use of this
Triplex glass is an absolute necessity.
Its extra margin of safety is something that every motorist
should look for in the purchase of a car—
especially where there are women and children.

• •

In essence, Ford should have known that the statements
were true or it should not have made them. In other words, Ford
was negligent. The court said:

> If a person states as true material facts . . . to
> one who relies and acts thereon to his injury, if the
> representations are false, it is immaterial that he did
> not know they were false or that he believed them to
> be true.

The automobile was represented as having a shatterproof
windshield. By examining the car, the average consumer would
not know if that representation was true. Statements of the
manufacturer would have to be relied on.

Since the concept of caveat emptor (buyer beware) was first
created, the complexity of doing business has undergone many
changes. Advertising has become a major factor in creating the
demand that causes goods to flow from manufacturer to ultimate
consumer. As we discussed earlier, the manufacturer is bound to a
form of strict liability to the buyer. Strict liability places absolute
liability on the manufacturer for a consumer's physical injury

resulting from a misrepresentation about the product. The manufacturer is liable to the buyer for representations that are proven to be false whether in advertisements, literature, or in a document that is passed along to the consumer by the dealer.

Let's look at a hypothetical situation. Acme Company manufactures hoists for cars. Acme distributes a manual that contains statements about the hoist's strength, lifting capacity, and so on. Mr. Jones goes into a local auto parts store and, after reading the literature, buys an Acme hoist. Jones uses the hoist to lift his car. The hoist does not have the lifting capacity that was stated in the literature, and as a result, the car crashes to the floor injuring him. Acme is subject to strict liability to Jones.

Similar situations may occur in almost any situation; the form that the representation takes is not important. In fact, a representation may be in the form of an advertisement on the radio or television, in the newspaper, or in other literature (labels on the product, packaging material, and etc.). It can be written or oral. For strict liability to exist, there must be an issue of fact in the advertising claim. In other words, the representation that the consumer relied on must be presented as a fact. This type of claim is more than just puffing, fantasy advertising, and the like. To illustrate this concept, let's go back to our earlier hypothetical example.

What if the hoist was advertised in the newspaper as "strong and safe for most uses," "the best available," "the best for the price," or even "the most desirable." Could these types of statements give rise to a legal action if the product fails? There is no definite answer, but the advertiser must be cautious. Even general statements can be considered to carry implications of fact. Such statements as a detergent being "kind to the hands" or a power tool being "rugged" have involved implications of fact, as we see in this chapter.

In *Procter & Gamble Mfg. Co. v. Superior Court*,[8] the claim of a detergent being kind to the hands was at issue. On February 3,

1953, Loretta and Robert Jones filed suit in the Marin County Superior Court of California asking for $60,000 in damages. Loretta had been injured, as she alleged, while using Procter & Gamble's product Cheer. Her injury was "a severe dermatitis and dermatosis, causing nervousness and illness and inability to perform her household duties for a six-month period, as well as permanent disfigurement of her hands, which prior to that time were beautiful and smooth." Proctor & Gamble lost the case.

Claims Of Quality Construction

In *Greenman v. Yuba Power Prods., Inc.,*[9] claims that a power tool was rugged were discussed. Mr. Greenman saw a demonstration of a product called a "Shopsmith." The Shopsmith was a combination power tool used as a drill, saw, and wood lathe. After studying a product brochure, Mr. Greenman decided that he wanted a Shopsmith. He told his wife this, and she purchased one for Christmas in 1955.

In 1957 Greenman purchased an attachment that would allow him to use the Shopsmith as a wood lathe. While working on a wood piece, it suddenly flew out of the lathe, striking Greenman in the head and causing serious injuries.

The jury returned an award for $65,000 in favor of Greenman after determining that Yuba Power Products had negligently constructed the Shopsmith. Expert witnesses testified that the set screws used to hold sections of the machine together were not adequate. Normal vibration would cause the screws to loosen, allowing the tailpiece of the lathe to move away from the spinning piece of wood, eventually allowing the wood to fly out of the lathe at high speed.

Here again, we see that the statements made in the manufacturer's product brochure were instrumental in determining the nature and extent of any express warranty that Yuba had made to the potential purchaser. As we saw earlier, an express warranty is created when any description, sample, model, fact, or promise is made by the seller to the buyer that relates to the goods and becomes part of the basis of the bargain. The express warranty is that the goods will live up to the promise. It does not matter that the advertiser knew or should have known that the express warranty was a misrepresentation.

The following information was contained in the Shopsmith brochure:

● ●
When Shopsmith is in Horizontal Position—
Rugged construction of frame provides rigid support
from end to end.
Heavy, centerless-ground steel tubing ensures perfect
alignment of components.
SHOPSMITH maintains its accuracy because
every component has positive locks that hold adjustments
through rough or precision work.
● ●

In this case, the court said: "A manufacturer is strictly liable . . . when an article he places on the market, knowing that it is to be used without inspection for defects, proves to have a defect that causes injury to a human being." Simply because the Shopsmith was placed on the market, the consumer could assume that it was safe for the jobs for which it was built.

Those jobs were detailed in the product brochure on which the consumer who purchases the product would rely. It does not matter that the manufacturer did not intend to mislead or cause harm. The harm occurred, and the manufacturer was liable. This holds true as long as the injury results from a defect in the product that appears when the product is being used as intended.

Liability For Commercial Loss

In February of 1962, Mr. Lonon purchased a Fordson Major Diesel tractor from the Haywood Tractor Company. Lonon was a farmer and needed a large tractor capable of performing certain tasks. He had visited the Ford tractor dealers in the area and had read the sales literature. He also had seen the many advertisements Ford published in farm magazines and ran on television. The literature contained information about the live power take-off, the power steering lift, and other full specifications.

Over a period of time the tractor failed to perform the functions that were claimed it could perform. The tractor was taken in for repairs on many occasions with no effect. It was defective from the time that it was purchased. Lonon sued Ford after failing to receive any satisfaction. In *Ford Motor Co. v. Lonon*,[10] the jury award of $4,000 was upheld. Lonon received $4,000 plus court costs for a tractor that originally cost him $4,243.10.

What makes this case interesting is that, unlike other products liability cases, there was no injury to the plaintiff. Most of the decisions hold the manufacturer liable for physical injury that was a direct result of the manufacturer's breach of warranty. In this case, we see that the courts can apply the same principle to commercial losses (losses of time and work as opposed to physical injury) that result from a defectively manufactured product or product part.

THE SEAMLESS STEEL ROOF CASE—
IMPLIED SAFETY CLAIMS

Mr. Bahlman, a traveling shoe salesman, bought a 1936 model Hudson Eight Sedan from the Hudson Motor Car Company, based in part on the claim that the car had a seamless steel roof. The manufacturer, in its promotional literature, had represented that the car had such a feature. In fact, the Hudson was touted as "A Rugged Fortress of Safety." However, in reality the roof was made of two separate parts. Typical of the advertising claims that Mr. Bahlman read were:

• •

Beneath the bigness and beauty, the safest car on today's
highway, with the world's first safety engineering.
Safeness combined with the first bodies all of steel.
Bodies introduced last year by Hudson and now brought to new
heights of strength and beauty with an improved
seamless steel roof.

How, What, Why about the 1936 Hudsons and Terraplanes.
A steel top which is a smooth, solid unit with the body shell.
There are no seams or joints in the roof and body structure,
just a complete steel body made from a single sheet of steel.

• •

In *Bahlman* v. *Hudson Motor Car Co.*,[11] the court held for the
plaintiff. Bahlman had been injured by a jagged edge of the welded
roof when his car overturned. Hudson had obviously conveyed an
impression of a safety characteristic in its literature by claiming
that the roof was one piece and therefore stronger than a welded
roof. The construction of the roof of the car was represented as a
specific safety feature, and specifically as protection against the
type of injury that Bahlman suffered.

The fact that Bahlman's own negligent driving caused the
accident was not significant because the safety feature existed to
protect the people in the car from what actually took place—a
crash. The safety features in a car are provided in the event of an
accident regardless of who or what caused the accident.

THE ABSOLUTELY HARMLESS TOY CASE

On the packaging of the Ronson revolver, a toy pistol, was
a picture of a small boy firing a Ronson revolver.

• • • • • • • • • • • •

In looks and action
just like the real thing.

B-A-N-G! F-L-A-S-H! S-M-O-K-E!
Absolutely harmless.
● ● ● ● ● ● ● ● ● ● ● ● ● ●

Shortly before Christmas in 1926, William Crist was demonstrating a Ronson revolver in the Crist Department Store window in Circleville, Ohio. William, a child of less than 10, was dressed in a Santa Claus suit, complete with beard. When William fired one of the Ronson revolvers, the sparks from the toy ignited the soft cotton material of the Santa Claus suit. In seconds the boy was enveloped in flames and seriously injured. The court in *Crist v. Art Metal Works*,[12] described the boy's injury as ". . . serious, painful, and permanent injuries, both externally and internally, about his head, face and limbs, . . . and . . . serious permanent disability and shock to his nervous system."

The interesting aspect of this case was that no defect in the product was alleged or discussed. In fact quite the contrary, the toy revolver operated perfectly. It was the claim that the toy was "absolutely safe" for a child that gave rise to the lawsuit. The advertising convincingly relieved all fear of possible injury to a child user. Here was a key example of where advertising plays a strong role in establishing the expectations of a product's performance. The product did not fail, but it failed to live up to its claim of safety.

There are cases in which the advertising or literature only suggests a safety quality. Other times a reference to safety is specific and direct, as in the case we just discussed. What is important for the advertiser to know is that the courts tend not to differentiate between these when looking at liability.

THE BASEBALL SUNGLASSES CASE

Richard Beck, the baseball coach at Oak Hill High School in Marion, Indiana, would not allow his players to wear sunglasses because he thought they were too dangerous. Yet, before the 1966 season he read the following in *Sporting News*:

● ● ● ● ● ● ● ●
PLAY BALL!
and Flip for Instant Eye Protection with
RAYEX
baseball
SUNGLASSES
Professional
FLIP-SPECS
Scientific lenses protect your eyes with a flip
from sun and glare anywhere . . .
baseball, beach, boat, driving, golfing, fishing,
just perfect for active and spectator sports
—world's finest sunglasses.
● ● ● ● ● ● ● ● ● ● ● ● ● ● ● ● ● ●

The product packaging stated: "Simply flip . . . for instant eye protection," and "Rayex lenses are guaranteed for life against breakage."

After reading the advertisement and packaging, coach Beck purchased Rayex flip-down sunglasses for his team. One of the teenage boys on the team, Michael Filler, wore the glasses while playing in a game. A batted ball struck the boy in the face, breaking the glasses. The shattered glasses splintered and damaged one of the boy's eyes so badly that it had to be removed. The court in *Filler* v. *Rayex Corp.*,[13] in awarding damages in excess of $101,000, said about the product:

Since they lacked the safety features of plastic
or shatterproof glass, the sunglasses were in truth
not fit for baseball playing, the particular purpose
for which they were sold.

There was no explicit advertising claim about the shatterproof quality of the glasses. The ad copy referred only to protection against sun and glare. But they were advertised in a sporting magazine, directed to athletes, and stated that they were safe for use in baseball. The obvious implication was that they were safe for use in that sport, even though the manufacturer had not made adequate tests to support that claim. This was a case of a safety claim being implied, but a safety claim nonetheless. Along with the sale, an implied warranty was created.

Regarding a point that we covered earlier, an implied warranty means that the warranty is implied with the sale of the product. As we have discussed, there are warranties of merchantability and fitness for a particular purpose. Merchantability refers to the fitness of the product for the ordinary purposes for which such goods are used. Fitness for a particular purpose implies a specific use by the buyer which is peculiar to the nature of his business.

THE OVERTURNED GOLF CART CASE

The Missouri Supreme Court upheld a $94,000 award in *Blevins* v. *Cushman Motors*[14] involving a man who was pinned under a golf cart that had overturned. Advertisements had appeared in golfing magazines promoting the Cushman golf cart. Typical of the ad's copy was:

• •
Talk about a turned on ride. Smooooth.
With a beefier, low-slung 3-point rubber suspension.
New rubber suspensions between power frame and main frame
lets the GC tool through turns with super ease,
super safety, super stability.
Low ground-hugging center of gravity makes
for wide stance, razor-honed handling.
Fat, ground-gripping, turf-protecting 9.50 x 8 Terra Tires

are standard.
This baby floats the course.
● ● ● ● ● ● ● ● ● ● ● ● ● ● ● ● ● ● ● ●

On the afternoon of July 15, 1969, Albert Blevins and a friend met for a round of golf at the Stayton Meadows Golf Course. The two men began play using their Cushman Golf Cart. On the 13th hole the cart was being driven at about five miles per hour when it crossed a wet, shaded area. The cart skidded and turned over, throwing Blevins's friend clear of the cart. Blevins, however, fell on the ground and was pinned and injured by the overturned cart.

In order to win his case, Blevins needed to establish that the accident and damage resulted from a use of the product that was "reasonably anticipated." Blevins was required to show that the golf cart was used as that—a golf cart which could negotiate a golf course. Here the advertising clearly convinced the court that that use was not only anticipated but encouraged. The advertising showed a "justified use and reliance by the driver" of the cart. In fact, the advertising tended to draw the purchaser into a false sense of security as to the use of the cart and its safety.

PUNITIVE DAMAGES

Increasing indications show that advertising is being considered heavily as an influential factor in imposing punitive damages in certain lawsuits. Punitive damages are awarded to punish the wrongdoer. They are also a strong deterrent for others to consider.

In *Leichtamer* v. *American Motors Corp.*,[15] a four-wheel-drive vehicle overturned while going down an incline. On April 18, 1976, Paul Vance and his wife Cynthia invited Carl and Jeanne Leichtamer to go for a ride in the Vances' Jeep CJ-7. The Vances belonged to an off-road club located near Dundee, Ohio, which had been converted from an old strip mine.

While the Vances' Jeep was descending a double-terraced hill, the vehicle's rear end pitched over. The Jeep had cleared the first embankment; and after clearing the second, it landed on the front wheels. At that point, the rear end continued over the front end of the Jeep. The Jeep landed upside down pointing back up the hill. Paul and Cynthia Vance were killed. Carl Leichtamer sustained a skull fracture, and Jeanne Leichtamer became a paraplegic.

During the trial it was acknowledged that Paul Vance's negligence caused the accident. However, it was claimed that the Leichtamers' injuries were "substantially enhanced, intensified, aggravated, and prolonged" as a result of the failure of the factory-installed roll bar on the Jeep. The roll bar was offered as optional equipment on the Jeep CJ-7 and was promoted solely for protection in the event of a rollover. The roll bar was not structurally sound enough to withstand the pitchover that the Vances went through.

Jeep, then a division of American Motors Corporation, had produced a multi-million dollar television campaign that encouraged people to buy a Jeep:

● ● ● ● ● ● ● ● ● ● ● ● ● ● ● ●
Ever discover the rough,
exciting world of mountains,
forests, rugged terrain?
The original Jeep can get you there,
and Jeep guts will bring you back.
● ●

This case illustrates the role advertising can play in the imposition of liability. Certain expectations that the consumer develops about the safety of a product are formed largely through the product's advertising. The manner in which a product's use is advertised is relevant to the use that the product is intended for.

The Jeep commercials depicted its qualities and safety in an off-road situation and stressed the Jeep's ability to negotiate steep hills. One particular spot challenged a young man, accompanied by his girl friend:

● ● ● ● ● ● ● ● ● ● ● ● ● ● ● ● ● ● ● ●
"You guys aren't yellow, are you?
Is it a steep hill?
Yeah, little lady, you could say it is a steep hill.
Let's try it.
The King of the Hill is about to discover the new Jeep CJ-7."
● ●

In fact, the advertising clearly depicted the Jeep going up and down steep and rugged terrain safely. Even the owner's manual claimed that the Jeep could "proceed in safety down a grade which could not safely be negotiated by a conventional 2-wheel drive vehicle."

The court felt that the advertising was a significant factor in supporting a finding for punitive damages since it showed the probable use of the vehicle while ignoring the danger that could likely result from that use saying: "The commercial advertising clearly contemplates off-road use of the vehicle."

The salesman's guide to the vehicle described the roll bar in the following terms: "Surround yourself and your passengers with the strength of a rugged, reinforced steel roll bar for added protection. A very practical item, and a must if you run competition with a 4WD club. Adds rugged good looks, too."

Given the foreseeability of roll-overs and pitch-overs, the failure of appellants to test to determine whether the roll bar "added protection" represents a flagrant indifference to the probability that a user might be exposed to an unreasonable risk of harm. For appellants to have encouraged off-the-road use while providing a roll bar that did little more than add "rugged good looks" was a sufficient basis for an award of punitive damages.

The Ohio Supreme Court granted a $2.2 million damage award in the case. Over half of the damages were punitive.

The Extent Of Punitive Damages

In 1982, the California Supreme Court affirmed a $9.2 million award in *Hasson* v. *Ford Motor Co.*[16] About $4 million were in punitive damages. The case developed because of a catastrophic brain injury suffered by the driver of a 1965 Lincoln Continental when the brakes failed on a hill. The driver established that the manufacturer failed to warn dealers and owners of a known (to Ford) problem with the brakes, and how to correct it, because it was protecting the model's reputation among customers. The manufacturer deliberately failed to test for the problem with the brakes and subsequently failed to install a dual master cylinder, which would have overcome the defect.

Deceit and fraudulent concealment—which we discussed at the beginning of this chapter—occur when the advertiser intends to mislead the consumer regarding a material fact about the product and the consumer relies on that information to his detriment. If the advertiser expressly misstates a fact, it is deceit. If the advertiser withholds information when he should give it out, it is fraudulent concealment.

The issue here was Ford's knowing disregard for the safety of the vehicle, something that its advertising convinced otherwise. Ford management had a policy of advertising that the Lincoln Continental was free from the need for service for a large portion of its components.

CONCLUSION

Advertisers must be aware of all areas of product liability. The portrayal of the product in advertising or promotional literature can be a major factor in claims against the integrity of the product. The stakes are high today in products liability litigation.

Now, proof of liability has become facilitated by recent legal activity in this area. Claims are higher. Awards are higher. Juries are more willing to award substantial punitive damages.

---

[1] *Klages* v. *General Ordnance Equipment Corp.*, CCH Prods. Liab. Rep. Paragraph 7664 (Pa. Super. 1976).

[2] Uniform Commercial Code, Section 2-313.

[3] Uniform Commercial Code, Section 2-314.

[4] Uniform Commercial Code, Section 2-315. Restatement of Torts (Second), Section 402A.

[5] Restatement of Torts (Second), Section 402A.

[6] *Rogers* v. *Toni Home Permanent Co.*, 167 Ohio St. 244, 147 N.E. 2d 612 (1958).

[7] *Baxter* v. *Ford Motor Co.*, 12 F2d 409, aff'd on rehearing, 15 P.2d 1118 (Wash. Sup. Ct. 1932).

[8] *Procter & Gamble Mfg. Co.* v. *Superior Court*, 268 P.2d 199 (Cal. App. 1954).

[9] *Greenman* v. *Yuba Power Prods., Inc.*, 377 F.2d 897 (Cal. Sup. Ct. 1963).

[10] *Ford Motor Co.* v. *Lonon*, 398 S.W.2d 240 (Tenn. 1966).

[11] *Bahlman* v. *Hudson Motor Car Co.*, 288 N.W. 309 (Mich. 1939).

[12] *Crist* v. *Art Metal Works*, 243 N.Y. Supp. 496 (1st Dep't. 1930).

[13] *Filler* v. *Rayex Corp.*, 435 F.2d 336 (7th Cir. 1970).

[14] *Blevins* v. *Cushman Motors*, 551 S.W. 2d 602 (Mo. 1977).

[15] *Leichtamer* v. *American Motors Corp.*, 424 N.E. 2d 568 (Ohio 1981).

[16] *Hasson* v. *Ford Motor Co.*, 19 Cal. 3d 530 (1977), CCH Prods. Liab. Rep. Paragraph 9398 (Sept. 16, 1982).

CHAPTER 5

THE RIGHTS OF PRIVACY AND PUBLICITY

Civilization is the progress toward a society of privacy.
—Ayn Rand

The year is 1913. The place is an empty horse barn recently converted into a "factory where pictures that move are made." It's daytime, but the inside of the big empty barn is dark. Only bright sunlight streams through a window at the end of the room. A few stagehands move camera equipment around in the distance. The air is dusty. The floor is covered with straw.

As the television commercial we're watching continues, a man's feet step into view. A megaphone sits on the floor in front of his feet. The name "Mr. DeMille" is stenciled on it. The legendary director rocks in place in his knee-high riding boots, tense in anticipation.

The camera moves around him while he clutches a pair of leather gloves behind his back. His hands squeeze the gloves with nervous excitement. DeMille takes in the activity happening within the room. We see, almost as if a ghost, the image of an early 1900's train approaching from the distance. Then we see the image of an early 1900's camera crew on the set.

We hear a recognizable voice: "In 1913, a young director prepared to step off the train in Flagstaff, Arizona. But it was raining. So he stayed on to the end of the line and shot his feature-length Western in a rented barn in a quiet farming town . . . called Hollywood."

The last of the crew members have moved away and the director moves out of the picture. Through the stark light of the window emerges the figure of a man. He walks toward us and becomes recognizable as Gene Barry, the actor. "Now, at the barn where it all began, you can relive those early days when Hollywood first met the movies." He turns toward DeMille.

"Ready, Mr. DeMille." The actor finishes: "The Hollywood Studio Museum. Where the legend lives on."

What you've just read is a script from a television commercial that I produced a few years ago promoting the site of the first feature-length motion picture—a little yellow barn, located in Hollywood and preserved as a historical landmark. The place where, literally, "Hollywood" began.

I've used this example (and we'll return to it later) because the commercial involves the subject of this chapter—the right of publicity and the right of privacy. Both rights protect a person against the unauthorized use of his or her identity. As we see in this chapter, each area of law covers different injuries and promotes different values. Whenever an advertiser uses an image, likeness, or name of another person in an ad or for trade, certain rights must be considered. Here, we explore two of these rights: The right of privacy and the right of publicity.

THE RIGHT OF PRIVACY

We start with the oldest of the two rights, the right of privacy. The concept of a specific right of privacy began to take shape in the late 1800's to protect individuals who truly desired privacy, mainly private citizens.

Here's a little sociology lesson. Individuals, by becoming a part of a society, give up many rights and privileges that they would be free to exercise in nature. In exchange for this, they receive the benefits of being part of a society. But all rights are not given up. There are matters that are private that any intelligent member of society can recognize, and there is a right of privacy in those matters.

The intent of the right of privacy laws is to protect the

essence of the individual person. To put it another way, privacy laws protect his or her persona from being taken and used without his or her knowledge or permission for the profit of another. The words Shakespeare wrote for Iago were straight to the point:

> Good name in man or woman, dear my lord,
> Is the immediate jewel of their souls;
> Who steals my purse steals trash;
> 'tis something, nothing;
> Twas mine, 'tis his, and has been slave to thousands;
> But he that filches from me my good name
> Robs me of that which not enriches him,
> And makes me poor indeed.

Individuals have the right to live their lives in any way they see fit so long as it does not invade the rights of others or violate public laws or policies. People may make themselves visible to the public when they desire and may withdraw from the public when they wish.

In Roman law we see the beginnings of what would become the right of privacy. Anyone who brought public attention to another on a public road or on the other's own private grounds would be punished. Shouting until a crowd gathered or following an honest woman or child were banned under Roman law. In those days the law recognized a right "to be let alone." Even though, at the time, it was considered a property right, and property was an extremely valuable commodity.

In *Semayne's* case,[1] one of the oldest English cases to be reported, we find the first legal maxim applied that "the house of every one is to him as his castle and fortress, as well for his defense against injury and violence as for his repose." Today, we find Semayne's maxim recognizable in our phrase "every man's home is his castle."

The unreported case of *Manola* v. *Stevens*, heard before the Supreme Court of New York in 1890, was the first case in this country where the right of privacy idea was used in an attempt to persuade the court that the lawful right existed. The complainant claimed that while the plaintiff performed on the Broadway stage in tights, she was photographed with the use of a flashlight. This was done without her knowledge or consent by the defendant sitting in a box seat. While the court permanently enjoined the display of the unauthorized photo, they steered clear of labeling this a right of privacy.

Right Of Privacy—The Early View

In 1902 the New York Court of Appeals rejected the existence of a common law right of privacy in *Roberson* v. *Rochester Folding Box Co.*[2] Abigail Roberson—at the time a child—sued for the unauthorized use of her photograph in posters (promoting a flour product) that were displayed in stores, warehouses, saloons, and so on. Even though the posters were complimentary—describing her as "The Flour of the Family"—the publication of the photo subjected her to "scoffs and jeers . . . causing her great distress and suffering both in body and mind."

In spite of this, the court refused to rule in favor of Roberson. They feared that this would open the flood gates once the principle of a privacy right was established. The court said:

> [T]he so-called right of privacy has not yet found an abiding place in our jurisprudence, and, as we view it, the doctrine cannot now be incorporated without doing violence to settled principles of law by which the profession and the public have long been guided.

However, the public reacted very strongly to what it considered to be an injustice and demanded that the legislature change the law. The New York legislature quickly enacted a statute prohibiting the use of a person's name, likeness, or picture, without prior written permission, for trade or advertising purposes.[3] This became the model law that other states have since followed.

The Right Of Privacy Becomes Law

The first court case to specifically recognize the right of privacy was *Pavesich* v. *New England Life Ins. Co.*[4] Paolo Pavesich's picture was published in a life insurance company's ad that had run in the *Atlanta Constitution* newspaper. His picture, that of a healthy and well-dressed man, appeared next to one of a sickly and badly dressed one. The caption above Pavesich read, "Do it now. The man who did." Above the sickly person ran the caption, "Do it while you can. The man who didn't." Below both pictures was the statement, "These two pictures tell their own story." Under Pavesich's picture was the following copy:

• • • • • • • • • • • • • • • • • • • •
"In my healthy and productive
period of life
I bought insurance
in the New England Mutual Life Insurance Co.
of Boston, Mass.,
and today my family is protected
and I am drawing an annual
dividend on my paid-up policies."
—Thomas B. Lumpkin, General Agent.
• •

The photo was used without Mr. Pavesich's knowledge or consent. The statement under his picture was also false; he never had a life insurance policy with the company. Pavesich asked for $25,000 in damages. He got it. In essence the court allowed Pavesich to recover damages for injured feelings.

The Pavesich case established for the first time the precedent for future actions under a right of privacy, and the court, in an opinion over 30 pages long, addressed the issue in detail. In its conclusion to the case it said:

> So thoroughly satisfied are we that the law
> recognizes within proper limits, as a legal right, the
> right of privacy, and that the publication of one's
> picture without his consent by another as an
> advertisement, for the mere purpose of increasing
> the profits and gains of the advertiser, is an invasion
> of this right, that we venture to predict that the day
> will come when the American bar will marvel that a
> contrary view was ever entertained by judges of
> eminence and ability.

Since the time of the *Pavesich* decision and the passage of
the New York statute, every state has developed (in one form or
another) a right of privacy. The U.S. Supreme Court, in fact,
established that the right of privacy stems from the specific
guarantees in the Bill of Rights.[5]

All right of privacy laws protect against one of four forms of
violations:

- The unauthorized use of another person's name or likeness
  for another's benefit;
- The invasion into an individual's seclusion;
- The public disclosure of embarrassing private facts; and
- The presentation of an individual in a false light in the
  public view. The common denominator between these four
  is the right to be left alone.

Waiver Of Privacy Rights

The right of privacy, like every other right of an individual,
may be waived by voluntarily allowing one's image to be used in
an ad. An advertiser must get written permission for such use in
order to avoid a violation. A person may also imply that he or she
waives privacy rights. A good example of this occurs when a
private citizen runs for public office. Here, the person's rights are

waived in order to allow the public to investigate how the candidate's private life is conducted. This is allowed to determine the person's qualifications for the office that the candidate wishes to hold. But the waiver of rights applies only to matters that affect competency for the office being sought. This type of implied waiver, however, is rarely involved in advertising situations.

THE RIGHT OF PUBLICITY

The right to privacy had its limitations. As years progressed, many people actually wanted publicity, not privacy. The right of publicity grew out of the need to aid people such as celebrities, entertainers, and athletes who wanted to protect the use of their marketable image.

Development Of The Right Of Publicity

Prior to the establishment of a right of publicity, it was not illegal for others to freely use entertainers' names or likenesses. Because entertainers sought publicity, they were making their lives public, and as such, waived their rights to privacy, it was felt.

In *O'Brien v. Pabst Sales Co.*,[6] a well-known football player claimed a violation of his right of privacy after Pabst used his picture on a calendar promoting its beer. While at Texas Christian University, David O'Brien was selected by Grantland Rice for his *Collier's* All American Football Team in 1938. O'Brien was probably the most publicized football player of the 1938-39 season. After graduating from TCU, he would play professionally for the Philadelphia Eagles.

Pabst Brewing Company published a calendar every year with the schedule of the entire football league included. Inland Lithographing Company printed 35,000 calendars for 1939 that used the picture of O'Brien in uniform. The headline read, "Pabst Blue Ribbon Football Calendar, 1939."

O'Brien claimed that he had not given his permission for

the use of his picture. In fact, he did not even know that it had been used until quite some time after its release to stores. He claimed that he was greatly embarrassed by the publication of his picture in connection with the sale of beer, a product he personally was against using.

The court, however, stated that:

[A]s a result of his activities and prowess in football, his chosen field, and the nationwide and deliberate publicizing with his consent and in his interest, he was no longer . . . a private but public person, and as to their additional publication he had no right of privacy.

The court decided that O'Brien had no case. He could not recover under a right of privacy claim because O'Brien was a famous National Football League figure and had purposefully publicized his name and photos. Because of this, he had waived his right of privacy. In fact the court said, "the publicity [he] got was only that which he had been constantly seeking."

Establishment Of The Right Of Publicity As Law

Essentially, celebrities had little chance of recovering damages for the appropriation of their names or likenesses for commercial use. However, this dim outlook was soon changed by the Court of Appeals for the Second Circuit. For the first time, a right of publicity was recognized in *Haelan Laboratories* v. *Topps Chewing Gum, Inc.*[7]

Haelan was a chewing gum company that had obtained the exclusive right to use a baseball player's photograph in connection with the sale of gum. The defendant Topps claimed that it had a contract for the use of the same ballplayer's photograph during that same time. Topps had, in fact, deceptively persuaded the ballplayer to enter into a contract with it while he was still bound by the contract with Haelan.

In this case, the court admitted that, in addition to rights of privacy, a person has a right of publicity. It protects a person's commercial interest in his or her identity, and that person has the right to authorize the publication of a picture of that identity. When this happens, it is an exclusive grant, and other advertisers are not allowed to use the picture. Haelan won its case because it owned the publicity rights to the ballplayer. Topps' contract was invalid.

Public Figures Do Not Waive Their Right Of Privacy

Public figures who do not market themselves commercially may suffer injury by being associated with commercial products. These people have not waived their rights of privacy simply by being public figures.

A good example of this occurred when the late Jacqueline Onassis won an action under a right of privacy claim in *Onassis v. Christian Dior, New York, Inc.*[8] What made the case unique was the way that Dior violated her right of privacy. Dior, through its ad agency, J. Walter Thompson, produced a campaign of 16 ads. Dior spent $2.5 million in publications including *Esquire, The New Yorker, Harper's Bazaar*, and the *New York Times*.

The ads featured a trio known as the Diors (one female and two men) who were to be the essence of the idle rich, decadent, and aggressively chic. The intent was to develop a group of characters that would become the most memorable personalities since Brooke Shields refused to let anything come between her and her Calvins. The copy for one of the ads read:

● ● ● ● ● ● ● ● ● ● ●
When the Diors
got away from it all,
they brought with them nothing except
The Decline of the West
and one toothbrush.
● ● ● ● ● ● ● ● ● ● ● ● ●

The ads led the reader through a progression of various situations that would include the marriage of two (but not the exclusion of the third), the birth of a baby, and their ascent to Heaven. One of the ads, the one for the wedding, ran:

● ● ● ● ● ● ● ● ● ● ●

Christian Dior:
Sportswear for Women and Clothing for Men.
The wedding of the Diors was everything
a wedding should be:
no tears, no rice, no in-laws, no smarmy toasts,
for once no Mendelssohn.
Just a legendary private affair.

● ● ● ● ● ● ● ● ● ● ● ● ● ● ● ● ● ● ●

The ad showed the trio along with their wedding party. Included in the group were movie critic Gene Shalit, model Shari Belafonte Harper, actress Ruth Gordon, and a secretary named Barbara Reynolds who bears an amazing resemblance to Jacqueline Onassis. All were obviously delighted to be at the event.

Dior knew that there was no chance of Ms. Onassis consenting to being in the ad. She has never permitted the use of her name or picture to be used in connection with the promotion of any commercial products, but only for public service, art, educational, or civic projects. So, the agency and photographer Richard Avedon contacted Ron Smith Celebrity Look-Alikes to supply someone who resembled Onassis. That they did with Barbara Reynolds. The use of look-alikes requires the permission of the actual celebrity, nonetheless.

Even though Onassis' name was not used in the ad, and the image was not actually of Onassis, the public would naturally assume that it was Onassis. A visual pun was used to catch the reader's eye and draw attention to the ad. What they had was a recognizable likeness, which was not consistent with reality.

Dior also contended that having Onassis attend the

wedding of the Diors was "no more than a touch of humor" and therefore was protected as a form of free speech. However, simply claiming that a statement was intended to be funny does not make it permissible to make the statement. In this case, the humor was used only to promote Dior products, so absolutely no freedom of speech privilege existed to justify its use.

What is ironic about this case, as the court noted, was that Dior was attempting to "pass off the counterfeit as a legitimate marketing device," when it had in the past, so adamantly tried to prevent others from deceptively obtaining the "fruits of another's labor." For example, in a previous case, *Dior v. Milton,*[9] Dior complained bitterly of the misappropriation of its good name and reputation that had taken so long to develop. Now the shoe was on the other foot.

Although Onassis was a public figure, even a celebrity, she purposely avoided any connection with commercial products. Embarrassment and annoyance were her injury rather than loss of economic opportunity.

As a side note, we'll look at another aspect of using celebrity look-alikes in Chapter 9. There, comparative advertising has become another area of law that is involved in certain situations that use look-alikes.

When Freedom Of The Press Overcomes The Rights Of Privacy And Publicity

In 1978, the movie *Magic* was released and subsequently grossed over $13 million. One of the stars of the movie was Ann-Margret. For only the second time in her career she appeared in a scene nude. She made the decision to disrobe for artistic reasons agreeing to do so only if there was a minimal crew at the filming and if no still photos were taken.

High Society magazine runs photographs of well-known women caught in revealing situations. In one particular issue, five pages were devoted exclusively to Ann-Margret. One of the photos was taken from the movie *Magic* and showed her nude from the waist up. After learning of this photo, suit was brought in *Ann-Margret v. High Society Magazine, Inc.*[10] for violation of her right of privacy and right of publicity.

There is no doubt that Ann-Margret is considered a celebrity, but simply because she is a celebrity she has not given up her right to privacy. However, she chose to appear in the motion picture, partially nude, knowing that the public would see her performance. The reproduction of scenes from that performance were faithful and accurate and not distorted, and therefore were not an invasion of her privacy.

The court said:

Undoubtedly, the plaintiff is unhappy about the appearance of her picture in [the] magazine. And while the court can sympathize with her feelings, the fact that she does not like either the manner in which she is portrayed, or the medium in which her picture is reproduced . . . [does] not expand her rights or create any cause of action . . .

As far as her claim of violation of her right of publicity, the court felt that it also had no merit. There is only an action when the use is for "advertising purposes or for the purposes of trade." The fact that the magazine is sold for profit does not constitute such a use. The mere use of the photos in an editorial context is acceptable. The case was dismissed.

When The Right Of Publicity Exceeds Freedom Of The Press

"Ladies and gentlemen, children of all ages, I present the great Zacchini." Hugo Zacchini practiced a form of entertainment developed by his father and performed by his family for over 50 years. Zacchini was a human cannonball, and over the years he performed at many public fairs and events.

In August and September of 1972, Zacchini performed his act at the Geauga County Fair in Burton, Ohio. The performance took place in a fenced area surrounded by grandstands. He was shot from a cannon into a net 200 feet away, and the performance lasted 15 seconds.

A freelance reporter for Scripps-Howard Broadcasting, owner of the local television station, visited the fair on August 30, 1972 where Zacchini was performing. Zacchini spotted the reporter carrying a video camera and requested that he not tape the performance, but on the next day the reporter returned and videotaped the feat anyway. The event was broadcast on the 11 o'clock news along with a commentary, which was very complimentary.

When Zacchini learned of the unauthorized broadcast, he sued for damages for showing and commercializing his act without his consent. This was the first case involving the right of publicity to reach the United States Supreme Court: *Zacchini* v. *Scripps-Howard Broadcasting Co.*[11]

Scripps-Howard argued that its broadcast of the event was protected under the 1st and 14th Amendments — freedom of the press. The TV station had the right to broadcast items of legitimate public interest. However, the TV station broadcast the entire act, from start to finish, along with a description of the event. If the station had broadcast that Zacchini was performing at the fair, commented on the performance, and showed his picture on TV, this could have been a very different case.

But as the Court said Zacchini:

[H]ad a right of publicity that gave him personal control over commercial display and exploitation of his personality and the exercise of his talents. This right . . . was said to be such a valuable part of the benefit, which may be attained by his talents and efforts, that it was entitled to legal protection.

Zacchini did not sue to stop the broadcast of his performance; he simply wanted to be paid for it. The Court agreed that Zacchini's commercial interest in his act was protected under his right of publicity.

DESCENDIBILITY OF THE RIGHT OF PUBLICITY

The right of publicity is a property right, separate and distinct from the right of privacy. The right of privacy is a personal right and is nondescendible; it terminates at death. The right of publicity is a property right, on the other hand, and can be inherited by or assigned to someone.

While some courts disagree, the trend is clearly toward descendibility. Since it is a property right, it survives after the death of the owner. A valid reason exists for recognizing this survivability. It motivates celebrities' efforts and creativity in encouraging them to develop their image so that their heirs will also benefit. It's money in the bank, so to speak. It may take many years to develop a talent, ability and reputation that will create large economic returns. Along those lines, non-related persons should not be able to benefit from the efforts celebrities put into developing their own images.

In practice, the various state courts have adopted one of three views regarding descendibility (see Table 5-1). One view says that the commercial use of the person's name or likeness shifts to the public domain after death. In other words, the right of publicity is never descendible.

Another view recognizes descendibility only if the right of publicity has been sufficiently exploited before death. What constitutes sufficient exploitation? Generally, it must be exploited by the celebrity through the creation of a second business or through the use of his or her name or likeness in connection with a product or service promoted by the person.

Finally, some courts recognize the descendibility of the right of publicity without any other conditions. Let's take a closer look at the three views. It is important to remember that the theory that applies to each case is determined by the state law used to decide that case.

TABLE: 5-1
State Interpretation of the
Descendibility of the Right of Publicity

State	Never Descendible To Heirs	Always Descendible: If Exploited During Life	Descendible: Public Domain
Alabama	√		
Alaska		√	
Arizona		√	
Arkansas			√
California	Δ		
Colorado		√	
Connecticut	Δ		
Delaware	√		
Florida		√	
Georgia	Δ		
Hawaii		√	
Idaho		√	
Illinois			√
Indiana			√
Iowa			√
Kansas	√		
Kentucky			Δ
Louisiana	Δ		
Maine	√		
Maryland	√		
Massachusetts	√		

State	Never Descendible To Heirs	Always Descendible: If Exploited During Life	Descendible: Public Domain
Michigan			Δ
Minnesota			√
Mississippi	Δ		
Missouri			√
Montana		√	
Nebraska			√
Nevada		√	
New Hampshire	√		
New Jersey	√		
New York	Δ		
North Carolina	√		
North Dakota			√
Ohio			Δ
Oklahoma			√
Oregon		√	
Pennsylvania	√		
Rhode Island	√		
South Carolina	√		
South Dakota			√
Tennessee			Δ
Texas	Δ		
Utah		√	
Vermont	Δ		
Virginia	√		
Washington		√	
Washington, D.C.	√		
West Virginia	√		

Δ = States where the descendibility issue has been decided.

√ = States where no appellate decisions have been made regarding descendibility. These states should be checked, since the accuracy of the position of these states may vary.

Nonsurvivable Theory— The Statue Of Elvis

The strict view of descendibility is illustrated in *Memphis Development Foundation* v. *Factors Etc. Inc.,*[12] an example of when the right of publicity is not descendible. Under Tennessee law the courts hold the opinion that the celebrity's right of publicity is not inheritable.

Elvis Presley died on August 16, 1977 in Memphis. In his honor, the Memphis Development Foundation, a nonprofit corporation, wanted to build a large bronze statue of Elvis in downtown Memphis. The foundation would collect the needed money from contributions. Contributors of $25 or more received an eight-inch pewter replica of the full-size statue.

The defendant, Factors Etc., was the assignee of Presley's right of publicity, and the company claimed that Memphis Development had taken away its right to market Presley's name and likeness. Memphis claimed that Factors' license did not allow for the distribution of the statuettes.

The court decided that, based on Tennessee law, Factors could not inherit Presley's right of publicity. It reasoned that "the basic motivations are the desire to achieve success or excellence in a chosen field, the desire to contribute to the happiness or improvement of one's fellows, and the desire to receive the psychic and financial rewards of achievement." Essentially, the court felt that this right should not be survivable to the heirs because the celebrity alone did not have complete control over developing the notoriety in the first place.

The court felt that the public was an integral element in the creation of an image. Therefore it had "serious reservations about making fame the permanent right of a few individuals to the exclusion of the general public." In conclusion, the court said: "Fame falls in the same category as reputation; it is an attribute from which others may benefit but may not own."

In other words, the right of publicity is not descendible, but rather becomes public domain after death. At least this is the case in Tennessee and other states that have adopted the same philosophy.

Descendibility If Exploited During Life

The second option is where there is no descendibility unless the right was sufficiently exploited during the person's life. To illustrate, let's look at a case involving Bela George Lugosi and his well-known character, Count Dracula, the legendary character created in 1897 by author Bram Stoker. In September of 1930, Lugosi entered into an agreement with Universal Pictures to star in the lead role in the film classic, *Dracula*.

The case was *Lugosi v. Universal Pictures*,[13] during which Justice Mosk rather sardonically stated, "not unlike the horror films that brought him fame, Bela Lugosi rises from the grave 20 years after death to haunt his former employer."

In this case, the heirs of Lugosi, his son and widow, claimed that Universal had taken property rights that the studio had not been given in the agreement for the production of *Dracula* in 1930. Between 1960 and 1966 Universal licensed many companies to manufacture items using the Count Dracula character. There was no doubt that the merchandising of the Count Dracula character was patterned after the likeness of Lugosi. It may well be true, also, that Lugosi is readily recognized as having been Count Dracula, even though Max Schreck, Christopher Lee, John Carradine, Lon Chaney, and others also have appeared in the role.

Yet, Lugosi never exploited the character of Dracula commercially during his lifetime. He also never exploited his own identity commercially. Let's assume, for the sake of argument, that Lugosi had opened a company named Lugosi/Dracula Enterprises. This company made T-shirts and hats with a picture of the actor made up as Dracula. Under the picture was printed "Dracula Lives . . . signed Bela Lugosi." This product created a large public awareness of the business. If the business existed and had not been sold before Lugosi's death in 1956, his heirs may have had a claim if the Dracula image was later misappropriated.

However, under California law at the time, the right to profit from one's name and likeness was personal and had to have been be exercised during lifetime in order for the right to survive after death. Since Lugosi hadn't used his name or likeness as Count Dracula in association with any business, service, or product (other than the part in the movie), he had no claim under the California interpretation of publicity rights. As a result, his heirs lost the case.

It is important to note that this case does not concern Lugosi's right of publicity for his likeness, but rather that of a character he played. Unless there is a contract to the contrary, merely playing a role creates no inheritable property rights— any more than George C. Scott has any rights to the character of General Patton, James Whitmore to that of Will Rogers, Gregory Peck of General MacArthur, or Charlton Heston of Moses.

The United States Court of Appeals for the Second Circuit agreed with the Lugosi decision when it decided a case involving three brothers Adolph, Julius, and Leo Marx. This case concerned the brothers' public image for which they were known as Harpo, Groucho, and Chico, respectively. The case was *Groucho Marx Productions, Inc. v. Day and Night Co., Inc.*[14]

At the New End Theatre in London, a play opened in January of 1979 called *A Day in Hollywood/A Night in the Ukraine*. In May of 1980, it came to Broadway. The second half of the play featured performers who simulated the Marx Brothers' unique style, appearance, and manner.

The Marx Brothers had assigned the rights to their names, likenesses, and style prior to their deaths; and subsequently their heirs transferred that right to Groucho Marx Productions, the plaintiff. The Marx Brothers, it can be said, made a profession of capitalizing on the unique characters they had created. Their fame arose directly from their efforts to create their instantly recognizable characters. The Marx Brothers' characters bore little resemblance to their actual personalities. This was a key issue in the case.

The Marx Brothers had capitalized on the commercial value of the artificial personalities they created. Every appearance and advertisement they took part in demonstrated their awareness of the commercial value of their images as Chico, Harpo, and Groucho. In fact, the Marx Brothers had promoted many products during their lifetimes, including Plymouth cars and Smirnoff vodka.

The play created a duplication, as faithfully as possible, of the Marx Brothers' performances. Granted, it devised a new situation and used new lines. But the essential style of humor of the Marx Brothers was accurately reproduced. The court said:

Although the [plaintiffs] may have intended to comment 'about 1930s Hollywood, its techniques, its stars, and its excesses,'. . . the content of the relevant portion of the play attempts to accomplish that objective exactly as would the Marx Brothers themselves.

The court found that indeed the Marx Brothers had established a commercial use of their names, likenesses, and images during their lifetimes. This allowed their right of publicity to survive them; to be passed on to their heirs. They had won their case.

Always Descendible Theory

The third approach makes the right of publicity always descendible. The case we see here was easier to determine than the Lugosi case because it featured actors playing themselves. Stanley

Laurel and Oliver Hardy developed their own characters, which were theirs alone and certainly not fictional.

The heirs of Laurel and Hardy brought suit for $250,000 against Hal Roach Studios, which claimed that the studio had been given the exclusive rights to the Laurel and Hardy characters. Roach contended that the rights had been acquired through contracts between the studio and the comedy team in 1923. However, the specific rights acquired were those of copyright for the Laurel and Hardy films, not the unlimited usage of the Laurel and Hardy names and likenesses. We'll look more closely at copyright in Chapter 6.

Roach also claimed that the names and likenesses of the comedy team are in the public domain. The court, in *Price* v. *Hal Roach Studios, Inc.*,[15] disagreed. Its only question was whether the right of publicity terminated on the death of Laurel and Hardy, or was it descendible.

The court felt that there was no reasonable basis to assume that the right was not assignable or that it should terminate with the death of the person. The court decided that the heirs of Laurel and Hardy were entitled to the commercial rights to the names and likenesses of the team. It also reasoned that the heirs were entitled to the actual damages sought in the lawsuit—for the appropriation of that right by Roach.

A further extension of the right of publicity for celebrities involved the late Dr. Martin Luther King, Jr., a public figure but not a celebrity. From 1955, Dr. King was the prime leader of the civil rights movement in the United States. For his efforts, he was awarded the Nobel Peace Prize in 1964. On April 4,1968, Dr. King was assassinated.

American Heritage Products manufactured plastic products. It developed the idea of marketing a bust of the late Dr. King. Although the company had asked permission for the endorsement of the product of the Martin Luther King, Jr. Center for Social Change (the nonprofit corporation that holds the rights to the

King estate), the center refused to participate.

Despite the lack of endorsement, American Heritage hired an artist to produce a mold for the bust. It also hired an agent to promote the product. American bought two half-page ads in the November and December 1980 issues of *Ebony Magazine*. The ad offered:

● ● ● ● ● ● ● ● ● ● ● ● ● ●
An exclusive memorial.
An opportunity to support
the Martin Luther King, Jr. Center for Social Change.
A contribution from your order goes to
the King Center for Social Change.
● ●

American also printed 80,000 brochures that were inserted in newspapers across the country. Two hundred busts had been sold with orders for 23 more when the lawsuit was initiated in *Martin Luther King, Jr. Center for Social Change, Inc. v. American Heritage Products, Inc.*[16]

Generally, the right of publicity is the distillation of celebrities' exclusive rights to the use of their names and likenesses. These celebrities are most often actors, musicians, athletes, comedians, or other entertainers. Although Dr. King was none of these, he still had the right to control the use of his image for trade purposes and advertising.

Indeed a public figure, Dr. King avoided having his name exploited during his life, and he was protected from having it exploited after death. Under Georgia law, individuals do not have to commercially exploit their names or likenesses during their lifetimes in order to have the right of publicity extend beyond life to their heirs. The Center won its case against American Heritage.

PROBLEMS RELATING TO CONSENT

The most appropriate method of avoiding suits involving

the right of privacy or publicity is to obtain the person's prior consent. Generally, this consent must be in writing, and it involves more than just the authorization to use a person's name, likeness, or image. Involved are questions of how the image is used, the media, the form, where and when it is used, and so on. The advertiser must make certain that these questions are answered by the consent release to avoid liability later.

Let's look at the different areas where consent problems are common.

Consent For A Specific Use

As a very successful fashion model, Christie Brinkley's photos have appeared on the covers of most major magazines including *Mademoiselle, Ladies Home Journal, Harper's Bazaar,* and *Sports Illustrated.* In September of 1979, John Casablancas, the president of Elite Model Management (Brinkley's agent), signed a licensing agreement with Galaxy Publishing. The agreement was to produce a series of posters of several models, including Brinkley.

Brinkley verbally agreed to the project and picked her own makeup artist, hair-stylist, and bathing suit for the photo session. Photographer Michael Reinhardt photographed Brinkley for the poster. Cable TV company Home Box Office (HBO) filmed the photography session for use in a special entitled: "Beautiful, Baby, Beautiful," on the careers of this country's top models. Brinkley gave her written permission to appear in the broadcast in the same pose and suit that was to be used for the poster.

After the session, Brinkley reviewed the photos and requested some retouching be done on the specific shot she had intended for the poster. This was done. At that point, Galaxy proceeded to print the posters. The problem was that Brinkley never signed a model release authorizing the publication of her pictures in a poster. Brinkley stated that she "agreed to participate in a shooting from which a poster *may* have been the result, depending of course on my final judgment of the final product."

She claimed that the printing and distribution of pinup posters was an unauthorized exploitation, for commercial purposes, of her name and image. The court agreed.

In *Brinkley* v. *Casablancas*,[17] Brinkley's consent for the use of her photo for a cable television show did not include consent for a poster of a different photo taken at the same session. There was no written permission given for that particular photo to be used as a poster.

Consent For A Specific Length Of Time

Another area where a problem can arise is the length of time allowed for the usage. In 1973 actor Charles Welch appeared in a television commercial for Mr. Christmas, a manufacturer of artificial Christmas trees. Welch was paid the sum of $1,000 for the commercial. According to the contract the $1,000 fee allowed the commercial to be run for no more than one year. However, the contract further provided for an additional year's option with the payment of an additional $1,000. Although Mr. Christmas had not paid Welch the additional fee to exercise the option for the second year, it allowed its distributors to air the commercial in 1974.

Welch found out about this and agreed to a financial settlement for the 1974 option. In March of 1975 Mr. Christmas was contacted by the Screen Actors Guild and cautioned that the spot could not be aired any longer without further negotiations. In spite of this warning, the commercial aired during 1975.

In the lawsuit that resulted, *Welch* v. *Mr. Christmas Inc.*,[18] the plaintiff was awarded compensatory damages of $1,000 and exemplary damages of $25,000. Here, the time limit was part of the original consent agreement. Using the commercial after the authorized period expired is the same as airing the commercial with no consent at all.

Mr. Christmas claimed as a defense that it did not use the commercial claiming that its dealers were expected to purchase their own air time and that it did not know or have control over the spots used by them. However, Mr. Christmas encouraged its dealers to get the maximum use of the commercial, and made no attempt to notify the dealers that the usage period had ended. All of this made Mr. Christmas liable.

As we have seen before, not taking action when you have a responsibility to do so is also negligent. Since the agreement was with the actor and Mr. Christmas, those are the parties who are responsible to each other. If the dealers had aired the spot after they were notified in writing by Mr. Christmas not to do so, the situation may have been different.

We'll discuss such responsibilities in greater detail in Chapter 11, The Client/Agency Relationship.

Usage In A Medium That Was Not Authorized

Frank Dzurenko is a model who participated in a photo session for Jordache jeans. At the end of the photo session, Dzurenko signed a model release inserting the phrase "magazine ad use only." His reason for adding the limitation was that in the photos he had posed with a female model who was wearing only a pair of jeans.

After the session one of those photos was blown up and produced as a poster, which was then distributed to retailers. This violated Dzurenko's right of publicity because the photo's use exceeded the limitations of the release. In *Dzurenko v. Jordache, Inc.*,[19] the court determined that a release can cover not only the use of a name, picture or likeness, but also the time, form, and media of its use. Dzurenko won the case.

Another interesting issue brought as a defense was that Dzurenko didn't sign the release with the limitation until after the photos had been taken. However, the court held that this didn't matter. Dzurenko had the absolute right to limit the usage of the photos in any way he desired, regardless of when the release was signed.

When Parental Consent Is Revocable

Another problem regarding consent can occur when a child's parent gives consent and then the child, on becoming an adult, attempts to withdraw it. This can pose a unique problem for advertisers. That was exactly what happened with Brooke Shields and Garry Gross.

In 1975 Brooke Shields was 10 years old. At the time she was registered with the Ford Model Agency, working as a child model (and a very famous one at that). One of the jobs she did was for Playboy Press that required her to pose nude in a bathtub. The intent was that the photos would be published in a publication called *Sugar and Spice*.

Before the photo session, Teri Shields, Brooke's mother, signed a consent for the photographer Garry Gross to "use, reuse and/or publish, and republish" the photos. Brooke's photos appeared in *Sugar and Spice,* as well as on posters and in other publications. Brooke even used the photos in a book about herself with the permission of the photographer. Gross, in fact, had shot Brooke on many occasions for *Penthouse* magazine, *New York Magazine*, and advertising for the Courtauldts and Avon Company.

In 1980 Brooke learned that the *Sugar and Spice* photos had appeared in the French magazine, *Photo*. At that point, she became disturbed by the publication of the photos and attempted to buy the negatives from Gross.

When that failed, she brought suit: *Shields* v. *Gross*.[20] The suit claimed, among other things, that her right of privacy had been violated and sought to cancel the consent given by her mother in 1975.

According to New York's Civil Rights Law, section 50, once the written consent is obtained, the photos can be published as agreed. If that person is a minor, his or her parents may give the consent.

Under common law, infants can disaffirm their own or their guardian's consent. However, where a specific statute permits a class of agreements to be made by a child, the discussion is ended, and the agreement is valid. Consent had been given, and it would stand under its original terms. Brooke lost her claim.

FORMS OF DEPICTION THAT CAN CAUSE LIABILITY

What type of depictions can cause trouble for advertisers? As we'll see, there are many. There is a difference between the right of privacy and the right of publicity regarding what depictions create a problem. The right of privacy is very specific, while the right of publicity is more broad.

Upholding Privacy Rights Requires Recognizability

The right of privacy generally requires that a visually recognizable likeness of the person is used even if the name is not. This right is narrower in scope than publicity rights because it protects citizens where there is a recognizability by others.

What constitutes a recognizable likeness? The New York Court of Appeals defined that in *Cohen v. Herbal Concepts, Inc.*[21] In 1977 on the July 4th weekend, a woman and her daughter were photographed while bathing in a stream in Woodstock, New York. The photo of Susan Cohen and her four-year-old daughter, Samantha, was photographed from behind while they bathed nude in the stream located on their friend's private property. Ira Cohen, the husband and father, saw the photographer taking pictures, became incensed, and chased him away. However, the photographer printed and sold the photos.

The photo showed the nude mother and daughter from behind and to the right in a full-length pose. The shot did not show their faces, but their backs and right sides are clearly visible, as was the mother's right breast. The photo later appeared in ads that ran in *House and Garden, House Beautiful,* and *Cosmopolitan* magazines.

The ad for Au Naturel, manufactured by Herbal Concepts, promoted a product intended to help eliminate body cellulite. As the ad said: "those fatty lumps and bumps that won't go away." While leafing through one of the magazines that contained the ad, Ira Cohen "recognized [his] wife and daughter immediately."

The issue here was whether a photograph of the nude mother and child constitutes a sufficiently identifiable likeness without showing their faces. The court established that it does. Features such as the mother's and child's hair, bone structure, body shape, stature, and posture all together could make the people in the photograph identifiable by someone familiar with them. The court ruled that the photo need not show the face. The plaintiff need only show that the photograph is reasonably recognizable. The photo was clear and sharp with no objects blocking the subjects. In New York, privacy claims are based on sections 50 and 51 of the Civil Rights Law. This statute, as with many other states, was designed to protect, not only name, portrait, or picture but a person's identity. The plaintiff must be "identifiable." The fact that Susan and Samantha were identified by Ira Cohen was acceptable.

THE MANY FORMS THAT CAN VIOLATE PUBLICITY RIGHTS

As for publicity rights, almost any form that can be devised can potentially cause trouble. Because of this, the advertiser must be very careful when using any form of celebrity or public figure in an ad. Name, image, likeness, voice imitations, commonly associated phrases, look-alikes, cartoons, even identifiable situations are potential problem areas. Now, let us explore some of these areas in detail.

Use of a Phrase

The use of a familiar phrase can be an infringement. In 1962 Johnny Carson began hosting *The Tonight Show* for NBC

Television. Carson was introduced five nights a week with the phrase "Heeeeere's Johnny." Johnny Carson is a well-known entertainer, and a large segment of the television viewing public associated him with the particular phrase.

In 1967 Carson authorized the use of this phrase by another business. He allowed it to be used by a restaurant chain called "Here's Johnny Restaurants." In 1970 Carson formed a clothing manufacturer and used the phrase "Here's Johnny" on its clothing and in its advertising. And in 1977 Carson authorized Marcey Laboratories to use the phrase as a name for a line of toiletries.

However, in 1976 a Michigan corporation was formed to rent and sell a product it called "Here's Johnny" portable toilets. The owner developed a clever tag line for the product:

"Here's Johnny Portable Toilets. The World's Foremost Commodian." The owner claimed that this made "a good play on a phrase."

Not long after this, Carson brought suit for, among other things, infringement of his right of publicity in *Carson* v. *Here's Johnny Portable Toilets, Inc.*[22] This was a case of an appropriation of Carson's identity without the use of his name—the phrase is so recognizable that when the public heard it, no one else but Carson came to mind. The phrase "Here's Johnny" is a symbol of Carson's identity, just as is a name or picture. The president of the toilet company even admitted that he used the name because it identified Carson.

A celebrity's right of publicity is invaded when his identity is intentionally appropriated for commercial purposes. The fact that the defendant did not use Carson's last name did not lessen the offense. In fact, no violation would have occurred if his name had been used.

The court gave as examples of names that would not have violated Carson's right of publicity: "J. William Carson Portable Toilet," "John William Carson Portable Toilet," and "J. W. Carson

Portable Toilet." The reason that these uses of his name would not have been violative of Carson's right is simple—there would have been no appropriation of Carson's identity as a celebrity. Even if his real name was used, the public would not have associated the two as the same person. Carson's full real name is not recognizable by the public anymore than Marion Michael Morrison would be for John Wayne's real name, or Creighton Chaney for Lon Chaney.

Use Of An Object

Here's another example of appropriation of an identity without the use of a name. This case involved an object commonly associated with a celebrity.

Lothar Motschenbacher was an internationally known race car driver. Part of his income came from product endorsements. Since 1966 all of Motschenbacher's cars were individualized to set them apart from other cars and to make them more recognizable as his. Each was red with a narrow white pinstripe, unlike any other car. The white background of his racing number 11 was always an oval, unlike the circular ones on other cars.

In 1970 R. J. Reynolds Tobacco Company and its agency William Esty produced a television commercial that used a stock photo showing several race cars on the track.

Motschenbacher's car was in the foreground. The driver could not be identified in the photo because of the helmet and driving suit.

The ad agency altered the photograph for the commercial. They changed the numbers on all of the cars; Motschenbacher's number 11 was changed to 17. A spoiler (wing) was attached to the car displaying the name of the product, Winston. All other product names were removed from the other cars.

The agency then filmed the slide adding a series of comicbook-type balloons with messages. Over Motschenbacher's car the balloon said: "Did you know that Winston tastes good, like a cigarette should?" The commercial was broadcast nationally.

Motschenbacher filed suit in *Motschenbacher v. R. J. Reynolds Tobacco Co.*[23] The court agreed that the plaintiff himself was not recognizable. However, the decoration of the car in the picture left little doubt that the car was Motschenbacher's, and implied that he was driving. Because of this, R. J. Reynolds lost the case.

Use Of A Performer's Style

Appropriation of a performer's style is another way that one's right of publicity can be violated. Guy Lombardo had invested 40 years in developing his image as "Mr. New Year's Eve." Add to this the combination of New Year's Eve, balloons, party hats, and *"Auld Lang Syne"* in the right context and you have an image that is unmistakable, and one that can be exploited commercially.

Doyle Dane Bernbach, the ad agency for Volkswagen at the time, entered into negotiations with Lombardo in late 1974 to obtain his appearance in a television commercial. The negotiations, however, fell through but the agency went on to produce the commercial featuring several products of the car manufacturer all set against the background of a New Year's Eve party.

Lombardo's name was never mentioned, but the actor used to portray the bandleader conducted the band using the same gestures and choice of music. Even the set resembled the one that Lombardo had become so closely associated with as "Mr. New Year's Eve." The case that resulted was *Lombardo v. Doyle Dane Bernbach, Inc.*[24] Lombardo won.

Use Of Three-Dimensional Objects

Eleanor Brown Young was, in 1941, a professional model of junior misses' clothes. She was employed by a department store and was asked to pose for the making of a mannequin. She allowed Greneker Studios to mold the mannequins in her image —her form, features, and likeness—for the exclusive use of her employer—the department store.

Later, it was learned that Greneker sold the mannequins to others. *Young v. Greneker Studios, Inc.*,[25] was the case that followed. Young alleged that Greneker manufactured and sold mannequins in her likeness, without her permission, for the purposes of trade.

Under New York Civil Rights Law, section 51, an action may be brought by "any person whose name, portrait, or picture is used . . . for advertising purposes or for the purposes of trade without the written consent first obtained." Even though Young gave her permission for her employer to make and use the mannequins in her image, she had not given permission to the company who manufactured them to sell them to anyone else.

What this case points up is that the courts give broad latitude to what form constitutes a "portrait or picture" of a person. As we have seen a picture is not limited only to a photograph of the person, but to any representation of that person. The representation can be two-dimensional or, as in this case, three-dimensional. The words "picture" and "portrait" are general enough to encompass any form of an image, from a photograph to a painting to a sculpture.

Use Of Photo-Illustrations

Another form that can create a problem involves photo-realistic illustrations. On February 15, 1978, Leon Spinks defeated Muhammad Ali in a 15-round split decision. Until then, Ali had been the heavyweight boxing champion of the world. In the February 1978 issue of *Playgirl* magazine a picture ran with an article entitled "Mystery Man," showing a nude black man seated in a corner of a boxing ring. The illustration fell somewhere between cartoon and realistic art. The article was not editorial, but rather fictional writing, using, as the court determined, the picture of Ali solely "for the purposes of trade."

There was no question that the portrait was of Ali. In the court's words: "The cheekbones, broad nose, and wide-set brown eyes, together with the distinctive smile and close-cropped black hair are recognizable as the features of . . . one of the most widely known athletes of our time." In *Ali v. Playgirl, Inc.*,[26] the court agreed that Ali's right of publicity had been violated.

One important thing to note here is that not only was the magazine liable for the violation of the right of publicity, but the artist who drew the portrait was named as a defendant as well.

Use Of Modified Photos

When a photograph or picture is modified or altered slightly, but still identifiable as a specific person, a problem can result. A situation such as this happened quite some time ago in 1917 when Gladys Loftus, a 22-year-old Ziegfeld Girl, appeared in the rose garden scene in *Midnight Frolics* wearing a special costume known as, "the rose costume" made by Lady Duff-Gordon.

Loftus had her picture taken wearing the rose costume by Alfred Johnson, a photographer employed to take pictures of some of the girls in the play, while in costume. Loftus became readily recognizable in her costume, and the public became very familiar with Johnson's photograph of her.

Sometime later The Greenwich Lithographing Company, a designer of theatrical and movie posters, was hired to produce a poster for the photoplay, *Shame*. The posters were distributed throughout the city of New York. The name *Shame* appeared very large on the poster along with copy that read:

• • • • • •
Coming
Soon
to your
local
theatre
John W. Noble presents
the photoplay of the hour

SHAME
featuring
Zena Keefe
(A story of the world's unjust condemnation.)
● ●

On the poster was a picture of a man pointing his right hand in scorn at a woman who had her head slightly bowing. Greenwich admitted that it had copied the photograph of Loftus to use as the model of the woman in the poster.

The artist, Ira Cassidy, used the rose costume picture when he painted the poster art for *Shame*, making only slight variations:

• Changing the tilt of the head;
• Lowering the hair;
• Altering the outline of the nose, chin, and neck; and
• Removing the right arm from view.

All other aspects of the photo were duplicated in the final painting.

The court determined, in *Loftus* v. *Greenwich Lithographing Co., Inc.*,[27] that the poster was not a direct copy of the photo, but the image of Loftus was duplicated in such a way as to make it easily identifiable as being Loftus. Loftus won her case.

Use Of A Voice Impersonation

Here again, the advertiser must be careful. A very popular trend, especially in radio commercials, is to produce spots using voice impersonators. At the end of these spots an announcer states "celebrity voice impersonated." This is done to clarify that the voice is an imitation and to avoid a violation of the celebrity's right of publicity.

In 1985, Ford Motor Company, through it agency Young & Rubicam, Inc., developed a campaign using the song "Do You Want To Dance." After getting permission to the copyright of the song, they hired a backup singer to record the song. They wanted to get a singer that could match singer Bette Midler's voice and style as close as possible. They did. The fact that the rendition of the song sounded exactly like Midler allowed her to win in court. When a distinctive voice that is widely known and recognized is deliberately imitated to sell a product, that person's identity is pirated.

THE HOLLYWOOD STUDIO MUSEUM COMMERCIAL

At the beginning of this chapter, I wrote about a television commercial that had been produced for The Hollywood Studio Museum. Now that you have read the chapter, I'm sure that you can see why I used the story to begin.

Let's analyze that commercial to see if and where a problem could arise. First, there is the image of the famous director C.B. DeMille. Do we have to be concerned with invasion of his privacy rights? What about his rights of publicity? Secondly, we must consider the rights of the actor who played DeMille in the commercial, Gene Barry. Think about these issues for a moment.

Let's start with DeMille. His privacy rights ended at the time of his death, so there is no problem. Regarding publicity rights, did we need the permission of the DeMille heirs to use his name and likeness? As we know, publicity rights are survivable under certain conditions. Under California law (that's where jurisdiction would have been), the publicity right is descendible, but only where it was exploited commercially during life. DeMille did, in fact, exploit his name and likeness during his life for commercial purposes. He was a very famous motion picture director, and his name alone sold many movies. Permission of the DeMille heirs was required and obtained.

As for Gene Barry, consent was required. Obviously, his appearance in the commercial was evidence of his consent to have his name and image used. However, there were questions of usage. Barry, through the Screen Actors Guild (SAG), authorized use for only one year. The consent was for television and radio (the voice portion) use only. Another required restriction imposed by Mr. Barry was that we clearly identify the spot as "a public service message." This was to clarify that he had donated his time and name and thereby not diminish his worth for commercials other than public service messages.

Noncompliance with any of these restrictions could give rise to a lawsuit for breach of his publicity rights and consent agreement.

As you can see, using a person's identity, and how it is used, brings with it many issues which must be considered.

---

[1] (5 Coke, 91), 1 Smith's Lead. Cas. 228.

[2] *Roberson* v. *Rochester Folding Box Co.*, 171 N.Y. 538, 64 N.E. 442 (1902).

[3] 1903 N.Y. Laws Ch. 132, sections 1-2
(codified as amended; N.Y. Civil Rights Law sections 50-51 (1976)).

[4] *Pavesich* v. *New England Life Ins. Co.*, 122 Ga. 190, 50 S.E. 68 (1905).

[5] See *Griswold* v. *Connecticut*, 381 U.S. 479, 85 S.Ct. 1678, 14 L.Ed. 2d 510 (1965).

[6] *O'Brien* v. *Pabst Sales Co.*, 124 F.2d 167 (5th Cir. 1941).

[7] *Haelan Laboratories* v. *Topps Chewing Gum, Inc.*, 202 F.2d 866 (2d Cir. 1953).

[8] *Onassis* v. *Christian Dior, New York, Inc.*, 122 Misc.2d 603, 472 N.Y.S.2d 254
(Sup. Ct. 1984).

[9] *Dior* v. *Milton*, 9 Misc.2d 425,155 N.Y.S.2d 443, aff'd. 2 A.D.2d 878,
156 N.Y.S.2d 996 (1956).

[10] *Ann-Margret* v. *High Society Magazine, Inc.*, 498 F.Supp. 401 (1980).

[11] *Zacchini* v. *Scripps-Howard Broadcasting Co.*, 433 U.S. 562, 97 S.Ct. 2849,
53 L.Ed 2d 965 (1977).

[12] *Memphis Development Foundation* v. *Factors Etc. Inc.*, 616 F.2d 956 (6th Cir. 1980).

[13] *Lugosi* v. *Universal Pictures*, 25 Cal.3d 813 (1979).

[14] *Groucho Marx Productions, Inc.* v. *Day and Night Co., Inc.*, 523 F. Supp. 485
(S.D.N.Y. 1981), rev'd, 689 F.2d 317 (2d Cir. 1982).

[15] *Price* v. *Hal Roach Studios, Inc.*, 400 F.Supp. 836 (S.D.N.Y. 1975).

[16] *Martin Luther King, Jr. Center for Social Change, Inc.* v. *American Heritage Products,
Inc.*, 694 F.2d 674 (11th Cir. 1983).

[17] *Brinkley* v. *Casablancas*, 80 A.D.2d 428, 438 N.Y.S.2d 1004 (App. Div. 1981).

[18] *Welch* v. *Mr. Christmas Inc.*, 57 N.Y.2d 143, 440 N.E.2d 1317 (1982).

[19] *Dzurenko* v. *Jordache, Inc.*, 59 N.Y.2d 788, 451 N.E.2d 477 (1983).

[20] *Shields* v. *Gross*, 58 N.Y.2d 338 (1983).

[21] *Cohen* v. *Herbal Concepts, Inc.*, 63 N.Y.2d 379, 472 N.E.2d 307 (1984).

[22] *Carson* v. *Here's Johnny Portable Toilets, Inc.*, 698 F.2d 831 (6th Cir. 1983).

[23] *Motschenbacher* v. *R. J. Reynolds Tobacco Co.*, 498 F.2d 821 (9th Cir. 1974).

[24] *Lombardo* v. *Doyle Dane Bernbach, Inc.*, 58 A.D.2d 620, 396 N.Y.S.2d 661
   (App. Div. 1977).
[25] *Young* v. *Greneker Studios, Inc.*, 176 Misc. 1027, 26 N.Y.S.2d 357 (Sup. Ct. 1941).
[26] *Ali* v. *Playgirl, Inc.*, 447 F. Supp. 723 (S.D.N.Y. 1978).
[27] *Loftus* v. *Greenwich Lithographing Co., Inc.*, 192 A.D. 251, 182 N.Y.S. 428
   (App. Div. 1920).

CHAPTER 6

COPYRIGHT REGULATION

Life is a copycat.
—*Heywood Broun*

Let's examine a situation involving an advertising agency.
We'll call the agency Doofus-Wazoo Advertising. One of its clients,
Acme Chemicals, made swimming pool chlorine and asked the
agency to create a television commercial for its product. The
creative team got together and devised a spot showing different
shapes and styles of pools with the tag line: "No matter what the
shape of your pool, Acme will keep it in shape."

The agency writer and creative director took the idea to Mr.
Wazoo, the agency president (and Acme account executive), and
explained that this could be a terrific spot with the right pools,
scenes, and camera angles. Mr. Wazoo loved the idea. He wanted
to produce an impressive commercial, but knew that the client
didn't have much of a budget. Therefore, filming the commercial
was out of the question.

So, Mr. Wazoo told the creative director to get a selection of
the best pool shoots he could find from a stock photo house. The
creative director ordered a group of 104 color slides. When the
slides came in, Mr. Wazoo and the creative director looked them
over and picked the best 14. But the fee for using the photos was
$300 each. Mr. Wazoo ordered all 104 slides to be sent out and
duplicated instructing the creative director to use the 14 best in
the commercial.

The creative director explained that the agency should not
have duplicated all of the slides without prior permission from the
stock photo house. He also explained that the agency could not
use the photos in the commercial unless it had permission and
paid the appropriate fee since the slides were copyrighted, and to

do so would be illegal.

Mr. Wazoo claimed that the client did not have $4,200 to pay for all 14 slides, so here's what he did. He sent the slides back to the stock photo house, but told them that the agency only needed to use and pay for one slide in the commercial. The agency, however, used all 14. Mr. Wazoo boasted, "They'll never find out, and if they do, we'll just pay the fee."

The creative director, under protest, produced the commercial using the 14 slides, only one of which was paid for. The commercial aired, and Acme was thrilled with the results. Doofus-Wazoo beamed with pride at its creative work. Mr. Wazoo gloated at producing the commercial for next to nothing and for making the client happy. Everyone except the creative director—who saw the light from the oncoming train—was very pleased.

Not long after, a United States Marshall walked into the agency and handed Mr. Wazoo a summons. The agency, the photo lab that duplicated the photos, the editing company that made the commercial, the distributors who were listed on the commercial, and the client were all being sued for copyright violations. The stock photo house claimed over $5 million in damages. And then depression set in.

Could such a blatant violation of copyright really happen? Would an agency be naive enough to think it could get away with such a thing? Could this story be real? Absolutely. I know, because I was the creative director. Ultimately, the case was settled out of court.

This type of copyright abuse occurs quite often—in fact, too often. In many cases, the agency just doesn't understand what can and can't be done legally. Some know the rules and still ignore them and, as in the situation I just described, some learn the hard way. Since forewarned is forearmed, let's take a look at the areas of copyright law affecting advertisers. Keep in mind as you read this chapter, and the next on trademark, the differences between the two areas of law. Each is based on different principles and, therefore, must be thought of separately.

THE COPYRIGHT ACT OF 1976

The Copyright Act of 1976 protects the creators of artistic works as an incentive to pursue their creative talents. The United States Constitution—Article 1, Section 8, provides that Congress shall have the power: "To promote the Progress of Science and useful Arts, by securing for limited Times to Authors . . . the exclusive Right to their ... Writings ...." The original Copyright Act was passed by the first Congress in 1790, shortly after the signing of the Constitution. The act has been amended over the years in 1831, 1870, 1909, and most recently in 1976.

In 1976 Congress updated the Copyright Act, which went into effect on January 1, 1978. Any work produced after that date was covered by the new law. Works created prior to that date are covered by the Copyright Act of 1909. In this chapter we deal with the current act.

REQUIREMENTS TO QUALIFY FOR COPYRIGHT PROTECTION

It is important to understand what can qualify to be copyrighted. There are conditions that must be met in order to apply for protection under copyright law. To qualify, a work must be the product of the original author and meet the requirement of originality. It must also be considered a "writing" and be fixed in a tangible medium. Let us look at each of these requirements separately.

Definition Of A "Writing"

To be eligible for copyright protection an item must be put in a written form referred to as a "writing." The common definition of a writing is much different than the legal definition. Under the

Copyright Act, the definition of a writing is quite broad encompassing anything that is "fixed in any tangible medium of expression, now known or later developed, from which [the original] can be perceived, reproduced, or otherwise communicated, either directly or with the aid of a machine or device."[1]

At the time the Copyright Act was first written, about the only means of performance was the stage. There were, of course, books, maps, and so on, which were specifically listed in the original act. But other than those forms of creative expression, the stage was all that was left. In those years, the only medium to record the stage performance was the mind of the audience. Today, a performance can be recorded in many ways with incredible realism. Protection of the creative work, therefore, has had to expand with technology to keep pace with the times.

Between 1970 and 1971 Mr. Goldstein and his associates purchased copies of record albums or tape cassettes at local record stores, duplicated them on tape, and distributed them to retail stores for sale to the public. Goldstein never asked for permission from, and made no payments to, the artists, writers, performers, producers, or any other person involved with the original recordings. No payments were made for the use of the artists' names or the titles of the original albums.

Eventually the state of California, where this occurred, arrested and prosecuted Goldstein in *Goldstein* v. *California*[2] for record piracy: the unauthorized duplication of major artists' performances. In this case, the United States Supreme Court established that a writing covered "any physical rendering of the fruits of creative, intellectual, or aesthetic labor." Records and tape recordings certainly qualified under this heading.

Fixed In A Tangible Medium

As we saw earlier, in order for an original work to be considered a writing, the work must exist in some tangible entity.

A tangible entity can be paper, video tape, film, computer disk, record, recording tape, compact disc, or almost anything else capable of maintaining its form. Under the copyright statute, material is protected when it is created and fixed into a concrete medium so that it can be perceived by others.

David Brown wrote a term paper for Professor Hagendorf's law course in 1977. In the fall of 1978, Hagendorf adopted Brown's paper in an article he wrote for Commerce Clearing House, a legal publisher. Brown sued—and won—for copyright violation in *Hagendorf v. Brown*.[3] Even a term paper can be protected by copyright. It is a tangible form that can be perceived by others.

Definition Of Author

Only the original author of a work can receive copyright protection. This was first discussed in *Burrow-Giles Lithographic Co. v. Sarony*.[4] In this case, photographer Napoleon Sarony took a picture of Oscar Wilde in January of 1882. Sarony claimed that he was the author of the copyright to that picture entitled, "Oscar Wilde No. 18." Sarony printed a copyright notice on each copy of the photograph which read: "Copyright, 1882, by N. Sarony."

Burrow-Giles had printed reproductions of the Oscar Wilde picture without Sarony's permission. Burrow-Giles argued that a photographer cannot be considered an author and therefore cannot hold the copyright to the photo. However, the Court disagreed and awarded Sarony $600 in damages (remember, this was 1883). At the time of this case, photography was a rather new medium and did not exist at the time the original copyright act was created.

This case defined an author as the person "to whom anything owes its origin; originator; maker . . . ." The Court in its opinion re-stated Lord Justice Cotton's earlier definition of an author: "In my opinion, author involves originating, making, producing, as the inventive or master-mind, the thing which is to be protected, whether it be a drawing, or a painting, or a photograph."

The author of a work protected under copyright has a variety of rights. These include the right to make and distribute copies of the work, to create adaptations, and to publicly display and perform the work.

Requirement of Originality

Copyright protection is available only to original works. But what is the definition of original? An original work must be the result of an independent effort. Here's an example.

United Card Company and Roth Greeting Cards were both in the business of manufacturing greeting cards for sale through gift and card stores. United president, Mr. Koenig, and vice president, Mr. Letwenko, produced a series of seven cards that bore an amazing resemblance to seven cards already produced by Roth. When Roth found out about this, *Roth Greeting Cards* v. *United Card Co.*,[5] resulted.

Roth's suit was for copyright infringement. While United claimed that the cards it produced were its own creations, it admitted to "visiting greeting card stores and gift shows in order to observe what was going on in the greeting card business." In addition, Roth had a complete staff of writers and artists, while United had none. In fact, most of United's work was done by Koenig and Letwenko themselves.

Although the United cards were not exact duplications of the Roth cards, they were "in total concept and feel the . . . same as the copyrighted cards of Roth," even to the casual observer. Since the Roth cards were the originals, they were protected by copyright. As a result, United lost the case.

THE SCOPE OF COPYRIGHT PROTECTION

Anyone who deals with advertising needs to understand

law copyright and what it protects. Certain works can be copyrighted, others cannot. Now we take a closer look at what can and cannot be protected.

Under the current definition, almost any form of expression can be covered under the Copyright Act. For the advertiser, the most common forms of copyright works include:

- Photographs, television commercials, videos, computer files and images;
- Illustrations, renderings, cartoons, prints, charts, models, mock-ups, drawings;
- Sound recordings, radio commercials, music;
- Ads, billboards, brochures, displays; and
- Literary works.

Generally, items that are not eligible to be copyrighted include the following:

- Works that have not been fixed in a tangible form. For example, if a person creates a song in his mind, it must be put in writing or some other tangible form to be copyrighted. The thought is not tangible because others cannot perceive it;
- Titles, names, short phrases and slogans, symbols, or design elements. These items could be protected under trademark law in certain cases however. See Chapter 7;
- Ideas, procedures, methods, systems, processes, concepts, principles, discoveries, devices, and machines. These, would be protected under patent law, if the item qualified; and
- Works that are only common property information and have no original authorship. This includes items such as calendars, rulers, public lists, etc.

Copyright Protects Only A Specific Item

Copyright, as we have seen, protects the work from

unauthorized duplication or copying. The work might be in any form from a brochure to a photograph, a drawing, a sign, or a television commercial. However, copyright protects only the tangible medium used. As an example, if a photograph of a house is copyrighted, only the specific photograph is protected, not the house that is depicted in the photograph.

This situation actually occurred in *Modern Aids, Inc.* v. *R. H. Macy & Co.*[6] Modern Aids ran newspaper ads for its product, a massage machine. Macy duplicated the machine almost exactly, which was legal since there was no patent on the machine. However, Macy also copied Modern Aids' ad, which was illegal. The Modern Aids ad was copyrighted and therefore protected. Yet the machine shown in the ad was not protected by copyright.

Objects Of Use Are Not Copyrightable

Items that do not in and of themselves convey information are considered items of use. While a blank account book cannot be copyrighted, a specific one with entries in it can be.

Objects which are only objects of use may not be copyrighted. Things like time cards, account books, diaries, bank checks, score cards, address books, and order forms fall into this category.

Copyright Of Compilations, Derivative Works, And Collections

Derivative works such as compilations or collective works, may be copyrighted in some cases. A derivative work may include a work based on one or a number of preexisting works: translations, abridgements, fictionalizations, a motion picture adapted from a novel, reproductions, or condensations. Collective works also include periodicals, anthologies, or encyclopedias where a number of separate works are brought together into one entity.

A compilation is a collection or assemblage of preexisting

works. According to the Copyright Act, a compilation is "data that are selected, coordinated, or arranged in such a way that the resulting work as a whole constitutes an original work of authorship."[7] It is important to keep in mind that in order for the derivative work or collection to be copyrighted, it must have enough originality in itself to merit protection. Also, it must not infringe any other existing copyrights. To avoid violations, permission must be obtained from the original authors.

A person who assembles these separate works into one unit would be considered the author of the collective work, and, if the work is copyrighted, that person would be the owner of that copyright. But the owner of the collection of works only owns the rights to the collection, not to the individual works composing the collection.

Rand McNally, in 1978 and again in 1982, produced the *Rand McNally Mileage Guides* for sale to the public. These guides listed mileage figures between various cities throughout the United States. Rand McNally gathered the distance figures for its guide from various city, county, and state maps in the public domain. It also examined road conditions, compensated for variations between map sources, and broke down the distances into smaller segments. Unavailable mileage figures between some cities were developed from scales between other cities. *Rand McNally Mileage Guides* were compilations and were copyrighted. As we saw earlier, individual facts cannot be copyrighted, yet certain compilations of facts can be protected under copyright.

A problem arose when Fleet Management System copied virtually all of the figures listed in the *Rand McNally Mileage Guides* to produce mileage guides of its own. This all came to light in *Rand McNally & Co.* v. *Fleet Management Sys. Inc.*,[8] where the court determined that Rand McNally held valid copyrights to the compilation and that Fleet Management had infringed on its copyright. Keep in mind that it was not the individual figures that were protected under the copyright but the collection of data that had been copied almost in total that constituted the violation.

PROTECTION OF COPYRIGHT

To be protected by copyright, the author must abide by certain rules.

Notice Of Copyright

When something is considered important enough to protect, it should be identified by a copyright notice. The notice must consist of three items: a "C" with a circle around it for visual works or a "P" with a circle around it for audio works (or the word "copyright" may be used), the year of first publication, and the copyright owner's name. Under the Copyright Statute, the following format should appear:

- Copyright 1987, John Doe & Company. All Rights Reserved; or
- ©1987 John Doe & Company. All Rights Reserved.

The phrase "all rights reserved," is not required in the United States, but is necessary for protection in foreign countries. Ideally, each copy of the material should bear this notice clearly and conspicuously. Proper notice shows the world that the owner claims the copyright to the work. Typically, copyright notice should be placed on:

- A photograph—printed on the back of the print;
- A slide or negative—attached to the sleeve;
- A TV commercial or video—legibly displayed on the screen at the beginning or end of the spot for at least two to three seconds;
- A magazine or newspaper ad—printed legibly in the corner of the ad;
- A radio commercial—printed on the box label and tape reel;
- Original artwork—printed on the back of the original; and

- A book, report, or other literary work—printed on the title page at the front of the work.

Publication Of Copyrightable Work

Publication is defined legally as "the distribution of copies . . . of a work to the public by sale or other transfer of ownership, or by rental, lease or lending. The offering to distribute copies . . . to a group of persons for purposes of further distribution, public performance, or public display, constitutes publication."[9]

In other words, when someone gives a copy of an original work to another in connection with a proposal, the original is considered published, so it is important that the original and any copies clearly display the copyright notice. Unless this is done, an inadvertent publication by another may cause loss of protection.

Registering For Copyright

Ideally, a copyright should be registered as soon as the work is fixed in a concrete, tangible form, but in any case, must be registered with the Copyright Office within five years of the date of first publication. If notice was not placed on the work, the author must make a reasonable attempt to add the notice to all works distributed after discovery of the omission.

Although registering a work is not required to secure protection under copyright, there are valid reasons why the author should do so. Most importantly, registration of the copyright protects the author by providing evidence of ownership. This is a crucial point for legal support of an author's claim to copyright protection. If a work is infringed upon, prior registration is required before a lawsuit may be initiated.

To register a copyright, the appropriate form must be completed. This form, along with copies of the work and a fee (currently $10) must be sent to the Register of Copyrights, Copyright Office, Library of Congress, Washington, D.C. 20559.

That office can be contacted to obtain the required forms.

Remember, there are different forms for different types of works, and it is important to use the proper one for registration. Here's a list of the current forms:

- **TX**: Nondramatic works, literary works;
- **SE**: Serials, successive items bearing numerical or chronological designations (newsletters, magazines, annuals, etc.);
- **PA**: Performing arts (musicals, dramatic works, motion pictures, audiovisual works, etc.);
- **VA**: Visual arts (pictorial, graphic works, sculpture, advertisements, etc.);
- **SR**: Sound recordings;
- **RE**: Renewal registration;
- **CA**: Corrections or amplifications; and
- **GR/CP**: Group contributions to periodicals.

Duration Of Copyright Protection

Copyright protection begins when the original work is fixed in some tangible form by the original author. Protection continues for the life of the author plus 50 years after his or her death. In works-for-hire situations, which we will discuss later in the chapter, the duration of protection is 75 years from the first publication date or 100 years from creation of the work, whichever is shorter.

TRANSFER OF COPYRIGHT TO OTHERS

The rights to a copyright are transferable, usually by assignment or licensing. The transfer of exclusive rights, i.e., where only the grantee (person to whom the rights are given) can use the rights, is valid only if made in writing and signed by the holder of the copyright, the grantor (person granting the rights). Transfer of nonexclusive rights need not be in writing. Remember though, whenever a copyright is transferred or licensed, it must be recorded with the Copyright Office.

Compulsory Licensing Of Copyright

Compulsory licensing covers certain works that others can use after the payment of a fee set by the Copyright Office, instead of the copyright owner agreeing to the use. This practice is common in the music industry. Here's how it works: If an agency wants to use a musical piece in a commercial, notice is served on the owner of the copyright, and monthly royalties are paid to the owner. Cable television can also obtain a compulsory license for the transmission of copyrighted works. Royalties are paid as a percentage of the gross receipts of the cable system to the Copyright Royalty Tribunal (a clearing house for accounting and disbursement of royalties) and later distributed to the owners.

Assignment Of Rights

Many authors assign their rights to organizations who, in turn, authorize usage by others for a fee. Organizations such as ASCAP (American Society for Composers, Artists and Publishers) hold copyrights for many musical works. Broadcasters and commercial users are required to pay a fee to ASCAP which is then distributed to the owners for the use of material.

THE "WORKS-FOR-HIRE" RULE

When an employer, person or company, has an employee or agent perform work, the employer is considered the author and the owner of the copyright of that work. Under copyright law this is called work "made-for-hire." In other words, when the work is made by an employee (work-for-hire), the actual person who created it does not own the copyright. The person who employed the worker does.

"Works-for-hire" include items produced by an employee within the scope of his employment. If an employee of the company is asked to photograph a product, the company is the owner of the copyright in the photograph and it is a work-for-hire. However, work created outside the scope of his employment is owned by the employee and not the employer. The concept or term also covers works specifically ordered or commissioned for a particular purpose, if there is an agreement in writing that the work was done for hire. However, a work-for-hire does not normally include routine professional services on behalf of a client, unless there is an agreement to the contrary.

Ownership problems can arise when an independent contractor is commissioned to create work. To illustrate, if a photographer is hired by a company to photograph a product made by that company, the photographer is the copyright owner. This is not considered a work-for-hire situation unless there is an agreement to the contrary.

The best way to avoid copyright ownership problems when dealing with independent contractors (including freelancers) is to have them sign a written document designating that all materials created by the freelancer are works "made for hire" and that the creator transfers and assigns all rights and interest to the company commissioning the work. This should be put into written form and given to the independent contractor to sign, prior to beginning work. One document can be prepared that will cover any work performed after the effective date of the agreement. Remember, the independent contractor must transfer rights, establishing that the work is made for hire in writing or ownership problems may arise.

COPYRIGHT AND PROTECTION OF IDEAS

One point about copyright must be made clear. Copyright does not protect an idea, *per se*. It does, however, protect the expression of an idea. If the expression of the original idea is recognizable in another work, to the extent that an infringement is created, a lawsuit may result.

I'll clarify this point. If Widget Manufacturing Company designed and built a new widget refurbisher, the company cannot copyright the machine. We saw earlier that devices may not copyrighted. If anything, the machine would need to be protected under patent law. However, to produce a brochure for its new product, Widget Manufacturing had a photograph taken of the machine. That picture could be copyrighted as it is an expression of the idea. But the copyright only protects the photo, not the widget. Let's take a closer look at this concept.

Copyright Does Not Protect Ideas, Per Se

As we saw in the previous section, copyright is limited in scope. It does not protect against the use of an idea. Copyright protection does not cover "any idea, procedure, system, method of operation, concept, principle, or discovery, regardless of the form in which it is described, explained, illustrated, or embodied in such work."[10]

Copyright Protects The Expression Of An Idea

Copyright might be used to stem an unauthorized expression of an idea. An expression of an idea can take almost any form. An advertisement, a movie, a book, even a video game can all be expressions of ideas. Unlike a patent, copyright protects only the expression the—tangible fixed form used to allow others to perceive the idea—not the idea itself.

Atari and Midway own the exclusive copyrights for a video game called "PAC-MAN." Atari markets a home video version of the game. Shortly after PAC-MAN hit the market, another company, North American Philips Consumer Electronics, hired independent contractor Ed Averett to create a video game, which was named "K. C. Munchkin." Averett was very well qualified for the task since he had developed over 21 other such games. Mr. Staup, who was the head of North American's video game development department, and Averett got together and visited various sites to see and play PAC-MAN.

The two men discussed the PAC-MAN game, its strengths and weaknesses, and decided to develop a version of the game for North American's Odyssey line of home video games. Averett began work on the project and when it was completed, he showed it to North American who examined the game and determined that it was totally different from PAC-MAN. However, its legal counsel told North American that the game should be changed even more to avoid any potential liability. Averett made a few changes to the game, which it was then produced and marketed to the public.

Stores in various cities ran advertisements promoting the new game. Typical of these ads were those in the *Chicago SunTimes* and the *Tribune*, which described the K. C. Munchkin game as "a PAC-MAN type game." The ads also claimed that it was "as challenging as PAC-MAN." When Atari learned of the new game, it produced its own response: *Atari Inc.* v. *North American Philips Consumer Elecs.*[11]

Atari sued for copyright infringement because North American's game was so similar to PAC-MAN. Atari argued that an ordinary consumer would assume that K. C. Munchkin was taken directly from PAC-MAN. Atari needed to prove that K. C. Munchkin was "substantially similar" to PAC-MAN. And it did just that.

The problem in cases like this is that there is no concrete rule or test to determine if an idea or the expression of an idea has been taken. It is a very subjective decision as was addressed in the Atari case. "Obviously, no principle can be stated as to when an imitator has gone beyond copying the 'idea,' and has borrowed its 'expression.'" The video board game "idea" cannot be protected. But the specific form, PAC-MAN, which is the expression of the game (idea), can be protected. It is the individual features of the game shapes, sizes, colors, sequences, arrangements, and sounds taken as a whole that form an expression. Exact duplication or almost exact duplication is not necessary. "[A]n infringement . . . includes also the various modes in which the matter . . . may be adopted, imitated, transferred, or reproduced, with more or less colorable alterations to disguise the piracy."[12]

The main consideration given by the courts in these situations is the overall similarities, not the minute differences between the works.

The features of K. C. Munchkin were very similar to PAC-MAN. Those of you who have played the game would instantly recognize it as a copy. The main "Gobbler" characters in both games are very similar in shape, mouth, and movement, as well as the sounds they make. The same applies to the other characters of the two games. The board field is also very similar as is the method of play and the rules and object of the game. The K. C. Munchkin game uses the same role-reversal and regeneration characteristics of PAC-MAN, as well. There was no doubt in this case that there was copyright infringement. Atari won a permanent injunction and substantial damages.

THE FAIR USE DOCTRINE

All holders of copyright are susceptible to the "fair use doctrine," which permits certain copying of copyrighted material for purposes of criticism, news reporting, teaching, or research. Generally, however, copying for commercial use violates the rights of the copyright holder. The fair use doctrine will not protect advertisers who try to use copyrighted material for commercial purposes without paying for it.

Fair use was developed to balance authors' rights to protection of their copyrights and accompanying economic compensation against the public's desire for a free flow of ideas and information. Basically, the doctrine tries to achieve a safe area between copyright protection and freedom of speech.

Fair Use Protection Against Infringement

The main issue that the courts look to in determining if the use falls under the fair use doctrine is whether the usage substantially diminishes the value of the work.

One of the most notable examples of fair use was shown in the landmark case involving Universal City Studios and its suit against Sony. This case discussed a then new area of copyright—copying by home video recorders—that Congress could not have conceived would occur when it enacted the first Copyright Act. Sony manufactured millions of its Betamax video tape recorders and sold them through many retail outlets.

Universal owned the copyrights to many of the movies, television programs, and other programming it broadcast over television stations across the country. In *Sony Corp. v. Universal City Studios.*[13] Universal claimed that by Sony providing the means to copy or record these shows from television, people were violating copyright laws. Universal was claiming essentially contributory infringement in its suit because although Sony could not infringe on Universal's copyrights directly, Sony contributed to it through consumers who bought and used the video recorders to record movies. However, Universal's argument in court was not valid under the Copyright Act. Contributory infringement did not exist here anymore than it would for a camera manufacturer or a photocopy machine manufacturer.

Sony further argued that the video recorders allowed the consumer to time-record from television. This allowed the consumer to watch the show when it was more convenient actually expanding the television viewing audience that would watch the program. Therefore, the copyright holder could not object to the home recording of copyrighted material. The key here was whether the home recording impaired the commercial value of the work now or in the future. In this case it was ruled that it did not.

The court determined, in a 22-page opinion, that

noncommercial home recording of copyrighted material broadcast over public television was fair use and did not constitute copyright infringement. Noncommercial is the operative word here because there would be no reduction in the market for the original work.

Although every commercial use of copyrighted material without permission is a copyright infringement, noncommercial uses are a different matter. In order to uphold a claim of infringement through noncommercial uses, it must be shown that allowing the use could cause some harm or could damage the potential market for the work. If the copyrighted material is used for commercial use, that likelihood is presumed, but for noncommercial use it must be shown. Universal tried to argue that by allowing its shows to be recorded at home, "live television or movie audiences will decrease as more people watch Betamax tapes as an alternative." The court disagreed and Sony won.

Here's an example that relates to advertising directly. *The Miami Herald*, published by Knight-Ridder Newspapers, developed an ad campaign to promote the new format of its magazine-style television supplement to the newspaper. The Sunday supplement was introduced in the newspaper in November 1977. The campaign included print ads and television commercials.

The focus of the *Miami Herald's* campaign was to compare its television magazine to *TV Guide* magazine. The print ads showed the covers of both magazines in actual size, with the headline which read:

● ● ● ● ● ● ● ● ● ● ● ● ● ● ● ● ●
The *Herald's* new TV book.
It's a little bit bigger
and a little bit better.
● ● ● ● ● ● ● ● ● ● ● ● ●

The message in the ad was that the *Miami Herald's* book was bigger, had more listings, was easier to read, and was more up-to-date than *TV Guide* magazine. In the television commercials, the message was the same. A typical spot, based on the Goldilocks and the Three Bears theme, went like this:

Narrator:
"This is the story of Sidney Bear, Cindy Bear, and Junior Bear."
"They all loved to watch TV, but ...."

Older man:
"This TV book is too small."

Child:
"This TV book is too big."

Older woman:
"This TV section is just right."

Narrator:
"It was the *Sunday Herald's* new TV book at no extra cost. The three bears loved the new, just-right size with its up-to-date and more complete listings. 'Til one day this little blonde kid—uh, but that's another story. Something for everybody. Everyday of the week."

When Triangle Publications, the owner of *TV Guide* magazine, heard about these ads, it brought suit. In *Triangle Publications* v. *Knight-Ridder*,[14] Triangle objected to the reproduction of a *TV Guide* cover in both print ads and television commercials. The issue was whether the use of the *TV Guide* cover in the Herald's ads was allowed under the fair use doctrine.

The court determined that the *Herald's* ads did not copy the essence of *TV Guide*, that is the articles, schedules, and features contained inside. The *Herald* reproduced only the cover of the magazine. This, the court reasoned, was not enough to determine that the commercial value of *TV Guide's* copyright would be diminished. In fact, if the *Herald's* ads drew customers away from

TV Guide, it would have been because of the validity of the message—the difference between the two publications rather than showing the *TV Guide* cover.

The court concluded by saying *TV Guide* "suffered no economic injury whatever from the alleged infringement of its copyright." The *Herald* won its claim of fair use. For a discussion of comparative advertising issues, which parallels this case, see Chapter 8.

When Fair Use Does Not Protect Against Infringement

The fair use doctrine has been used to allow certain forms of parody, i.e., when the "style of . . . [a] work is closely imitated for comic effect. . ."[15] But the advertiser must understand the limits of the doctrine. To determine whether the use made of a copyrighted work can be considered fair use, the following need to be considered:

- The purpose and character of the use, including whether such use is of a commercial nature or is for nonprofit educational purposes;
- The nature of the copyrighted work;
- The amount and substantiality of the portion used in relation to the copyrighted work as a whole; and
- The effect of the use upon the potential market for or value of the copyrighted work.[16]

On the other hand, in the advertising area, a parody can fall outside the fair use doctrine when another company's theme, tag line, or primary characteristic is taken. Sambo's restaurants found this out when Dr. Pepper sued it for copyright infringement.

Dr. Pepper developed its *"Be a Pepper"* campaign in 1978. Within four years the company had spent over $100 million on the campaign and had realized tremendous results. Dr. Pepper was so pleased with the results that it planned for the campaign to run another 10 years.

In many cases, success breeds imitation. Here, Dr. Pepper was the success, Sambo's was the imitation. While the Dr. Pepper campaign was in its fourth year, Sambo's ad agency, Bozell & Jacobs, developed a campaign called *Dancing Seniors.*

Both commercials started with one person (the leader) dancing and singing the beginning of a jingle. In the Dr. Pepper commercial, the leader sang, "I drink Dr. Pepper and I'm proud. I'm part of an original crowd." In the Sambo's commercial: "I eat at Sambo's Restaurants every day. I get a special deal on my dinner meal." Both commercials used people dancing along with the leader to a chorus:

For Dr. Pepper; "Wouldn't you like to be a Pepper, too?"

For Sambo's; "Don't you want to be a senior, too?"

The Sambo's commercials first aired in late 1980, and when Dr. Pepper learned of this in January 1981, it sued in *Dr. Pepper Co.* v. *Sambo's Restaurants, Inc.*[17] Dr. Pepper held copyrights to its television commercials and to the *"Be a Pepper"* jingle. As a defense to the case, Sambo's claimed that it was entitled to parody the Dr. Pepper commercial under the fair use doctrine.

However, any commercial use has a tendency to contradict the fair use doctrine. This is a very risky area for advertisers. Because of Sambo's use of the essence and substance of the Dr. Pepper commercial, it diminished that spot's value, uniqueness, and originality. This took the infringement out of the fair use arena. Sambo's impact on the useful life of the *"Be a Pepper"* campaign was an infringement and Sambo's lost.

What about fair use of copyrighted material that was not another commercial? Parody or satarization is a common and legal practice in all forms of entertainment and social commentary under the fair use doctrine. However, it is not allowed in advertising.

Miller Brewing Company, their advertising agency Backer & Spielvogel, and comedian (the performer in the commercial) Joe Piscopo were sued by a rap music group, the Fat Boys. The case,

Tin Pan Apple, Inc. v. Miller Brewing Co., Inc.,[18] involved a television commercial that infringed the copyright of some of the Fat Boys' songs. Miller argued that the similarity between the Fat Boys composition was allowed under the Fair Use Doctrine because the commercial was simply a parody of rap music in general, and of the Fat Boys in particular. In Miller's argument, they discounted the fact that the music and action used in the commercial was "substantially similar," the test for copyright infringement, to the Fat Boys' songs and performances.

Miller tried to use a 1989 case where a federal court ruled that a song entitled "I Love Sodom," used in a skit on the television program Saturday Night Live, did not infringe the copyrighted song "I Love New York." This was clearly because the purpose of the skit was to satirize the way in which New York City had attempted to rectify its rather tarnished image through the use of a comprehensive advertising campaign. This form of parody was protected under the fair use rule because it was used for social satire, rather than commercial advertising.

Although the parody defense is viable in situations where parts of the copyrighted work are used for social comment or criticism, the defense did not apply in the Miller case because their use was solely for the purpose of promoting the sale of a commercial product; in this case, beer. Commercial advertising cannot use the doctrine of fair use to defend an illegal use of copyrighted material.

As we have just seen, the more unique the concept of the commercial, the greater the protection required against infringement. If the commercial is based on more general situations, greater latitude will be allowed. Any car commercial may use a showroom as its setting with a car salesman speaking to the audience. However, if the bulk of the commercial shows a salesman announcing claims about the car, which are obvious and blatant lies, and subtitles are shown (as in the past Isuzu commercials), the courts will be more inclined to consider this type of use an infringement.

COPYRIGHT PROTECTION RELATING TO ADVERTISEMENTS

Copyright law can, as in the Dr. Pepper case, be used against an ad or commercial derived substantially from another piece. This goes back to the "expression of an idea" concept discussed earlier, i.e., that is, if the other commercial takes the same basic feeling or premise. Devising a concept for an advertisement is an idea. A specific ad is an expression of that idea and can be copyrighted.

When An Ad Takes The Expression Of Another Ad

To illustrate this point, let's take, for example, McDonalds' campaign developed directly from the H. R. Pufnstuf cartoon characters. When McDonalds' agency, Needham, Harper & Steers, developed the McDonaldland concept, it was patterned after the characters in the *H. R. Pufnstuf* TV show. The Pufnstuf television series, which began in 1969, featured a boy named Jimmy, who lived on "Living Island"—a fantasyland inhabited by mayors with large round heads and oversized mouths, Keystone-Cop-type assistants, crazy scientists, multiarmed evil creatures, animated trees having human faces, and talking books. The McDonaldland image used the same location, characters, and elements.

McDonald's even used the people who designed and constructed the sets and costumes for Pufnstuf, as well as some of the same voice people for the campaign. The set itself was the same Living Island concept used in Pufnstuf. In January 1971, the McDonaldland commercials began to air.

The Pufnstuf cartoon characters had previously been licensed for Kellogg's cereal, the *Ice Capades*, as well as other toys and games. In fact, the Ice Capades actually replaced the Pufnstuf characters with the McDonaldland characters after the McDonalds' campaign began.

The creators of Pufnstuf sued McDonald's for copyright infringement in *Sid & Marty Krofft v. McDonald's*.[19] Even though the specifics of the McDonald's campaign were not identical, they were substantially similar enough to have captured the look and feel of the Pufnstuf characters. McDonald's lost, was required to stop using the ads, and had to pay $50,000 in damages. The credibility of the Pufnstuf characters had been eroded. Pufnstuf even showed loss of licensing (*Ice Capades*) as a direct result of the McDonaldland ad campaign.

When There Is Not Enough Similarity Of Expression

Certain cases show a lack of similarity and therefore no infringement of copyright. The creators of the Pink Panther character tried at one time to sue Lincoln-Mercury for copyright infringement. When Lincoln-Mercury developed an animated cat character for use in its ads, the creators of the Pink Panther sued because of the similarities between the Lincoln-Mercury cat and the Pink Panther. It was claimed that both of the cats had human characteristics and mannerisms as well as elongated tails. But this was not enough to cause infringement.

Lincoln-Mercury had used a live cougar as its identity for many years prior to the alleged infringement. Also, the Lincoln-Mercury cat had a strong masculine personality as opposed to the glitzy Pink Panther personality. In fact, many companies have used animated cats including Exxon, B. F. Goodrich's Tigerpaws tires, Kellogg's Tony the Tiger, Le Tigre shirts, and others.

LEGAL REMEDIES

Obviously, one should not take the copyrighted work of someone else and use it without permission. Congress, in creating the Copyright Act, felt that there were two good reasons for making this unauthorized use illegal. First, the author may have future plans to license the work. And infringement could severely interfere with these plans. We saw this in the Dr. Pepper case. Second, the author may consider that commercial exploitation of his work may demean his creative efforts and thereby erode its credibility. This is especially true in the case of literary works, although we saw the advertising version of this in the *Pufnstuf* case.

If actual damages cannot be shown, the statute provides for not less than $250 or more than $10,000 per infringement. This can be increased up to $50,000 for willful infringement. There is a wrinkle to the "per infringement" fine. If we go back to the Doofus-Wazoo story at the beginning of this chapter, you'll recall that the agency was slapped with a $5 million lawsuit. In that case the TV commercial used 14 copyrighted slides, and the use was willful; that's $50,000 multiplied by fourteen.

Also, each time the commercial airs another 14 infringements occur. It adds up fast!

Remedies for copyright violation include injunction, seizure, impounding and destruction of infringing items, damages and profits, and in many cases attorney's fees. Indeed, advertisers should be careful where copyright infringement is concerned. The penalties are very severe, as we have seen.

[1] 17 U.S.C. section 102(a)(1982).

[2] *Goldstein* v. *California*, 412 U.S. 546, 93 S.Ct. 2303, 37 L.Ed. 2d 163 (1973).

[3] *Hagendorf* v. *Brown*, 699 F.2d 478 (9th Cir. 1983).

[4] *Burrow-Giles Lithographic Co.* v. *Sarony*, 111 U.S. 53, 4 S.Ct. 279, 28 L.Ed. 349 (1884).

[5] *Roth Greeting Cards* v. *United Card Co.*, 429 F.2d 1106 (9th Cir. 1970).

[6] *Modern Aids, Inc.* v. *R. H. Macy & Co.*, 264 F.2d 93 (2d Cir. 1969).

[7] 17 U.S.C. section 101.

[8] *Rand McNally & Co.* v. *Fleet Management Sys. Inc.*, 600 F.Supp. 933 (N.D. Ill. 1984).

[9] 17 U.S.C. section 101.

[10] 17 U.S.C. section 102.

[11] *Atari Inc.* v. *North American Philips Consumer Elecs.*, 672 F.2d 607 (7th Cir. 1982).

[12] *Universal Pictures Co. Inc.* v. *Harold Lloyd Corp.*, 162 F.2d 354, 360 (9th Cir. 1947).

[13] *Sony Corp.* v. *Universal City Studios*, 52 U.S.L.W. 4090 (U.S. Jan 17,1984) rev'g 659 F.2d 963 (9th Cir. 1981).

[14] *Triangle Publications* v. *Knight-Ridder*, 626 F.2d 1171 (5th Cir. 1980).

[15] *Webster's New Collegiate Dictionary* (Springfield, Mass.: Merriam-Webster Inc., 1976).

[16] 17 U.S.C. section 107.

[17] *Dr. Pepper Co.* v. *Sambo's Restaurants, Inc.*, 517 F. Supp. 1202 (1981).

[18] *Tin Pan Apple, Inc.* v. *Miller Brewing Co., Inc.*, 737 F.Supp. 826 (S.D.N.Y. 1990).

[19] *Sid & Marty Krofft* v. *McDonald's*, 562 F.2d 1157 (1977).

CHAPTER 7

TRADEMARK REGULATION

I hate the man who builds his name
On ruins of another's fame.
—*John Gay*

Within 20 years after the Civil War, a Columbus, Georgia pharmacist named John S. Pemberton had invented, manufactured, and sold a variety of products. These ranged from Globe of Flower Cough Syrup and Indian Queen Hair Dye to Triplex Liver Pills, Gingerine and Extract of Styllinger.

Pemberton later moved to Atlanta where he created a drink that combined an extract of kola nut, fruit syrup, and extract of coco leaf. In 1886 he took his syrup to Jacob's Drug Store in Atlanta where, on a trial basis, he was allowed to sell his drink at the soda fountain. The drink became modestly popular with the patrons of Jacob's Drug Store.

Eventually, Pemberton became disillusioned with the drink and sold out to a man named Asa Chandler. Pemberton made $1,750. With his new product in hand, Chandler first advertised the drink as a "Wonderful Nerve and Brain Tonic and Remarkable Therapeutic Agent." By 1893, Chandler had sold 48,427 gallons of his tonic. A year later, soda water was added to the mixture, and it was bottled.

Chandler's tonic grew in popularity. In fact, the more a person drank, the more that person wanted. In part this was because of the caffeine and small amounts of cocaine that remained in the syrup after the brewing process. As sales of the drink grew, it became apparent to Chandler that he needed to market the product on a larger scale. So, in 1906 he hired the Massingale Agency in Atlanta to advertise his product. From that point on, Chandler's drink (which was named by the Jacob's Drug

Store bookkeeper) soared into marketing history on the wings of a trademark the likes of which has not been seen since. The drink was Coca-Cola.

The strength and value of a trademark to identify goods and distinguish them from others cannot be overstressed. As Coca-Cola proved, a successful business gets that way by investing much of its efforts in building a favorable identity for itself and its products. This can be called *reputation*, and in many cases it is called *good will*. The public's knowledge of this image—what we in advertising work so hard to build and maintain—will draw first-time buyers and continue to bring back repeat buyers.

Once the buyer, let's say Ms. Jones, is satisfied with a product, she will seek it out to buy again. Ms. Jones seeks out the same product because of qualities she found in it before, and hopes to find again. Sociologists tell us that these qualities can range from actual product performance to ego gratification. Regardless, the consumer finds fulfillment in some form. This satisfaction in a brand also draws attention to new products introduced by the same manufacturer. It can create a built-in satisfaction with the product, even before it's purchased.

Take, for instance, the Chevrolet Corvette. Since the car's inception in 1953, its popularity has grown steadily. Even in the mid-1970s when oil prices were climbing, the 55 MPH speed limit was invoked, and the V-engine was dying, demand for the Corvette continued to grow. Over the years, this demand has increased. Today, even before a new Corvette model is released, many people place orders for one. This demand exists, in large part, because of the reputation that the Corvette name has built over the years. I know from personal experience that this is true. I've owned eight of them.

Trademarks are an important part of indicating the origin of the product. They make the product recognizable and identifiable by the consumer. Often, the trademark can say more than any photo or amount of ad copy. The old adage claims that pictures speak louder than words. Well, a reputable trademark can speak louder than both. Take the Volkswagen ads in the early 1970's. One such ad ran the headline: "Here's What to Do to Get Your Volkswagen Ready for Winter." The rest of the page was blank— except for the Volkswagen logo. That shows how strong the Volkswagen trademark is.

When a consumer sees a product with a particular trademark on it, that person should be able to rely on the image that the name conjures up and to trust the quality of a product that carries a certain trademark. After all, trademark laws were created to support that trust. A trademark is intended to distinguish one manufacturer's goods from another's. That's why a company must protect its trademark, and also why a company must be careful not to let its trademark infringe on another company's mark. These are concerns both the advertiser and its agency must heed.

While reading this chapter, the advertiser should be most concerned with how to protect its own mark while not infringe another's mark. It is not my desire here to teach the reader how to search trademarks. That should be left to a competent trademark attorney.

QUALITIES OF A TRADEMARK

There are many aspects of trademark law that advertisers must understand. One of the first concerns the qualities need to exist in a trademark. The following section discusses this important issue.

The Difference Between A Trademark And A Trade Name

Under the Federal Trademark Act of 1946, trademarks may be registered, but trade names may not.

[A trademark is] word, name, symbol, or

device or any combination thereof adopted and used by a manufacturer or merchant to identify his goods and distinguish them from those manufactured by others. [Trade names are] "individual names and surnames, firm names and trade names used by manufacturers, industrialists, merchants, agriculturalists, and others to identify their businesses, vocations, or occupations.[1]

To distinguish the two terms, a trademark refers to products or services, and a trade name refers to the business entity itself. For example, Beatrice (the company) is a trade name while its product, Hunt's Ketchup, is a trademark; Kodak is a trademark while Eastman Kodak Company (the manufacturer) is a trade name.

Types Of Trademarks

The term "trademark" actually covers a number of marks of various uses. There are trademarks, service marks, certification marks, and collective marks. A trademark, as we have just discussed, is used in connection with a product.

A service mark is used when referring to the sale of a service. Since services rarely have anything concrete to place a name or mark on, the service mark generally identifies the business itself. In this case, what would usually be considered a trade name would be registered as a service mark. As an example, if Acme Auto Repair Service, Inc. desired to protect its name, it would have to register it as a service mark. These services are identified with an "SM" symbol. The category of service marks also includes slogans, titles, characters, and symbols.

Another form of mark is called a "certification mark," which calls attention to the origin, material, nature, method of manufacture, accuracy, quality, or labor source of a product. Examples include the Good Housekeeping Seal of Approval, the mark used for the AFL-CIO, or the mark used by the cotton industry to designate 100% cotton composition of the item.

Collective marks, another form of trademark, are marks used to show membership in an organization or group. A collective mark has no relation to a specific product or service, but merely shows affiliation with the group. The marks used by the Elks' Lodge or the American Association of Advertising Agencies are prime examples.

STRONG MARKS AND WEAK MARKS

As far as trademarks are concerned, there are two strengths of marks: strong and weak. The law offers different protection for each type so it is important for the advertiser to be aware of the difference between the two types of marks.

Strong Marks

Strong marks can receive protection under trademark law simply because they are distinctive. Marks in this category can include those that are suggestive of the product. A strong mark is coined or fanciful, such as "Kodak," "Xerox," or "Exxon." "Sure" for deodorant, "Raid" for insect spray, and "Drano" for clogged drains are other examples of strong marks. Strong marks, while they are suggestive, are more than just descriptive of the product.

Weak Marks

Weak marks do not automatically qualify as trademarks and will be permitted protection only if the Trademark Office allows it. A weak mark would be composed of words that praise or describe a quality like "best" or "premium." However, a weak mark, as such, will be granted protection as a trademark only if it has acquired a secondary meaning. This implies that the consumer makes an automatic connection between the product or service that the mark refers to and its source. The consumer must associate the product and the mark with the manufacturer. If this connection can be shown, then protection can be afforded the mark. For example, when you hear the term "Big Mac," what do you think of? McDonald's of course. That's secondary meaning.

Another category of weak marks include the use of geographical names. Unless secondary meaning could be established, names using "Swiss" for watches, "Columbian" for coffee, "California" for oranges, and so on would not be protected under trademark law. These names only designate the geographic origin of the item, and a manufacturer cannot take such a designation for its own to the exclusion of others.

Weak marks also include surnames. Common names like Johnson, Smith, White, and Jones have probably already been trademarked at some time. If another company has already trademarked a surname, a manufacturer runs the risk of infringing on that mark. Even if the name is the person's legitimate one, it can still infringe on another's trademark.

Let's say that Smith's Oil begins manufacturing its product and trademarks the name. It runs a high risk that another trademark already exists under that name. If time goes by, and no claims are brought, consumers may become accustomed to associating Smith's Oil with the product. In this case, the name develops a secondary meaning. If another manufacturer begins selling an oil product under that same name, in the same marketing area, it would be infringing on Smith's trademark.

Marks that use descriptions of praise as trademarks also fall into the weak mark category. "Premium," "World's Finest," and others are very weak unless secondary meaning can be attributed to the trade name. However, this does occur, as we see later. Products such as Pabst Blue Ribbon beer, Gold Medal flour, and others have achieved this secondary meaning status through heavy and continued usage of the marks for many years within the market. As a result, they are protected under trademark.

REGISTRATION OF MARKS

Trademarks are registered with the U.S. Patent and Trademark Office in Washington, D.C. The importance of registering a mark is that doing so notifies others that the owner of the mark "claims" the exclusive rights to its use. But registering the mark alone is not enough to protect it. Notice of registration must be used along with the mark. Keep in mind that registering a mark does not create an unlimited legal right to ownership; rather it's a claim of ownership. To be protected, the mark must not infringe on another's mark. Until 1989, federal trademark law said that a company must actually use a trademark before it could be registered. However, in 1989, the statute was amended to allow trademark registration by showing an "intent to use" the mark, which may be inferred from marketing, advertising and distribution plans.

Length Of Registration

Once a trademark is registered, the claim is established for 10 years. After obtaining registration, the company has six months to begin using the trademark in commerce. Registration may thereafter be renewed for unlimited 10-year periods. An application must be filed within six months before the expiration of a trademark. As an alternative, a mark can be renewed up to three months after expiration if a penalty is paid.

Trademark Registers

Trademarks can be recorded in one of the two registers of the Trademark Office: the Principal Register or the Supplemental Register. All applications for registration go first to the Principal Register. If the mark does not meet the requirements of that register, it is passed on to the Supplemental Register for possible acceptance. This is an automatic process used by the Trademark Office.

It is important to note that, unlike copyright, registering a trademark does not provide any right of ownership. Any such right exists through common law as a property right. Because of this, many marks that are not registered are still afforded trademark status. We'll look at this later.

Also, some marks that are registered can have their trademark status revoked if challenged by a company that previously registered and used the same mark. The registers only provide a place where marks can be listed for public record. This doesn't mean that there are not good reasons to register a mark. Indeed there are, and we look into these reasons later.

The Principal Register accepts only marks that meet certain standards but keep in mind that the Trademark Office does not search for similar marks that have already been registered. The applicant must perform its own search or hire someone, such as a trademark attorney to do this. The Trademark Office only judges a mark against the standards of the office for acceptance, not against other marks already registered—that's the applicant's responsibility. Standards for acceptance include:

- The mark must be distinctive;
- The mark must not be immoral, deceptive, or scandalous;
- The mark must not consist of a flag, emblem, or insignia of the United States or other country;
- The mark must not consist of the picture or signature of an individual without prior consent;
- The mark must not resemble another mark;
- The mark must not be merely descriptive of the product;
- The mark must not be geographically descriptive of origin; and
- The mark must not be a surname.

The Supplemental Register is more lenient. All four of these requirements must be met for registration:

- The mark must be unqualified for registration on the

Principal Register;
- The mark must be able to distinguish the product;
- The mark must not fall into any category above for the Principal Register, except numbers 6, 7, or 8; and
- The mark must have been used in commerce for one year without opposition from another trademark owner.

NOTICE OF REGISTRATION

It is important to place a notice of registration along with a trademark. A notice of registration of a mark allows damages to be recovered if infringement of the mark occurs. Without that notice damages cannot be awarded; only the infringing usage of the mark may be stopped. Notice also lends credibility, which should help deter potential infringers. Registration notice also helps establish that the mark is a trademark rather than a generic term.

The Trademark Act states that ". . . a registrant of a mark . . . *may* give notice that his mark is registered by displaying with the mark as used . . . the letter 'R' enclosed within a circle."

The act goes on to say: ". . . in any suit for infringement under this chapter by such a registrant failing to give such notice of registration, no profits or damages shall be recovered . . . *unless the defendant had actual notice of registration* . . ." (emphasis added).[2] There are two alternate notice forms, which are acceptable, but seldomly used because of their sheer bulk: "Registered in U.S. Patent and Trademark Office" and "Reg. U.S. Pat. & Tm. Off."

Marks that are not yet registered, but for which application has been made, can be identified with a "TM." Be aware that it is legal to use a notice of actual registration "®" only after a certificate of registration has been issued.

The registration notice may be placed anywhere in relation to the mark and in any style. If a trademark is used more than once in an ad, it is not necessary for the notice to appear every time the mark appears, but it should appear with the mark that is used first or appears most prominent. Of course, the notice itself should be large enough to be readily recognizable and readable.

Another important consideration is that when using another company's trademark in your ad, always use the appropriate notice with the mark. Also, when you use someone else's trademark in an ad, capitalize the mark. For example, use "XEROX" or "Xerox," not "xerox." In other words, capitalizing lets the reader of the ad know that the mark is the trademark of another company. This may need to be clearly identified elsewhere in the ad if there is any chance of confusion, such as a credit line stating: "Acme is the registered trademark of Widget Manufacturing Company."

Using A Trademark Notice With A Mark That Has Not Been Registered

If a notice is placed with a trademark that is not registered, severe problems can result. Most importantly, the right to register the mark in the future can be lost. A trademark known as *Four Roses* is a good example. In 1925, Small Grain Distilling Company applied for and was granted the trademark *Four Roses* for its high-grade whiskey. *Four Roses* was a widely known brand name at the time.

Early in 1926 another company, Four Roses Products, began placing a notice of registration on its product of malt syrup used in making liquor. The name *Four Roses* was used on the product packaging along with the notice "Trade-Mark Reg. U.S. Pat. Off." When Small Grain learned of this, it brought the case to court in *Four Roses Products Co.* v. *Small Grain Distilling & Drug Co.*[3]

The fact was Four Roses Products had never received a registration of the trademark for "Four Roses:" It had applied for registration but had been denied. Four Roses Products used the registration notice even though it knew it had no registration. The court determined that Small Grain's trademark of Four Roses was legitimate and Four Roses Products' mark was not. Essentially, Four Roses Products tried, through the use of the registration notice, to imply that its product was authentic and that any other, including Small Grain's, was an infringement. This was not accurate.

Since Four Roses Products used the registration notice on an unregistered mark, it lost the case, had to pay damages for infringement, and lost any chance for future registration. As a side note, this must have been a heated case in court considering the time it occurred—not long after the 18th Amendment to the Constitution was adopted. The amendment repealed prohibition.

There is another reason not to use a registration notice if the mark has not been registered. The right to stop another company from using the same mark can be lost. Fox Photo learned about this in 1972. The company provided photo developing and finishing services to the public. The Fox Photo logo consisted of a red fox running with the name Fox Photo across it. Fox Photo also used, as part of its logo, a red "R" in a circle.

Sometime later, Harry Otaguro began publishing a photo magazine called *FOX*. Fox Photo decided that Otaguro's magazine infringed its trademark because of the similarity in the names and the fact that both products were in the same field— photography. *Fox-Stanley Photo Products, Inc.* v. *Otaguro*,[4] resulted. Unfortunately Fox Photo had never registered the Fox Photo mark. That, however, did not deter it from placing a registration notice with the logo to imply registration of the mark.

Fox Photo lost its case at the outset simply because it did not own the trademark. Because it had used a registration notice on a mark that had not been registered, Fox also lost its right to be granted a trademark registration for its logo in the future.

ANOTHER FORM OF ERRONEOUS USE OF A TRADEMARK

Other than the situations described above, there is an additional form of trademark misuse that can cause problems. This involves using a mark with goods different from those for which it was registered. A trademark can be used only with the product or product line that it was registered for, i.e., registering a mark for use with a specific product does not automatically allow that mark to be used with other products. Here's an example. If Bonzo Company manufactures and owns a trademark for its line of cars, it cannot use that trademark for its new line of dishwashers.

In 1965 Cumberland Packing Company wanted to register the mark for *Sweet 'N Low*. The low-calorie sugar substitute was to be marketed to the public in packet form. Cumberland had been assigned the rights from the inventor, May MacGregor.

Another company who sold only to the trade, Duffy-Mott Company, also owned a trademark to use the name *Sweet 'N Low*. It, too, had been assigned rights to the name by MacGregor for use of her sugar-substitute formula in canned, frozen, and fresh fruits; vegetables; pudding; and cake mixes. Duffy-Mott opposed the registration of the mark for Cumberland's packet version of *Sweet 'N Low*, claiming that it would infringe Duffy-Mott's use of the mark. *Duffy-Mott Co.* v. *Cumberland Packing Co.*,[5] was the case.

Duffy-Mott argued that by allowing registration of *Sweet 'N Low* for the sugar substitute sold in packets, its mark would be eroded. However, the court reasoned that the issuance of a registration for Cumberland would not infringe on the mark used by Duffy-Mott because Cumberland's mark would be directed to the public in raw form. On the other hand, Duffy-Mott's mark was directed to the trade to be included in a finished product. Since the product lines and markets were different for each company, the court allowed registration for Cumberland.

GENERICIDE: WHAT CAN HAPPEN WHEN A MARK IS MISUSED

Ultimately, when a mark is misused, it can be lost to the forgotten world of generic terms. The consumer may begin to consider a trademark as the name of the product line in general.

Then the trademark no longer identifies and distinguishes the product of a particular manufacturer. Instead of standing for one particular brand of the product, the mark stands for the type of product. This is called "genericide."

When a trademark is not handled properly, it can be weakened to the point that it is no longer protected as a trademark. Therefore, an advertiser must be very cautious. The manufacturer's own promotion, labeling, and advertising are at fault when this happens. Genericide has been the demise of many trademarks, which we now consider product lines, including "cellophane," "celluloid," "kerosene," "lanolin," "linoleum," "milk of magnesia," "dry ice," and (as we'll soon see) "aspirin," "thermos bottles," "escalators," and "PROMS." These trademarks were allowed to deteriorate to the point that they became synonymous with the product rather than the manufacturer.

The key to understanding this process is this: genericide happens in the mind of the consumer, not to the product. Yet, there is something that the advertiser can do to control how the consumer perceives the trademark. The easiest way to avoid genericide and to protect a trademark would be to use the word *brand* in connection with the name and product, i.e., "Xerox brand copiers" or "IBM brand computers," to forestall any assumption by consumers that the trademark is a generic term.

The Headache That Aspirin Caused

How many brands of aspirin can you think of? Bayer, Johnson & Johnson, Excedrin, Bufferin, and Anacin are some of the major ones. This is the problem that Bayer had to deal with in the early 1920's, because "aspirin" was originally a trademark.

"Aspirin" was the trademark for the drug acetyl salicylic acid, a powder that was patented by Bayer Company in 1898. In 1904 the name of the drug was changed to momoaceticacidester of salicylic acid. Bayer began allowing chemists, druggists, and physicians to make the powder into tablets for sale under names such as "Squibb Aspirin," "Smith, Klein & French Aspirin," or "United Drug Company Aspirin." United Drug, in particular, sold over 19 million tablets in its first two years. The consumer could not possibly have known the manufacturer of the drug, only the name on the bottle.

In 1915 Bayer changed its policy and discontinued selling to other manufacturers. From that time on Bayer prohibited others from manufacturing or selling the drug. It began selling aspirin itself in tablets to the general public. Tablets were sold in tin boxes with the legend:

● ● ● ● ● ● ● ● ● ● ● ● ● ●
The Trademark "Aspirin"
(Reg. U.S. Pat. Office)
is a guarantee that the momoaceticacidester of salicylic acid
in these tablets is of the reliable Bayer manufacture.
● ●

But it was too late; the harm had been done. Because of this change in policy, United Drug sued Bayer claiming that the name *aspirin* had become a descriptive name, free for anyone to use. The case was *Bayer Co. v. United Drug Co.*[6] While the druggists knew that aspirin was a trademark, the general public did not. Its only knowledge of the product was through the over-the-counter brands that were available, especially since many manufacturers had used the name alone in labeling and advertising—all allowed by Bayer.

Bayer understood that the term "aspirin" had become generic. When it began to sell to the public in 1915, its labels read: "Bayer—Tablets of Aspirin." This meant that the tablets were Bayer's make of the drug known as "aspirin."

The public could not have known that "aspirin" was a trademark for momoaceticacidester of salicylic acid; it thought that *aspirin* was the name of the drug. By allowing this confusion to occur, Bayer failed to protect the trademark as such, and the

Trademark Office declared the trademark not valid as of 1918. The court in its decision agreed with both the Trademark Office and United Drug in determining that the name "aspirin" had become a generic term.

The Moving Stairway

Trademark registration number 34,724 was issued to Charles D. Seeberger in 1900. The trademark was for the term "escalator." Seeberger had invented the device and assigned the trademark to the Otis Elevator Company a number of years later, which manufactured not only elevators, but escalators as well.

A typical ad for Otis from a 1946 issue of *Architectural Forum* magazine contained the following:

• • • • • • •
Otis (logo)
THE MEANING OF THE OTIS TRADEMARK.
To the millions of daily passengers on the
Otis elevators and escalators, the Otis
trademark or name plate means
safe, convenient, energy-saving transportation.
To the thousands of building owners and managers,
the Otis trademark means the utmost in safe,
efficient, economical elevator and escalator operation.
• •

Obviously, the Otis name was treated as the trademark, and the names "escalator" and "elevator" were merely descriptive of the product. This was plain from the ad copy. As a result, the Haughten Elevator Company attempted, in the late 1940's, to have the name "escalator" declared generic.

Haughten succeeded with its efforts in *Haughten Elevator Co.* v. *Seeberger.*[7] Here, the court determined that the term "escalator" was a generic term for a moving stairway. The court reasoned that the term "escalator" described any moving stairway made by any company. Otis, in large part, allowed this to occur through its literature and advertisements. The term "escalator" was not used by Otis to identify it as the originator and only source of an escalator. The word "escalator" became a generic term for any moving stairway. Trademark number 34,724, held by Otis, was cancelled.

Keeps Hot Things Hot And Cold Things Cold

A German company named Thermos-Gessellschaft M.B.H. manufactured vacuum-insulated containers that were adopted from Dewar's vacuum flask invention of 1893. In 1907 the German company sold out to a new American company, The American Thermos Bottle Company, which produced the now well-known thermos bottle. Initial sales were $114,987 in 1907, and by 1960 the company grossed $13,280,164 for the year.

As early as 1910, American Thermos was promoting the fact that "thermos" had become a household word synonymous with "vacuum-insulated;" thus Thermos bottle. The public adopted this term, and began referring to the thermos bottle as if it were a type of product.

A competitor, Aladdin Industries, also manufactured vacuum-bottles. When it started calling its product a "thermos bottle," American Thermos sued to stop this use in *American Thermos Products Co.* v. *Aladdin Industries, Inc.*[8] The court determined that "thermos" had become the generic term for the vacuum bottle. American Thermos used the combination of "Thermos bottle," not "Thermos brand bottle," or "Thermos vacuum-insulated bottle." American Thermos could still use the name, but so could anyone else.

The court stated that American Thermos, during the early 1900's, welcomed the public's conception that "Thermos" was synonymous with vacuum-bottle. American Thermos "recognized this as an 'enormous amount of free advertising' worth, at that time, between three and four million dollars . . . ." On the other hand, it paid a high price for the free advertising; it lost its trademark protection forever.

The PROM That Never Was

Most losses of trademark protection to genericide occurred in the years when marketing and advertising techniques were young. As we have seen, many early trademarks were lost because of poor handling. But today's company is still at risk when it comes to trademark protection as clearly seen in a recent example involving the computer revolution and one of its components, the "PROM."

High-tech afficionados love to use initials for the names of components. For computer memories, RAM stands for Random Access Memory, SAM for Simultaneous Access Memory, CAM for Content-Addressable Memory, ROM for Read-Only Memory, and PROM for Programmable-Read-Only Memory.

The Harris Semiconductor Division of Radiation, Inc. developed the first field programmable-read-only memory. Harris adopted the acronym "PROM" for the product and put that name on its merchandise. Soon after, other companies developed similar programmable-read-only memories and also used the designation "PROM." Harris attempted to stop the other manufacturers from using the name claiming that "PROM" was a trademark for its own products. Harris then attempted to register the term "PROM" as its trademark.

When this occurred, Intel (one of the other competitors) brought an action to stop Harris from acquiring the trademark. In *Intel Corp. v. Radiation, Inc.*,[9] the issue was whether the term "PROM" should be trademarked. Essentially, the court determined that "PROM" was merely the "descriptive letters [that] constitute the initials or abbreviations of the common name of the product."

In fact, the trade had already become well-acquainted with the term "PROM." The acronym had been used extensively by publications within the trade and in promotional materials of various manufacturers. It was common practice in the electronics industry to use abbreviations as an easy method for identifying the different components. It was also well known that these acronyms did not denote the manufacturer of the component. Indeed, "PROM" was only a descriptive name or acronym for the specific type of memory. Harris was not granted a trademark for the term "PROM"—it was a generic name.

HOW TO AVOID GENERICIDE

Al Ries and Jack Trout, in their inspiring book, *Positioning: The Battle for Your Mind*,[10] extol the virtues of positioning a product so that the brand name becomes generic with the product. It's the basis for positioning strategy, and anyone in advertising knows it. Let's take a short step back to our Bayer case. In their book Trout and Ries use it as an example to discuss the power in a name:

> The tablets in a bottle of aspirin are Bayer. Not aspirin manufactured by a company called Bayer.... The great strength of a generic brand name is this close identification with the product itself. In the consumer's mind, Bayer is aspirin, and every other aspirin brand becomes 'imitation Bayer.[11]

The strength of positioning strategy cannot be questioned. But what is good for marketing may be terrible for protection of a trademark. The advertiser must be careful not to destroy a trademark in the process of building brand awareness.

The best method an advertiser can use to avoid genericide is to treat a trademark as a trademark. In other words, distinguish it from the type of product. How can you accomplish this? For copywriters, a trademark should always be an adjective that modifies the product name. It is not a noun; the noun names the type of product. Actually, the trademark is a proper adjective modifying a proper noun—allowing both words to be capitalized.

As an example, let's take a fictitious company called

Metropolis Manufacturing. It makes a car called the Metromobile. Now "Metromobile" is a trademark. In its advertising, to protect the trademark, Metropolis must not refer to its car merely as a Metromobile. It should refer to it as a Metromobile Automobile or Metromobile Car. (Also, note that a trademark is not a verb since you can't Metromobile to work.)

Here's the test to see if a trademark is treated as a trademark therefore avoiding possible genericide. A typical advertisement headline to accomplish this might read: "Enjoy the Freedom of the Road in a Metromobile Car." If you eliminate the trademark, "Metromobile," does the remaining sentence make sense? Aside from the fact that it would be a horrible headline, it would read: "Enjoy the Freedom of the Road in a Car." The headline still makes sense grammatically. Compare this to an incorrect usage of the mark. If the type of product were left out, the headline would read, "Enjoy the Freedom of the Road in a Metromobile." Now remove the trademark from this version, and the headline would make no sense: "Enjoy the Freedom of the Road in a ___." The sentence must make grammatical sense if the trademark is removed.

But let's be realistic. Not all advertisers follow these rules. One reason is that some trademarks are so strong the consumer invariably knows exactly what product is being referred to. How is it that a consumer can drive a Ford, smoke a Salem, use a box of Tide, drink a Coke, or wear a pair of Nikes? It happens because some trademarks are very well understood by consumers. They know exactly what product is being referred to when the term is used. This is the secondary meaning we discussed earlier. The consumer places the generic name with the trademark automatically in his mind. We saw this earlier when we discussed positioning. Yet, all trademarks are not so fortunate as to have that status. Only in cases where the generic term is understood so thoroughly can the advertiser feel secure that the trademark can stand alone. For new products, or lesser-known ones, habitual use of the trademark without mention of the generic product should be avoided. When Bayer first heard people ask, "What brand of aspirin do you use?," it should have seen what was coming.

SLOGANS

In some cases slogans may be trademarked. But those situations are controlled by strict guidelines. Slogans, if they qualify for protection, fall into the category of service marks. A trademark may consist of any slogan, but it is allowed protection only if it distinguishes the product.

In 1932 American Enka adopted the mark of a black rectangle with a thread extending through it. Below the logo was the name American Enka; above the logo was the slogan, "The Fate of a Fabric Hangs on a Thread." By 1939 Enka had modified its mark. The slogan remained, but the logo became a tag with the words "Fashion Approved" in it. Underneath the tag were the words "Enka Rayon."

Then in 1947 Enka applied for registration of its mark with the slogan. The Commissioner of Patents and Trademarks, John Marzall, declined to register the slogan. Enka then filed suit in *American Enka Corp.* v. *Marzall*,[12] to decide the matter.

The court determined that Enka could register its slogan with the logo. Enka was the only user of the slogan, and it had become widely known to identify its rayon yarn from any other. The slogan unquestionably indicated the origin of the mark.

Indeed, certain word combinations can operate as trademarks when they are so distinctive. The fact that the words comprise a slogan does not bar them from trademark status.

"We Smile More"

Marriott began using the slogan, "We Smile More," as an advertising and promotional line in 1964. In 1968 the hotel chain applied for registration of the slogan as a trademark after it learned that Ramada Inns had begun using the same line.

The case went to trial in *In re Marriott Corp.*,[13] where it was determined the slogan did qualify to be registered. A slogan does not have to be unique in verbiage to qualify. "[A] capability of identifying and distinguishing the source of goods or services is all that is required to support registration."

The court went on to say that "the function of a . . . mark is to indicate continuity of quality of services, i.e., that the quality of services rendered in connection with a particular mark is controlled by a single entity." Marriott showed that customers were aware of the slogan and recognized the mark as belonging to it. These consumers substantiated that they knew the slogan referred to Marriott, and only to Marriott. Indeed, the slogan indicated the source. The court allowed the registration of "We Smile More" as a trademark.

The Slogan That's A Mouthful

Everyone in advertising will no doubt remember McDonald's campaign in the mid-1970s that used the slogan:

• •

"TWOALLBEEFPATTIESSPECIALSAUCELETTUCECHEESE PICKLESONIONSONASESAMESEEDBUN."

• •

McDonald's began using the slogan in its advertising in late 1974. It spent over $2 million in advertising, using the slogan as its theme through the end of 1975. The advertising campaign included almost every media available from TV, radio, newspaper, magazine, billboards, through point-of-purchase, contests, and premiums.

In essence, McDonald's saturated the market with "TWOALLBEEFPATTIESSPECIALSAUCELETTUCECHEESE-PICKLESONIONSONASESAMESEEDBUN."

McDonald's applied for registration of its slogan as a

trademark in 1975, and *In re McDonald's Corp.*[14] resulted. At the hearing the argument was made in opposition to the application that the phrase was no more than a descriptive list of ingredients of a Big Mac sandwich. However, the phrase is a unique "and somewhat catchy arrangement and combination which in its entirety creates a commercial impression quite different from that of the individual words as they are ordinarily used."

Through its massive advertising campaign, McDonald's also met the second requirement for registration, that of knowledge of origin by the public. At the time, everyone who knew the name McDonald's, knew the slogan. There was little doubt the public knew that the phrase meant only McDonald's.

"America's Freshest Ice Cream"

When a slogan is a mere statement, puff, or irrelevant phrase, it will not be allowed protection. A good example of this is evident in the case, *In re Carvel Corp.*,[15] involving Carvel Ice Cream. Carvel wanted to register its slogan, "America's Freshest Ice Cream," which it had been using since 1978, along with its logo. However, as the court put it, the mark "is not a mark capable of distinguishing [Carvel's] goods from like goods of others . . . ."

Carvel attempted to argue its point that because it used the word "*fresh*" in relation to ice cream it is a distinctive mark. It felt that the word *fresh* was not normally associated with ice cream, and therefore it was distinctive. The court was not convinced. This simple expression of praise was not capable of functioning as a trademark. A common expression, such as the one Carvel used, could not indicate anything other than a motive toward high quality. It certainly could not indicate the origin of the mark to the general public. Hypothetically though, if it could have been proven that the slogan was well understood by the public to mean Carvel, and only Carvel, the outcome may have been different.

Strictly speaking, the Trademark Act does not prohibit expressions of praise (even if they are self-inflicted) from being registered. But in order for one to be registered, there must be enough originality or uniqueness to set it apart from other marks in the consumer's mind. It must distinguish the origin or owner of the mark for the consumer. Clearly, Carvel's slogan failed to accomplish this and therefore was refused registration.

Typical Slogans That Have Been Refused Registration

The following list presents a few more examples of typical slogans that have been refused registration.

"Best and Biggest Cigar"	Lewis Cigar Company
"America's Finest Overall"	Levi Strauss
"Tender Fresh"	Nash-Finch Fresh Cut Chicken
"Sudsy"	Parsons Ammonia
"Champagne"	Demos Salad Dressing with Champagne
"The Professional Health Care People"	Career Employment Services
"More Gun for the Money"	Mossberg Firearms
"America's Most Luxurious Mattress"	Englander Mattress Company
"For a Day, a Week, a Month or More!"	Brock Residence Inns

CONSIDERATIONS IN CHOOSING A TRADEMARK

When a company develops a new product, it generally creates a new name for it—and possibly a trademark. In many cases the ad agency is involved in choosing the name, so it's important to know what to consider in selecting a trademark.

Marks That Infringe Existing Marks

The most important concern in developing a new mark is establishing that it does not infringe on an existing mark. The new mark must not be the same as another existing mark or confusingly similar to an existing mark.

Believe it or not, there is no single place where the applicant can look to find a list of all trademarks. Simply checking with the Trademark Office isn't enough. One reason for this is that some marks may be registered in a particular state (we look at this later in the chapter). Another reason is that a mark may have been used for many years without being registered. The original mark would be allowed protection in many cases under common law (refer to the section "Trademark Registers" for an explanation). There are, however, professional trademark search services. These services are fairly thorough and use a number of sources to determine if the mark already exists as a trademark. But beware: They are not 100 percent conclusive.

It is important to check new trademarks before putting them into use, as Goodyear found out. Goodyear is the world's largest tire manufacturer;. in 1974 its net sales reached over $5.25 billion. A minor competitor, Big O Tire Dealers, manufactured a private label tire of its own. In late 1973, Big O named its line of tires "Big Foot." The name appeared on the sidewall of each tire.

In July of 1974 Goodyear adopted the name "Big Foot" for its new Custom Polysteel Radial tire. The name also appeared on the side of the tire. The firm hired a trademark search firm to investigate any existing trademark conflicts. None were shown. Feeling secure, Goodyear developed an advertising campaign to promote its new tire, Big Foot. Within a year, Goodyear had spent over $9.6 million on the advertising of this single product. Typical headlines from Goodyear ads were:

• •

Bigfoot, the new Polysteel Radial.
Bigfoot. The Polysteel Radial that keeps
its feet even in the rain.
Only from Goodyear.

• • • • • • • • • • • • • •

In August of 1974, Goodyear learned of the existing and previous trademark held by Big O Tires. Goodyear tried to buy the rights to use the name from Big O, but the offer was not accepted. When Big O refused the offer, it mentioned the possibility of a lawsuit if Goodyear did not stop using the trademark "Big Foot." As stated in court, Goodyear informed Big O president Norman Affleck, that if Big O did bring suit, "the case would be in litigation long enough that Goodyear might obtain all the benefits it desired from the term 'Big Foot.'"

In fact, Big O Tires did sue in *Big O Tire Dealers, Inc.* v. *Goodyear Tire & Rubber Co.*[16] The problem occurred because Goodyear, through their search firm, failed to verify an existing trademark for "Big Foot." Since there was such a trademark, Goodyear lost the case.

At trial it came to light that when Goodyear learned of the Big O trademark, not only did it not discontinue its ad campaign, which claimed exclusiveness, it continued to willfully infringe upon the existing mark. Goodyear basically thumbed its huge corporate nose at Big O. Because of Goodyear's action and its disregard for Big O's trademark, the court awarded $678,302 in compensatory damages and $4,069,812 in punitive damages.

Marks That Cannot Be Registered

There are a few areas that could disqualify a mark from registration. These were listed earlier in the section on the two registers and their requirements to qualify for registration. Now let's take a closer look.

Confusing or Deceptive Marks. Marks cannot be registered that are "likely . . . to cause confusion, or to cause mistake, or to deceive."[17] This could also occur through the use of a similar or exact duplication of another trademark.

Marks that Are Descriptive of a Place or Function. Marks cannot be registered as trademarks if they are only functionally or geographically descriptive, or if the mark is only a surname. In other words, the mark must be distinctive.

Use of Flags or Insignias. Marks cannot use flags, coats of arms, insignia of cities, states, the federal government, or foreign countries.

Use of Names or Personal Identities. Marks cannot use the name, image, or signature of a person, unless written permission is given.

Use of Immoral Marks. Marks cannot be "immoral" or "scandalous."[18] This includes names that are contemptuous or disparage a person, institution, established belief, or national symbol.

Protection Only for a Specific Category of Use

Keep in mind that a mark can only be registered for the specific category in which it is used. We saw this illustrated earlier in the *Sweet 'N Low* case. The Patent and Trademark Office maintains records for the classification of trademarks under the specific category of goods or services for which the mark is used.

The name Johnnie Walker has meant high quality Scotch Whiskey since 1880, when the trademark was created. Since its inception, the name was heavily advertised and promoted. As a result, the name Johnnie Walker has gained an excellent and very recognizable reputation. I think I can safely say almost every adult knows the name "Johnnie Walker," and quickly associates it with whiskey.

In the early 1950's, Tampa Cigar Company began marketing one of its cigars under the name Johnnie Walker. This irritated John Walker & Sons (the whiskey company) enough to file a lawsuit: *Tampa Cigar Co. v. John Walker & Sons, Ltd.*[19] Clearly, the use of "Johnnie Walker" on cigars was an infringement. Tampa tried to take advantage of the fame and reputation built on the Johnnie Walker name. In effect, Tampa Cigar tried to create the impression that the makers of the whiskey were the makers of the cigars. This is called "palming off."

Tampa argued that because the products were different, it should be allowed to use the name. "That," the court said, "we decline to do." While the products, whiskey and cigars, are different, they are often sold to the public at the same time and in the same stores. Bars, liquor stores, restaurants, markets, convenience stores all sell these items. Johnnie Walker whiskey and cigars could literally be placed side by side and sold to the same person at the same time. Even though the products were different, the cigar's use of the mark was an infringement.

On the other hand, there are cases where no infringement exists. A good example of this can be seen in *Holiday Inns, Inc. v. Holiday Out In America.*[20]

Holiday Inns had developed a considerable reputation with the public for its chain of travel motels. Its reputation was one of consistent high quality. Keeping close watch over its marks of "Holiday Inn, Holiday Inns of America," and "The Nation's Innkeeper," Holiday Inns, Inc. guarded its service marks.

In 1966 another company opened a series of trailer parks under the name "Holiday Out" and "Holiday Out in America." Holiday Out registered its trademark on January 23, 1967, describing its business as "maintaining and operating campground facilities for campsite owners." When Holiday Inn learned of this, it filed suit in July of that year.

The court found that there was no likelihood of the consumer being confused by the two trademarks. They were totally different markets, and no proof was shown to validate Holiday Inn's claim of infringement. The court felt that allowing both trademarks to be used "is not reasonably calculated to cause confusion or mistake or to deceive." Holiday Out was allowed to retain its trademark.

DECEPTIVE FORMS OF TRADEMARKS

In addition to the Trademark Office's regulations, the FTC can become involved if the trademark or trade name used is deceptive. The FTC's concern is any form of deception of the consumer, whether in an ad or a name. Having a trademark registered does not protect it against causing other violations of the law. In cases where the name does fall into the deceptive or false advertising arena, the FTC can force the company to stop using the name.

A rental car company using the trade name "Dollar-A-Day Car Rental" was brought into court by the FTC in *Resort Car Rental System, Inc. v. F.T.C.*[21] It was shown that the name created an obvious impression to the public. The court said: "The 'Dollar-A-Day' slogan carries strong psychological appeal. Its connotations are obvious." The consumer could expect to be charged $1 per day for a rental car. This was certainly not true, however.

This case turned on the issue of deceptive advertising. The point here is that trademark registration did not create a shield to protect what was essentially a deceptive claim in the guise of a trade name. Dollar-A-Day was required to change its name.

FOREIGN WORDS AS TRADEMARKS

Another area to consider is the use of foreign words in trademarks. Some companies try to register marks using foreign words in place of the English version that they could not ordinarily register in English. If the words are descriptive of the product in that foreign language, then the United States will also consider them not qualified to be protected under trademark law. The guide should be that if the mark would not qualify in English, for whatever reason, it wouldn't qualify using another language either.

On another point, if a company desires to market its product in other countries, it must consider the trademark laws of those governments. They all vary and may have a large impact on the choice of a trademark. A specialist should be consulted in this case, since the requirements of foreign countries far exceed the scope of this book.

RESTRICTIONS IMPOSED BY STATE LAW

While the Trademark Act grants protection of trademarks on a federal level, the separate states can also grant trademark registration. However, only trademarks for professional services may be registered by the state. This applies only to businesses that the state categorizes as "professional" (doctors, attorneys, certified public accountants, etc.). These firms which are prohibited from using fictitious names may trademark their firm name even though they are using surnames. The regulations of the respective state should be considered in these situations.

Cities, counties and states also maintain registers of business names. While these are not federal trademark registers, a company should consult these sources for any conflicts of name, origin or identity, which could cause legal problems.

---

[1] Trademark Act of 1946, section 45, 15 U.S.C., Section 1127 (1976).

[2] 15 U.S.C., section 1111.

[3] *Four Roses Products Co.* v. *Small Grain Distilling & Drug Co.*, 29 F.2d 959 (D.C.Cir. 1928).

[4] *Fox-Stanley Photo Products, Inc.* v. *Otaguro*, 339 F. Supp. 1293 (D. Mass 1972).

[5] *Duffy-Mott Co.* v. *Cumberland Packing Co.*, 154 U.S.P.Q. 498 (TTAB 1967).

[6] *Bayer Co.* v. *United Drug Co.*, 272 F. 605 (SDNY 1921).

[7] *Haughten Elevator Co.* v. *Seeberger*, 85 U.S.P.Q. 80 (Comm'r 1950).

[8] *American Thermos Products Co.* v. *Aladdin Industries, Inc.*, 169 U.S.P.Q. 85 (D. Conn. 1970).

[9] *Intel Corp.* v. *Radiation, Inc.*, 184 U.S.P.Q. 54 (TTAB 1974).

[10] Al Ries and Jack Trout, *Positioning: The Battle for Your Mind*
(New York: McGraw-Hill).

[11] *Positioning: The Battle for Your Mind*, Page 105.

[12] *American Enka Corp.* v. *Marzall*, 92 U.S.P.Q. 111 (D.C.Cir. 1952).

[13] *In re Marriott Corp.*, 517 F.2d 1364 (C.C.P.A. 1975).

[14] *In re McDonald's Corp.*, 199 U.S.P.Q. 490 (TTAB 1978).

[15] *In re Carvel Corp.*, 223 U.S.P.Q. 65 (TTAB 1984).

[16] *Big O Tire Dealers, Inc.* v. *Goodyear Tire & Rubber Co.*, 561 F.2d 1365 (1977).

[17] 15 U.S.C., section 1052(d).

[18] 15 U.S.C., section 1052(a).

[19] *Tampa Cigar Co.* v. *John Walker & Sons, Ltd.*, 222 F.2d 460 (5th Cir. 1955),
110 U.S.P.Q. 249 (Com. Pat. 1956).

[20] *Holiday Inns, Inc.* v. *Holiday Out In America*, 481 F.2d 445 (5th Cir. 1973).

[21] *Resort Car Rental System, Inc.* v. *FTC*, 518 F.2d 962 (9th Cir. 1975).

CHAPTER 8

COMPARATIVE ADVERTISING

One man's ceiling is another man's floor.
—*Paul Simon*

The year was 1949, June to be exact. At 350 Madison Avenue in New York, Ned Doyle, Maxwell Dane, and William Bernbach, along with 13 employees, started an ad agency with a simple philosophy of Bernbach's: "Don't be slick. Tell the truth." Bernbach had a clear and deliberate approach to advertising. He felt that most advertising was dull and failed to motivate the consumer. "Business is spending money for advertising," he would say, "and is achieving boredom with typical American efficiency."

Doyle Dane Bernbach has produced its share of memorable ad campaigns over the years since its inception. In the beginning, the agency took on clients like Ohrbach's, Levy's Rye Bread, Polaroid, El Al Airlines and in 1959, Volkswagen. Doyle Dane Bernbach created the Volkswagen campaign that stands as one of the industry's best.

Then, in the fall of 1962, Avis moved its $1.5 million account from McCann-Erickson to Doyle Dane Bernbach. At that time Hertz was the car-rental leader and pulling way ahead of Avis. So, Doyle Dane Bernbach gathered art director Helmut Krone and copywriter Paula Green together. They came away with the first of a new series of Avis ads.

The first ad read:

● ●
Avis is only No. 2 in rent-a-cars.
So why go with us?
"We try harder. (When you're not the biggest, you have to.)

We can't afford dirty ashtrays. Or half-empty gas tanks.
Or worn wipers. Or unwashed cars. Or low tires.
Or anything less than seat-adjusters that adjust.
Heaters that heat. Defrosters that defrost.
Obviously, the thing we try hardest for is just to be nice.
To start you out right with a new car, like a lively
super-torque Ford, and a pleasant smile.
To let you know, say, where you can get a good, hot
pastrami sandwich in Duluth.
Why?
Because we can't afford to take you for granted.
Go with us the next time.
The line at our counter is shorter.

• •

Before the client was shown the new ad, Bernbach
commissioned a consumer survey to pretest the ad. It scored very
poorly. Nonetheless, Bernbach sold the client on the ad. Two years
later Avis had increased its market share by 28 percent.

While Avis never mentioned who it tried harder than,
everyone knew. Hertz was the number one car rental company at
the time. Because of this, the Avis ads have become acknowledged
as the first major comparative advertising campaign.

While the Avis campaign might have been the first
comparative ad campaign, many more have followed, and they
have run the gamut. My personal favorite started life in the late
1970's. The commercial depicted a small, bulbous store owner
standing in his electric light bulb store. On the phone he
proclaims: "If those bulbs aren't here tomorrow morning, I am out
of business!" In the next scene, Dingbat Air Freight pulls up in
front of the store, two days late. The courier scurries around
frantically looking at the front door. A sign across the front of the
store reads, "OUT OF BUSINESS."

Federal Express took on the giants of air freight, Emery,
United Parcel, and even the United States Postal Service.

Its slogan, "Twice as good as the best in the business," became fighting words for Federal Express. The company started in 1971, and promptly fell $30 million into debt. But by 1983, Federal Express had broken the $1 billion mark in annual revenue. The Federal Express ads, created by Ally & Gargano Advertising, were classics of comparative advertising. They did the job, and did it very well.

When a company compares its product to another, both are identified either by name, implication, or reputation. The use of another company's identity involves the use of its image trademark, or trade name. If this use is truthful, honest, and accurate the law allows products to compare themselves. On the other hand, if Bunko Company compares its product as being superior to Binko's product and a deception results, the image and therefore value of Binko's trademark can suffer. As we saw in Chapter 7, a company's trademark is of great value, and can be protected by its owner under the law.

Therefore, comparative advertising is based on trademark law. In fact, comparative advertising is controlled by a section of the Trademark Act, which will be discussed later. Under this law there is nothing illegal about comparing a product to that of a competitor unless a deception is created. When this happens, there are basically two avenues of court action for victims. One is under federal law: Section 43(a) of the Lanham Act.[1] The other is under state law: Antidilution statutes. We examine the advantages and disadvantages of both in this chapter.

THE DEVELOPMENT OF COMPARATIVE ADVERTISING

Today, comparative advertising bombards the consumer. But this hasn't always been the case. For the most part, comparative ads were not used prior to the 1970's. One main reason was that mentioning a competitor's name gave recognition to it and, in effect, free publicity. For this reason, major companies rarely had any interest in comparative ads. These companies felt that nothing was to be gained from mentioning competitors.

Many companies also felt that showing a competitor in a bad light would create consumer sympathy for the competitor, thereby causing consumers to buy its products. As a result, companies did not want to be pictured as a "big bully picking on the little kid."

Taking part in comparative advertising was also considered by many advertising agencies to be unethical, hitting below the belt so to speak. Many advertisers and their agencies also shied away from this practice for moral reasons. The main deterrent, however, was that the FTC and the television networks would not allow comparative ads.

There was a concern over the use of advertisements that compared products. Until 1972 two of the television networks and some major print publications banned comparative ads altogether. But in 1972 the FTC came out in favor of comparative ads, and the media changed its stance. The media finally accepted comparative advertisements. The FTC proclaimed that by having the ability to compare the features of various products, the consumer could make a more informed and intelligent purchasing decision, as long as the comparison was fair and accurate.

The FTC Policy Statement established the commission's position on comparative advertising. The commission has supported the use of brand comparisons where the bases of comparison are clearly identified. Comparative advertising, when truthful and nondeceptive, is a source of important information to consumers and assists them in making rational purchase decisions. Comparative advertising encourages product improvement and innovation, and can lead to lower prices in the marketplace.[2]

Suave Shampoo's comparative advertising is a good example of the FTC's position. The ads for Suave compared it to other leading brands and claimed that Suave performed as well, but at half the price. The consumer benefited because that person could purchase a product that would do the same job at a lower cost. Because of its campaign, Suave Shampoo increased its sales from $10 million to $50 million in just four years.

Comparative advertising also contributed to a 20 percent increase in sales in one month for Wendy's Restaurants. Wendy's superb "Where's the Beef?" campaign compared its single to McDonald's Big Mac and Burger King's Whopper.

Comparative advertising can have positive benefits for both the consumer and the advertiser, but it must be fair, truthful, and accurate. Otherwise it can be a dangerous instrument. This is why the FTC and the courts keep a very watchful eye on comparative ads.

The television networks, to help assure truthful comparative advertising, have established guidelines for advertisers to follow. The National Broadcasting Company's (NBC) guidelines are reproduced as an example in Exhibit 8-1 below.

EXHIBIT 8-1:
NATIONAL BROADCASTING COMPANY
DEPARTMENT OF BROADCAST STANDARDS

Comparative Advertising Guidelines

NBC will accept comparative advertising which identifies, directly or by implication, a competing product or service. As with all other advertising, each substantive claim, direct or implied, must be substantiated to NBC's satisfaction and the commercial must satisfy the following guidelines and standards for comparative advertising established by NBC:

1. Competitors shall be fairly and properly identified.

2. Advertisers shall refrain from disparaging or unfairly attacking competitors, competing products, services or other industries through the use of representation or claims, direct or implied, that are false, deceptive, misleading or have the tendency to mislead.

3. The identification must be for comparison purposes and not simply to upgrade by association.

4. The advertising should compare related or similar properties or ingredients of the product, dimension to dimension, feature to feature, or wherever possible be a side-by-side demonstration.

5. The property being compared must be significant in terms of value or usefulness of the product or service to the consumer.

6. The difference in the properties being compared must be measurable and significant.

7. Pricing comparisons may raise special problems that could mislead, rather than enlighten, viewers. For certain classifications of products, retail prices may be extremely volatile, may be fixed by the retailer rather than the product advertiser, and may not only differ from outlet to outlet but from week to week within the same outlet. Where these circumstances might apply, NBC will accept commercials containing price comparisons only on a clear showing that the comparative claims accurately, fairly and substantially reflect the actual price differentials at retail outlets throughout the broadcast area, and that these price differentials are not likely to change during the period the commercial is broadcast.

8. When a commercial claim involves market relationships, other than price, which are also subject to fluctuation (such as but not limited to sales position or exclusivity), the substantiation for the claim will be considered valid only as long as the market conditions on which the claim is based continue to prevail.

9. As with all other advertising, whenever necessary, NBC may require substantiation to be updated from time to time, and may reexamine substantiation, where the need to do so is indicated as the result of a challenge or other developments.

Challenge Procedure

Where appropriate, NBC will implement the following procedures in the event a commercial is challenged by another advertiser.

1. If an advertiser elects to challenge the advertising of another advertiser, he shall present his challenge and supporting data to NBC in a form available for transmittal to the challenged advertiser.

2. The challenged advertiser will then have an opportunity to respond directly to the challenger. NBC will maintain the confidentiality of the advertiser's original supporting data which was submitted for substantiation of the claims made in the commercial. However, NBC will ask the challenged advertiser to provide it with a copy of its response to the challenger and, where the response is submitted directly to NBC, the challenged advertiser will be requested to forward a copy of its response to the challenger.

3. Where NBC personnel do not have the expertise to make a judgment on technical issues raised by a challenge, NBC will take appropriate measures in its discretion to assist the advertiser and challenger to resolve their differences, including encouraging them to obtain a determination from an acceptable third party.

4. NBC will not withdraw a challenged advertisement from the broadcast schedule unless:

a. it is directed to do so by the incumbent advertiser;

b. the incumbent advertiser refuses to submit the controversy for review by some appropriate agency when deemed necessary by NBC;

c. a decision is rendered by NBC against the incumbent advertiser;

d. the challenged advertiser, when requested, refuses to cooperate in some other substantive area; or

e. NBC, prior to final disposition of the challenge, determines that the substantiation for the advertising has been seriously brought into question that the advertising can no longer be considered substantiated to NBC's satisfaction.

5. NBC may take additional measures in its discretion to resolve questions raised by advertising claims.

(Excerpt courtesy of National Broadcasting Company, Inc. © 1987. National Broadcasting Company, Inc. All Rights Reserved.)

TYPES OF COMPARATIVE ADVERTISEMENTS

There are basically three types of comparative ads. The most obvious type includes ads that specifically name the competitor and the product. One form of this can be seen in Suave's advertising claim that it's as good as five other named shampoos at half the price. This includes ads that attack the other product. Here are some examples: Scope mouthwash ads claim that Listerine gives "medicine breath," and Minute Maid lemonade ads label Country Time as being the "no lemon lemonade."

The second type of comparative ad is more subtle. It does not name the competitor, but rather implies it. The Avis ad campaign discussed earlier falls into this area because Avis does not name the competitor, but the implication is understood by everyone; there's no doubt that it is Hertz.

The last type involves ads that do not identify the competitors. Comparisons between "our product" and "Brand X" are good examples. This type of comparative ad was very popular in years past, probably because it was safe.

THE LANHAM ACT

The federal government has developed a policing resource through private court action that can overcome the inherent drawbacks to an FTC suit for deception. Section 5 of the FTC Act allows the government to sue companies for deceptive advertising. But what about the company that was the victim of the deception?

The Lanham Act allows one company to sue another

company directly for damages due to deception and also serves as a way of avoiding the red tape, time, and expense of an FTC action. However, to qualify under the Lanham Act, the deceptive claim must involve a comparison of products. The Lanham Act provides for private litigation for "all actions . . . without regard to the amount in controversy or to . . . the citizenship of the parties."[3]

Congress passed Section 43(a) of the Lanham Act in 1946 providing:

> Any person who shall . . . use in connection with any goods . . . any false description or representation, including words or other symbols tending falsely to describe or represent the same, and shall cause such goods or services to enter into commerce . . .shall be liable to a civil action by . . . <u>any person who believes that he is or is likely to be damaged</u> by the use of any such false description or representation. (Emphasis added.)

The real power here is in the phrase, "believes that he is or is likely to be damaged." The important word is "likely." Unlike many other areas of law that we've seen, the Lanham Act does not require that proof of actual damage be shown, only that damage is likely. This is a very broad concept, which gives the act tremendous strength.

Another benefit to the Lanham Act is expressed in the phrase "any person." This means Section 43(a) actions are available not only to companies who are in competition, but individual consumers as well. For this reason, advertisers must be very aware of the Lanham Act and its provisions. The reasons a company may decide not to sue a competitor, even if it is the victim of a deceptive comparison, usually won't apply to the consumer. Deceived consumers, now, are a concern to advertisers.

The courts originally placed severe limitations on actions brought under Section 43(a) of the Lanham Act. As we have seen before, it takes time for courts to adjust to new legislation. Just as water seeks its own level, laws also need a period of adjustment to find their level in society. For example, the courts initially refused to act unless 30 or more cases were reported against an advertiser. However, all this changed in 1954 when the Lanham Act found its level as a result of the following case.

L'Aiglon Apparel manufactured and sold through an ad campaign a distinctively styled ladies dress for $17.95. In its advertisements, L'Aiglon pictured its dress along with the price. This combination of picture and price became very identifiable with the public at the time.

Lana Lobel, a retailer, sold a different dress of much lower quality. Lobel advertised its dress in a national magazine for the price of $6.95, available through mail order. The Lobel ad showed an actual photographic reproduction of the L'Aiglon dress. This fraudulently represented to the buying public that the L'Aiglon dress was being sold at $6.95—a representation that was not true.

Lobel's ads provoked L'Aiglon to sue in *L'Aiglon Apparel, Inc. v. Lana Lobel Inc.*[4] L'Aiglon alleged that two forms of damage existed. First, Lobel's misrepresentation "caused some trade to be diverted" from L'Aiglon to Lobel. And, second, other trade was lost by L'Aiglon because of the inaccurate impression given to the public that L'Aiglon had been selling a dress worth only $6.95 for $17.95.

The resulting lawsuit was filed under Section 43(a) of the Lanham Act. And, the court gave a new and clear interpretation for future cases to follow. The court said:

> It seems to us that Congress has defined a statutory civil wrong of false representation of goods in commerce and has given a broad class of suitors injured or likely to be injured by such wrong the right to relief in the federal courts.

This case interpreted the Lanham Act to mean that a single

individual or company could bring suit. The earlier requirement that there be a minimum of 30 victims before a suit could be initiated was abolished. L'Aiglon won its case against Lobel and helped establish the Lanham Act as a versatile tool against deceptive comparative advertising. The decision established the way the Lanham Act would be interpreted from then on— the way it is today.

The Trademark Law Revision Act Of 1988

On October 19, 1988, Congress passed the Trademark Law Revision Act of 1988. Although the 1988 act deals primarily with trademark matters, it also changed advertising law in several respects. Certain changes may prove significant, but whether they will actually have a material affect on advertising litigation remains an open issue.

Section 43(a) of the Lanham Act has been amended to read as follows:

(a) Any person who, on or in connection with any goods or services, or any container for goods, uses in commerce any word, term, name, symbol, or device, or any combination thereof, or any false designation of origin, false or misleading description of fact, or false or misleading representation of fact, which—

(1) is likely to cause confusion, or to cause mistake, or to deceive as to the affiliation, connection, or association of such person with another person, or as to the origin, sponsorship, or approval of his or her goods, services, or commercial activities by another person, or

(2) in commercial advertising or promotion, misrepresents the nature, characteristics, qualities, or geographic origin of his or her or another person's goods, services, or commercial activities, shall be

liable in a civil action by any person who believes
that he or she is or is likely to be damaged by such
act.

As amended, section 43(a) will make illegal any advertising
that disparages "another person's goods, services, or commercial
activities." This change was intended to circumvent decisions in
cases holding that section 43(a) extended only to false statements
concerning the advertiser's own products and did not apply to
claims that merely disparaged the products of another.

Disparagement (often referred to as trade libel or injurious
falsehood) is a false and deliberate attack on the advertiser's
product. This disparagement tends to diminish the respect,
confidence or esteem in the product that is attacked.
Disparagement exists where the quality of the advertiser's product
is impugned, and violates the Lanham Act. While this a new
element in section 43(a), it is one that the advertiser must be
aware of.

Another change to section 43(a) was its application to false
representations pertaining to, among other things, the
"commercial activities" of the advertiser or of another person.
Section 43(a) previously applied only to false representations
pertaining to the "inherent quality or characteristics" of the
defendant's "goods." After the 1988 amendment however, the
section applies to false representations pertaining to any
"commercial activities."

GROUPS THAT CAN SUE UNDER THE LANHAM ACT

As mentioned earlier, under the Lanham Act any "person"
may bring a civil suit "who believes that he is or is likely to be
damaged by the use of any such false description or
representation." This broad definition creates a huge group of
people who are potential litigants. Under the Lanham Act the term

"people" covers businesses, groups, or individuals. In the following sections we will examine consumer and business groups separately.

The Consumer's Standing To Sue

Although an individual consumer may bring suit under the Lanham Act, in practice, this is not very common, mainly because the cost of a court battle is so high.

Some, but not all, courts feel that individual consumers must show a "commercial interest" in order to bring suit. In the case that follows we see how the court dealt with both issues.

Arneson, an inventor, brought suit against the Raymond Lee Organization, a patent service. The suit claimed that Raymond Lee had lured clients through misleading advertisements. The case was *Arneson* v. *Raymond Lee Organization, Inc.*[5]

The court felt that the wording in the act should be taken literally, i.e., "any person" could bring an action under the Lanham Act. Arneson was "any person" and was allowed to sue Raymond Lee. That is what the act says, and that is what it means. After all, consumers can be injured by deceptive comparative advertising, as well as competitors. An ad can clearly compare two products, pointing out the flaws in one but if this is done through incorrect, misleading, or deceptive statements, the consumer will be damaged when the claim is relied on to make the purchase. As a result, the consumer will purchase the product based on incorrect information, and a commercial interest will become involved.

A Company's Standing To Sue

The most common Lanham Act issue involves direct competitors in business; companies having a commercial interest that is directly threatened by deceptive comparative advertising. Situations that are most likely to create court actions involve companies or products who compete directly for the same market. We see this in most of the cases illustrated throughout the rest of this chapter.

A company may however, have a commercial interest even though it does not compete directly with the other company. As an example, two companies may be in totally different industries, selling to completely separate markets. Yet, one company may create a deception that affects the other company's name or image.

The best example I can recall to illustrate this point occurred in 1978. This is also one of the more unique cases we discuss in this book. In November of that year, Pussycat Cinemas began showing an X-rated movie called *Debbie Does Dallas*. The film was described by the court as "a gross and revolting sex film whose plot, to the extent that there is one, involves a cheerleader at a fictional high school, Debbie, who has been selected to become a Texas Cowgirl." (Courts sometimes make editorial opinions.) The movie ends with a scene showing Debbie in a cheerleader's uniform bearing a striking resemblance to the outfit worn by the Dallas Cowboys Cheerleaders. In fact, 12 minutes of the film shows Debbie engaging in various sexual acts while wearing all, or part, of the uniform.

The movie was promoted with a poster showing Debbie wearing the same outfit, i.e., a combination of white boots, white shorts, blue blouse, white star-studded vest and belt, all of the same style and cut as that used by the Dallas Cowboys Cheerleaders.

As soon as the Dallas Cowboys Football Club learned of the movie, the organization filed suit under the Lanham Act in *Dallas Cowboys Cheerleaders, Inc. v. Pussycat Cinema, Ltd.*[6] seeking an injunction to prohibit the distribution and showing of *Debbie Does Dallas* because of the movie's use of the Dallas Cowboy image and trademark.

The actual Dallas Cowboys Football Club employs 36 women who perform as the Dallas Cowboys Cheerleaders. *The Dallas Cowboys Cheerleaders, Dallas Cowgirls,* and *Texas Cowgirls* are all registered trademarks. The group has gained world-wide exposure (excuse the pun) and has made many public appearances outside of football stadiums. As a result, the Dallas Cowboys organization has earned substantial revenue from its commercial ventures involving the Cheerleaders.

The Dallas Cowboys wanted the movie banned because it felt that the public was likely to be deceived by the representations in the movie and promotional poster. Pussycat claimed, as a defense, that the public would not be confused about the origin of the film. Such confusion is a requirement the courts look for in Section 43(a) actions. Yet, the court said about the existence of consumer confusion, "the public's belief that the [trademark's] owner sponsored or otherwise approved the use of the trademark satisfies the confusion requirement."

Simply put, the issue here was the association between *Debbie Does Dallas* and the Dallas Cowboys Football Club—or, more accurately, the assumed association between the two. In fact, a commercial interest existed even though the two "products" did not directly compete. The movie did create a confusion in the consumer's mind and injured the Dallas Cowboys' business, name, and reputation. The Dallas Cowboys Cheerleaders won their case.

REQUIRED ELEMENTS THAT CREATE A LANHAM ACT VIOLATION

The concept of the Lanham Act is very simple. When an ad claims a superiority over another product, a comparison is used. This occurs many times in today's advertising— Mitsubishi compares itself against Toyota, Hebrew National against Oscar Mayer, and Chrysler against Ford.

However, if that comparison is disparaging, deceptive or misleading, a lawsuit may be brought by the victim. But certain specific conditions must exist in order to create a violation of the act. In fact, there are five elements that must exist:
- A false statement about the product must be made;
- The advertising must have actually deceived or have the

tendency to deceive;
- The deception must be material;
- The advertised product must have entered interstate commerce; and
- There must be injury or a likelihood of injury.

One case where all of these requirements developed involved two power tool manufacturers, Skil and Rockwell. The two companies manufacture portable electric drills and jigsaws for sale to the consumer. In 1973, Rockwell began a major national advertising campaign using television, magazine, and newspaper. It was estimated that the campaign reached approximately 80 million people.

The Rockwell campaign revolved around a comparison of product testing, which had been done by an independent testing lab. Under "supposedly normal-use situations," Skil, Rockwell, and other manufacturers' tools were tested. The results of this independent testing was used in Rockwell's ad campaign. In the ads, Skil products were clearly shown and were identifiable by their labels.

The Lanham Act was violated because Rockwell's ads were not factually accurate regarding the performance of the Skil product line. Mainly, the test results used to compare product performance were biased. The testing was not conducted under normal-use conditions. The Skil products were put through much more demanding test conditions than would have been encountered in normal use, which was not disclosed in the advertising.

As a result, Rockwell used false, misleading, deceptive, and incomplete claims in its ads about Skil. When Skil realized the content of Rockwell's ads, it filed suit in *Skil Corp.* v. *Rockwell International Corp.*[7]

Skil not only sought an injunction against Rockwell, it also wanted damages for its loss of profits and damage to its name, which would affect future earning power. This one case developed the guidelines for the five elements required to bring a lawsuit under the Lanham Act. Now let's examine each requirement.

1. Making False Statements About A Product

The first requirement to bring suit under the Lanham Act is that the ad must create a deception in one form or another by making disparaging, false or partially correct claims, or failing to disclose material facts about its product.

Going back to our case, Rockwell made false statements about the performance qualities of Skil tools. The facts used in its ads were supposedly the result of testing the tools under normal-use conditions. This was not the case, however, so the results used in the ads were clearly false, misleading, and deceptive.

2. Requirement That Advertising Actually Deceived Or Has A Tendency To Deceive

The second element required is that the advertisement actually deceived consumers or had a tendency to deceive a substantial portion of the intended audience. This also refers to the confusion requirement we saw in the *Dallas v. Pussycat* case. Confusion is another way of saying "tendency to deceive."

Consumers who buy power tools base their decision on many factors: price; the features of the tool; performance; and durability. If a consumer buys a Rockwell power tool over a Skil tool, it would be for one or more of these reasons. If, as in this case, the consumer buys the Rockwell product based on the performance features it claims to have over Skil, the consumer has been clearly deceived. Since the Rockwell ads gave factually incorrect information in the comparison of Skil products, actual deception occurred.

3. The Deception Must Be Material

The third requirement necessary to bring suit is that any

deception created must be a material one. That is, it must have been likely to have influenced the purchasing decision. We saw this in Chapters 2 and 3 in the discussion of deception and the FTC Act. The same reasoning applies here.

In the Rockwell case, its false and misleading claims involved the performance of Skil products. This is a primary criterion for purchasing a power tool, as discussed in the previous section. Statistics about the durability and performance of a power tool would weigh heavily in the consumer's decision to purchase or not to purchase a specific brand of product. Rockwell's deceptive statements were, without question, material.

4. The Advertised Product Must Have Entered Interstate Commerce

The fourth element required under the Lanham Act is that the goods advertised were involved in interstate commerce. Simply, the product must have been engaged in commerce between two or more states. At first glance this may seem to disqualify many products. However, the courts feel that if any portion of the product—during any stage of its manufacture—crossed state lines, (or even if the product has an "effect" on interstate commerce) then the product is considered to have entered interstate commerce.

It is not just the final product that can meet the interstate requirement. If any part of the tool, say the power cord, is purchased out of state, then interstate commerce is involved. This means that many more products qualify under the interstate commerce requirement than would first appear.

In the case of Rockwell, both its and Skil's finished products were sold in every state and therefore were clearly involved in interstate commerce; there was no need to look into the manufacturing of either product to see if a more subtle form of interstate commerce was involved.

5. Injury Or Likelihood Of Injury Must Exist

The final requirement that must be present in order to sue under this act is that the advertisement has injured, or is likely to injure. Actual injury can result either from the diversion of sales or by the weakening of good will belonging to the product or service.

In the Rockwell case actual injury occurred in both forms. For Skil, the injury involved sales (lost profits) that were lost due to the deception. Skil also suffered potential future injury because, in the consumer's eye, Skil products were of a lesser quality as a result of Rockwell's deceptive advertising. In essence, the future selling power of Skil's long established name and reputation had been diminished. By the way, Skil won its case. It received an injunction and was awarded damages.

TYPES OF CLAIMS THAT VIOLATE THE LANHAM ACT

As the use of comparison advertisements grew, certain types of claims began to appear. Of those, a certain group has emerged that can violate the Lanham Act—claims that a product does something that others don't do. If the product claims are true, accurate and can be supported, this is legal.

However, claims that unjustifiably attack another product's qualities or performance or do so without support are another matter. There are a few different forms that this can take. The claim may be implied or it may be created, for example, through the use of a survey, disclaimer, or trademark.

Implied Claims

Certain claims are literally true but create a misleading impression as seen in the FTC's interpretation of deceptive advertising. This can also occur from a comparative advertising standpoint. A good example can be seen in a series of ads run by Hertz in early 1984 that contained the following copy:

• • • •
Hertz
has more new cars
than Avis has cars.
If you'd like to drive some of the newest
cars on the road, rent from Hertz.
Because we have more
new 1984 cars than Avis
or anyone else has cars—new or old.
Hertz. The #1 way to rent a car.
• • • • • • • • • • • • • • • • • • • •

The above ad was produced by Hertz's ad agency Scali, McCabe & Sloves. Obviously, the objective of the ad was to lure renters away from Avis and to Hertz. The lure was based on the claim that Hertz had more cars available for rental. Therefore, Hertz implied that it had an advantage over Avis, an advantage that consumers should exploit. The reality though was quite different. While the statements were literally accurate, they painted an inaccurate picture for the consumer.

Here's the problem. As of the time the ad ran, Hertz had a total of 97,000 (1984 model) cars. Avis, on the other hand, had a total of 95,224 (1984 model) cars. So, literally, the claim that Hertz had more 1984 model cars than Avis was true. However, of the 97,000 Hertz cars, only 91,000 were available for rental: The others were part of Hertz's licensee fleet. Although Hertz did own them, these cars were not part of the cars available to rent.

When an "apples-to-apples" comparison was made (that is, cars available for rental), Hertz had only 91,000 compared to Avis' 95,224. That is why the claim was misleading. The ad claimed that Hertz "has more new cars." But the impression on the potential car renter—to whom the ad was directed—was that Hertz "has more rental cars" than Avis. Because of this ad campaign, Avis sued Hertz for violation of the Lanham Act in *Avis Rent-A-Car* v. *Hertz Corp.*[8] Avis won.

Using Consumer Surveys To Establish Deception

One of the difficulties in succeeding in a Lanham Act case involves proving that a comparative ad is deceptive, or is likely to deceive. One method is by using market research or consumer surveys as evidence to prove that the consumer was deceived or is likely to be deceived. For this reason consumer surveys are widely used in Lanham Act cases.

A good case in point involved Coca-Cola. In early 1984 Tropicana Products began airing a television commercial for its orange juice product. Olympic athlete Bruce Jenner was shown squeezing an orange and claiming: "It's pure, pasteurized juice as it comes from the orange." In the next scene, Jenner poured the fresh-squeezed juice into a Tropicana carton while continuing: "It's the only leading brand not made with concentrate and water."

When the ad came to their attention, Coca-Cola the makers of Minute Maid orange juice filed suit in *The Coca-Cola Company* v. *Tropicana Products, Inc.*[9] In this case, Tropicana's claim was blatantly false. The ad claimed that Tropicana contained unprocessed, fresh-squeezed juice. In fact, it was pasteurized (heated to 200 degrees) and then frozen prior to being packaged. In the commercial, Jenner claims that Tropicana is "pasteurized juice as it comes from the orange." Well, pasteurized juice doesn't come from oranges. The representations in the commercial were clearly untrue.

Tropicana and Minute Maid, at the time, were the top selling ready-to-serve orange juices on the market. If Tropicana's advertising were allowed to mislead consumers into believing that its juice was better because it was fresh-squeezed and unprocessed, then Minute Maid would lose a significant share of the market.

Prior to the trial, Coca-Cola commissioned a consumer reaction test to be conducted by ASI Market Research, Inc. to measure consumer recall of the commercial. At trial, Coca-Cola produced this evidence showing that a "significant number of consumers would be likely to be misled" by the Tropicana ad.

The court ruled in favor of Coca-Cola.

This does not mean that any survey can be used effectively in court. On the contrary, courts are very critical about the credibility and thoroughness of any survey brought into court as evidence. The intent of the court is to make certain that damage amounts are calculated accurately. Surveys are acceptable as evidence only if they accurately reflect the consumers' true impressions.

Using Consumer Surveys As Comparison

Until now we've looked at surveys as a way of showing the existence of deception. However, surveys can also be used in an ad as a way of comparing products. Using consumer-survey information as part of a comparative advertisement may create a deception. This can occur if the results or methodology are misrepresented.

In the mid 1970's, two of the leading cigarette manufacturers in the United States were Phillip Morris and Lorillard (which was owned by Loew's Theatres). In 1972 Phillip Morris introduced Marlboro Lights, and in 1975 it introduced Merit. Merit was supported by an intensive ad campaign pushing a claim of good taste in a low-tar cigarette. In 1979, Lorillard began marketing its low-tar brand, Triumph.

In April of 1980, Lorillard hired SE Surveys to conduct "A National Taste Test: Triumph Menthol versus Winston Lights, Marlboro Lights, Vantage and Merit Non-Menthols." The results of that test were used in Triumph's advertising. Lorillard's ads for Triumph claimed:

●●●●●●●●●●●●●●●●●●●●●●●●●

"Triumph. National Taste test Winner.
Triumph tastes as good or better than
Merit, or . . . Marlboro Lights.
In rating overall product preference,

> more smokers independently
> chose Triumph over Merit,
> or . . . over Marlboro Lights."
> • • • • • • • • • • • • • • • • • • •

As a result of these ads, Phillip Morris filed suit for an injunction. The case was *Phillip Morris, Inc.* v. *Loew's Theatres, Inc.*[10] At the time of the trial, Merit was the largest selling low-tar cigarette in the United States generating over $350 million in revenue. About $80 million was spent on advertising that one brand alone.

The actual issue in this case revolved around the use of a taste test. Lorillard claimed that its brand Triumph was the "National Taste Test Winner." Yet, actual test results revealed that: 36 percent preferred Triumph over Merit for taste; 24 percent considered the two brands to be equal; 40 percent preferred Merit.

Obviously, from the test results, Merit not Triumph was preferred for taste. The ad failed to inform the consumer that, based on the same criteria, 64 percent stated that Merit tastes as good or better than Triumph. In other words, Triumph stated a statistic, which was true, and implied that the figure made it the winner. In reality, the other brand scored higher, which the ad failed to report.

Obviously, the results of the taste test were not used accurately in the Triumph advertisements. Phillip Morris submitted evidence at trial that consumers believed credible tests had proven that Triumph tasted better than Merit. As a result, the court stated: "there is convincing evidence that consumers are being deceived by Triumph's false claim of taste superiority."

Using Disclaimers in a Comparative Advertisement

There are situations in which an advertiser adds a disclaimer to an advertisement to offset what would otherwise be a deceptive claim. In 1984 the FDA authorized the sale of the drug ibuprofen in over-the-counter 200 mg. tablet form. American Home Products marketed the aspirin substitute under the brand name "Advil." A competitor, Upjohn, marketed the drug under the brand name "Nuprin." Prior to the over-the-counter release of ibuprofen, Upjohn manufactured and sold ibuprofen only as a prescription under the trademark of "Motrin." Now, who's on first?

American Home Products produced an ad campaign for Advil through its ad agency, Young & Rubicam. The campaign included magazine ads and television commercials. In the ads, an Advil tablet was shown. The tablet was orange in color and the same size and shape as the prescription drug Motrin. Copy in the ads exclaimed: "ADVIL contains ibuprofen, the same medicine as the prescription drug MOTRIN now in nonprescription strength."

When Upjohn learned of the ads, it contacted American Home Products requesting that it change them to avoid any confusion for the consumer. American Home Products changed the color of its Advil tablets to brown. It also changed the disclaimer used in its ads to read: "ADVIL contains a nonprescription strength of ibuprofen, the medicine found in the prescription brand, MOTRIN." American Home Products also added a visible line of copy to the television commercial that Advil is from Whitehall (a division of American Home Products) and that Motrin is manufactured by another company.

The revised print ads read:

● ●

ADVIL IS ADVANCED MEDICINE FOR PAIN
ADVIL isn't Tylenol and it isn't aspirin.
Advil contains ibuprofen—the medicine in the prescription brand
Motrin, the product of another company.
Now ibuprofen is available in nonprescription strength
in Advil. Ibuprofen has been proven so effective in relieving
many types of pain that doctors have already
prescribed it over 130 million times.
● ●

After American Home Products made these changes and added the disclaimers, Upjohn went to court requesting an injunction in *Upjohn Co. v. American Home Products Corp.*[11] Upjohn felt that the consuming public would still be misled and confused by American Home Product's ads for Advil. Upjohn wanted to stop any implication that Advil tablets were the same color as Motrin, that Advil was manufactured by Upjohn, that Advil was the equivalent of Motrin, or that the ingredient in Advil was Motrin.

The court examined these issues and determined that the new changes and disclaimers used in the Advil ads were sufficient. For the trial, consumer reaction surveys were instituted to determine the effect of the revised ads on the public. The surveys found that a higher percentage of consumers polled recalled the disclaimers as opposed to those who felt that Advil and Motrin were made by the same manufacturer. The court said: "[s]uch disclaimers are preferred to an absolute prohibition of the potentially misleading reference as a means of alleviating consumer confusion . . . ."

The important point to remember is that consumer confusion can be alleviated through the use of disclaimers or qualifying language. However, if this is challenged in court by the competitor, consumer surveys will be relied on and the survey will be used to determine whether use of the disclaimer alleviates the majority of consumer confusion.

Fair Use Of Trademarks In Comparative Advertising

There is nothing illegal, *per se*, in referring to another company's trademark. But this is true only if the use is informational and not likely to cause confusion about the source of the product or its qualities. We see many instances where an ad will make reference to, or show another company's product. In most cases this is done fairly and to compare qualities or features that one product has making it distinctive from the other. These comparisons must be true and accurate. Comparisons must not be deceptive or mislead the consumer, and proof to support the claim must exist prior to making the claim.

Here is another example of deceptive comparisons. Johnson & Johnson Company is a major manufacturer of Johnson's Baby Oil, Johnson's Baby Powder, and Johnson's Baby Shampoo. Quality Pure also manufacturers skin oil, skin powder, and shampoo. Its products are packaged in containers that exhibit an amazing resemblance to the J & J products. In fact, at a quick glance, the competing product packages look the same. Such similarity can be an infringement of trademark. This close similarity, known as "palming off" involves the use of another company's trademark to cause a likely confusion as to the origin of the product.

As an example, let's look at the shampoo products. The Johnson & Johnson Baby Shampoo bottle is elongated and made of clear plastic. The clear, yellow shampoo can be seen through the container. The Quality Pure shampoo package was almost identical to J & J's down to the style and color of label. The J & J label contained a tear drop with the slogan, "No More Tears," while the Quality Pure label used three tear drops on the label with the words "Tear Free."

The packaging of all of the Johnson & Johnson products was distinctive and unique. Suffice it to say that Quality Pure was in competition with Johnson & Johnson. But the competitor is not allowed to package its product so as to ride on the coattails of the image, reputation, and goodwill built over many years by Johnson & Johnson.

Quality Pure produced and aired a 30-second commercial to promote its new line of products. In its commercial an actress, Jane Paley, claimed that Quality Pure Shampoo "gave me the same lather" as Johnson & Johnson Baby Shampoo. The commercial also claimed that "both were extremely mild." The gist of the commercial was that while the products gave the same results and had the same qualities, Quality Pure was cheaper than Johnson &

Johnson.

As a result Johnson & Johnson brought suit in *Johnson & Johnson* v. *Quality Pure Mfg., Inc.*[12] Two items were at issue in this case: the similarity of the packaging; and, the advertising claim of equal performance and lower price. The court expressed its opinion that competing on a price level is perfectly acceptable. Yet it is not acceptable to "sell a competing product on the basis of a lower price and at the same time use [packaging] designed and calculated to fool the customer into the belief that he is getting someone else's product." See Chapter 3 for more on labeling requirements.

Further, Quality Pure had no basis for the claims used in its commercial. Quality Pure conducted a "survey" by handing out samples of competing shampoos to shoppers at shopping centers. The competing shampoos were unidentified except for a mark on each bottle either X or Y. Then Jane Paley was given the samples and, after using them, scored them as equal. This result is what appeared on the television commercial.

The problem rests on the credibility of the "survey." There was no way of determining which brand of shampoo was in which bottle, or even if the products were different. The test was rigged and without any substantiation, and in the court's eye "had far too much resemblance to three-card monte to be accepted . . . ."

REMEDIES AVAILABLE UNDER THE LANHAM ACT

Originally, there were essentially three remedies available under the Lanham Act: an injunction against the deceptive ad; corrective advertising by the company that ran the deceptive ad; and monetary damages. In order to recover damages or require corrective advertising, however, it must be shown that the buying audience was actually deceived. If only a likelihood of deception can be shown, an injunction is the sole remedy allowed.

The 1988 act made the damage remedies set forth in

section 35 of the Lanham Act applicable to actions under section 43(a).

Section 35(a) provides as follows:

When a violation of any right of the registrant of a mark registered in the Patent and Trademark Office, <u>or a violation under section 43(a)</u>, shall have been established in any civil action arising under this chapter, the plaintiff shall be entitled . . . subject to the principles of equity, to recover (1) defendant's profits, (2) any damages sustained by the plaintiff, and (3) the costs of the action. (Emphasis added.)

Prior to the amendment, most courts that had considered the question held that section 35(a) applied to actions under section 43(a), although most of those cases involved unregistered trademarks rather than advertising issues.

The 1988 act authorizes courts to apply the remedies provided in section 35, and provides damages and profits should continue to be "rarely assessed" in actions under section 43(a). The 1988 act also makes the remedies provided for in section 34 (injunction) and section 36 (destruction of infringing copies) applicable to actions under section 43(a). Injunctions, however, have always been available in false advertising cases.

Injunction As A Remedy

This is the most common (and quickest) remedy under the Lanham Act. Essentially, an injunction bans the ad from running. The most important function of an injunction is that it stops the publication of the deceptive ad.

Most people have the view that the legal system moves very slowly. It may be refreshing to learn that a preliminary injunction can be obtained within months or even weeks of filing a complaint. This can be a major consideration to the company who is the victim of an advertisement showing its product in an unfavorable, disparaging or misleading way.

Discussed earlier, one of the features of an injunction is that it stops further damage. The negative side, though, is that it does not remove the deception already created. Further, an injunction does not compensate the victim for injury either.

In order to be granted an injunction, the person or company requesting one must show the court that irreparable damage will be suffered if the injunction is not issued. Actual lost sales need not be proved, but it must establish that there is more than a belief of injury. If the advertising claim is explicitly false, no other proof is required. However, if the advertisement is less than explicit, some other evidence must be shown that establishes that the claim is likely to deceive the consumer.

The Toro Company and Jacobsen Manufacturing (a division of Textron) are manufacturers of various labor-saving machines for consumer use. A few years ago a controversy arose when Jacobsen produced an ad directed toward dealers. The ad showed a performance comparison between its Sno-Burst snow thrower and Toro's Snow Master. In the ad Jacobsen's Sno-Burst appeared to come out ahead in the categories rated.

When Toro learned of this, it filed suit seeking an injunction against the ad. Toro obviously felt the ad was deceptive. The court, in *Toro Co.* v. *Textron, Inc.*,[13] discussed whether the ad misled dealers about the features of both machines. The ad headline claimed: "The New Jacobsen. You Get More To Sell." The ad then proceeded to compare categories such as reserve power, engine size, starter priming, gas/oil ratio, wheel size, snow-throwing distance, fuel capacity, auger housing, handle adjustment, and warranty.

The basis for Jacobsen's comparison, however, proved to be insignificant and arbitrary. Here are some examples. Regarding the category under "starter," Jacobsen claimed that its machine didn't need to be primed to start, while the Toro did. The court found that, in fact, the Jacobsen required pulling the starter cord a number of times before the machine would start just as with the Toro model. This, the court reasoned, constituted priming. The comparison was considered false.

Some of the other claims by Jacobsen were literally true, but they were insignificant as a valid comparison. Jacobsen claimed that its handle was adjustable and Toro's was not. A true statement. However, on closer examination, the Jacobsen handle was only adjustable one inch. The claim that the handle on the Jacobsen was adjustable was truly misleading.

As you can see, a number of the compared features between the two machines were found to be false or so insignificant that there was a likelihood of confusion of the buyer. While Toro could not show that purchasers were actually deceived (a requirement for damages), it could show that the ads had a tendency to deceive. In order to obtain an injunction, "[Toro] need only show that the misrepresentations of which it complains 'have a tendency to deceive' . . . the three claims found to be false do have a tendency to mislead consumers into purchasing a Jacobsen rather than a Toro, and injunctive relief is, therefore, appropriate."

Toro was granted an injunction against Jacobsen for making the deceptive claims.

Corrective Advertising

This type of remedy is essentially an award of money. The company who created the deception is ordered by the court to use its own money to produce advertising that will offset the originally deceptive ads.

The intent of corrective advertising is for the new ads to correct the confusion created by the deceptive ad. The company must produce its own ads with a message that effectively counters the previous, deceptive message much like a public apology.

Durbin Brass Works is a manufacturer of brass lamps selling its lamps through, among other outlets, The Sharper Image stores and catalog. In the early 1980s, Richard Schuler also sold lamps of the same style and design as Durbin's. The Schuler lamps were sold through, among other outlets, the American Express Company catalog. Schuler's lamps were manufactured in Taiwan as opposed to Durbin's lamps, which were manufactured in the United States.

Durbin filed suit in *Durbin Brass Works, Inc. v. Schuler*[14] claiming that Schuler's lamps caused a decline in sales of its lamps because of consumer confusion between the two manufacturers. In other words, due to the identical appearance of the two brands of lamp, consumers were drawn to buy the cheaper version while believing that they were buying the original Durbin lamp.

Schuler sold over $60,000 worth of imitation lamps before Durbin brought suit. The court agreed with Durbin that these sales were a result of the public's confusion. Durbin testified at the trial that it would cost his company $10,000 in advertising to offset the deception created by the Schuler ads. The court concluded that Schuler's actions created actual consumer confusion, and therefore an award of corrective advertising was appropriate. Durbin was awarded $10,000 as damages plus court costs. It was ordered, by the court, that the $10,000 be spent by Schuler on corrective advertising to offset the deception that it had originally created.

Monetary Damages As A Remedy

Until the early 1980's no court had awarded monetary damages to a plaintiff under Section 43(a) of the Lanham Act. All prior awards were either injunctions or corrective advertising. This, however, was to change when a case came to court that was able to prove a direct loss of sales or potential sales. In seeking damages, two things must be shown: actual consumer deception; and consumer reliance on the false claim.

Another section of the Lanham Act, Section 35, has been utilized in comparative advertising cases. This has given even more punch to an already strong law by expanding the damages allowed. Under Section 35, the lost profits, actual damages, and the cost of the lawsuit may be recovered. Treble (three times) damages and attorney's fees may also be recovered in certain extreme cases. The largest award in such case occurred in 1984.

Ryder System was in the car and truck rental business. In the mid-1970's, James A. Ryder began to lose control of the company that he had begun. New internal management had largely ignored him for a few years.

Even though Ryder was over 60 years old, he decided to leave Ryder System and start a new company to compete with Ryder. The new car and truck rental company was originally named "Jarpool," but was later renamed Jartran. Originally Jartran, with only mediocre results, leased large truck and trailer units to businesses. Seeing the potential in consumer rentals, Mr. Ryder wanted to expand into the self-move rental field. This would bring the new company directly into competition with the leader, U-Haul.

In order to put his plan into motion, Mr. Ryder went heavily into debt to acquire the vehicles that he needed. Once Jartran obtained its vehicles, it needed to get them on the road fast. And that meant competing head-to-head with U-Haul for customers. As anyone in advertising knows, it is extremely difficult to dislodge the number one company in any field. But Jartran was determined to do it.

So, Jartran, through its ad agency Sandra C. Tinsley Advertising, created an ad campaign to generate consumer rentals. The campaign was designed to compete on a price advantage over U-Haul. Did the campaign work? Jartran's gross revenues in 1979 (its first year) were $3 million. In 1980 however, gross revenue rose to $58 million, and in 1981 to $95 million. Yes, I'd say it worked. Within months Jartran had taken over more than 10 percent of the market.

The campaign worked so well that it won the Gold Effie award from the American Marketing Association, for "its overall marketing effectiveness." In Mr. Ryder's opinion the campaign "knocked the competition (U-Haul) on their ass."

How did this affect U-Haul? In 1979 U-Haul had almost all of the self-move rental business in the United States. Others had entered the field over the years but with very little effect. U-Haul's largest competition came, coincidentally, from Ryder System in 1979. However, U-Haul's revenue began to decrease after Jartran's campaign broke. In 1981 U-Haul saw, for the first time, its revenue decrease with a loss of $49 million. To stem the tide, U-Haul tried to counteract Jartran's efforts with $13.6 million spent on advertising between 1981 and 1982.

Without its concentrated and comparative ad campaign, directed at U-Haul, Jartran would not have gained the market share that it did. The ads were simple. The headlines claimed:

●●●●●●●●●●●●●●●●●●●●●

U-Haul It to Dallas for $0000.

. . . Jartran It to Dallas for $000.

Save big money . . . to almost any city.

●●●●●●●●●●●●●●●●●●●●●●●●●●

The price stated for Jartran was always less than the stated U-Haul price. In the ads, a picture of each company's rental truck was shown. However, the size of the U-Haul truck used in the ad was smaller to make it look less attractive.

In June 1980, U-Haul filed suit to stop Jartran's campaign. *U-Haul International, Inc. v. Jartran, Inc.*[15] was the case. U-Haul claimed that Jartran's price comparison ads were false and that Jartran knew it. The court agreed.

The Jartran rental prices shown in the ads were "special promotion prices," although this very important point was never mentioned. The intent, which worked, was to convey that the advertised price was Jartran's regular price. Actually, the rates advertised were considerably lower than those stated on Jartran's one-way price sheet. Conversely, the price Jartran quoted for U-Haul rentals was its regular price plus a distribution fee. Again this was not disclosed in the ad. In fact, a distribution fee is charged in only certain unique rental cases.

The price claims that Jartran made were blatantly false and were intended to mislead the consumer into renting from Jartran instead of U-Haul. A series of consumer surveys were used as evidence to substantiate that: "The false and deceptive statements contained in the Jartran ads were material in influencing rental decisions of a substantial segment of the public interested in renting self-move equipment."

The claims in the Jartran ads were published deliberately. They were known by Jartran to be false, and they were intended to damage U-Haul by taking business away through deception. Under the Lanham Act, "a court may award additional damages, up to three times the amount awarded for actual damages according to the circumstances of the case."

In this case, the court awarded actual damages of $20 million to U-Haul. In addition, the court felt that Jartran's advertising was "willful, malicious or in reckless disregard of the rights of [U-Haul]," and an additional $20 million was awarded— $40 million in all. U-Haul was also awarded court costs and attorney's fees.

ANTIDILUTION STATUTES: STATE ACTION AND COMPARATIVE ADVERTISING

What we've seen up to now is federal control over comparative advertising. But many states have also gotten involved by enacting what are termed "antidilution statutes." See Exhibit 8-2 for a complete list. In practice through use of these statutes each state controls deceptive comparative advertising within its borders. Since these are state laws, the necessity for interstate commerce is not a requirement.

Dilution is defined basically as any whittling away or general eroding of the trademark's selling power. In other words, any non-owner use of a trademark or trade name that diminishes the selling power of that mark violates the statute. As we saw with the Lanham Act, a comparative ad, if untrue, can diminish the selling power of the competitor's trademark.

Antidilution actions can take place under three situations: generic usage; unrelated usage; and comparative advertising. The first is generic usage. This situation exists when a competitor uses another trademark to denote a class of product, in other words, using another's mark as if it were the generic type of product.

The second area, unrelated usage, covers use of a trademark on products that do not compete and have no connection. Here again this type of use erodes the value of the mark. We saw this earlier in *Dallas Cowboys Cheerleaders, Inc.* v. *Pussycat Cinema, Ltd.* Although that case was brought under the Lanham Act (federal law), the principle is the same.

EXHIBIT 8-2:

State Antidilution Statutes

Alabama	Alabama Code, section 8-12-17 (1975)
Arkansas	Arkansas Statutes Annotated, section 70-550 (1979)
California	California Business & Professions Code, section 14330 (West Supp 1980)
Connecticut	Connecticut General Statutes, section 35-11i (1979)
Delaware	Delaware Code Annotated, section 3313 (Supp 1978)
Florida	Florida Statutes Annotated, section 495.151 (West 1972)
Georgia	Georgia Code, section 106-115 (1978)
Idaho	Idaho Code, section 48-512 (1977)
Illinois	Illinois Revised Statutes Chapter 140, section 22 (1975)

Iowa	Iowa Code, section 548.11(2) (1979)
Maine	Maine Revised Statutes Annotated, Title 10, section 1530 (1964)
Massachusetts	Massachusetts General Laws Annotated Chapter 11OB, section 12 (West Supp 1980)
Montana	Montana Annotated Statutes, section 417.061 (Vernon 1979)
Nebraska	Nebraska Revised Statutes, section 87-122 (1976)
New Hampshire	New Hampshire Revised Statutes Annotated, section 350-A:12 (Supp. 1979)
New Mexico	New Mexico Statutes Annotated, section 57-3-10 (1978)
New York	New York General Business Law, section 368-d (McKinney 1968)
Oregon	Oregon Revised Statutes, section 647.107 (1971)
Rhode Island	Rhode Island General Laws, section 6-2-12 (Supp. 1980)
Tennessee	Tennessee Code Annotated, section 47-25-512 (1984)

The final area involves literal comparative advertising. As in federal cases, comparative advertising can injure a product's selling ability by re-directing the trademark's image to another company's product. This violates antidilution statutes because consumers no longer associate the reputation of the trademark exclusively. In other words, a dilution of the mark has occurred.

CELEBRITY LOOK-ALIKES AND THE LANHAM ACT

In Chapter 5 look-alikes that can violate a celebrity's right of publicity or privacy were discussed. In 1985 the issue of look-alikes was taken one step further. It crossed over into the comparative advertising realm.

Early in 1984, a man named Phil Boroff appeared in an ad for National Video, a video rental service. Boroff was hired through his agency, Ron Smith's Celebrity Look-Alikes in Los Angeles, California, because he bore a striking resemblance to Woody Allen.

In the National ads, Boroff appeared behind the counter where two of Woody Allen's films were displayed. The headlines for two of the ads claimed:

• •
We'll Make You Feel Like A Star.
You Don't Need A Famous Face
To Be Treated To Some Famous Service.
• •

These ads ran in national magazines including National Video's own publication and *Video Review* magazine. In the *Video Review* issues the ad carried the disclaimer: "Celebrity double provided by Ron Smith's Celebrity Look-Alikes, Los Angeles, Calif."

Allen was not amused by this. He filed suit in *Allen v. National Video, Inc.*[16] What made that case unique was that it was the first time that a suit of its type succeeded under the Lanham Act. Allen claimed a violation of Section 43(a). He argued that a likelihood of confusion existed between Boroff and himself.

Even if some consumers realized that the person in the ad was not Allen himself but a look-alike, these same people most probably will assume another possibility. That is, the public "may be led to believe by the intentional reference to [Allen] that he is somehow involved in, or approves of their product."

You might say that there was a disclaimer in the ad stating that the person was a double for Allen. Yet, a small disclaimer at the bottom of an ad was not sufficient to offset an overall deceptive advertisement.

The result of this case was that an injunction was issued, stopping the use of any of the ads with Boroff as Woody Allen. National Video paid Allen $425,000, and Boroff was barred from appearing as a look-alike for Allen in any advertising that "creates the likelihood that a reasonable person might believe that he was really [Allen] or that [Allen] had approved of the appearance."

However, Boroff could appear in advertising only if a "clear and bold" disclaimer or clarifying body copy was used.

While this case is relatively recent, not to mention revolutionary, it shows a trend. Other courts may follow; they may not. Only time will tell. Yet, the Lanham Act was effectively used to stop the use of a look-alike who in essence created a false impression by comparing Boroff to Allen. And after all, that's what the Lanham Act was created for. The moral of this story is that the deceptive comparison can be that of people as well as of products.

---

[1] 15 U.S.C., Section 1125(a).

[2] S. Kanwit, *Regulatory Manual Series*, Federal Trade Commission, Section 22.17 n. 13 (1985).

[3] Section 39 of the Lanham Act, 15 U.S.C. Section 1125(a).

[4] *L'Aiglon Apparel, Inc. v. Lana Lobel Inc.*, 214 F.2d 649 (3rd Cir. 1954).

[5] *Arneson v. Raymond Lee Organization, Inc.*, 333 F. Supp. 116 (C.D. Cal. 1971).

[6] *Dallas Cowboys Cheerleaders, Inc. v. Pussycat Cinema, Ltd.*, 604 F.2d 200 (1979).

[7] *Skil Corp. v. Rockwell International Corp.*, 375 F. Supp 777 (N.D. Ill. 1974).

[8] *Avis Rent-A-Car v. Hertz Corp.*, 782 F.2d 381 (2nd Cir. 1986).

[9] *The Coca-Cola Company v. Tropicana Products, Inc.*, 690 F.2d 312 (1982).

[10] *Phillip Morris, Inc. v. Loew's Theatres, Inc.*, 511 F. Supp. 855 (S.D.N.Y. 1980).

[11] *Upjohn Co. v. American Home Products Corp.*, 598 F. Supp. 550 (S.D.N.Y. 1984).

[12] *Johnson & Johnson v. Quality Pure Mfg., Inc.*, 484 F. Supp. 975 (D.N.J. 1979).

[13] *Toro Co. v. Textron, Inc.*, 499 F. Supp. 241 (D. Del. 1980).

[14] *Durbin Brass Works, Inc. v. Schuler*, 532 F. Supp. 41 (E.D. Mo. 1982).

[15] *U-Haul International. Inc. v. Jartran, Inc.*, 601 F. Supp. 1140 (D. Az. 1984).

[16] *Allen v. National Video, Inc.*, 610 F. Supp. 612 (S.D.N.Y. 1985).

CHAPTER 9

CONTESTS AND LOTTERIES

This is essentially a people's contest . . .
—to afford all an unfettered start, and a fair chance,
in the race of life.
—*Abraham Lincoln*

The summer of 1955 brought the era of the game show. All across America people tuned in to watch an immigrant welder win a fortune through his knowledge of art or a file clerk dazzle the audience with her grasp of opera trivia—the common citizen getting the chance to become richer than his or her wildest hopes. The things dreams are made of—to win a fortune on such shows as "Twenty-One" (portrayed in the movie *Quiz Show*), "The $64,000 Question," "Tic-Tac-Dough," "Name That Tune," "Dotto," and "The Big Surprise." That moment of glory. As Andy Warhol said, ". . . everyone will be world famous for fifteen minutes."

To assure honesty, the questions were guarded so that no one could discover them, or their answers. The audience was sure that contestants could not possibly have known what they would be asked. On many shows isolation booths were used so that the contestants could not get help from the audience. Some shows went so far as to use bank officials accompanied by armed guards to hand deliver the questions to the host. The questions had been locked in a bank vault until that time.

The tension would build with each question, and the audience would sigh with relief after each correct answer. The appeal of the game show was what appeared to be the unrehearsed spontaneity of the shows, and that the contestants were masters of certain areas of knowledge, memory, and intelligence. These game shows were a spectacle to behold. The audiences became engrossed in the show, and they were just that—all show.

In July 1958, the Federal Communications Commission (FCC) was drawn into the scene when a contestant of "Dotto" complained that the show was deceptive. Not much resulted from this investigation. The station denied any wrong-doing, and the case was dropped. But news had leaked out, and the game show scandal began to draw public attention. In late 1959, a subcommittee of the House Committee on Interstate and Foreign Commerce opened hearings on the matter.

Witnesses (previous contestants) who were called before the subcommittee testified that they were given the questions and in many cases the answers as well. Some were given scripts to memorize. Even the theatrics of their responses were coached. Despair, agony, exuberance, elation were all prerehearsed to create the desired effect for the audience.

Good-looking contestants were promoted to increase the television audience; unattractive ones were routinely eliminated (or so the producers would try). Dr. Joyce Brothers, the now well-known psychologist, was one such contestant. The producers of the game show tried to get her to lose the game, but her knowledge of boxing was so extensive that she answered every question they threw at her.

Quite obviously the game shows were fixed, and the advertising community was also involved. The advertisers and their agencies were the ones who were truly in control of the purse-strings. At that time it was common for a single advertiser to sponsor an entire show, therefore wielding a tremendous amount of control over the show and its content to the point where the advertiser actually directed the contestant briefing.

The television game show scandal caused the networks to re-think their priorities. As a result of the bad press, television began to move away from game shows and in their place came the era of the Western. "Gunsmoke," "Wagon Train," "Have Gun, Will Travel," "Bonanza," "Wanted Dead or Alive," and many others saw the sun set on the era of the game show.

Since then, contests of every kind have drawn acute attention from the networks, the FTC, and courts, alike. That is why it is very important for advertisers and their agencies to understand the laws that apply to contests. Sometimes they are called games, sweepstakes, games-of-chance, or just contests. Regardless of the name, the intention is obvious. The advertiser expects that the consumer will enter the contest and be drawn to its product.

In other words, contests generate interest because they get the consumer involved. They appeal to a basic human trait—the desire to get something for nothing. The real intent, then, is to transfer this desire to the product and, with that, increase sales.

Somewhere, right now, people are filling out entry forms and dreaming of what they'll do with the money if they win. Winning a fortune in a contest is a dream of many Americans, an easy reward for very little effort. Yet, the odds of winning a contest are extremely low. For example, the odds to win first prize in the January 1969 *Reader's Digest* sweepstakes were about 1 in 480,000.[1]

But what does the advertiser need to be concerned with when creating and promoting a contest? Actually, the answer is very simple. There are guidelines that must be followed to run a contest and to prevent it from becoming a lottery. This chapter examines those guidelines. If the contest is structured according to the guidelines, these games are legal.

However, if the game falls outside the guidelines, it will be considered a lottery—which is gambling and illegal (unless state sponsored). To prevent an illegal lottery, there are specific and stringent laws that control contests. This heavy regulation evolved because contests closely resemble lotteries. In the states that permit this form of gambling, it is very heavily regulated. For the advertiser, a contest must not be allowed to cross over the line and become a lottery.

WHAT CONSTITUTES A LOTTERY

Recently, many of the states have sponsored lotteries to raise funds for various government institutions. In California, for example, the proceeds from the lottery were intended to benefit public education. In Colorado, lottery profits were intended to benefit state parks and recreation areas. With the growth and popularity of these lotteries, many companies have jumped on the contest band-wagon. Companies that had not been involved with contests in the past have begun promoting their products through contests and sweepstakes of every kind.

In order to remain within the boundaries of a legal contest, it is important to understand what situations will be considered an illegal lottery. The generally accepted definition of a lottery is "a chance or chances taken, for a consideration, in the hope or expectation that something would be obtained of greater value than that which was given up, but with the full knowledge that nothing at all might be obtained . . . ."[2]

As mentioned earlier, contests are legal, but lotteries are not. The difference between a contest and a lottery is quite simple, and advertisers must understand the difference. Let's take a look at the three basic conditions that create a lottery:

- A prize must be offered;
- The entrant must give up something (consideration) in order to participate; and
- Winning must involve an element of chance rather than skill.

If one, or more, of these elements is missing, a lottery does not exist. All three are required for a lottery. Two elements occur in most all games of chance: a prize and chance. The tricky element, as you'll see, is consideration. We'll look into each of these areas in more detail.

In the late 1930's the government confiscated 83 cases of merchandise marked "Honest John," "Wonder Store," and "Diamond Store." Each of these boxes contained smaller boxes with a number on each. On the main display case were small pull-tabs, which a consumer would remove to reveal a number underneath.

The consumer purchased a chance to remove one pull-tab for 1, 2, or 5 cents. After the pull-tab was removed to reveal a number, the consumer got the prize in the small box that had the same number on it. Each box contained a small amount of inexpensive candy and some other trinket. The value of the items in the prize boxes was only a few cents, and each box contained a prize of equal value.

Now the question is, was that a legal contest or an illegal lottery? That question was answered by the court in *U.S. v. 83 Cases of Merchandise Labeled "Honest John."*[3] The court examined the three elements that needed to exist in order for this to be a lottery: a prize, consideration, and chance. In this case, "there is no single prize, no group of prizes, but a prize given for every chance that is taken."

In a lottery, the consumer takes a chance on winning a prize that is much greater than the price paid to participate. In this case there was no substantial difference between the amount of money that the participant paid and the value of what would be received. In essence there was no "prize" involved.

No chance was involved either, because all participants received an item for their participation in the game. This game, then, was a legal contest because it did not meet all three of the elements required of a lottery.

Prize As An Element

Most games of chance end with a winner, or a couple of winners, who receive a prize. A prize is a special item given to the winner. It is also what is used to induce the consumer to enter the game.

Prizes can range from cash, to cars, vacations, merchandise, to just about anything. A few years ago Zerex antifreeze, made by

DuPont Corporation, offered as first prize in its contest a radiator filled with Zerex antifreeze. What made this prize worth winning was the fact that the radiator was installed in a new Rolls-Royce.

If every entrant receives a gift of equal value, and in the same way, then no "prize" is awarded. We saw this in the case just discussed. If the gifts have different values, the game is considered a lottery (if the other two elements also exist).

In the early 1900's, a company in Georgia named Purvis Investments offered a plan to customers. The plan involved offering a loan on very favorable terms to the first few people who mailed in an investment of a specific amount. However, the investment return was not as good as other savings institutions at the time. The main feature of the scheme was the possibility of obtaining a loan at better than average rates. That was the incentive for entering the "contest" and paying the investment amount. The customer's payment of the investment constituted consideration.

When entries were received at the company, they were opened and numbered. But if a batch of entries were received in the same day's mail, it would be pure chance which envelope was opened first. So, we have the element of chance. When this scheme made its way to the courts in *United States* v. *Purvis*,[4] the court said, "it was of course a mere matter of chance as to which the . . . clerk . . . should take up first, as he opened and entered them."

The final element necessary for this to be a lottery was the existence of a prize. In this case the prize was an opportunity to obtain a loan on favorable terms. "It was the desire to obtain loans on the very attractive terms proposed . . . which made these contracts so much favored and which induced the purchase of these loan contracts." The investment return itself was not particularly attractive. Better returns could have been achieved at other savings institutions. But the chance to obtain one of the loans was a thing of value. It also made this qualify as the element of a prize. The scheme was held to be a lottery.

Consideration As An Element

The next element of a lottery is consideration. If the other two elements exist but there is no consideration, then there is no lottery. But what is the definition of consideration? Many acts can constitute consideration. Even a forbearance (a promise to not do something) can be consideration. Yet, the most obvious form of consideration is money. There are others, and we look at those here.

It is extremely important to understand that what we are discussing are general rules under federal law. Each state has specific laws concerning what it feels qualifies as consideration in relation to a lottery. We'll look at these later in this chapter. Without exception, the advertiser should check into the laws of any state in which it intends to promote a contest.

As just explained, the exact definition of consideration varies from state to state. But generally, consideration can be money or anything of value. It can also be an act such as exerting substantial time and effort in some way. In Wisconsin, which is unique in this respect, consideration is defined by statute as "anything which is a commercial or financial advantage to the promoter or a disadvantage to any participant."[5] What this means is that some states (including Wisconsin) feel that any burden put on the participant constitutes consideration. But, generally, the requirement that a consumer visit the store to obtain game pieces is not interpreted as consideration.

Around 1950 George Wagner was the Postmaster of Garden City, New York. Mr. Wagner wanted to ban the mailing of a card that he felt constituted a lottery. Here's how the game worked. The consumer who received the card in the mail would remove the coupon portion which contained a number. Then the consumer kept the coupon and mailed the other portion of the card to the Garden City Chamber of Commerce.

Later, the consumer visited the stores that participated in the game. If the consumer saw an article in the store window that had the same number as the person's coupon, the store would give the item as a prize. In essence, this was a treasure hunt.

The question is, does the act of visiting stores create a consideration which would make this a lottery? That question was answered in *Garden City Chamber of Commerce* v. *Wagner*.[6] The court agreed with the Postmaster who brought the suit and stated "consideration is present in the substantial amount of time and effort involved in examining the various prizes to ascertain whether one holds a winning ticket."

As seen earlier, consideration can take the form of a payment of money, purchase of a ticket, or the expenditure of substantial time or effort. The basis of the controversy in this case is whether the act of visiting a store "actually involves an expenditure of substantial effort and time." The court ruled that it did not, saying: "[We] have found no case in which the element of consideration has resided in walking or driving to look in a window."

Generally, situations that are not classified as consideration include requiring participants to:
- Visit a store to enter;
- Return to store to learn of winners;
- Visit different stores;
- Witness a demonstration or take a demonstration ride; or
- Pay postage.

Once again, it is important to consult specific state statutes for exact regulations.

Now let's look at typical situations where consideration does exist.

Use Of Consumer's Name Or Likeness

Requiring the authorization to use the name or likeness of a participant or winner could be held to mean that consideration was given because there is consent to do something in the future. It is consideration notwithstanding the future performance aspects of the consent.

The Gift Enterprise

In many cases the consumer must purchase the advertiser's product to qualify for the contest. Then usually a proof of purchase in the form of a box top, wrapper, facsimile, or the like is sent in to register for the contest. This is known as a "gift enterprise."

Even though the price of the product remains the same, there is consideration because the consumer is required to do something. The consumer is required to make a purchase.

Therefore, a gift enterprise scheme involves the element of consideration. This explains the common "No purchase required" disclaimer used in many contests.

There is another situation that is very closely related to a pure gift enterprise. That involves games where a lottery is created when a customer must promise to buy a product to enter a game. A good example of this situation occurred in 1976, with a radio promotion called "Dial-a-Discount."

Don J. Plumridge Advertising in Washington, D.C. developed a radio campaign for one of its clients, Allyn's Pants Ranch. A typical commercial read:

● ●

Dial your own discount on a pair of pants.
This is our Pants Ranch Wheel of Fortune.
On it are various dollar amounts.
Two dollars, three dollars, four, five, and ten dollars.
After you purchase any pair of pants—and the Pants Ranch
has over 40,000 to choose from—
you get to dial your own discount.
What you spin on the wheel is what you save
on the purchase of your first pair of pants.

If the wheel stops on "freebie," lucky you!
Cause there's no charge.
The pants are on us!
• • • • • • • • • • • • •

The concept of the game was pretty straightforward. The customer took a pair of pants to the counter where the Wheel of Fortune was spun. Wherever the wheel stopped was the amount of the discount off the purchase price of the pants.

When the Federal Communications Commission found out about the game, a complaint was initiated: *In the Matter of Metromedia Inc.*[7] The commission discussed the following:

Whether a 'Dial-a-Discount' participant's commitment to purchase a pair of pants alone [constituted] the requisite element of consideration, since if money has not yet changed hands, any participant may refuse to pay after spinning the discount wheel and return the pants to the shelf.

However, the game rules required this agreement to pay in order to participate, and therefore, consideration existed because there was an "agreement" to pay at least the regular price of a pair of pants in order to participate. This game was an illegal lottery because it required that the consumer purchase the pants without knowing, in advance, the amount of the discount. Metromedia lost the case and was required to pay a $16,000 fine for promoting an illegal lottery.

Presence At The Drawing

Here again there is a difference of opinion. But most courts feel that requiring participants to be present in order to win a drawing is consideration.

Obstacles In Obtaining Entry Blanks

If free entry blanks for a game are offered but the company

has irregular office hours, a problem can result. Also, if the participant must, let's say, purchase a newspaper to obtain entry forms, an illegal lottery exists. The purchase of the newspaper is consideration. In other words, entry forms must be made readily available, and a purchase must not be required in order to obtain an entry form. Otherwise, consideration is given.

The following case provides a good example of obstacles for participants. Dreem Arts, Incorporated published a newspaper in Chicago called *Nightmoves*. The paper cost $2 and contained a game called "Pick and Play." The idea of the game was for the reader to pick the winners of upcoming professional and college football games. All upcoming games were listed, along with the point spread. Participants mailed in their entry blank listing the teams they picked to win. If an entrant picked 10 winning teams, the prize was $1,000 in cash. Other prizes were available if a person picked at least four winning teams. The advertised contest rules were as follows:

> Free contest entry forms are available at office of publisher. Please send stamped self-addressed envelope and free entry form will be mailed to you; a reasonable hand-drawn facsimile can be used—in addition to stores and news stands, copies of Nightmoves are available at Chicago public libraries for your inspection (no limit to number of contest entries.) . . . No purchase necessary—tax liabilities for all prizes are the sole responsibility of winners.

Late in 1985 the Chicago Police Department confiscated newspapers from various locations, and *Dreem Arts, Inc. v. City of Chicago*[8] was the result. A detective investigated the case and found that the *Nightmoves* offices had no sign displayed. The office was closed, and no employees were present. He was unable to obtain the "free entry form." The detective also tried to obtain an entry blank by mail, but none was ever received. Another detective visited over 24 Chicago libraries, none of which had ever subscribed to the newspaper.

If the consumer is allowed to submit a reasonable facsimile for an entry, no consideration exists. There is a problem, though, when the consumer can't get a copy from which to make a facsimile without buying something. That was the case here.

Obviously the publisher devised the rules to "purposely [make] it more difficult to obtain free entry forms than to pay the $2 newsstand price of *Nightmoves*." The court found that the obstacles in obtaining free entry blanks made this option inordinately difficult. Because the only realistic way to enter the game was to pay the $2 price of the newspaper, this was consideration, and that made the game a lottery.

Chance As An Element

Chance is another element that must exist in order to qualify as a lottery. If chance dominates the game, rather than skill or judgment, it becomes a lottery. Chance is usually involved in games in which the participant must guess something to win— from guessing the number of beans in a jar to guessing the number of people that will attend a grand opening event. (There are other ways chance can create problems, and we look at those later.)

Chance is an interesting element. Pure chance is not the issue in most cases that have gone through the courts. Rather, the courts look to whether chance is the controlling factor in awarding prizes. For example, a dice game involves pure chance. On the other hand, a chess game involves pure skill. In the middle are card games, which are games of chance. They do not stop being games of chance simply because some element of skill is involved. Card games are still predominantly controlled by the luck of the draw.

One of my favorite examples of a game of chance involved a trade newspaper, the *United States Tobacco Journal*. The case occurred about 1900 and involved an advertisement for a game advertised in the newspaper. The ad read as follows:

● ●

The United States Tobacco Journal
SAVE OUR BANDS
Another free Distribution of
$142,500.00
Will be made in December, 1903
Based on the Month of November, 1903
TO SMOKERS OF
[Here follow the names of 30 brands of cigars.]
How many cigars (of all brands, no matter by whom
manufactured) will the United States collect taxes on
during the month of November, 1903?
(Cigars bearing $3.00 tax per thousand)
The persons who estimate nearest to the number of cigars
on which $3.00 tax per thousand is paid during the month of
November, 1903, as shown by the total sales of stamps made
by the United States Internal Revenue Department during
November, 1903, will be awarded as follows:
To the person estimating the closest . . . $5,000 in cash.

● ●

The list continued for the number of people who guessed
next closest in descending order. At the end of the list were people
who won $5 or a box of free cigars. In theory, over 35,000 people
could win something. Obviously, because of the newspaper's
audience, the game was directed to retail sellers of cigars and other
tobacco products. These retailers could make four estimates for
every 100 cigar bands sent in.

The game was sponsored by a cigar manufacturer, the
Florodora Company. As part of the rules, the company allowed
each Florodora cigar band to count as two for the purpose of
entering the game. Suffice it to say that the purpose of Florodora
was to increase sales of its brand of cigar. There is nothing wrong

or illegal in this.

Yet, the State of New York felt that the game was an illegal lottery, so they arrested the magazine publisher, Ismar Ellison. In many states, operating a lottery is a criminal offense; in this case it was a misdemeanor. The case was *People ex rel. Ellison v. Lavin.*[9]

According to the elements of a lottery, this game provided for awarding prizes. It also possessed the element of consideration by requiring the dealer to purchase cigars from which to get the bands required to enter the game. "Therefore," said the court, "the only question presented by the case is whether the distribution is made by chance or not."

This game was a lottery because the outcome was based primarily on chance. That is not to say that there is no skill or judgment involved, but it is slight compared to the chance involved. "A lottery," said the court, "does not cease to be such . . . because its result may be affected, to some slight extent, by the exercise of judgment." In this case, the controlling factor in receiving a prize was chance, rather than skill or judgment.

Earlier in this chapter we looked at a case that involved picking the winners of upcoming football games. Surely chance is involved in that game, you may think. Not so. Let's look at a situation to explain why that is.

Charles Rich and Frank Camarrata ran a game for which they were essentially bookmakers. The two men solicited bets or wagers on the outcome of sporting events from horse racing to baseball. They also took bets on elections. A complaint was filed against these two men charging that they were operating an illegal lottery in *United States v. Rich.*[10]

The participant wagered an amount by placing a bet. The requirement of consideration was met. The participant also stood to win a large return if the right team won. That meant that the requirement of a prize was also present. What was left to be determined was whether the game involved chance. That was the issue that the court was left to ponder.

The court said about "chance" that, ". . . the word has reference to the attempt to attain certain ends, not by skill or any known or fixed rules, but by the happening of a subsequent event, incapable of ascertainment or accomplishment by means of human foresight or ingenuity." Obviously, a blindfolded man pulling a winning ticket from a jar involves pure chance. Here, though, it's a different story.

The government argued that choosing the winner of a horse race or baseball game offered extremely narrow odds. Because of the huge amount of uncertainty, the winner could attribute the win to nothing more than a guess.

The court, however, felt that "there is always something more than a mere guess" involved, and they said:

> The odds may often be long, and the chance of winning small so as to tempt the ignorant and the greedy to risk amounts small or large on the chance of getting a much larger return, and yet in every case there is a race or a game of skill or an election or something in which natural forces are involved and upon which knowledge, skill and judgment are brought into play.

In the case of a horse race, bets are placed on races that may be run quite some time in the future. Yet, the bets are placed based on information that can be obtained about the horses in advance. The stable that the horse comes from, the owner, the jockey, and the track are all considerations on which knowledge, skill, and judgment can be used to make a selection. There is no pure chance here as applied to lotteries. The government lost its case.

But chance in determining the winner is not the only way this element can be involved to turn a contest into a lottery. Chance is also created when the amount of the ultimate prize is unknown or undetermined. That is, when the amount of the prize is to be determined by some event yet to happen, like the dollar sales of a particular store on a certain day in the future. Another situation could exist when the prize depends on the number of people who ultimately enter the contest.

In 1963 Boris Zebelman was a car dealer in Gardner, Kansas. He developed a game to promote his dealership, which he advertised through the mail. He claimed that anyone who bought a car from him would become an "automobile owner representative." This rep would then submit names and addresses of others who would be potential buyers. For each person whose name was submitted and who purchased a car, also becoming a rep, the original rep would receive $100 in cash. Also, the original rep would receive $50 for each person whose name was submitted by the new participant, if that person bought a car and participated as a rep.

In other words, let's say Mr. Smith bought a car from Zebelman and became a rep. He would submit names of others including Ms. Jones. Now Ms. Jones buys a car and becomes a rep, and Mr. Smith receives $100. Then Ms. Jones submits the name of Mr. Adams, who buys a car and becomes a rep. In that case, Ms. Jones would receive $100, and Mr. Smith would receive $50. If this sounds like a pyramid scheme, it is.

Zebelman was caught and charged with 15 counts of running a lottery. The case was *Zebelman* v. *United States*.[11] The question here is tricky. Is chance involved? In the case of the original purchaser rep, the answer is no. In this phase of the game, chance is not the controlling factor. The person has control over this part of the game.

The chance element enters into the picture because "the original purchaser has no control over the payment or receipt of the $50 since it is the person whose name he submits that must locate another buyer." This situation requires, in large part, the element of chance, and this makes the scheme a lottery.

Use Of Skill

If skill or judgment is dominant, then the game is not a lottery. In games that ask for the "best letter," "best essay," or "best name," no chance is present. Also, as we saw in the *Rich* case involving sports games, skill or judgment is required because picking the winner is determined in part by the skill of the entrant.

As long as the winners are determined on the basis of a comparison of the skill of the entries, it is legal. In these games if a tie exists, both winners must receive prizes of equal value; otherwise chance enters into the picture again.

In 1912 the Armstrong-Byrd Music company in Oklahoma City, Oklahoma, ran a promotion for a give-away of one of its pianos. The company ran ads promoting the contest. The object of the game was to complete a puzzle by filling in spaces with numbers to make a total of fifteen. The puzzle was quite simple, but the challenge was to submit an entry that was the neatest or most unique design.

On May 10, 1912, a group of judges gathered together to pick the winner from the 6,500 entries. Most were simply filled in puzzles from the entry blank supplied in the newspaper ad. But a few were very original. One was actually made out of burnt wood, and another was embroidered on a pillow. The five most unique and original were awarded the promised prizes.

When the winners were notified of their prizes by mail, the Postmaster, H. G. Eastman, filed suit to stop what he considered an illegal lottery. The case was *Eastman* v. *Armstrong-Byrd Music Co.*[12] The court determined that the contest winners were picked based on a use of their skill and judgment. As the court said, "There was no element of chance in this scheme or plan." This contest was not a lottery and therefore legal.

AGENCIES THAT HAVE REGULATION OVER CONTESTS

There are basically four federal agencies with control over contests and how they are promoted. The U. S. Postal Service has control over any contest that uses the mail in any way. The Federal Trade Commission has control over any activity which is deceptive or unfair, including contests. The Federal Communications Commission controls any contest advertised over radio or television. The Bureau of Alcohol, Tobacco and Firearms controls contests which affect those items. And, finally, each state has specific statutes that govern the use of contests, as do each of the television networks. We'll look at each of these in the remainder of this chapter.

U. S. Postal Service

The first form of regulation over gambling activities took place in 1868 in the form of postal regulations.[13] These laws were created in an attempt to curb the fraud and abuse in state sponsored lotteries after the Civil War.

Under current law, it is a criminal offense to mail any advertisement of any lottery, gift enterprise, or similar scheme where prizes are awarded based on chance. Violation of this law carries a fine of $1,000 or two years in prison, or both.[14] In addition, the Postal Service is authorized to issue a cease-and-desist order and refuse processing any such advertisement in the U.S. mail.[15] Violation of a cease-and-desist order carries a civil fine of up to $10,000 per day.

Contests that use the mail in any way must be approved by the General Counsel, Mailability Division, U.S. Postal Service, Washington, D.C. 20006. When I say "contests that use the mail," I mean anything from mailing entry forms to mailing notification to winners after the contest.

We've seen cases earlier where the Postal Service brought

suit because the mail was used in the scheme. *United States v. Purvis, Garden City Chamber of Commerce v. Wagner, Dreem Arts, Inc. v. City of Chicago, People ex rel. Ellison v. Lavin* and *Eastman v. Armstrong-Byrd Music Co.*, are good examples of cases where the Postal Service became involved.

Compliance with Postal Service rules, however, is going to be more difficult in the future. Effective January 2, 1985, it no longer issues "no action letters" to advertisers who wish a ruling on whether or not their proposed contests are lotteries, and so would be challenged by the Postal Service under the postal lottery laws.[16] Its reason: Over the years the "number and complexity" of requests for such letters had increased dramatically.

Until recently, a game of chance enclosed in a product package violated the postal lottery law unless it was disclosed clearly in the advertising and on the package that a person could enter the contest by merely sending in a "facsimile" in the form of a 3 x 5 card with the product's name or some other words or phrases written or printed by hand. However, in 1979 the Postal Service, by means of a "no action" letter, approved a promotion involving an in-pack game piece, if the package itself contained a notice of "no purchase necessary" and advised that a free game piece was available to persons who requested one by mail. In the view of the Postal Service this message offered potential entrants an accessible free entry alternative and that, therefore, persons who chose to enter by purchasing the package would be doing so voluntarily. In other words, the equivalent free entry offer eliminated the lottery element of consideration. Contrast this with the *Dreem Arts* case we looked at earlier, where it was much more difficult to obtain information with which to send in a facsimile entry.

Federal Trade Commission

The FTC, in 1925, began issuing cease-and-desist orders against lotteries. Since then the FTC has established rules that apply to contests. It requires the following:

- Disclosure of the exact number of prizes to be awarded;
- Disclosure of the odds of winning;
- Disclosure of the area within which the game will exist;
- Disclosure of the length of the contest;
- That all game pieces must be distributed to stores on a totally random basis; and
- That the game cannot end until all game pieces are handed out.

Also, any game that continues beyond 30 days must disclose the number of unredeemed prizes and revised odds on a weekly basis. Successive games must be separated by 30 days or the length of the previous game, whichever is shorter.

These rules do not apply to broadcast media; however, the same information must be made available to consumers. The company must disclose where the consumer can go, or write, to get complete contest information.

R. F. Keppel & Brothers operated a business which manufactured and placed in retail stores a candy game known as Break and Take. In the early 1930's, Keppel promoted its game in stores located near schools. It displayed the game in a way that would be attractive to children. The company earned about $234,000 a year from the game.

The game involved an assortment of wrapped candy. The participant would pay one cent and pick a piece of candy from the 120 pieces in the display. The candy would be opened to discover if it contained a penny as a prize, or a slip of paper with a purchase price of 1, 2, or 3 cents. In reality, only four pieces contained a penny. The other pieces of candy contained prices of 1 to 3 cents each. If the candy contained a ticket, that was the price that the participant had to pay. There was a possibility that the person could win back the initial penny investment and get the candy free. But the odds were very low.

Obviously, this game qualified as a lottery. All three

essential elements were present: consideration, prize, and chance. Yet, the Federal Trade Commission brought suit in *Federal Trade Commission v. R. F. Keppel & Bros. Inc.*,[17] because of the game's effect on children. They were the audience at which the game was directed.

The Supreme Court, in upholding the FTC's decision, felt that "the method of competition adopted . . . induces children, too young to be capable of exercising an intelligent judgment of the transaction, to purchase an article less desirable in point of quality or quantity than that offered at a comparable price."

That is why the FTC became involved with the lottery. The method exploited children who were unable to protect themselves. The FTC, as we saw in Chapters 2 and 3, concerns itself with deception and unfairness. As the Court said, "It would seem a gross perversion . . . to hold that the method is not 'unfair.'" Keppel lost the case.

In many cases, the FTC may issue a cease-and-desist order for games that are not deemed to be literally illegal lotteries. Remember that the FTC has the authority to stop any activity that is unfair or deceptive, even if it does not violate specific lottery regulations.

A good example of this involved the *Reader's Digest* Sweepstakes. Entry forms were mailed to members of the public. The entry forms contained a number and a ticket with the same number printed on it. The participant was to return the ticket to *Reader's Digest* where it would be compared against preselected winning numbers. If the number on the ticket matched a winning number, that prize would be awarded.

The intent of the sweepstakes was to build sales in its products. To promote its sweepstakes, *Reader's Digest* made claims about the contest, including:

- Participants only needed to mail in their ticket to receive their prize if they were winners;
- Participants had a reasonable chance of winning;

- All advertised prizes had been purchased by *Reader's Digest* prior to the contest;
- Consumers who received entry forms were "selected," "chosen," or were "one of the few people to be invited;"
- Entry forms were mailed on a limited basis; and
- In January 1969 (a typical contest), 101,751 prizes were offered worth $999,000.

This well-known sweepstakes ran into trouble when the FTC stepped in and filed suit in *In the Matter of Reader's Digest Assn.*[18] The FTC took action, not because this was an illegal lottery, but because the sweepstakes was deceptive.

In reality, the claims that *Reader's Digest* made in its advertisements and promotion were not accurate. Participants were not "one of the few to be invited." In fact, millions of copies of the *Reader's Digest* Sweepstakes entry forms were mailed to consumers. In the January 1969 contest, there were not 101,751 prizes worth $999,000. In reality there were 40,517 prizes worth $441,789. Also, winners were required to do more than send in their ticket to receive a prize. They were required to do other undisclosed things—for example, submit to interviews by a private detective before being allowed to obtain their prize.

In addition, there was no "reasonable opportunity to win" in *Reader's Digest* Sweepstakes. As noted at the beginning of this chapter, the odds of winning first prize were about 1 in 480,000. The *Reader's Digest* Sweepstakes was simply not what it was promoted to be. Because of the deception, the FTC issued a cease-and-desist order.

Generally, there are specific situations regarding contests that the FTC does not allow. The following list represents a general outline of practices that are prohibited by the FTC as they apply to contests:

- Making false representations of the value of a prize;
- Promising cash and awarding merchandise instead;
- Failing to follow contest rules as established; and

- Offering a number of prizes that differ from those advertised.

In addition, the FTC does have a rule governing contests in the food retailing and gasoline industries. Issued in the wake of complaints that games were allegedly rigged, the commission adopted a rule, that is almost impossible to live with, requiring that the game pieces must be updated frequently;[19] this is difficult in a game that might be run by as many as 10,000 retail gas stations.

Federal Communications Commission

Congress first attempted to regulate the airwaves under the Radio Act of 1927.[20] However, lotteries were not regulated in broadcast until the Federal Communications Act of 1934.[21] Later these regulations were made a part of the Criminal Code as Section 1304.[22]

Under current law, Section 1304, it is a criminal offense to broadcast by radio or television any advertisement for a lottery, gift enterprise, or similar scheme. Specifically, the statute prohibits:

Any advertisement of or information concerning any lottery, gift enterprise, or similar scheme, offering prizes dependent in whole or in part upon lot or chance, or any list of the prizes drawn or awarded by means of any such lottery, gift enterprise, or scheme, whether said list contains any part or all of such prizes . . . .[23]

A good example of this occurred in 1973. The University of Florida radio station WRUF in Gainesville, Florida, broadcast a radio commercial for its client, Shaw and Keeter Fordtown. Any person who purchased an automobile from the dealership received a prize. Here's the radio copy:

• •
Shaw and Keeter has an extra bonus for you . . .
A U.S. Savings Bond with every new car or truck delivered!
At least a $25 bond . . . it might be a $50 bond . . .
it could be a $500 bond!
After purchase, check the sealed envelope in the glove box
with the sealed envelope in the office.
It will be a $25 bond . . .
it might be a $50 bond . . . it could be a $500 bond!
Offer ends March 31st!
Hurry to Shaw and Keeter Fordtown,
downtown at 238 West University Avenue!
• •

When the FCC learned of the commercial, it filed a complaint against the school. The FCC held that a violation of lottery restrictions was created with *In the Matter of University of Florida*.[24]

All three elements of a lottery existed in this case. A prize was offered in the form of a savings bond. While every purchaser received a bond, values varied of the bonds considerably. Consideration existed since the consumer was required to purchase a car or truck before being eligible to win a savings bond. Finally, chance was present as to which bond would be won. Since the University of Florida created, produced, and aired the spot, it was required to pay a fine of $2,000.

In any case where broadcast media is involved the advertisement should include information on the following:

• Who may participate;
• Type of entries required;
• Where, when, and how the entry is to be submitted;
• Number and nature of prizes;
• The existence of duplicate prizes in the case of ties;
• The closing date; and
• Where complete contest details can be obtained.

Bureau Of Alcohol, Tobacco And Firearms

The Bureau of Alcohol, Tobacco and Firearms (ATF) has jurisdiction over what's contained in, attached to, or printed on packages of certain tobacco products, such as cigarettes. The ATF view differs from the U.S. Postal Service's as to what constitutes a lottery. The ATF believes, for example, that the element of consideration exists even if no purchase of a tobacco product is required to take part in a contest. The statute in question, is a section of the Internal Revenue Code of 1954,[25] providing that no certificate or coupon representing a "ticket, chance, share or interest in or dependent, the event of a lottery" shall appear in or "on any package of tobacco products or cigarette papers or tubes."

The ATF also issues advisory letters involving the lottery aspects of proposed promotions. However, unlike the Postal Service, it has steadfastly refused to permit any kind of game promotion in which the game price is enclosed in the package with cigarettes or cigars.

STATE REGULATION

Each of the states is in agreement as to what constitutes an illegal lottery, as we've discussed in the previous part of this chapter. They agree with the federal guidelines in most all cases. The difference shows up in how the states interpret the requirements. What constitutes "chance," "a prize," and especially "consideration" is where the states vary in some ways.

Each state has legislated specific requirements for contests. The current state statutes or amendments, regulation or case law should be consulted before creating an advertisement involving a contest. It would also be wise to consult with an attorney in the applicable state The following is a review of the law in many key states.

Alaska

Pyramid schemes occur where purchasers get consideration in the form of rebates or commission payments when they cause others to participate in the program. These are prohibited.[26]

Arizona

Pyramid schemes are programs where purchasers get consideration in the form of rebates or commission payments when they introduce other persons into participation in the program. These schemes are prohibited.[27]

Arkansas

Pyramid schemes are prohibited in Arkansas. These schemes occur where purchasers get consideration in the form of rebates or commissions when they bring others into the program. These schemes are prohibited.[28]

California

A leading case that extensively discusses the element of consideration when some participants receive a game chance with a purchase is: *California Gasoline Retailers v. Regal Petroleum Corp.*[29]

California also requires that a form to completed and filed with the State Department of Justice if telephone solicitation implies that a consumer may win a prize.[30]

California has anti-deception statutes that prohibit misrepresentations about the chances of winning a contest, the number of winners, and the value or availability of the prizes .[31]

In California, there are disclosure requirements where a prize is offered as an inducement to either attend a sales presentation or visit a location.[32]

Pyramid schemes where purchasers get consideration in the form of rebates or commission payments when they introduce other persons into the program are illegal. These are prohibited.[33]

Connecticut

This state has certain minor restrictions concerning the disclosure of prizes.[34]

Connecticut requires certain disclosures for contests relating to promotion of time-share plans.[35]

Pyramid schemes are illegal where purchasers get consideration in the form of rebates or commission payments when they induce other persons to participate in the program.[36]

Florida

In Florida the following are required for a game promotion:
- All rules and regulations must be filed with the Department of Legal Affairs thirty days in advance of game commencement;
- Rules and regulations must be posted in every retail outlet and published in all advertising copy;
- The promoter must establish a trust account or obtain a bond equivalent to the total value of all prizes offered;
- The promoter must provide the Department of Legal Affairs with a certified list of the names and addresses of all persons who have won a prize of more than $25 within sixty days after such winners have been determined;
- A list of winners must either be provided to persons who request it or published in a Florida newspaper of general circulation; and
- The promoter must hold all winning entries submitted for a period of ninety days after the close or completion of the game.[37]

This statute applies only to games in which the total value of the prizes exceeds $5,000 but, applies to all game promotions, not only those offered by retailers. A non-refundable filing fee of $100 must accompany the advance registration papers. Florida provides forms to aid game promoters in making the required filings.

Florida prohibits anyone connected with a game promotion from coercing a retail operator to participate in a promotion.[38]

Florida also has anti-deception statutes prohibiting misrepresentations about the chances of winning a contest, the number of winners, and the value or availability of the prizes.[39]

Florida prohibits the use of chance contests relating to promotion of time-share plans.[40]

Florida also prohibits promoters from notifying a person that he/she has won a prize or gift if the person must pay any money, do any act, or submit to a sales promotion effort.[41]

Georgia

Georgia has disclosure restrictions where a prize is offered as an inducement to either attend a sales presentation or visit a location.[42]

Georgia requires certain disclosures for contests relating to promotion of time-share plans.[43]

Hawaii

Hawaii prohibits telephone solicitors from offering prizes as a promotional device.[44]

Illinois

Illinois has conflicting precedents on the legality of grocery store promotions, but has not enforced any lottery restrictions against game promotions.

Louisiana

In Louisiana, there are disclosure requirements when a prize is offered as an inducement to either attend a sales presentation or visit a location.[45]

Louisiana requires certain disclosures for contests relating to promotion of time-share plans.[46]

Maine

Maine forbids gas station games.[47] It is also illegal to award liquor as a prize in a contest.[48] This state also restricts the distribution of some live animals as prizes.[49]

Here again, pyramid schemes are prohibited.[50] In these programs purchasers get consideration in the form of rebates or commission payments when they introduce others into the program.

Maryland

Maryland prohibits promoters from notifying a person that he/she has won a prize or gift if the person must pay any money, do any act, or submit to a sales promotion effort.[51]

This state specifically limits the ability of gas station operators from using games of chance as promotions.[52]

Maryland also requires certain disclosures for contests relating to promotion of time-share plans.[53]

Massachusetts

Massachusetts forbids gas station games.[54] This state also restricts the distribution of some live animals as prizes.[55]

Michigan

Michigan requires disclosure of the prizes and information concerning the number of prizes to be awarded. Michigan prohibits anyone connected with a game promotion from coercing a retail operator to participate in a promotion.[56]

Minnesota

Minnesota specifically prohibits "in-package" promotional

games unless participation is available free, without purchase of the package.[57]

Missouri

The Missouri electorate amended the state constitution to permit games of chance. The Supervisor of Liquor Control permits promotional games on the premises of licensees if consideration is not required for "participating in such games or contests or for receiving the award or prize therefrom."[58]

This language tracks part of the language of the constitutional amendment approved by the voters in November 1978. Section 39 (9) appears to outlaw games in which a purchase is required after the participant had been declared a winner.

However, the constitutional amendment also contains a definition of "lottery or gift enterprise," stating that these terms: ". . . shall mean only those games or contests whereby money or something of value is exchanged directly for the tickets or chance to participate in the game or contest."

The Division of Liquor Control will enforce regulations against food stores and others who have a license to sell 5 percent beer and, therefore, a retail game which requires a purchase "for receiving the award or prize" is unlawful for such licensees.

Missouri requires certain disclosures for contests relating to promotion of time-share plans.[59]

Montana

Pyramid schemes, programs where purchasers get consideration in the form of rebates or commission payments when they introduce other persons into participation in the program, are prohibited.[60]

Nevada

This state specifically limits gas station operators from using games of chance as promotions. [61]

Pyramid schemes are programs where purchasers get consideration in the form of rebates or commission payments when they introduce other persons into participation in the program. These schemes are prohibited.[62]

New Hampshire

Like Nevada, this state specifically limits gas station operators from using games of chance as promotions.[63]

New Jersey

Insofar as gasoline station promotions are concerned, it is immaterial in New Jersey whether consideration is or is not present because its Unfair Trade Practices (UTP) law[64] flatly prohibits "games of chance, in connection with the sale of motor fuels." The courts have ruled that the definition of a lottery contained in the state's anti lottery law, which makes consideration an indispensable element of a lottery, does not control the interpretation or affect the application of its UTP law to gasoline retailers. See *United Stations of New Jersey* v. *Getty Oil Co.*[65]

New Jersey also prohibits promoters from notifying a person that she has won a prize or gift if the person must pay any money, do any act, or submit to a sales promotion effort.[66]

New Mexico

Pyramid schemes are programs where purchasers get consideration in the form of rebates or commission payments when they introduce other persons into participation in the program. These schemes are prohibited.[67]

New York

New York's General Business Law requires registration of promotional games with the Miscellaneous Records Section of the

Department of State.[68] To register a game, you must complete an application form and enclose a $50 fee. The application form includes requests for the names of promoters, the odds of winning, and a copy of the rules. A trust account must be established or bond posted sufficient to cover the amount of the prize to be distributed in New York state. Winners must be disclosed to the New York Department of State within ninety-days of the conclusion of the contest.

Contrary to many other states, New York does permit promoters to notify a person that has won a prize or gift when the person must pay some money, do an act, or submit to a sales promotion effort. But this is only allowed if the operator explicitly informs the person of these conditions to the receipt of the prize.[69]

New York prohibits anyone connected with a game promotion from coercing a retail operator to participate in a promotion.[70]

North Carolina

Pyramid schemes are illegal in North Carolina. These are programs where purchasers get consideration in the form of rebates or commission payments when they introduce others into participation in the program. These schemes are prohibited.[71]

North Dakota

North Dakota addresses an ambiguity in the common law of lottery. The issue was: In a game promotion that requires only some contestants to give a consideration to enter, has one established a lottery against those who do not pay? In North Dakota if some patrons receive free chances to enter, their participation in the game may be prohibited if others have to pay.

Pyramid schemes are programs where purchasers get consideration in the form of rebates or commission payments when they introduce other persons into participation in the program. These schemes are prohibited.[72]

Ohio

Similar to New York, Ohio does permit promoters to notify a person that he/she has won a prize or gift when the person must pay some money, do an act, or submit to a sales promotion effort. But this is only allowed if the operator explicitly informs the person of the conditions to the receipt of the prize.[73]

Oregon

Oregon has anti-deception statutes prohibiting misrepresentations about the chances of winning a contest, the number of winners, and the value or availability of the prizes.[74]

Pyramid schemes are illegal here where purchasers get consideration in the form of rebates or commission payments when they induce others into participation in the program. These schemes are prohibited.[75]

Pennsylvania

Pennsylvania requires certain disclosures for contests relating to promotion of time-share plans.[76]

Rhode Island

Rhode Island has registration requirements similar to the laws of New York and Florida in that it only applies to games conducted by retail establishments. However, Rhode Island law applies to situations where the prize totals as little as $500.

Games by retail gasoline stations are not prohibited in this state. However, state law prohibits retail gasoline dealers from using games of chance or awarding any prizes which "permit any purchaser to obtain motor fuel from such retail dealer at a net price lower than the posted price applicable at the time of the sale."[77]

Pyramid schemes are programs where purchasers get consideration in the form of rebates or commission payments when they introduce other persons into participation in the program. These schemes are prohibited under *Roberts* v. *Communications Inv. Club*.[78]

Additionally, state law prohibits coercion of retail dealers to participate in a game of chance.[79]

Tennessee

Tennessee requires certain disclosures for contests relating to promotion of time-share plans.[80]

Pyramid schemes are programs where purchasers get consideration in the form of rebates or commission payments when they introduce other persons into participation in the program. These schemes are prohibited.[81]

Texas

Texas has anti-deception statutes prohibiting misrepresentations about the chances of winning a contest, the number of winners, and the value or availability of the prizes.[82]

Texas requires certain disclosures for contests relating to promotion of time-share plans.[83]

Utah

Pyramid schemes are prohibited in Utah. These occur where purchasers get consideration in the form of rebates or commission payments when they introduce others into the program. These schemes are prohibited.[84]

Vermont

Vermont's anti-deception statutes prohibit misrepresentations about the chances of winning a contest, the number of winners, and the value or availability of the prizes.[85]

Pyramid schemes are programs where purchasers get consideration in the form of rebates or commission payments when they introduce other persons into participation in the program. These schemes are prohibited.[86]

Virginia

Virginia requires certain disclosures for contests relating to promotion of time-share plans.[87]

Washington

Article II, Section 24 of Washington's constitution was amended in 1972 to read in part: "lotteries shall be prohibited except as specifically authorized upon affirmative vote of 60% of the members of each house of the legislature . . . ." The statute[88] defines the term "lottery" as meaning "a scheme for the distribution of money or property by chance, among persons who have paid or agreed to pay a valuable consideration for the chance."

Further, the statute states that the term "valuable consideration" does not include listening to or watching a television or radio show, filling out and returning a coupon or entry blank received through the mail or published in a newspaper or magazine, sending in an entry blank, visiting a business establishment to obtain a game piece, expending time, thought, attention and energy in perusing game materials, or merely registering at a place of business or making or answering a telephone call.

The law provides that a "drawing" conducted by a retail outlet may not last more than seven consecutive days and only one such drawing can be conducted within a year. This does not prevent retailers from conducting other types of games, such as "instant winner" rub-off games and bingo games.

Pyramid schemes are programs where purchasers get consideration in the form of rebates or commission payments when they introduce other persons into participation in the program. These schemes are prohibited.[89]

West Virginia

Pyramid schemes are programs where purchasers get consideration in the form of rebates or commission payments when they introduce other persons into participation in the program. These schemes are prohibited.[90]

Wisconsin

Wisconsin is a state in flux regarding lotteries. In 1965, Wisconsin adopted a constitutional amendment. The state's attorney general then issued a decision that only skill contests were permissible. In 1982, however, Wisconsin courts upheld a bottle-top game in *Coca-Cola* v. *LaFollette*.[91] In 1983, another decision, *State* v. *Dahik*,[92] declared that chance must be the dominant element in a lottery. Yet, one remnant of the old view on lotteries is probably *Kayden* v. *Murphy*,[93] which offered that a game requiring a store visit would be void.

Pyramid schemes are programs where purchasers get consideration in the form of rebates or commission payments when they introduce other persons into participation in the program. These schemes are prohibited under *State* v. *Dahik*.

Wisconsin specifically prohibits "in-package" promotional games unless participation is available free, without purchase of the package.[94]

NETWORK STANDARDS

All major television networks have special rules to monitor ads that promote contests. Each has specific review procedures covering such advertising.

The advertiser of a proposed contest should present the storyboard and the game details, along with rules, entry prizes, game pieces, and any other elements to the network involved for approval.

CBS's Procedures

At CBS, the rules are outlined in *CBS Television Network Advertising Guidelines*. A proposed ad will be reviewed initially and a questionnaire mailed out. Ad agencies are required to complete the form and enclose a copy of the official rules as they will actually be used, an entry blank and playing pieces, and a detailed breakdown of all prizes awarded during the contest. All related point-of-sale displays and print media ads must also to be enclosed.

CBS will review the following points:

- The final date by which one can enter the contest or claim a prize. This date must be clearly stated in the commercial;
- Where entry blanks and rules will be available and the manner in which they may be obtained without purchase;
- When the commercials will be aired and in what geographic area the contest will be promoted;
- What prizes are to be awarded and who will supply them (advertiser or prize company);
- Eligibility requirements must be clearly disclosed in the commercial. For example, whether one must be a licensed driver to enter;
- Any limitations on the number of times one can enter a contest;
- Whether a contest is limited to "participating dealers," there will be sufficient sources where contest materials will be available;
- What print media will be running ads relating to the contest. (However, it does not need to know if another network will carry the ads.);
- Whether the commercials will be used in children's programming. If children are the target of a game, they must be informed very clearly what the odds of winning are. The commercial must show the prizes that will be awarded;

- Whether the contest is based on skill or chance. If the contest is based on chance, CBS wants to know whether the winners will be chosen by a random drawing. If so, where, when, and who will supervise the contest?;
- Will the winning contestant have to consent to use of his/her name to receive a prize?;
- If the contest is skilled in nature, the criteria for judging, the list of judges, and their qualifications must be disclosed;
- Will duplicate prizes will be awarded. If not, how will ties be broken?; and
- Will the public be able to obtain records of the contest, the list of correct answers, and the names of winners?

NBC's Procedures

The *NBC Broadcast Standards for Television* provide for review of advertising of contests to assure that the proposed contest "is not a lottery, that the material terms are clearly stated, and that it is being conducted fairly, honestly and according to its rules." The following will need to be addressed:

- Submission of complete details of the program to the Broadcast Standards Department at least ten business days prior to the first public announcement of the contest (not the first NBC airing of the commercial);

- Submission of a complete copy of the contest rules, the entry blank, a complete questionnaire (similar to that outlined for CBS), all promotional material, and any print media ads and proposed broadcast copy;

- On-air contest disclosures are similar to CBS's. However, the criteria in which station call-in or call-out quizzes are handled must be explained;

- Game procedures must be free of tampering. NBC is very concerned with the security procedures used throughout the contest to maintain integrity and insure that contest rules are followed fairly; and

• NBC also wants to know if any aspect of the contest could alarm the public over an imaginary danger; cause crowds, traffic violations or result in damage to public or private property or divert police officers from their normal duties; or result in significant numbers of telephone calls to government agencies or private lines.

ABC's Procedures

The *ABC Advertising Standards* allows advertising of contests as long as the contest offers a fair opportunity to all qualified contestants, it complies with all relevant laws and regulations, and it is not contrary to the public interest.

While ABC does not have a specific questionnaire procedure, the complete proposed ad and all details of the contest rules, prizes, and a copy of the entry blank must be approved by ABC's department of Broadcast Standards and Practices. ABC reviews the following points:

• A free means of entering the contest must be provided if there is an element of chance involved;
• All contestants must have an equal chance of winning a chance-based contest;
• The network will refuse to broadcast any information concerning a private lottery;
• Methods of judging a contest must be disclosed; and
• Sweepstakes may be aimed at children if they have a fair chance of winning and the prizes are appropriate. The address to submit entries in children's sweepstakes must be both displayed visually and given in the audio portion of the commercial.

GUIDELINES IN CREATING CONTESTS

When developing contests there are certain items to consider. We've looked at these throughout this chapter. Here is a quick reference list of points to think about when developing contests and promoting them in ads. This is only a starting point. The specifics of the contest will determine what must be included..

Contest development should include the following:

- A description of the judging method;
- A statement that entries will not be returned;
- A statement that entries become the property of the company;
- A statement that winners will be notified by mail, if applicable;
- A statement regarding the limit on the number or frequency that a person may enter;
- A statement as to who may or may not enter the contest (i.e., children under 18, employees of the company);
- A list of places where the contest is void;
- A list of the prizes, including the retail value and cash substitute option if any;
- A clarification regarding whether certain prizes will only be given to parents or guardians, when a minor is the winner;
- A list of where entries may be sent, as well as where contest rules, a list of winners and a list of prizes, may be obtained;
- A statement that the company reserves the right to use names and likenesses of entrants or winners for publicity purposes;
- A deadline (by final postmark date) for receipt of entries;
- Disclaimer of liability for any applicable taxes, licensing or other fees on prizes;
- Disclaimer of liability for lost or stolen prizes;
- Disclaimer of liability for prizes supplied by others; and
- The termination date of the contest.

[1] *In the Matter of Reader's Digest Assn.*, 79 F.T.C. 696 (1971).

[2] *United States* v. *83 Cases of Merchandise Labeled "Honest John,"* 29 F. Supp. 912, at 915 (D.C. Md., 1939).

[3] *U.S.* v. *83 Cases of Merchandise Labeled "Honest John,"* 29 F. Supp. 912 (D.C. Md., 1939).

[4] *United States* v. *Purvis*, 195 F. 618 (N.D. Ga. 1912).

[5] Wisconsin Statutes Annotated, section 945.01(2)(b)(1)(1981).

[6] *Garden City Chamber of Commerce* v. *Wagner*, 100 F. Supp. 769 (E.D.N.Y. 1951).

[7] *In the Matter of Metromedia Inc.*, 60 F.C.C.2d 1075 (1976).

[8] *Dreem Arts, Inc.* v. *City of Chicago*, 637 F. Supp. 53 (N.D. Ill. 1986).

[9] *People ex rel. Ellison* v. *Lavin*, 179 N.Y. 164 (1904).

[10] *United States* v. *Rich*, 90 F. Supp. 624 (E.D. Ill. 1950).

[11] *Zebelman* v. *United States*, 339 F.2d 484 (10th Cir. 1964).

[12] *Eastman* v. *Armstrong-Byrd Music Co.*, 212 F. 662 (8th Cir. 1914).

[13] 15 Stat. 194 (1868).

[14] 18 U.S.C., section 1302 (1982).

[15] 39 U.S.C., section 3001, 3005 (1984 Supp.).

[16] 18 U.S.C. §1302; 39 U.S.C. §3005.

[17] *Federal Trade Commission* v. *R. F. Keppel & Bros. Inc.*, 291 U.S. 304, 54 S.Ct. 423, 78 L.Ed. 2d 814 (1934).

[18] *In the Matter of Reader's Digest Assn.*, 79 F.T.C. 696 (1971).

[19] 16 C.F.R. 419.

[20] 44 Stat. 1162 (1927).

[21] H. R. Rep. No. 72-2106, 72 Cong. 2d Sess. (1933).

[22] 18 U.S.C., section 312 (1982).

[23] 18 U.S.C., section 1304.

[24] *In the Matter of University of Florida*, 40 F.C.C.2d 188 (1973).

[25] 26 U.S.C. 5723(c).

[26] Alaska Stat. §45.50.471.

[27] Ariz. Rev. Stat. Ann. §44-1731.

[28] Ark. Stat. Ann. §41-3285.

[29] *California Gasoline Retailers* v. *Regal Petroleum Corp.*, 330 P.2d 778 (Cal. 1958).

[30] Cal. Bus. & Prof. Code §17511.3.

[31] Cal. Bus. & Prof. Code §17537.1.

[32] Cal. Bus. & Prof. Code. §17537.1.

[33] Cal. Penal Code. §327.

[34] Connecticut Statutes §53-290(a).

[35] Conn. Gen. Stat. Ann. §42-103-103bb.

[36] Conn. Gen. Stat. Ann. §42-145.

[37] Fla. Stat. Ann. §849.094.

[38] Fla. Stat. Ann. §849.094(7).

[39] Fla. Admin. Code Ann. 2-9.007.

[40] Fla. Stat. Ann. §721.111(2).

[41] Fla. Stat. Ann. §817.415.

[42] Ga. Code Ann. §16-12-36.

[43] Ga. Code Ann. §44-3-188.

[44] Haw. Rev. Stat. §468-4.

[45] La. Rev. Stat. Ann. §51:1721.

[46] La. Rev. Stat. Ann. §9:1131.12(g).

[47] Me. Rev. Stat. Ann. tit 17-2304.

[48] Me. Rev. Stat. Ann. tit 28, §305.

[49] Me. Rev. Stat. Ann. tit. 7, §3972.

[50] Me. Rev. Stat. Ann. tit. 17, §2305.

[51] Md. Com. Law Code Ann. §13-305.

[52] Md. Ann. Code Art. 56 §144A.

[53] Md. Real Prop. Code Ann. §11A-119.

[54] Massachusetts Statutes 271 §6c.

[55] Mass. Gen. Laws Ann. Ch. 272, §80F.

[56] Michigan Statutes §750.372a.

[57] Minn. Stat. Ann. §609.75.

[58] 11 CSR 70-2. 140.

[59] Mo. Ann. Stat. §407.610.

[60] Mont. Code Ann. §45-6-319.

[61] Nev. Rev. Stat. Ann. §1598.799.

[62] Nev. Rev. Stat. Ann. §598.100.

[63] N.H. Rev. Stat. Ann. §287-B:1.

[64] N.J. Stat. Ann., 56: 6-2 (f).

[65] *United Stations of New Jersey* v. *Getty Oil Co.*, 246 A.2d 150 (1968).

[66] N.J. Stat. Ann §56:8-2.3.

[67] N.M. Stat. Ann. §57-13-4.

[68] N.Y. Gen. Bus. Law §369(e).

[69] N.Y. Gen. Bus. Law §369(ee).

[70] N.Y. Gen. Bus. Law §369-e(7).

[71] N.C.. Gen. Stat. §14-291.2.

[72] N.D. Cent. Code. §51-16-01.

[73] Ohio Admin. Code §109:4-3-06.

[74] Or. Rev. Stat. §646.608(p).

[75] Or. Rev. Stat. §646.608.

[76] 63 Pa. Cons. Stat. Ann. §455.604(a)(18).

[77] R.I. Gen Laws §31-37-14.

[78] *Roberts* v. *Communications Inv. Club*, 431 A.2d 1206, 1212 (R.I. 1981).

[79] R.I. Gen Laws §11-50-7.

[80] Tenn. Code Ann. §66-32-133.

[81] Tenn. Code Ann. §39-6-625.

[82] Tex. Penal Code Ann. §32.42.

[83] Tex. Rev. Civ. Stat. Ann. art.6573c.

[84] Utah Code Ann. §76-6a-3.

[85] Vt. Admin. Proc. Comp. §109.01.

[86] Vt. Admin. Proc. Comp. §101.01.

[87] Va. Code Ann. §55-374.1.

[88] RCW 9.46.020.

[89] Wash. Rev. Code Ann. §19.102.010-020.

[90] W. Va. Code §47-15-2.

[91] *Coca-Cola* v. *LaFollette*, 316 N.W.2d 129 (Wisc. 1982).

[92] *State* v. *Dahik*, 330 N.W.2d 611 (Wisc. 1983).

[93] *Kayden* v. *Murphy*, 150 NW2d 447 (Wisc. 1967).

[94] Wis. Stat. Ann. §100.16.

CHAPTER 10

GUARANTEES AND WARRANTIES

Guarantees . . . are not worth the paper they are written on.
—Johann Bernhard

When someone mentions the word "guarantee," most people think of a piece of paper that comes with their new car, dishwasher, or compact disc player. In that case, the guarantee explains what the manufacturer will do if certain parts of the product fail within a certain time. This type of product guarantee is very common in today's market economy.

But there are other guarantees. Probably the most important and powerful one ever created was devised by a group of 55 men who met at a convention in Philadelphia. The first to show up for the meeting was a 36-year-old educator from Virginia named Jim Madison. The others who joined the meeting later were people from business, government, shipping, farming, education, and law. In fact, more than half of them were lawyers.

The group had the task of creating a guarantee for a new product. It was a different, rather revolutionary product,so they had to consider new situations that might arise and what would happen if they came about. This group continued their meeting for almost 17 weeks before they had ironed out the conditions of their guarantee. Finally, they were satisfied. And, then as with all good guarantees, they put it in writing so that anyone who needed to could rely on it, should a claim become necessary.

The guarantee that I have been discussing was written sometime ago—in 1791 to be exact. And it's still in effect today. It's called the Bill of Rights—the first ten amendments to the Constitution of the United States. It's a guarantee for the people, a guarantee of personal freedom. It is probably the most powerful (the *Magna Carta* being the only other that comes close) and yet misunderstood guarantee ever written.

Although most people don't consider the Bill of Rights to be a guarantee, it surely is one. It guarantees the people of the United States certain "inalienable rights" that cannot be taken away or overlooked. Of all the cases that the U. S. Supreme Court hears involving constitutional liberties, most of them involve breaches of the Bill of Rights.

Since this chapter deals with guarantees, I thought it appropriate to start with the first ever written in this country. The Ninth and Tenth Amendments essentially say, "we mean what we said." Specifically, the Tenth specifies that powers not delegated are reserved. The Ninth guarantees, "The enumeration in the Constitution, of certain rights, shall not be construed to deny or disparage others retained by the people." For over 200 years this guarantee was ignored until the Supreme Court used it to announce that the privacy of the bedroom involved an "unenumerated" right. Specifically, the issue was contraception.

The Eighth Amendment disallows cruel and unusual punishment, as well as excessive bail and fines. The Seventh guarantees the right to a jury trial in civil cases "where the value in controversy exceeds twenty dollars." The Sixth begins, "The accused shall enjoy the right to a speedy and public trial . . . ." That word "enjoy" still bothers me.

The Fifth Amendment declares two guarantees. The first specifies that no person "be subject for the same offense to be twice put in jeopardy of life and limb." Today we call this "double jeopardy". The other guarantee is that no person "shall be compelled in any criminal case to be a witness against himself." We call this "self-incrimination." This Amendment has caused the greatest amount of activity in the courts, from the "Communists-are-everywhere" era of Joe McCarthy and Richard Nixon to the "read-him-his-rights" era of the *Miranda*[1] rule in 1966.

The Fourth Amendment guarantees protection ". . . against unreasonable search and seizures." The Third touches on a person's right of privacy in his or her home. The Second Amendment specifies a guarantee that a "well regulated Militia being necessary to the security of a free State, the right of the people to keep and bear Arms shall not be infringed." This originally applied to the right of a militia to keep and bear arms, not the individual citizen.

The First Amendment, although it lay dormant for over 130 years, guarantees freedom of speech, freedom of the press, the right of people to peacefully assemble, and the right to practice one's religion. We will revisit the First Amendment and its impact on advertising more in Chapters 12 and 13.

So there you have it. The first guarantee written in this country. And yet it wasn't unanimously adopted by every state until 1939. Massachusetts, Georgia, and Connecticut were the hold-outs.

All guarantees have the same purpose: They are intended as a protection. They give confidence to people who must rely on a claim. But the guarantees we are concerned with here are simpler. They are guarantees that involve the state of the marketplace, rather than the state of the Union.

In the fall of 1986, American Express started an ad campaign promoting its "Buyers Assurance Plan." American Express would automatically extend the manufacturer's warranty on any purchases made on its charge card. In some cases the manufacturer's warranty was extended for up to a year. The campaign was intended to run for only four months, but it was so successful that it was continued through 1987. The plan was instituted because American Express was used mostly for such business and travel purchases as air fare, hotels, and meals. But the company wanted to increase sales of retail merchandise with its charge card. As a result of the extended warranty, consumer use of the card increased considerably.

In the spring of 1987, Lufthansa German Airlines began a program for first class and business class passengers guaranteeing to pay $200 for any missed connecting flights or late baggage due to the airline's fault. Passenger ticket sales increased, as a consequence, with only minimal claims filed.

These examples show just how dominant the use of guarantees has become. Entire ad campaigns are built around them. Today, an increasing number of companies are turning to guarantees and warranties to increase sales. Companies recognize the value of customer satisfaction and tie that into their products with stronger guarantees. Airlines, appliances, banks, cars, computers, hotels, and many others are developing strong guarantees for products and services and advertising the fact heavily. Warranties and guarantees have become a part of comparative advertising and are major elements that one company can use to position itself against the competition.

Most of the car manufacturers now offer 6-year or 60,000 mile power-train warranties. A few years ago Ford offered a lifetime service guarantee covering major repairs for as long as the customer owns the car. Advertisements that exclaim "money-back guarantee," "quality assurance," "customer satisfaction," or "extended warranty," have become strong selling tools. Clearly, the advertiser must understand the legalities of promoting guarantees and warranties in its ads.

DIFFERENCE BETWEEN A GUARANTEE AND A WARRANTY

The terms "warranty" and "guarantee" are often used interchangeably. In reality there is very little difference between the two, but there is a distinction. To be technical, a warranty is an assumption by the seller of the quality, suitability, character, and performance of the product. On the other hand, a guarantee is the agreement that comes with the purchase of the merchandise that, if the product fails to live up to the claims, the seller will remedy the situation in some way.

A warranty is, simply put, a promise that becomes a contract between the manufacturer and the buyer. The contract goes into effect at the moment the consumer makes a purchase.

A guarantee is a promise that if something goes wrong with the product, the manufacturer will do certain things.

Let's say a roll of photographic film claims that it is "free from defects in workmanship and materials." That's a warranty. If the film turns out to be defective, the guarantee states that "if defective it will be replaced with a new roll of equivalent film free of charge." The warranty states what the manufacturer claims the product will do. The guarantee states what the manufacturer will do if the product fails to live up to the warranty.

THE SCOPE OF WARRANTIES AND GUARANTEES

As seen in Chapter 4 on the role of advertising in products liability actions, there are different forms of warranties. Warranties can be expressed, that is clearly stated, or they can be implied. I would recommend a review of that chapter to examine the ways in which warranties can have an impact on advertising.

Here, however, we will deal mainly with how guarantees should be advertised rather than discussing the legalities of developing guarantees. The balance of this chapter will be devoted to considerations about using guarantees in advertising.

REPRESENTATIONS MADE IN ADS ABOUT GUARANTEES

When advertisements discuss product guarantees the advertiser must be concerned with making certain representations. When claims are made in an ad about the quality, results, or effects of guaranteed merchandise, the advertiser must do certain things—identify the guarantor and state the characteristics, performance, duration, conditions, and charges involved.

Identifying The Guarantor

In Maryland in the early 1960s, World Wide Television Corporation sold television sets and appliances to the public. As part of its promotion the company advertised in newspapers and on radio, focusing on a guarantee for its products.

The company had a unique way of selling its products. World Wide's giant screen Olympic console televisions were controlled by a coin meter, called the "Metermatic Plan." Instead of making monthly payments for the appliance, the purchaser would insert coins in a box to turn on the unit, similar to a coin-operated laundry. The purchaser couldn't use the appliance unless money was put in. A typical ad stated that the products were guaranteed. Here's what was claimed:

● ●

**BRAND NEW GIANT SCREEN OLYMPIC
CONSOLE TELEVISION**
WITH ONE FULL-YEAR GUARANTEE including picture tube.
Service is fully guaranteed!
Service guarantee included!
The Metermatic Plan is better because service is guaranteed.

● ●

In truth, the Olympic televisions were guaranteed by Siegler Corporation, the makers of the television, and not World Wide. Yet this was not stated anywhere in the ads, but only in the instruction booklet included with the television set. The implication in the ad was that World Wide was guaranteeing the television sets. The consumer could not have known the true identity of the guarantor until after the television was delivered. This was deceptive.

There's another unique thing about World Wide's service guarantee. Service was guaranteed because if the company didn't fix a broken set, it couldn't be used by the consumer—and the company wouldn't get paid. That's the only reason service was fully guaranteed. The FTC, learning of the situation, filed a complaint, *In the Matter of World Wide Television Corp.*[2]

In that case the commissioner stated:

[World Wide's] products are not unconditionally guaranteed for one year. Said guarantee is subject to numerous requirements, limitations, and restrictions. The advertised guarantee fails to set forth the nature, conditions and extent of the guarantee, the manner in which the guarantor will perform . . . and the identity of the guarantor.

The commissioner ordered that World Wide could not claim its products were guaranteed unless the nature, extent, and duration were clearly stated. Further, World Wide had to clearly state the name and address of the guarantor.

Stating The Characteristics Or Attributes To Be Guaranteed

An advertiser can build whatever guarantee it wants into a product. In other words, an advertiser may create the limits of any guarantee on its products. However, it must state the characteristics, attributes, and limitations in its guarantee. But simply using the word "guaranteed," alone and without clarification must be avoided.

One of the earliest situations to establish this involved the Parker Pen Company. Parker manufactured fountain pens and sold them to the public. In 1946 Parker ran advertisements for its pens that contained a statement "Guaranteed for Life by Parker's." The specific terms of the guarantee were spelled out elsewhere in the ad: "Pens marked with a Blue Diamond are guaranteed for the life of the owner against everything except loss or intentional damage, subject only to a charge of 35 cents for postage, insurance and handling, provided complete pen is returned for service."

The Federal Trade Commission filed a complaint against Parker because it felt that by charging 35 cents a deception was created as to the "Lifetime Guarantee." The FTC claimed that the 35 cent charge limited the guarantee. The case was appealed to the Federal Circuit Court of Appeals in *Parker Pen Co. v. F.T.C.*[3]

There the court voiced its opinion. "Ordinarily the word, guarantee, is incomplete unless it is used in connection with other explanatory words." To say a pen or other object is guaranteed is meaningless. What is the guarantee? Is it a limited guarantee? Is it an unlimited guarantee? The answer to these questions gives meaning to the word "guaranteed." The same is true of the words "Guaranteed for Life" or "Life Guarantee."

In this case, Parker advertised its guarantee, claiming that it would make needed repairs during the life of the original buyer, if that person paid 35 cents per repair. There is nothing wrong with that. It clearly spelled out the terms of its guarantee. Parker won its case.

Specifying How The Guarantee Is To Be Performed

Another element of the claim that a product is guaranteed involves how the guarantee will be honored. In other words, what will be done if the product fails to perform as promised.

Capitol Manufacturing Company in New York offered watches represented as manufactured by Hamilton and Gruen Watch Companies. In reality, Capitol did not sell Hamilton or Gruen watches, but rather cheap imitations. In its ads, Capitol made statements about its watches, including:

•••••••••••••••••••••••••••••••••••

ELECTRA TWO-YEAR SERVICE GUARANTEE
We guarantee this watch for two years from date of purchase against defects in material and workmanship.

•••••••••••••••••••••••••••••••••••

This guarantee appears to name a company called Electra as the guarantor. It claims that any obligations that the company has under the guarantee will be performed fully, satisfactorily, and promptly. The ad also states that the watch will operate properly for at least two years.

Capitol's guarantee came to the attention of the Federal Trade Commission. Since the guarantee did not specify how the guarantor would fulfill the guarantee, filed a complaint, *In the Matter of Capitol Mfg. Corp.*,[4] charging that the guarantee was deceptive. The watches sold by Capitol were so cheaply made that "[f]ew, if any, . . . will operate for at least the two year period represented in the guarantee."

The problem with this guarantee was its failure to state what Capitol would do if the watch broke within the two-year period. Would it repair the watch? Would it replace the watch? Would it refund the purchase price? None of this was stated. In truth, it wasn't going to do anything. This is probably how the FTC learned about the situation in the first place.

When any guarantee is claimed, the "manner in which the guarantor will perform . . . [must be] clearly and conspicuously set forth in immediate connection therewith." Since Capitol failed to provide this information with its guarantee, the FTC issued a cease-and-desist order.

Duration Of The Guarantee

A guarantee should specify a limit as to the length of time it will be honored by the manufacturer. Advertisers can get into trouble with guarantees described as "for a season of use," or "for the year." The guarantee should specify when the time of the guarantee starts. For example, a statement such as, "guaranteed for one year from the date of retail purchase," leaves little to interpretation.

Another way to list the duration of a guarantee is to state its termination date. Let's go back to our example of photographic film, which is commonly guaranteed in this way. Film generally lists an expiration date for the "guaranteed" use of the product such as "not good after . . . ."

A common way to start the clock running on a guarantee is through a mail-back registration card. Many products are guaranteed only after a registration card is filled out and returned to the manufacturer. Many home appliances, stereos, cameras, and watches are commonly guaranteed in this way.

In the late 1950's, a sewing machine manufacturer placed ads in national consumer magazines including *McCall's* magazine. The manufacturer, International Stitch-O-Matic in Chicago, promoted its guarantee in these ads. The guarantee stated that the product was backed by a "money-back" guarantee on the entire machine for 25 years. When it turned out that this was false, *In the Matter of International Stitch-O-Matic Corp.*[5] resulted. The guarantee claimed that the entire machine was covered for 25 years. In fact, only the motor was guaranteed, and for just one year. The Stitch-O-Matic guarantee had limitations, including time, which were blatantly misstated in its ads.

Stating Conditions Of The Guarantee

In the late 1960's Universe Chemicals, Incorporated manufactured and sold a water-repellent paint by the name of "Kleer-Kote" and "Kolor-Kote." The sales demonstration of the product was quite impressive. Various items were shown to the prospective buyers, and they were told that the items were coated with Kleer-Kote or Kolor-Kote.

A piece of sheet metal, coated with Kolor-Kote, was shown, and the prospect was told that the paint would not crack, peel, or break even if the metal was bent. In another example, a treated brick showed the repellent quality of the coating when water was poured over it. The coating was heated with an infrared bulb to demonstrate its heat resistance. A sieve was coated with Kleer-Kote and was shown to hold water without leaking.

The product appeared to be truly amazing, and the demonstrations were convincing. Kleer-Kote and Kolor-Kote even came with a "10-year, unconditional guarantee." Unfortunately, the product failed to live up to its claims, and the guarantee turned out to be not much of a solution. The Federal Trade Commission became involved and filed *In the Matter of Universe Chemicals, Inc.*[6]

While the wording in the Kleer-Kote brochure stated that the product was "unconditionally guaranteed for 10 years," this was not the case. When a guarantee is claimed to be unconditional, it means just that: no conditions. If there are any conditions, the guarantee is not unconditional. In that case, it should be stated as a "limited guarantee," and then the limits must be specified.

Actually, in Universe Chemicals' case the company would only replace the product if defective. In certain cases the product was replaced, but in many cases the company refused. "The guarantee," said the commissioner, "was clearly not unconditional, and the conditions were not stated in the advertising."

Stating Charges Involved In A Guarantee

Western Radio Corporation manufactured pocket-sized radio transmitters and advertised them in such magazines as *Popular Science* in the mid 1960's. Its Radi-Vox transmitter was advertised with a "Money-back guarantee." However, the company failed to inform the consumer that a service charge applied to the guarantee.

The case went to court in *Western Radio Corp.* v. *FTC.*[7] There, the court said the advertising had the capacity and tendency to mislead the public, "by failure to disclose a service charge in connection with the advertised unconditional guarantee."

When a guarantee is advertised as a money-back guarantee, it means just that. Any guarantee must state "the terms and conditions of such guarantee . . . clearly and conspicuously . . .

including the amount of any service or other charge which is imposed."

PROBLEMS WITH ADVERTISING GUARANTEES

The most obvious problem encountered in advertising a guarantee is whether the ad creates a deception about the actual guarantee. When there is a difference between the guarantee and the way it is advertised or where it is a blatant falsehood, the Federal Trade Commission can step in.

Variations Between An Advertised Guarantee And An Actual Guarantee

Montgomery Ward offered rebuilt car engines through its chain of retail department stores in the 1960's. In its advertisements the engines were promoted as having an unconditional guarantee. The customer would read the ad, go to the store, and purchase the engine only to learn later that the guarantee had quite a few restrictions.

The Montgomery Ward guarantee was not unconditional. It actually covered only a period of 90 days or 4,000 miles:

• •
FOR A PERIOD OF NINETY DAYS
from the date installed or four thousand miles
(whichever comes first) we warrant this
rebuilt assembly for passenger car service
against defects in material and factory workmanship
provided our installation and
operating instructions are followed.
• •

The guarantee also contained other restrictions. For instance, the guarantee only provided for the following:
• Replacement of parts, no labor;

- A claim for engines installed by Wards;
- A claim if required checkups are made;
- A claim if damage was not caused by misuse or accident; and
- A claim if a valid certificate was on file.

Eventually, the FTC learned of Montgomery Ward's guarantee and a complaint was filed; *Montgomery Ward & Co.* v. *FTC*.[8] Montgomery Ward argued that it had a policy of honoring claims for defective merchandise even though its guarantee stated many restrictions. In fact, the court acknowledged that there was no evidence "that any customer had any claim under any guarantee . . . or that [Wards] failed to satisfy any claim under its guarantees."

The point, however, was that Ward's actual guarantee placed many restrictions, which were not revealed in its advertising. Plain and simple, this is deceptive. If you'll recall from Chapters 2 and 3, the FTC does not require a showing that actual deception occurred, only that the ad has the likelihood to deceive.

"The capacity [or under current interpretation, likelihood] to deceive," said the court, "involved in Ward's advertisements lies in the inducement to buy created by the unlimited, advertised guarantee." It is clear from this case that an advertiser must specify the terms of its guarantee in an ad, unless it truly offers an "unconditional" guarantee. The advertising of a guarantee must clearly express the actual guarantee that the consumer will get with the purchase.

False Statements Regarding A Guarantee

Certain industries place specific restrictions and requirements on guarantees of quality, origin, and authenticity of merchandise. Industries such as alcohol, tobacco, medicines, textiles, and others have such regulations. An advertiser should consult the specific regulations of these industries.

M. Reiner & Sons was a fur dealer in New York. In 1969

the company advertised and sold furs with the guarantee that the furs were authentic and in compliance with specific laws governing the fur trade.[9] The company claimed that the proper guarantee, as required by the Fur Products Labeling Act, was on file with the Federal Trade Commission.

It was learned later that this was not the case; therefore, a complaint was filed by the FTC; *In the Matter of M. Reiner & Sons.*[10] The commission discovered that Reiner had no certificate of guarantee on file and therefore violated the law by creating a deception about its guarantee.

The commission stated that Reiner:

[F]alsely represented in writing that [it] had a continuing [guarantee] on file with the Federal Trade Commission when [it] in furnishing such guarantees had reason to believe that the fur products so falsely guaranteed would be introduced, sold, transported, and distributed in commerce.

As a result, Reiner was ordered to cease-and-desist from such practices.

TYPES OF GUARANTEES

There are many different types of guarantees. Among the most common are money-back, satisfaction, lifetime, repair, limited, and refund or replacement guarantees. The type of guarantee offered is dependent on the manufacturer. Now let's take a look at each of these.

Money-Back Guarantees

This is one of the most common. A money-back guarantee means just that. If the consumer is not satisfied, a full refund must be given. This type of guarantee must be honored in a timely manner. If a customer asks for a refund, he must not be made to make numerous attempts to collect the refund.

This guarantee can be offered in a number of situations, and should be clearly stated in any ads as well as on the packaging of the product. Typical money-back guarantees clarify what the manufacturer will do under the following situations:

- If the consumer is not satisfied with the product;
- If it can be purchased elsewhere for less;
- If it fails to perform a specific job; and
- If it does not do its job better than its competition.

Satisfaction Guaranteed

If an ad claims "satisfaction guaranteed," without any clarification, then the consumer is entitled to determine if the product satisfies or not.

In cases where the claim is "satisfactory-fit guaranteed" the consumer is still able to determine if satisfaction resulted from the purchase of the product. Satisfaction is a subjective judgment call, and the purchaser is allowed to use his or her judgment as to whether satisfaction exists.

Lifetime Guarantees

Lifetime guarantees are legal, but the terms of the guarantee should be clearly spelled out. The guarantee must be stated as "conditional" if charges are applied for service or replacement parts. A full disclosure of any conditions or service charges must accompany the guarantee. Terms such as "guaranteed forever" should not be used unless the manufacturer intends to live up to the claim, literally. The Sears Craftsman tool guarantee is a good example of a valid lifetime guarantee.

Claims that should not be made include the following:

- Guaranteed to last through the ages;
- Guaranteed to give a lifetime of service;
- Guarantee of a lifetime;
- Guaranteed for a lifetime; and

• Guaranteed forever.

Repair Guarantees

Certain guarantees involve service repairs. These guarantees, usually found with appliances or automobiles, should be carefully explained. The following elements should be included in any repair guarantee:
- Time restrictions;
- Service charges;
- Cost of repairs;
- Party responsible for repairs; and
- Types of defects that are covered.

Limited Guarantees

As seen earlier, any guarantee that is not unlimited is limited. If a guarantee is claimed in an ad and it is not unlimited, then it must be called a limited guarantee.

A good example of a limited guarantee can be found in our earlier example of film. Typically the manufacturer provides that if the film is defective the original roll of film will be replaced. But no other obligations exist; the company cannot be made to pay for loss of the photographic images or the costs to reshoot.

Refund Or Replacement Guarantees

Some guarantees may specify whether the manufacturer will refund the purchase price (sometimes pro-rated) or replace the item. The manufacturer may make this decision, but the term must be specified in the guarantee.

THE FTC GUIDES FOR ADVERTISING OF WARRANTIES AND GUARANTEES

The commission has produced the *Guides for the Advertising of Warranties and Guarantees*[11] to help advertisers avoid unfair or deceptive practices in the advertising of warranties and guarantees. These supplement the issues just discussed.

Under these guides, an advertiser generally is not required to mention a warranty or guarantee offered on an advertised product, but is required only to disclose certain information if the warranty is mentioned. An advertiser should mention that a product is warranted or guaranteed only if the seller or manufacturer "promptly and fully performs its obligations under the warranty or guarantee."

In issuing the guides, the FTC stressed that the Federal Trade Commission Act is still the "ultimate legal standard governing warranty advertising." The commission's intent is for the guides to aid advertisers in avoiding violations of the law. Based on FTC case law, the guides also reflect the changes effected by the Magnuson-Moss Warranty Act.[12] That act will be discussed later in this chapter.

Advertising of written warranties on consumer products must also conform, where applicable, to the commission's rule on the "Pre-Sale Availability of Written Warranty Terms."

Written Warranties On Consumer Products

If an advertisement for a consumer product costing more than $15 mentions a written warranty, the FTC's *Guides for the Advertising of Warranties and Guarantees* states:

> The advertisement should disclose, with such clarity and prominence as will be noticed and understood by prospective purchasers, that prior to sale, at the place where the product is sold, prospective purchasers can see the written warranty or guarantee for complete details of the warranty coverage.

If an advertisement in a catalog or other solicitation for mail order or telephone sales mentions a warranty, the advertisement must prominently and clearly, in close proximity to the description of the warranted product or in a clearly-referenced information section, set forth the full text of the warranty or disclose that prospective buyers can obtain complete details of the written warranty or guarantee free of charge upon specific written request from the seller or "from the catalogue or other solicitation "

Warranty Disclosure Requirements

Originally, the guides required disclosures of virtually all warranty terms in ads mentioning warranties. However, the FTC decided that to require disclosure of all warranty terms in ads might deter advertisers from mentioning warranty coverage at all. Since the Pre-Sale Availability Rule assures that warranty terms are available to consumers at the store, the FTC also concluded such detailed disclosures in ads are not needed. Instead, the revised guides recommend disclosure in warranty ads promoting a product covered by the Pre-Sale Availability Rule 8, of the fact that the warranty document is available for examination before purchase of the product.

The guides contain a similar approach for mail-order and catalog sales ads. One provision in the FTC guides calls for mail-order or catalogue sales to disclose "information sufficient to convey to consumers that they can obtain complete details on the written warranty free upon specific written request, or from the catalogue or solicitation (whichever is applicable)."

The guides also state (concerning disclosures), that text in the ad will clearly and prominently specify that "warranties are available for inspection prior to sale."

Television ads will comply with the guides if the ads:
Make the necessary disclosure simultaneously with or immediately following the warranty claim.
The disclosure can be presented either in the audio portion or in the video portion as a printed

disclosure, provided that a video disclosure appears on the screen for at least five seconds.

However, disclosures called for by other guide provisions may require advertisers to use additional methods. For example, the FTC guide states:

It may be necessary for multiple disclosures of the material limitations on a satisfaction guarantee to be disclosed in the audio portion of an advertisement, or to be disclosed for a longer period of time than five seconds in order for the disclosures to be clear and prominent.

Satisfaction Guarantees

Satisfaction guarantees are very popular in advertising, particularly on television and in mail-order. The guides state that "satisfaction guaranteed" claims should be used only if you plan to refund the full purchase price at the buyer's request. The guides also suggest that, if this type of representation is subject to material limitations or conditions (an express limitation of duration, or a limitation to products returned in their original packaging), the ad should disclose that limitation or condition.

"Lifetime" Representations

The guides suggest that use of the term, "lifetime" in describing the duration of a guarantee or warranty can mislead consumers unless clarified as to the definition of "life." The guides require clarification of the life to which the claim refers, i.e., whether or not it refers to the buyer's life.

Warranty Performance

The guides promote "that a warrantor or guarantor should ensure performance on advertised warranties or guarantees."

SELF-REGULATORY BODIES

If you're planning to advertise a warranty, be aware of the various self-regulatory bodies. The most important industry self-regulatory mechanism is the Better Business Bureau's (BBB) National Advertising Division/National Advertising Review Board (NAD/NARB). An important pamphlet to read is the BBB's *Code of Advertising*. This contains basic advertising standards issued for the guidance of advertisers, ad agencies, and the advertising media. In particular, section 8: Warranties (or Guarantees) of that code provides:

a. When the term "warranty" (or "guarantee") is used in product advertising, the following disclosure should be made clearly and prominently: a statement that the complete details of the warranty can be seen at the advertiser's store prior to sale, or in the case of mail or telephone order sales, are available free on written request.

b. (1) "satisfaction guarantee," "money back guarantee," "free trial offer," or similar representations should be used in advertising only if the seller or manufacturer refunds the full purchase price of the advertised product at the purchaser's request.

b. (2) When "satisfaction guarantee" or similar representations are used in advertising, any material limitations or conditions that apply to the guarantee should be clearly and prominently disclosed.

c. When the term "lifetime," "life" or similar representations are used in advertising to describe the duration of the warranty or guarantee, the advertisement should clearly and prominently disclose the life to which the representation refers.

d. Sellers or manufacturers should advertise that a product is warranted or guaranteed only if the seller or manufacturer promptly and fully performs its obligations under the warranty or guarantee.

e. Advertisers should make certain that any advertising of warranties complies with the Consumer Products Warranty Act, effective July 4, 1975, relevant Federal Trade Commission requirements and any applicable state and local laws.

NETWORK GUIDELINE'S RELATION TO THE ADVERTISING OF WARRANTIES

As with any network commercial, consult the network's clearance department before producing a commercial. Both ABC and NBC have extensive guidelines pertaining to the advertising of warranties or guarantees. Both networks will require clear and conspicuous disclosure in the commercial referring to a warranty or guarantee, whether the warranty is full or limited. In addition, both networks require additional disclosures in the audio or video portions of a commercial, or in both. ABC requires that the ad disclose: "specific duration, major limitations (e.g., parts excluded or costs or responsibilities the customer must undertake), and see dealer for details" statements.

Under NBC's broadcast standards requirements, the ad must disclose: "the nature and extent of the guarantee; the identity of the guarantor; the manner in which the guarantor intends to perform; information concerning what a purchaser wishing to claim under the guarantee need do before the guarantor will perform pursuant to its obligations under the guarantee."

In addition, ABC has guidelines for "satisfaction or your money back" representations, "savings guarantees," "guarantees as a representative," "lifetime guarantees," and "prorated adjustment of guarantees."

THE MAGNUSON-MOSS WARRANTY ACT

When Congress enacted the Magnuson-Moss Warranty Act, it gave the federal government a potentially dominant role in warranty law. While the act still hasn't lived up to initial expectations, it is, nonetheless, a major force to be reckoned with when offering a warranty or guarantee on a product or service. An initial determination should always be made whether the Magnuson-Moss Warranty Act applies. Magnuson-Moss is applicable to written warranties.

Essentially, there are two types of written warranties under the act: "full" and "limited." If you decide to offer your customers a "full" warranty, it means, among other things, that:

- You will fix or replace a defective product for free within a reasonable time;
- You won't require your customer to do anything unreasonable to get warranty service;
- Your warranty is good for anyone owning the product during the warranty period; and
- You will give your customer the choice of a new product or his or her money back if the product can't be fixed or hasn't been fixed after a reasonable number of attempts.

If you offer a "limited" warranty, it means you're offering less than what a full warranty provides. For example, a limited warranty may cover only parts and not labor, or cover only the first buyer, or charge for handling.

If a manufacturer or retailer offers a written warranty, the Magnuson-Moss act demands substantial analysis and compliance.

To get a copy of the Magnuson-Moss Act, implementing regulations, and explanatory pamphlets on the law, you should write to: the Federal Trade Commission, Washington, D.C. 20580.

[1] *Miranda v. Arizona*, 384 U.S. 436, 86 S.Ct. 1602, 16 L.Ed. 2d 694 (1966).

[2] *In the Matter of World Wide Television Corp.*, 66 F.T.C. 961 (1964).

[3] *Parker Pen Co. v. FTC*, 153 F.2d 509 (C.C.A. 1946).

[4] *In the Matter of Capitol Mfg. Corp.*, 73 F.T.C. 872 (1968).

[5] *In the Matter of International Stitch-O-Matic Corp.*, 54 F.T.C. 1308 (1959).

[6] *In the Matter of Universe Chemicals, Inc.*, 77 F.T.C. 598 (1970).

[7] *Western Radio Corp. v. FTC*, 339 F.2d 937 (7th Cir. 1964).

[8] *Montgomery Ward & Co. v. FTC*, 379 F.2d 666 (7th Cir. 1967).

[9] Fur Products Labeling Act, 15 U.S.C. § 69 et seq. (1988).

[10] *In the Matter of M. Reiner & Sons*, 77 F.T.C. 862 (1970).

[11] 16 C.F.R. §§ 239.1-.5 (1987).

[12] 15 U.S.C. § 45 (1988).

CHAPTER 11

THE CLIENT/AGENCY RELATIONSHIP

The client is, of course, god. And so it has been ever since the days of the first great ad man Jesus Christ.
—*Robert C. Pritikin*

If you'll allow me, I have a short story to tell you. A very long time ago, let's say somewhere around 10 million B.C., there lived a man we'll call Urr. He lived a simple life, mainly concerned with providing for his family. Back in those days, life could be pretty rigorous. Even cutting firewood could be a major ordeal. So, in order to make the job easier, Urr designed a crude but effective device, which he called for lack of a better name, a tree cutter. With it, the first tool was invented.

Everything went along fine until one day a fellow named Ogg happened by and saw Urr working with his tree cutter. Realizing that he could make excellent use of this device for his own daily chores, and being quite a bit larger in stature than Urr, Ogg used this advantage to negotiate for the cutter. As you'd expect, he took possession of it, thereby carrying out the first business transaction in history.

Thoroughly frustrated, Urr thought that there had to be a better way to do business. He soon realized that since he had built something that Ogg wanted, perhaps others would also want his invention. Urr reasoned that rather than letting others steal his device, he could make more and offer them in exchange for items other people possessed that he needed. Setting his plan into motion, he soon found to his pleasure that it worked.

Yet, it was only a matter of time before Urr became aware of a growing problem, competition. As expected, other people began making and selling their own brand of tree cutter. With salespeople cropping up (excuse the pun) everywhere, Urr knew that he had to do something. So he called on his cousin Aad.

Being a good salesman, Aad got the word out that Urr's tree cutters were better than any of the other cheap imitations on the market. Finding out that he had a real skill at this sort of thing, Aad decided to go into business promoting other products. He called his company The Aad Agency, and a new industry was born.

If you don't believe my version of how the first agency came about, here is another that can be better documented.

A common practice in Italy around 1250 was to sell wine by the flask. Many unscrupulous wine merchants filled the bottom of their bottles with wax, thereby reducing the amount of wine in the bottle and improving the profit margin substantially. When the public found out about this deception, wine sales dropped rapidly. So the legitimate wine merchants began sending agents out into the streets promoting wine with placards saying "Sine Cere," which means "without wax." From this phrase comes our word "sincere," and from this practice comes one of the earliest examples of an organized advertising agency.

THE ADVERTISING AGENCY

A professional agency is a business that acts on behalf of others. Attorneys, accountants, brokers, factors, auctioneers, and, yes, advertising agencies may fall into this category. Any profession—if it qualifies as an agent—is regulated by the same laws. As a result, some of the cases we examine in this chapter do not involve advertising agencies, but the principles are binding on any agency relationship.

First, there are a couple of terms that need to be clarified. An *agent* can be an individual alone, a group of people, a large corporation, or a full-time employee. A "principal" can be the client or the employer. But for purposes of clarity, we refer to the *principal* as the "client" throughout this chapter.

Advertising agencies that want the legal benefits of being an agency must abide by the duties that go along with the title. Simply calling a company an "advertising agency" does not mean that it is one legally. The legal relationship is what exists, not what is claimed. It must act like a true agency to be treated as one. We will examine this idea more closely in the balance of this chapter.

Now you may ask why ad agencies are called "agencies" if they are not. It's more out of tradition than for any other reason. The title creates a trade name more than an establishment of legal status. It is actually a misnomer; a throwback from the early "space-broker" days when advertising agencies were merely brokers of media space.

The alternative to being an agency is being an independent contractor. Here's an example to illustrate. A person owns a Chevrolet dealership in Los Angeles. This dealer sells Chevrolet cars and trucks, and the business is referred to as a Chevrolet agency. However, this dealer is not an agent. The person simply sells Chevrolet products as an independent contractor, he does not work on the behalf of others.

The distinguishing feature between an "agent" and "independent contractor" is the amount of control retained by the client over the physical conduct of the person performing the service. The independent contractor obligates herself or himself to produce a result, and is free to pursue her or his own methods in the performance of the work.

For example, if Acme Company wants a new machine, it can use its own employees to build it. Or, it can contract with Bosco Corporation to build the machine according to Acme's specifications, and at an agreed-on price. If Acme hires Bosco to build the machine, Bosco is an independent contractor. Bosco has been hired to produce a result: a specific machine at a specific price. Acme has no physical control over how Bosco produces the machine.

However, in most cases advertising agencies are true agencies in the legal sense. They don't have the independent contractor's freedom of control. The ad agency is subject to direct control by the client. In the advertising business, most clients reserve the right to select, approve, confer, and be advised of the work of their advertising agencies during every stage of the process. Anyone who has ever worked in an agency can vouch for that. So most courts have maintained that agencies have, in fact, acted as agents for their clients.

DUTIES OF THE ADVERTISING AGENCY

An advertising agency is able to commit the client to contracts, and at the same time it owes a duty of confidence and trust (fiduciary) to the client. Duties that the agency owes to the client fall into one of two areas: specific duties that are spelled out in a written contract, and duties that are imposed by law. Specific duties can be anything so long as they do not violate a law, and that the client and agency want to make a part of the contract.

Even if no written contract exists between the client and agency, the agency's duties imposed by law still exist. These include the following:
- High level of skill required of agency;
- Full disclosure to client;
- Obligations regarding competitive accounts;
- Trustee of client, and handling of funds;
- Accountability to client;
- Duty to cooperate with client;
- Obligation to preserve trade secrets; and
- No undisclosed interest in suppliers.

Now let's look at each of these duties in more detail.

High Level Of Skill Required Of Agency

An advertising agency represents itself as being an expert in its field. When an ad agency makes a presentation to a prospective client, it goes out of its way to impress upon the client that it possesses a tremendous degree of skill in both the area of advertising and that of the client's product. Once stated, the agency is then obligated to deliver. It must not merely show a general level of skill, but it must demonstrate the level of a highly skilled professional.

It is not enough that an advertising (or any other) agency apply the usual degree of care to the business entrusted it by its client. It must put forth its best efforts using its skill, experience, and knowledge to the best of its professional ability. When an agency fails to deliver on this, breach of contract may exist. The breach may be cause for the client to terminate the contract, or in some cases, bring suit for damages.

On the other hand, it is true that an agency is not required to guarantee the success of the advertising that it produces, only to put forth all of its best efforts toward the success of it. That means not doing anything that would diminish its chance for success.

Full Disclosure To Client

An agency owes its clients complete loyalty. This may seem simple to accomplish, but it can affect an agency in many ways. Part of this loyalty includes a responsibility to inform the client of any fact or occurrence that affects the client in any way. For instance, if the agency has been late in paying a supplier, who in turn threatens to cut off services, the agency is under a duty to inform its client. As unpleasant as this may be, the client is legally entitled to be informed quickly and thoroughly on all such matters.

Let me give you a good example. The disclosure required of an agent was discussed in *Crocker* v. *United States*.[1] Frank Crocker owned a company, which had a contract to furnish mail-carrier satchels to the U.S. Post Office. His company did so, but something happened to cause the Postmaster General to rescind the contract and refuse to pay for the satchels.

Two employees of Crocker, Mr. Lorenz and Mr. Crawford, made a secret agreement with Mr. Machen, who was superintendent of the division that needed the satchels. Machen arranged for the contract to go to Crocker's company in exchange for half of the profits. Crocker got the government contract, with Machen getting half the profits from the sales. The company furnished over 10,000 satchels before the Postmaster General learned of the collusion.

Lorenz and Crawford were agents of Crocker, and were acquiring the contract at the company's request. They were trying to secure the government contract by working out a fraudulent deal with Machen. By virtue of the agency relationship, Crocker in essence sanctioned what they did. Because the contract was obtained fraudulently, Crocker lost his claim for payment.

Obligations As To Competitive Clients

A problem arises when an agency tries to serve two clients who are in competition with each other. The agency can't serve both unless it has the consent of the two parties in advance. This became the issue in *Joyce Beverages of New York, Inc.* v. *Royal Crown Cola.*[2]

Joyce Beverages was a licensee, and as such an agent, of several soft drink manufacturers, including Royal Crown Cola, 7-Up, Diet 7-Up, A&W Root Beer, Sugar-Free A&W, Perrier, Nestea, Hawaiian Punch, and Nehi drinks. Royal Crown's licensing agreement with Joyce stated that Joyce must use its best efforts to build, maintain, and expand the sales of the Royal Crown drinks to Royal Crown's satisfaction.

The contract between the parties would not allow Joyce to distribute any soft drinks that were "substantially or reasonably similar" to Royal Crown products. The contract further provided that: "any cola shall be deemed substantially or reasonably similar to any . . . cola [and] any diet cola to any . . . diet cola."

One of the ways Joyce could breach this agreement was to take on a competing drink. That's exactly what it did. In 1982, Joyce began marketing "LIKE," a decaffeinated cola drink manufactured by the 7-Up Company.

By handling another competitive cola in its market area, Joyce created "inevitable and corrosive divided loyalty and effort and made impossible a continued relationship . . . of confidence and cooperation." In essence, Joyce would be selling a new product to old customers, with advertising and promotion practices that it established for the old product. This breaches the duty of an agent not to handle competing clients without consent.

Joyce argued, in its defense, that Royal Crown would not be put in a position to "sink or swim" by itself, Joyce also claimed that Royal Crown wouldn't "go down the drain." This points out a common misconception, i.e., Joyce's duty to its client is to vigorously promote the product—to expand its market share, not simply to keep it alive. The court agreed and allowed Royal Crown to rescind the contract.

Sometimes it is not easy to determine whether two clients compete with each other. Clients compete, basically, when their products are similar or interchangeable or where one product may replace the need of the other. Such products that could replace the other might be toothpaste and dental cleaning powder, floor wax and a product that eliminates the need to wax, or bandages and a cut spray that replaces a bandage.

Another area of competition is situations in which products are advertised and sold in different geographic areas. In these cases there may be no direct competition of products, yet clients may not be pleased. Clients may claim that information obtained from one company is being used to benefit the other. While this may not violate any duty, the agency could have some very irritated clients on its hands. The best practice is to inform the agency's existing client and get its approval beforehand.

However, many agencies do represent different clients in

competition for the same market. These agencies promote the fact that they specialize in a certain area: banking, real estate, or medical, for example. In many fields, this agency specialty is preferred by clients. In these cases, clients who know of this are considered to have consented to the agency's representing other competitors. If the client is told about representing other competitors in the same field before it becomes a client, it will have very little to complain about later. The point is that the client must be made aware of, and give its consent to, this multiple representation.

Trustee Of Client And Handling Of Funds

Handling Of Funds

The financial aspect of a client/agency relationship can be a major source of aggravation for both, especially in the area of commingling of funds, i.e., mixing the money that belongs to the agency with that which belongs to the client. The agency is the trustee of the funds taken in on behalf of the client, and must treat that money accordingly.

Basic agency law requires that an agent must keep money belonging to its client separate from its own. The only time that this does not need to happen legally is when the client has knowledge and has consented in advance.

The common practice, however, is to the contrary for a number of reasons. When a client sends money to the agency, rarely does it identify what it should be applied to. It is very uncommon that a client will send a separate check for each type of payment. However, payments intended to cover the agency's fees and costs need not be kept separately. But, money that merely flows through the agency on the way to suppliers or media, less commissions, should not be mixed with the agency's money. To avoid problems later, this subject should be specifically addressed in the client/agency contract.

The best way to protect the agency is to have separate bank accounts: one as a trust account for the client's money, which can be drawn on as needed, and another for the agency's money, which is not subject to accountability to the client.

Trustee Of Rights And Materials

Everything that the agency creates for its client belongs to the client; the agency holds these items in trust for the client. This could include such materials as photographs, artwork, videotapes, or rights such as copyright, trademark rights, rights of publicity.

The agent does not own these items or rights, but it has a duty to guard them for its client. Here's an example which occurred between the Molle Company and its agency, Stack-Goble Advertising, in 1933.

Molle manufactured shaving cream and, through Stack-Goble, wanted to develop radio advertising. Stack-Goble hired Sedley Brown to produce and direct a program with Molle as the sponsor. We must remember that years ago it was common for advertisers to sponsor shows by themselves, and it was the job of the advertising agency to put the shows together. For example, "Amos 'n Andy" sold Pepsodent, "The Story of Mary Marlowe" sold Kleenex, "Fibber McGee and Molly" for Johnson's Glo-Coat floor wax, "The Rhythm Boys" (featuring a youngster named Harry Lillis Crosby, later to be known as Bing) for M. J. B. Coffee, and the list went on and on.

But back to Molle. As part of producing the show, Brown created a jingle out of Molle advertising slogans and set the words to the music of E. L. Gruber's, "West Point Caisson Song." The jingle went:

● ● ● ● ● ● ● ● ● ●
Mo-lle, Mo-lle,
The way to start your day,
As your razor goes sliding along,
Over cheek, over chin,

> You don't have to rub it in,
> As your razor goes sliding along.
> Then it's sing, boys, sing,
> Good-bye to pull and sting,
> Your whisker troubles quickly fade away,
> You can shave close and clean with this
> brushless shaving cream,
> So remember the name
> Molle, Molle.
> • • • • • • • • •

Brown produced the first radio show on September 25, 1933, and continued to do so until late December when he left the show. The show, along with the theme song, continued to air without any protest from Brown. In April 1934, Brown filed a copyright for the words to the song and gave notice to Molle of his claimed ownership in September of that year.

When Molle refused to acknowledge his claim, Brown brought suit for copyright infringement in *Brown* v. *Molle Co.*,[3] claiming ownership of the rights to the jingle. While it was true that the words were written by Brown, they belonged to Stack-Goble, who held them as trustee for Molle. Brown was employed by Stack-Goble to produce the program, including the theme song. Brown was an employee of Stack-Goble, and as such, anything he created as part of his duties became the property of Molle. When an agent creates work for, and at the direction of the client, it gives up, along with the work, any right to the work. Brown lost his case.

Accountability To Client

An agency is under a strict duty to account for all funds passing through the agency, or controlled by it, on behalf of its client. The client has the right to inspect books, records, papers, invoices, orders, receipts, and any other items that apply to its account with the agency. These must be made available to the client, at any time, for its inspection. Along these lines, the client can demand an accounting of all commissions or discounts, received from or credited by third parties (suppliers, media, etc.) to the agency on the client's account.

One major problem area regarding accountability involves hidden profits. This constitutes a serious breach of the agency's duty. Legally, this is called "fraudulent concealment." I have known of a few agencies that made a practice of stating in their contracts that they charged a 17.65 percent markup on third-party bills. Yet, the estimates and invoices given to clients actually included an undisclosed but considerable markup in excess of 30 percent.

If an agency makes a purchase for a client based on an estimate, and the actual billing comes in lower, the agency must pass this savings on to the client. It cannot legally keep the difference. At some agencies, the policy is to estimate a job and get the client to sign the estimate. Then the agency pre-bills the client for that amount before beginning the project, often receiving payment before the project is completed. Sometimes the final cost of the project comes out lower than the estimate. If the ultimate costs are lower than the estimate, and the difference is not returned to the client, the agency is breaching its duty.

If pre-billing must be done, the best practice is to provide a recap of the project showing any amounts billed in excess of the estimate and credit them back to the client.

Purchase Orders

Another important duty is that the agency should document all purchases for its client with a written purchase order. The purchase order must establish what has been ordered and what will be paid. It should also establish that the order is being placed on behalf of the client. Exhibit 11-1 is a sample purchase order for reference.

Duty To Cooperate With The Client

Rarely do we hear mention of the duty of obedience when discussing the relationship between agency and client. This may be due to the fact that advertisers are usually inclined to bow to the expertise of the agency. Or it may be attributable to good business sense on the part of the agency. Whatever the reason, this is an area that needs to be discussed, nonetheless.

An advertising agency has a duty to do its best to cooperate with the client. Sometimes this can be difficult when an agency is determined to sell a campaign to its client. Let's say that the agency submits a campaign plan to its client. The client has the right to disapprove of the campaign plans—media, copy, art, or any other proposals of the agency—simply because it does not like them. An agency cannot force the client to produce advertising that it does not like or has not approved. The client cannot be deprived of the right to reject the agency's creative work in a campaign or in an individual ad.

Such a situation became the subject of *Medivox Productions, Inc. v. Hoffman-LaRoche, Inc.*[4] Hoffman-LaRoche, a well-known pharmaceutical manufacturer, entered into a contract with Medivox Productions as its agent in the production of a series of radio programs entitled "Milestones of Medicine." The contract called for 260 programs to be created and produced during one year at a total cost of $140,000. These programs were to be dramatic episodes depicting important medical events in history. Hoffman-LaRoche was to have a credit line in each episode. The intent was that of enhancing the public's image of those connected with medicine and health, while at the same time promoting the importance of drugs.

The contract stated that before being produced and broadcast, scripts would be submitted to Hoffman-LaRoche for their review and approval. Even without a contract this would be required. By the time Medivox had produced 135 of the programs (which the client had approved), Hoffman-LaRoche terminated the contract, having paid only $63,000. Medivox sued for breach of contract and sought to be allowed to complete the shows and receive the balance due on the contract. Hoffman-LaRoche claimed that they were entitled to terminate the contract because Medivox produced poor quality scripts.

Hoffman-LaRoche was dissatisfied with the scripts because they were inaccurate factually, and many of them discussed events that were not in keeping with the "Milestones of Medicine" theme. Medivox failed to satisfy its client, and as a result, Hoffman-LaRoche terminated the relationship. The court ruled that Medivox could not force the continuation of the relationship (legally this is called "specific performance") or collect the balance due on the contract. However, Hoffman-LaRoche could not recover the money that it had paid Medivox because it had accepted, used, and received the benefits of the 135 programs.

The client has the right, in an agency relationship, to approve or reject the work of its agency. Termination of the relationship, then, is based on the genuineness of its dissatisfaction, not necessarily on the reasonableness of it. Generally, the client makes this determination. Keep in mind, when the client expects satisfaction, the agency must allow the client to be the sole judge of its satisfaction.

The agency also has a duty to obey the instructions of its client in all but extreme situations. The agent has the right to refuse under certain extreme conditions without liability for damages. However, the client also has the right to terminate the contract if the agent does refuse to perform.

The four situations when the agent can legally refuse to obey its client are listed below.

1. The Instructions Are Unlawful

The agency has the right to refuse to produce advertising that is illegal—that is, advertising that violates any rights of others (including such things as publicity rights, copyrights, and trademarks), or when it would be engaging in unfair methods of competition or deception.

2. The Instructions Conflict With Other Duties Of The Agency

The agency may refuse to perform any instruction, such as the client's demand that the agency hold off paying certain media bills. Yet, this would be valid only if it would be a conflict of an agency duty. The agency may also refuse if the client demands that the agency take on a new product made by the existing client, which competes with another existing client of the agency.

3. The Instructions Defeat The Agency's Right To Protect Its Own Interests

A good example would be demanding the agency accept work on a speculative basis, with payment contingent on the client's sales or profits.

4. The Instructions Are Unreasonable

This fourth area may cause some problems, as we saw in the aforementioned *Medivox* case. What is considered unreasonable becomes the question. In many situations agencies feel that creating an ad it knows to be ineffective is unreasonable. An agency is hired for its expertise in a certain area, and should be allowed to use its judgment. Logically, this may be true; legally, it may not.

Basic agency law states that, barring one of the above exceptions, an agent must obey the instructions of its client. Failure to abide by the instructions of the client could result in agency liability for damages. On the other hand, the agency may terminate the relationship at any time, with proper notice given, if it does not want to abide by the instructions.

The Obligation To Preserve Trade Secrets

Frequently it is necessary for a client to familiarize its agency with many matters it desires to keep secret. An advertising agency is under an obligation, both during and after its employment, to preserve those trade secrets, i.e., secrets that were disclosed or learned during the relationship.

Originally the issue was discussed in *E. I. Du Pont de Nemours Powder Co.* v. *Masland.*[5] A former employee, Mr. Masland (an agent), was sued to prevent him from disclosing or using secret trade processes learned while in the employ of Du Pont. Masland intended to open a company to manufacture artificial leather. He admitted that he intended to use processes related to those learned while employed with Du Pont. Masland's former employer did not want any of its secret trade processes divulged, and it had the right to enforce this. Masland had learned the facts about Du Pont's processes through a confidential relationship.

It is difficult to define what a trade secret is. However, some examples would be a specialized manufacturing process as we just saw, or special ingredients in a product such as Coca-Cola or Dr. Pepper. It seems that courts are more interested in the unfair use of the information than by the nature of the information itself.

The best story I can recall about trade secrets occurred a number of years ago. I was working for an agency that handled the Mitsubishi Electronics account. One day we got the news that two Mitsubishi executives had been arrested by the FBI. Evidently, Mitsubishi had paid $26,000 to undercover FBI agents, who posed as grey-market electronics dealers. The money was paid in exchange for confidential trade secrets about IBM's newest computing products. This event was dubbed "Japanscam" by the press.

Note, any information that is easily accessible through other sources cannot be a trade secret. Lists of customers would be a good example. As a general rule these are not considered trade secrets because they are readily obtainable through such other public sources as trade publications.

There's another area to consider. Some years ago, Chiat/Day Advertising was in the running for the Godfather Pizza Parlor account. In order to prepare a speculative presentation to Godfather, the agency was given access to confidential information by the restaurant chain. A number of Chiat/Day employees were given this information, which contained many trade secrets.

Before the presentation was made to Godfather, Chiat/Day declined the account in favor of the Pizza Hut account. At that point, Godfather went to court to stop the use of the confidential information that Chiat/Day had obtained. The California Superior Court judge granted an injunction against Chiat/Day. The injunction stated that Chiat/Day could not use any of the confidential information it obtained from Godfather. In addition, the injunction banned the Chiat/Day employees involved in the Godfather presentation from being involved in any way with the Pizza Hut account. The point here is that, even at the presentation stage, the duty to preserve trade secrets is in force, and courts are backing this up by issuing injunctions.

Lastly, the agency has a continuing duty, even after termination, not to disclose or use trade secrets or other confidential information obtained during the course of its professional relationship.

No Undisclosed Interest In Suppliers

Another area of concern involves suppliers, vendors, or media that provide work for the agency's clients. The agency cannot have an undisclosed financial interest such as part ownership, kickback arrangement, etc., in these companies. Let's say that Acme Advertising produces brochures for its client, ABC Company. Bogus Photography Studio photographs ABC's products for the brochure. However, Acme Advertising owns 33 percent of Bogus Photography, and ABC doesn't know it. This would breach Acme's duty as an agency and make it impossible for the agency to make decisions in the client's best interests. The agent cannot perform as a true, impartial, and unbiased agent for its clients. Or at least it couldn't convince a court that it could.

Two other areas of this type of conflict of interest need to be discussed. First, the agency must not contract with suppliers who use them as their agency. To go back to our earlier example, if Bogus Photography uses Acme Advertising as its agency, Acme cannot let ABC Company's brochure be photographed by Bogus. Second, the agency must not perform work itself that it has been instructed to contract out. Again, let's say Acme is told by ABC Company to have Bogus photograph its brochure. Acme Advertising cannot photograph ABC's brochure itself, in-house.

Although these types of situations do exist, it is usually without the client's knowledge. If the agency has the client's consent, in writing, then it is not a breach of the agency's duty, since no trust has been violated.

DUTIES OWED BY CLIENTS TO THEIR AGENCIES

The most important duty the client has to its agency is to make the payments it owes to the agency. There are other duties, however, such as furnishing information to the agency and approving or disapproving programs or ads. The client must perform its duties within a reasonable time so as not to cause the agency additional delay and expense. It should make its decisions based on reason and good faith, not on a whim. Further, as seen earlier, the client does not have a right to demand the agency produce advertising that violates any laws. Finally, the client is bound by any contracts made by the agency on its behalf, again, provided the agency acted within the scope of its authority.

In 1869 the advertising agency was beginning to gain respect as a true agent of the client instead of a common space broker. In that year in Philadelphia, a man named Francis Wayland Ayer took $250 and opened an agency named after his father, N. W. Ayer & Son.

One of Ayer's clients, Devlen, manufactured Dent's Toothache Gum. In 1905 Devlen instructed Ayer to place an advertisement in daily newspapers. He also informed Ayer that he wanted "full position" (only editorial around the ad) for his small-space ad. Ayer informed its client that it was impossible to guarantee full position for a very small ad, and that in some papers such position was available only at an increased rate.

As the ad began to run, Devlen noticed that he was not getting full position in all newspapers. He complained to Ayer about this, but the ads continued to run for many months. Devlen also continued to make payments for the ads that ran.

In October 1907, Ayer terminated the contract with Devlen and in *Ayer v. Devlen*,[6] asked the court for damages of $3,801.22 for the balance of the media charges. Devlen had wanted his ads to receive a certain position in newspapers and although he had been told that this was not possible in most cases he authorized the placement of the ads for some time, while still demanding full position. The main issue here was whether Devlen had a contract for his ads to be placed in full position only. The court decided that Devlen did not, and he was ordered to pay the back media charges.

BREACH OF CONTRACT SITUATIONS

In the most simplistic terms, a contract is based on a promise, or promises. When the promise is broken, a breach of contract can exist and a lawsuit can result. The client/agency contract can be breached when either party fails to perform in some area. For the agency, this can occur when it fails to comply with a duty, written in the contract or required by law. Placing an ad that the client had not approved, or taking more than the amount of commission stated in the contract are examples. The client can also breach the contract if it fails to live up to its duties. Failure to pay the agency's bills is the most obvious example.

Generally, remedies for a breach of contract claim are

recision (canceling the contract), damages, specific performance (forcing the other to fulfill the contract), or termination. Specific performance does not apply to personal service situations; that is called slavery, and there are laws against that now. The two main remedies left are recision and damages. A party may find that recision is more realistic than seeking damages. And termination is always a remedy available to both parties.

In breach of contract cases the most common problem is not whether the contract has been breached, but rather determination of the amount of damages. Here's a good example of a breach of contract situation.

An ad agency, William B. Tanner Company, bought space from Action Transit Ads. Action sold space on buses and subways in New Jersey. Tanner, at the request of its client, Tanya Hawaiian Tanning Oil, entered into a contract for three years, 1969 through 1971. The contract provided for three things: the advertising was for Tanya, the agency would receive a 15 percent commission, and the contract could be canceled at the end of each year.

In mid-1971, another contract was entered into between Tanner and Action for Tanya for the years 1972 through 1974. As with the previous contract, Action was to be paid $22,500 per year. However, the difference here was that Tanner did not have the permission of its client to enter into this new contract. At the end of 1972, when Tanya refused to pay the bills, Tanner notified Action that it was terminating the contract. As a result, Action sued in *Action Ads, Inc. v. William B. Tanner Co.*[7]

William Tanner was authorized by Tanya to purchase the transit ads for the first three years, 1969 through 1971. However, it was not authorized by Tanya to make the second three-year contract. Because of that, Tanner was acting on its own in entering into the 1972 through 1974 contract: Tanner had breached its contract with its client and was itself liable for the $22,500 for the 1972 contract with Action.

DURATION OF CONTRACTS

In all written contracts the length of time that the agreement is to run must be stated. If it is indefinite, that should be stated as well. All contracts between advertising agencies and clients should be made in writing. Oral contracts are not a good idea for a variety of legal reasons mainly because they can be found to be unenforceable in many situations.

TERMINATION OF CONTRACTS

Notice Of Termination

When a contract is terminated, the first thing to consider is the amount of time that must be given to the other party as notice. This "grace period" is built into client/agency contracts to allow the agency time to restructure for the change, and for the client to settle its business with the agency. In other words, no undue hardship should be placed on either party.

The length of the notice period, according to industry trade custom, is usually 60-to 90-days, although it can be any period of time that both parties agree to. (A trade custom is law because of the length of time that the practice has been accepted and used.) To be on the safe side, the notice period should be stated in the contract. On this subject, Doyle Dane Bernbach tried to recover $126,729 for advertising from a former client, Avis Flowers, in *Doyle Dane Bernbach, Inc. v. Warren E. Avis*.[8]

Doyle Dane also handled the Avis Rent-A-Car account, which was started by the owner of Avis Flowers, Warren Avis, and later sold to a conglomerate. Avis Rent-A-Car put the agency on notice that it had to choose between the two clients due to the similarity in names and identity. Obviously, Doyle Dane opted to keep the Avis car account.

When Doyle Dane terminated the agreement with Avis Flowers in November 1977, it gave 90 days notice. During the notice period, Doyle Dane contacted the flower company to arrange for the transfer of the account to another agency. Even though it had given a notice of termination, Doyle Dane continued to handle the Avis Flowers account through the end of 1977, placing ads in *People* magazine that had been approved prior to when notice was given.

Avis Flowers claimed that Doyle Dane placed the ads after termination (breach of contract) and, therefore, was liable for any media charges incurred after the agency gave notice for those insertions. In fact, there was no written contract, so there was no stated notice period. However, the 90-day notice period is standard in the advertising industry, and is accepted as a trade custom—one that Avis should have been well aware of. Doyle Dane gave Avis a sufficient amount of notice—the standard amount in the industry—and continued to perform through the notice period. As a result, Avis was required to pay the media fees incurred during the 90-day period.

Commissions Due After Termination

As just illustrated, certain post-contractual liabilities and duties are imposed on both parties. If the agency had entered into contracts with third parties on behalf of the advertiser before the relationship was terminated, the agency would be entitled to the commissions that it would have received.

In 1952 Hansman-Joslyn Advertising entered into a contract with Uddo & Tormina Company, makers of Progresso Italian foods. Hansman, as its agent, entered into a contract with WBOK radio. The one-year radio contract with Progresso was canceled after only a few months, causing the radio station to charge a "short rate" amount for the time because the full contract period was not used. The short rate policy is a trade custom in the advertising business.

In *Hansman* v. *Uddo and Tormina Co.*,[9] the court said:
Contracts made with any kind of advertising

media . . . providing therein a short rate
cancellation, that is to say, the advertiser contracts to
use the media for a stated length of time at a certain
rate . . . if the advertiser sees fit to cancel the
contract prematurely, then he is obligated to pay the
rate which would be applicable had the contract . . .
been for the number of advertisements actually
used.

Uddo was ordered to pay the amount due the media.

Now, for the case of media contracts that were entered into
by the previous agency. If the client takes its business to a new
agency, the client is liable to the old agency for the media
commissions, unless a contract agreement covers this occurrence.

To illustrate, let's go back to the hypothetical situation used
earlier. Acme Advertising had placed media for an ad for its client,
ABC Company, in *American Widget Monthly* magazine. A week later
ABC notifies Acme that it is moving its account to a new agency,
Dinkum Advertising, in 30 days. Even though Dinkum produces
the ad and coordinates with the magazine, ABC must still pay
Acme the amount of commission it would have received.

What if the client uses material from the former agency in
preparation for another advertising campaign, after the
termination of the relationship? If that material was never used or
paid for, the client must compensate the original agency for its
efforts. It cannot use the fruit of the agency's labor for future
advertising without paying for it. In legal terms this principle is
known as *quantum meruit*. In simpler terms, you don't get
something for nothing.

When ABC Company transferred its account over to
Dinkum Advertising, it also gave them campaign concepts and
layouts that were developed by Acme Advertising. Acme had
prepared the campaign on a speculative basis, but it was never
approved by ABC. Since ABC never paid for the concepts and

layouts, if it produces the campaign through Dinkum, it must compensate Acme for the work. On the other hand, if ABC had paid for the campaign to be created, the company would be free to produce it without further compensating Acme.

Soliciting New Accounts After Giving Notice Of Termination

When notice of termination has been given, can the agency service a competing account? It is certainly free to do so after termination. What is doubtful, though, is whether the agency is free to associate with prospective new clients who are in competition with the current client before termination becomes effective. The best advice would be that the agency should not jeopardize itself by creating a potential liability.

Limit To Use Of Information Gained

In the natural course of the advertising business an agency becomes familiar with the workings of its clients. It obtains a certain expertise in each client's line of business. There can be no doubt, however, that intimate knowledge of a client's trend of thought and method of doing business can become part of the agency's general knowledge and expertise.

Therefore, the post-contractual duty not to divulge or use details of the client must be restricted to actual trade secrets and the kind of confidential information that is separate from the general knowledge about a trade or business.

Here's a strong case in point. Murray Salit and other employees of Irving Serwer Advertising were sued by Serwer in *Irving Serwer, Inc. Advertising* v. *Salit*.[10] This occurred after the employees left the agency to open their own shop, Salit & Garlanda Advertising. Serwer claimed that Salit and the others had taken accounts over to the new agency by obtaining confidential information while in its employ and that they "entered into a course of conduct and conspiracy to destroy [Serwer's] business."

However, the court held that simply gaining information about clients while working for an agency does not, in and of itself, constitute learning trade secrets or confidential information. As a result, Serwer lost his case.

While this situation involves employees of an agency, this reasoning applies to agencies who use knowledge gained from other clients. If the information does not constitute a trade secret and is not confidential (as discussed earlier), the agency cannot be stopped from making use of the knowledge.

LIABILITY TO MEDIA

Is a client liable for media commitments by the agency? There is a conflict here, but the general feeling is that the ultimate liability is on the advertiser. In essence, if the media knew who the client was and knew that the agency was acting in its behalf, any claims would be against the client. The agency would not be liable on the contract as long as it entered into the agreement with the client's knowledge and consent. One exception to this is a sole liability clause, which we'll discuss later in this chapter.

American Manufacturers Mutual Insurance contracted, through its agency Clinton E. Frank Advertising, to sponsor a news broadcast entitled "ABC Evening Report." At the end of one broadcast on November 9, 1962, a promotional announcement was run that displeased American Manufacturers. The announcement promoted a show called "The Political Obituary of Richard M. Nixon." American Manufacturers terminated its sponsorship of the "ABC Evening Report," and refused to pay the media fees.

American Broadcasting Company filed suit for the amount due for media charges: *American Broadcasting-Paramount Theatres v. American Manufacturers Mutual*.[11] In this case, Clinton E. Frank Advertising was named as one of the defendants, but was held not to be liable for the media fees. Even though Clinton Frank was the agency and placed the order, it was not liable for any damages because ABC knew Frank was acting as the agency for American Manufacturers. ABC also knew that the agency had entered into the contract on behalf of its client. ABC won the suit for breach of contract, and American was liable for the media.

The client/agency relationship may exist only with the knowledge and consent of both parties. The client who hires an agency voluntarily empowers it to bind the client to contracts with others. Simply put, when someone hires an agency it creates an implied acknowledgment that the client intends to be bound by any contract or transaction that the agent must enter into to fulfill his agency duties. Parties who deal with a known agent generally assume that the client intends to be bound by the agency's commitments.

In 1971 Lennon & Newell was the ad agency for Stokely-Van Camp foods company, as it had been for the previous 17 years. Lennon & Newell had purchased media space for Stokely on CBS. In 1967 the agency began to suffer substantial losses and by 1970 was in severe trouble. It had been paid by Stokely for media billings but had not, in turn, paid the media. By the end of 1971 Lennon owed CBS $714,000 out of total payables of $3 million, and could not make its payments. About that time, Lennon & Newell filed for bankruptcy.

Because of the situation, CBS filed suit, *Columbia Broadcasting System, Inc. v. Stokely-Van Camp, Inc.*,[12] directly against the client. This was a case of liability when an agent goes bankrupt owing money to media. Does the media have a claim against the client? In this case, it did even though the client had paid the agency for the media.

In 1978 Sander Rodkin/Hechtman/Glantz Advertising purchased television time for its client Climate Control, an air conditioning distributor. At the time, Sander was having financial problems. When the agency received money from Climate Control for media, it did not pay the media. Climate Control, however, had paid its total bill and documented each payment. The final payment for $15,000 was designated as "final payment for WLS-TV air time."

WLS-TV was the local ABC affiliate in Chicago. It sued Climate Control for the amount due in *American Broadcasting Companies, Inc. v. Climate Control Corporation.*[13] It was not until December 1979 that ABC contacted Climate Control and told them that it was liable for the unpaid balance. Right after that, this lawsuit was initiated.

In this case, Sander was the agency for Climate Control, and as such, bound Climate Control to any contracts it had made for the client. Climate Control was liable for the unpaid balance to ABC. Sander Rodkin went out of business.

For reference, I've included a sample media insertion order form (Exhibit 11-2). The format is typical of insertion order forms used in many agencies. This should serve as a general format for others to adapt and use as their needs dictate.

Sole Liability Clauses

The advertising agency is directly liable to the media under certain conditions. One is when the agency voluntarily agrees to be directly liable for media bills. The other is when the media contract contains a "sole liability" clause, to which the agency has committed. In both cases the agency accepts full liability for media costs.

The sole liability clause, which is included in many media contracts, says that the agency is solely liable for the debts incurred on behalf of the client. As a consequence of the sole liability clause, the agency can impose on the client a duty to pay the media charges to the agency prior to the media's due dates. Failure to make these payments on time can easily lead to cancellation of the media space, as well as substantial damage claims by the agency against the client.

LIABILITY FOR ADVERTISING

As seen in other chapters, the agency can be liable along with the client, for the advertising it produces. If the advertising makes deceptive or unfair claims, the agency as well as the client can be held liable for those claims. This has been proven many times in court. Claiming, as many agencies do, that they only did what the client told them to do does not relieve the agency's liability. The courts generally consider that an advertising agency should know what its clients are doing.

Other areas where the agency can be liable involve defamation (libel and slander), copyright and trademark infringement, violation of privacy and publicity rights, in addition to others. In general, advertising agencies must realize that the courts look on them as the professionals. This idea goes back to the "higher degree of skill" concept discussed earlier. More and more, agencies are being held liable for the joint actions stemming from the client/agency relationship. It is very important that agencies understand this idea.

The Invisible Window Case

A manufacturer of automobile windows set about to demonstrate how much clearer its windows were, compared to those of its competition. The commercial exaggerated the demonstration by distorting the competition's windows with a coat of Vaseline. The clarity of the advertiser's windows was additionally enhanced by simply rolling down the window for the commercial.

When the FTC filed an action, the manufacturer's defense was that it had instructed its advertising agency to "present a fair commercial." The court reasoned, when it upheld the FTC's previous ruling in *Libbey-Owens-Ford Glass Co.* v. *FTC*,[14] that this statement did not allow the advertiser to escape liability by delegating the responsibility for the commercial to its agency.

ELEMENTS OF THE CLIENT/AGENCY CONTRACT

While it is not imperative that a written contract be created, it is the much wiser option. When the rights, duties, and intentions of both parties are fixed in writing, there is less interpretation and guesswork involved if a problem arises.

There are certain considerations that should be addressed when the contract provisions are made. The following list includes the most important ones:

- Appointment as the agency;
- Nature and extent of services to be provided;
- Compensation (commission, fees, etc.);
- How supplier contracts are to be handled;
- Rights upon termination of contract;
- Indemnity against claims;
- Handling of competitive clients; and
- Liability to media.

I have included a sample contract (Exhibit 11-3) and a project proposal (Exhibit 11-4) that are commonly used. The contract and project proposal work together and make reference to each other. The contract covers the general provisions of the relationship. The project proposal is used as an estimate for each specific project. While every agency should consult an attorney to have its specific contract drawn up, Exhibits 11-3 and 11-4 will serve as general formats to follow.

EMPLOYEE RELATIONS WITHIN THE AGENCY

One of the areas that agencies need to be aware of involves situations when an employee leaves and takes accounts. Account piracy is a growing internal problem for ad agencies. Many agencies are dealing with the problem by adopting restrictive covenants in employment contracts to prevent this.

Let's say that you own the Acme Advertising agency and your employees become increasingly dissatisfied with you and the way you run the agency. Some of the key people get together and decide that they will give you an ultimatum: sell them the agency and get out, or they will leave and take some of the accounts with them. Is this legal?

Let's take a look at just that type of situation to find the answer. The Duane Jones Company was an ad agency founded in 1942 by Duane Jones, who was the president and operating head of the agency until August 1951. At that time, the agency billed $9 million annually from about 25 accounts. But what happened in August, 1951 threw a wrench into the machinery of the agency.

About that time the agency lost three accounts and $6,500,000 with them. Along with that, three executives and numerous staff people resigned from the agency because, as the employees claimed, Duane Jones "had been guilty of certain behavioral lapses at his office, at business functions, and during interviews with actual and prospective customers. As a result . . . several of [Jones's] officers and directors expressed dissatisfaction with conditions—described as 'intolerable.'"

In June 1951, a private meeting had been held at a hotel in Manhattan between a number of the agency's officers, directors, and employees, led by one of the officers, Mr. Hayes. It was decided that these people would make an ultimatum to Jones: either sell them the agency or they would resign "en masse." Hayes told Jones of this plan and informed him that certain clients of the agency had been presold on the idea of leaving with the employees. Jones responded, "In other words, you are standing there with a Colt .45, holding it at my forehead, and there is not much I can do except to give up?" Hayes replied, "Well, you can call it anything you want, but that is what we are going to do."

At first, Jones decided to accept the buy-out of the agency, but negotiations fell through in August 1951. That same month, six officers and directors resigned from the agency. A few days later the former employees of Jones opened a new agency, Scheideler, Beck & Werner, Inc. This agency employed 71 of the 132 Duane

Jones employees. Within a few weeks, the new agency had as accounts Manhattan Soap Co., Heublein, International Salt, Wesson Oil, C. F. Mueller Co., The Borden Co., Marlin Fire Arms, McIlhenny Corp., Haskins Bros., and Continental Briar Pipe—all former clients of Duane Jones.

When one acts as an agent or employee—the legal relationship is the same for either—a duty of loyalty, trust, and good faith is owed to the client or employer. We discussed this duty earlier. As a result, Duane Jones filed suit in *Duane Jones Co.* v. *Burke, et al.*[15]

The court awarded damages to Jones and said: "defendants . . . while employees of [Jones], determined upon a course of conduct which, when subsequently carried out, resulted in benefit to themselves through destruction of [Jones's] business, in violation of the fiduciary duties of good faith and fair dealing imposed on defendants . . . ."

There are situations in which taking accounts away from a former employer is acceptable, however. One example of such an occurrence is found in the case of *Nationwide Advertising Service, Inc.* v. *Kolar*.[16] Here, Nationwide sued a former employee, Martin Kolar, and his new employer Bentley, Barnes & Lynn for acquiring former accounts of Nationwide. Both agencies specialized in recruitment advertising. Not until after Kolar left Nationwide and became employed with Bentley did he solicit accounts of Nationwide. This was acceptable.

One of the issues in this case involved an implied covenant binding Kolar not to compete with his former employer. But this covenant covered only confidential information gained through his employment, and then used for his benefit, to the detriment of the employer. This was not the case here.

Granted, an agency's interest in its clients is proprietary by nature, but this is valid only when the client/agency relationship is near permanent. In the advertising business, this is a rare claim. In the recruitment advertising business, it is almost nonexistent.

Further, Nationwide's client list was not confidential, and no trade secrets were used to solicit the accounts. Kolar did not solicit any accounts until after leaving the employ of Nationwide. The court held that no breach of trust or confidence occurred; Nationwide lost the case.

Restrictive Covenants

Probably the best solution to account piracy involves the use of restrictive covenants in written employment contracts. This is the only way to legally enforce damages against former employees for account piracy.

Under an agreement containing a restrictive covenant, the employee agrees not to serve or contact any client of the former agency for a specific period of time. It is crucial that a specific period of time be stated in the agreement; otherwise it will be unenforceable. Also, the time must be reasonable, usually one to two years.

Restrictive covenants must be agreed to at the beginning of the employment. If an agency wishes to add restrictive covenants to existing employment situations, some additional consideration must be given. This can be any valuable offering: extension of employment, stock options, money, etc.

AGENCY LIABILITY FOR CHILDREN

This is a very important subject for advertisers and their agencies. Almost every ad agency has dealt with children in the course of producing an ad, television commercial, billboard, or brochure. Any agency that works with children needs to understand the applicable restrictions and requirements. Few photographers and fewer art directors are aware of the current child labor laws governing employment of children.

The Problem

You're at the photo studio to photograph a client's project. Everything is going fine. The set looks good, the kids are great in their costumes, and the collie is behaving just fine. All of a sudden, the photo assistant kicks a light stand and the dog, startled, turns and bites one of the children. The child falls, knocking over a prop stand causing the entire set to crash down on top of another child. About then you wonder what else could go wrong.

Well, if the children were working without a valid work permit, you've only begun to hear your world come crashing down around you. If you, or your client, did not have the proper work permits, you could face criminal or civil prosecution, resulting in lawsuits, fines, and even jail. If the child is working without the proper permits, liability insurance could be useless. Insurance companies can deny coverage if a law was violated that led to the injury.

This was something John Landis learned the hard way. While filming the movie *Twilight Zone*, two child actors and actor Vic Morrow were killed when a helicopter crashed. The children were employed illegally for four reasons. First, they were working at 2:30 a.m. Second, they were in an extremely dangerous situation. Third, the children did not have work permits as required by California law. Fourth, no social worker was present. Had one been, the filming would probably not have been allowed. Had the laws been obeyed, the accident would not have killed the children or Morrow, since they would not have been on the set at that time.

Child Labor Laws

In the early 1900's child labor laws were created in response to an increase in serious injuries of children. Most of these injuries were the result of severe conditions in mills, sweatshops, and mines where children were used as cheap labor.

Child labor laws created restrictions on minimum wages, hours of employment, and working conditions. While some laws are federal, the most important are state statutes. The individual states have become more involved in this area and have adopted very stringent laws to protect children. New York and California are at the head of this list.

Note: anyone can be held liable—the photographer, the director, the ad agency, or the client. Each must protect itself by making sure that the proper permits are obtained and working conditions are met.

Guidelines For Working With Children

- **Check with the state agency** that oversees child labor laws to determine the state's requirements. For example, in California, it is the California Division of Labor Standards.
- **Obtain the proper permits** from the state where the photography takes place.
- **Abide by the hours of employment** allowed by law. For example, in California, children 6 to 18 years old can only work a maximum of four hours a day and not after 6:30 p.m. A one-hour lunch break must be provided no later than 1 p.m. For sessions out of the studio, lunch must be provided free to the child and teacher or welfare worker.
- **Provide the required supervision**. Again, in California, a studio teacher or welfare worker must be hired and present during any session.
- **Check insurance coverage**. Make sure that the photographer has valid workers' compensation and liability insurance.
- **Report any injury** that occurs to a child immediately to the insurance carrier and the state Workers' Compensation Board.
- **Medical attention**. Make sure that the child gets immediate medical attention.

- **Parents cannot waive liability**. Remember, a parent or guardian cannot give a release of liability by law. Even a written release will not protect you.

The Chilko River Incident

Over the years, Al Wolfe organized fishing and river rafting trips for many of his employees and clients. As Wolfe would later say of his trips: "If you could get away from the titles and pretense and really get to know each other, there would be a bond formed."

In 1987, Wolfe put together one such trip while he was the president of DDB Needham Worldwide's Chicago office. The plan was to take a group of eleven friends and business acquaintances for a weekend fishing and rafting trip on the Chilko river in British Columbia, Canada.

On a Saturday in August, the group set off down the Chilko, some of the roughest rapids in the world. Suddenly, after entering a stretch of river known as the "White Mile," the raft hit a rock and overturned. Five of the eleven perished in the river.

Those who never returned included Robert Goldstein, VP/advertising for Procter & Gamble; retired agency executive Richard O'Reilly; retired DDB Needham Senior VP James Fasules; Stuart Sharpe, Senior DDB Needham VP account manager; and, Gene Yovetich, Senior DDB Needham VP account manager.

The disaster, dramatized in the HBO movie *White Mile*, affected not only the participants but the agency as well. DDB Needham was sued by Mr. Fasules' family for his death due to the inadequate safety precautions and the negligence of Wolfe (in his capacity as president of DDB Needham). Fasules was not an employee of the agency at the time and therefore the family could bring a negligence suit directly against DDB Needham. The agency employees, however, were limited to recover damages under workers' compensation actions. While the U.S. District Court determined that Fasules was 45 percent responsible for his own death, they also found that DDB Needham was 55 percent responsible. The court awarded Fasules's family $1.1 million in damages to be paid by DDB Needham.

The Chilko case illustrates how an action can bring liability to an agency, even if it did not actually involve work within the agency. Agencies (like any other company) can be held liable for the actions of their employees, at any time, when they are acting within the course and scope of their employment.

Avoiding Liability For Use Of Unsolicited Ideas Submitted By Outsiders

Occasionally, someone outside an agency or client may approach the company with an offer of a new idea for the company. While this is a common occurrence for advertising agencies, these situations present risks since subsequent use of the ideas can lead to an obligation to reasonably compensate the person who submitted the idea. This applies to creative ideas for ads, as well as marketing and product development ideas. A good example is, Procter & Gamble who received an idea from an outsider for putting a blue substance in a laundry powder. Later, when P&G marketed "Blue Cheer," liability was imposed by the court for using the submitted idea. The court in *Galanis* v. *Procter & Gamble Corp.*,[17] could have imposed liability on an express or implied contract theory, or on a misuse of trade secret theory, but they used a theory of unjust enrichment and ruled that Procter & Gamble was obligated to pay the outsider for the value of the idea it had received.

Although subsequent use by a company of information or ideas submitted to it is always somewhat risky, use of the information is not invariably illegal. Before liability is imposed, courts will insist that the outsider's idea be both novel and concrete; liability will not be imposed for use of vague and general ideas (unless, of course, there is a clear, express contract covering the matter). While the line between concrete and vague ideas is ambiguous, it's more prudent to err on the safe side to avoid the problems that can result from accepting unsolicited idea submissions. Formal records should be kept as to the date the idea was received and its specific content. Also, a written response should be made to the person submitting the idea explaining the company's position on not accepting unsolicited outside ideas.

If an outsider submission is accepted, it is wise to make a specific written agreement between the parties as to the use of, and compensation for, any ideas to be submitted. If an outside person submits an idea that had already been developed internally, there is no liability to compensate for the same suggestion. However, to guard against a possible argument that subsequent use of an internally developed idea actually came from an outsider, firms should keep accurate records as to the time and place of, and employees involved in, the discovery and development of new ideas and trade secrets.

CONCLUSION

As we have seen throughout this chapter, the ad agency has a lot to consider in the operation of its business. The agency business is a fascinating one indeed, but it also has many risks and pitfalls. An agency must deal with many areas of law in the operation of its business. While it has certain rights of its own, it also has duties to its clients and suppliers, as well as duties to the public and to its employees. And all of those parties have rights and duties of their own.

EXHIBIT 11-1
SAMPLE AGENCY PURCHASE ORDER

Purchase Order

ACME ADVERTISING

1234 Main Street
Hometown, CA 10000
(310) 555-1234

VENDOR:		
	PURCHASE ORDER NO: _____	
	DATE:	
ATTENTION:	CLIENT:	
To Vendor: This order is placed by our agency as agents for our client as referenced on this order. All appropriate Sales Taxes must be billed on invoice. All invoices received after the 25th of the month are deemed to be the subsequent month's liability. Submit all invoices in triplicate. Job number and P.O. number must appear on invoice to receive payment.	JOB TITLE:	
	JOB NO:	
	TERMS:	

QUANTITY	DESCRIPTION	DUE DATE	PRICE QUOTED

SPECIAL INSTRUCTIONS:

DELIVERY INSTRUCTIONS:

ORDERED BY:_____ DUE DATE:_____

EXHIBIT 11-2
SAMPLE MEDIA INSERTION ORDER

Insertion Order

ACME
ADVERTISING
1234 Main Street
Hometown, CA 10000
(310) 555-1234

DATE:

PUBLISHER:

INSERTION ORDER NO:

ADVERTISER:

PRODUCT:

RATE:

PUBLICATION:

DISCOUNT ALLOWED: _____

SALES REPRESENTATIVE:

This is a Change. ☐

This is a Cancellation. ☐

PLEASE INSERT OUR CLIENT'S ADVERTISING AS SPECIFIED BELOW:

SPACE	COLOR/BLEED	ISSUE DATE EDITION	CANC DATE	CAPTION	AD NUMBER	GROSS AMOUNT	NET AMOUNT

POSITION:

MATERIAL:

Billing Instructions:
☐ Client to be billed direct at net by Media as Agency receives commission via monthly service fee. The Client, not Agency is liable for all payments regarding this insertion.
☐ Agency to be billed direct at net by Media.

SPECIAL INSTRUCTIONS:

FOR AGENCY: _____

FOR CLIENT: _____ DATE

EXHIBIT 11-3
SAMPLE AGENCY CONTRACT

THIS AGREEMENT, entered into this____day of_____,
19__, by and between ACME ADVERTISING, a California
corporation, ("Agency") and_____
_____, ("Client").

ARTICLE I
ADVERTISING REPRESENTATION AND SERVICES

1.01 <u>Term of Agreement</u>. This Agreement shall become
effective as of the execution date hereof and shall continue in effect
until terminated as provided herein.

1.02 <u>Appointment and Authorization of Agency</u>. Client
agrees to retain and appoint the Agency, as its agent, to represent it
in carrying out its advertising program, subject to the terms and
conditions of this Agreement. The Agency is authorized to enter
into contracts with third parties to effectuate the purposes of this
Agreement. In instances when a written project-proposal(s) shall
be submitted for approval by Client, the terms and conditions of
such project-proposals shall become a part of this Agreement.

1.03 <u>Agency Services</u>. Agency agrees to act as the Client's
advertising representative and to perform, upon authorization by
Client, any and all of the following services to the extent necessary
to meet the Client's needs.

(a) Study, research and analyze the Client's business and
products or services and survey the market therefor.

(b) Develop and implement an advertising and marketing
program designed to meet the Client's needs and budgetary
limitations.

(c) Counsel the Client on his overall marketing and
advertising program or make plans therefor.

(d) Determine and analyze the effect of the advertising

used.

(e) Plan, create, write and prepare layouts and the actual copy and art to be used in advertisements of all types.

(f) Analyze all advertising media to determine those which are most suitable for use by the Client.

(g) Make contracts with the advertising media for space or time and with others to effectuate the advertising program and obtain the most favorable terms and rates available.

(h) Check and follow up on all contracts with the various media for proper performance in the best interests of the Client, including the appearance, accuracy, date, time, position, size, extent, site, workmanship and mechanical reproduction, as appropriate to the advertisements used.

(i) Negotiate, arrange and contract for any special talent and services required for all photography, cinematography, animation, models, special effects, layouts, and art work, and for all printing, including any required photography, separations, typography, film production, video and audio production, and any other necessary technical material for use in the advertising program.

(j) Make timely payment to all persons or firms supplying goods or services in connection with the advertising program.

(k) Advise and bill the Client for all amounts incurred by the Agency on behalf of the Client's account and maintain complete and accurate books and records in this regard.

1.04 <u>Prior Approval of Client</u>. Agency shall not incur any obligations or provide any services for the Client's account without first obtaining the approval from Client. The Agency shall submit a written project-proposal(s) to the Client, whenever possible, containing full descriptions of the proposed advertisements and estimates of the cost of obligations or services involved, including media costs, costs of preparation of the advertisement, costs of production, and any additional costs.

All estimates shall be submitted on the Agency's standard

project-proposal forms with sufficient copies to meet the needs of the Client.

The Agency shall not be responsible for missed deadlines, closing dates or insertions caused by the delay of the Client in approving the advertisements to be used in connection therewith.

Production schedules shall be established and adhered to by Client and Agency, provided that neither shall incur any liability or penalty for delays caused by force majeure.

1.05 <u>Property and Materials</u>. All materials, sketches, copies, artwork, dummies, type, art, dies, photographs, illustrations, negatives, film stock, video tapes and other items supplied by Agency shall remain the exclusive property of Agency and no use shall be made, nor any ideas obtained therefrom may be used, except upon compensation to Agency to be determined by Agency. All such items shall remain the sole and exclusive property of Agency until compensation is made to Agency.

1.06 <u>Delivery of Materials</u>. Unless otherwise specified, any price quoted is for a single shipment without storage, F.O.B., local Client's place of business or F.O.B. printer's platform for out-of-town Clients. Proposals are based on continuous and uninterrupted delivery of complete order, unless specifications distinctly state otherwise. Charges related to delivery from Client to Agency or from Client's supplier to Agency are not included in any quotation unless specified.

<u>ARTICLE II</u>
COSTS AND PAYMENTS

2.01 <u>Advertising Costs and Expenditures</u>.

(a) Client shall reimburse Agency for all costs incurred and expenditures made on behalf of Client for approved advertising, for which client shall compensate the Agency as provided in Section 2.02.

(b) Client shall pay the Agency for its direct costs of

mailing, packaging, shipping, taxes and duties, telegrams and telephones incurred by the Agency in connection with its performance under this Agreement.

(c) Client shall pay all of Agency's costs for any necessary travelling done on behalf of Client.

(d) In the event media or any other charges increase or decrease after the Agency has submitted an estimate, the Client shall pay for such increase or be given a credit for such reduction, as the case may be. In the event the Client, after having approved any planned advertising, cancels all or any part thereof, the Client shall pay for all costs incurred therefore to date of cancellation and any unavoidable costs incurred thereafter, including any noncancelable commitments for time or space. In addition, the Agency shall receive any commissions it would have earned had the proposal been fully performed.

2.02 Agency's Compensation.

(a) Agency shall receive a commission of fifteen percent (15%) of all gross media charges. The Agency shall charge an amount which, when added to the net cost of media allowing no commission or less than 15% commission, will yield 15% of the Agency's total media bill to the Client.

(b) The Agency shall receive a commission of fifteen percent (15%) of the charges made by third parties with whom the Agency has contracted for products or services which are to be used to implement the advertising approved by the Client.

2.03 Billing and Payment. The Agency shall bill the Client from time to time, and payment for which shall be made within thirty (30) days of the invoice date. Final billing to Client shall be adjusted based upon final invoices from vendors, plus Agency's commissions. Bills and project-proposals estimating the costs involved may be initially used, but final, detailed bills, supported by invoices of charges of third parties and showing all adjustments and credits, will be submitted to the Client as soon as available.

2.04 Internal Labor. All internal labor of Agency shall be

charged at an hourly rate for: creative time, concept, design, art direction, copywriting, trademark, logo-type, mock-ups, research and development, market research, media research and planning, broadcast production, product development, analysis and public relations. Internal labor rates shall be as follows: [specify rates].

2.05 <u>Speculative and Experimental Work</u>. Speculative and experimental work performed by Agency for Client, at Client's request, such as sketches, research, drawings, composition, film and materials, including labor, will be charged Client at current rates and may not be utilized by Client without the prior written consent of Agency, and upon compensation to Agency.

<u>ARTICLE III</u>
TERMINATION OF AGREEMENT

3.01 Either Party may terminate this Agreement by giving the other Party written notice of at least ninety (90) days prior to the effective date of termination. Upon receipt of notice of termination, the Agency shall not commence work on any new projects or advertisements, but it shall complete and place all projects and advertisements previously approved by the Client. All the rights and duties of the Parties shall continue during the notice period, and the Client shall be responsible to the Agency for the payment of any contract obligations incurred by the Agency with third parties during this period.

3.02 In the event the Client of Agency desires to terminate all work in progress on all projects and advertisements commenced before receipt of notice of termination, it may be so agreed upon by the Parties' mutual consent and determination of the compensation to be received by the Agency for partially completed work.

3.03 <u>Billing Upon Termination</u>. Upon termination of the Agreement, the Agency shall bill the Client for all amounts not previously billed and due the Agency at that time under the terms of this Agreement.

Agency shall be entitled to payment for services and commissions for advertisements approved by Client prior to the effective date of termination.

ARTICLE IV
COMPLIANCE WITH LAW

4.01 Any controversy or claim arising out of or relating to this Agreement, or any project-proposal submitted pursuant to the terms of this Agreement, may be settled by arbitration in accordance with the rules of the American Arbitration Association, any judgment upon the award rendered by the arbitrator(s), may be entered in any court of competent jurisdiction. In the event of such claim, the prevailing party shall be awarded its reasonable attorney's fees and costs.

4.02 Neither Party may assign any rights or delegate any duties hereunder without the expressed prior written consent of the other.

4.03 This writing contains the entire Agreement of the Parties. No representations were made or relied upon by either Party, other than those expressly set forth herein. No agent, employee, or other representative of either Party has the power to alter any of the terms hereof, unless done in writing and signed by an authorized officer of the respective Parties hereto.

4.04 Validity, interpretation and performance of this Agreement shall be controlled by and construed under the laws of the State of California.

4.05 All notices pertaining to this Agreement shall be in writing and shall be transmitted either by personal hand-delivery or through the facilities of the United States Postal Service. The addresses contained herein for the respective Parties shall be the places where notices shall be sent, unless written notice of a change of address is given.

4.06 You represent and warrant that the information and materials provided Agency and which may be included in the work performed, will not at any time infringe upon or violate any copyright, artistic, personal, dramatic or any other rights, legal or equitable of any person. You agree to indemnify, defend and hold Agency harmless from any liability, claim or action arising out of or pertaining to the foregoing warranty. In the event of any such claim or action against Agency, you shall defend Agency with attorneys of your own choice, and at your own expense, and we agree to cooperate in all respects in connection with said defense.

IN WITNESS WHEREOF, the Parties have caused this Agreement to be executed on the date first hereinabove set forth.

"AGENCY"

BY:_____

"CLIENT"

BY:_____

EXHIBIT 11-4
SAMPLE AGENCY PROJECT PROPOSAL

Date:
To:

In accordance with your request, ACME ADVERTISING is pleased to submit the following project-proposal. Agency agrees to act as the Client's advertising representative and to perform any and all of the following services to the extent necessary to meet the Client's needs:

Our proposal is based upon estimates supplied by vendors. Final billing is subject to receipt of vendors' final invoices. This proposal does not include any applicable commissions, ACME ADVERTISING fees, expenses and costs, all of which will be contained in the final billing.

We shall furnish all elements and facilities necessary for the completion of the above-described work, except the following items which you shall provide:

This proposal shall remain valid for thirty (30) days from the date indicated, after which it may be withdrawn, or revised by ACME ADVERTISING. Any changes subsequent to approval of the proposal may affect the prices quoted and, therefore, must be approved by both parties. In the event of cancellation of the proposal by client after acceptance, ACME ADVERTISING shall be reimbursed for any expenses incurred and shall be paid any commissions it would have earned had the proposal been fully performed.

You represent and warrant that the information and materials provided ACME ADVERTISING and which may be included in the work performed, will not at any time infringe upon or violate any copyright, artistic, personal, dramatic or any other rights, legal or equitable of any person. You agree to indemnify, defend and hold ACME ADVERTISING harmless from any liability, claim or action arising out of or pertaining to the foregoing warranty. In the event of any such claim or action against ACME ADVERTISING, you shall defend ACME ADVERTISING with attorneys of your own choice, and at your own expense, and we agree to cooperate in all respects in connection with said defense.

Any disputes arising out of or pertaining to this agreement may be pursued in accordance with the rules of the American Arbitration Association, and any award made with respect to such arbitration shall be enforceable in any Court of competent jurisdiction. In the event of any such arbitration or any litigation arising out of or pertaining to this proposal, California law shall govern and the prevailing party shall be awarded its reasonable attorneys fees and costs.

All unpaid invoices in connection with the foregoing work shall bear interest at the rate of ten percent (10%) per annum until paid. All materials and/or other items produced and/or supplied by ACME ADVERTISING shall remain the exclusive property of ACME ADVERTISING and no other use or reproduction shall be made by client, without first obtaining the consent of ACME ADVERTISING, which consent shall include reasonable compensation to ACME ADVERTISING.

Very truly yours,
ACME ADVERTISING

BY:_____

ACCEPTED AND AGREED TO BY CLIENT:

BY:_____   _____DATED:_____

[1] *Crocker v. United States*, 240 U.S. 74, 36 S.Ct. 245, 60 L.Ed. 533 (1916).

[2] *Joyce Beverages of New York, Inc. v. Royal Crown Cola*, 555 F.Supp. 271 (1983).

[3] *Brown v. Molle Co.*, 20 F.Supp 135 (1937).

[4] *Medivox Productions, Inc. v. Hoffman-LaRoche, Inc.*, 107 N.J. Super. 47, 256 A.2d 803 (1969).

[5] *E. I. Du Pont de Nemours Powder Co. v. Masland*, 244 U.S. 100, 37 S.Ct. 575, 61 L.Ed. 1016 (1917).

[6] *Ayer v. Devlen*, 179 Mich. 81, 146 N.W. 257 (1914).

[7] *Action Ads, Inc. v. William B. Tanner Co.*, 592 S.W.2d 572 (1979).

[8] *Doyle Dane Bernbach, Inc. v. Warren E. Avis*, 526 F.Supp. 117 (1981).

[9] *Hansman v. Uddo and Tormina Co.*, 76 So.2d 753 (La. App. 1955).

[10] *Irving Serwer, Inc. Advertising v. Salit*, 17 A.D.2d 918 (1963).

[11] *American Broadcasting-Paramount Theatres v. American Manufacturers Mutual*, 42 Misc.2d 939, 249 N.Y.S.2d 481 (Sup.Ct. 1963), aff'd 251 N.Y.S.2d 906, aff'd 17 N.Y. 2d 849 (1966).

[12] *Columbia Broadcasting System, Inc. v. Stokely-Van Camp, Inc.*, 522 F.2d 369 (1975).

[13] *American Broadcasting Companies, Inc. v. Climate Control Corporation*, 524 F.Supp. 1014 (1981).

[14] *Libbey-Owens-Ford Glass Co. v. FTC*, 352 F.2d 415 (6th Cir. 1965).

[15] *Duane Jones Co. v. Burke, et al*, 281 N.Y.A.D. 622, (1953), aff'd 306 N.Y. 172 (1954).

[16] *Nationwide Advertising Service, Inc. v. Kolar*, 329 N.E.2d 300 (1975).

[17] *Galanis v. Procter & Gamble Corp.*, 153 F. Supp. 34 (S.D.N.Y. 1957).

CHAPTER 12

SPECIAL ADVERTISING CONCERNS

You can tell the ideals of a nation by its advertisements.
—*Norman Douglas*

"The case is too hard for man," Maitland said, "so it is left to the judgment of God." That is how laws were tested for centuries. This is Occam's Razor in action. Actually it wasn't William of Occam, or Ockham, but Duns Scotus who created the Razor. Occam's Razor says that where there are several ways to account for a thing, the theory that involves the fewest hypotheses is to be preferred. And, around the 1300's, this was a handy way to dole out laws, indeed.

Laws were interpreted by God, the only one who could make such determinations as guilt and punishment. This was shown in the old concept of trial by ordeal which existed to let God determine such matters in his own way. The judges didn't presume to have the power or knowledge to do so on their own. And, after all, the judges answered only to the church.

Then, five hundred years later the U. S. Constitution separated church and state. Man now has to decide all the intricate details of law. All the interpretations, the subtle nuances, the social ramifications. The drafters of the Bill of Rights could never have anticipated the consideration of issues like abortion, pornography, and commercial speech.

The First Amendment we are very aware of today. For a hundred and fifty years, however, it was rarely noticed. Not because there was perfect freedom of speech and press, but because nobody thought there ought to be.

The First Amendment has been treated for about a hundred and fifty years as a wicker basket that could not carry a heavy burden. In recent years however, it has been treated more as a catch-all. Yet, recent events under the First Amendment dramatize the pendulum swings of history, and the dangers of doctrine, and tendency of doctrinaires to fight past wars.

Here, we are going to take a look at First Amendment issues regarding commercial speech: that is advertising. We'll look at the Commercial Speech Doctrine. We'll also look at other issues which have involved First Amendment issues such as attorney advertising and political advertising.

THE NEW COMMERCIAL SPEECH DOCTRINE UNDER THE FIRST AMENDMENT TO THE U. S. CONSTITUTION

While it has not always been that way, the Supreme Court now recognizes that "commercial speech" (advertising falls into this category) is protected under the First Amendment to the U. S. Constitution. This means, among other things, that certain advertising of products and services cannot be banned by the government. Today, advertising and other forms of commercial speech are still not held in the same high regard as political or religious speech. Yet, the good news is that because of this change, fewer restrictions are being placed on advertisers. Those restrictions that are in place, or are considered, continue to cause debate on First Amendment issues. This is especially evident in recent efforts to completely ban tobacco advertising.

The New And Improved Commercial Speech Doctrine

Until 1975 commercial speech was virtually unprotected by the First Amendment. However, in that year, the Supreme Court overturned a criminal conviction for violation of a certain statute on the books in Virginia making it a misdemeanor to distribute any publication that encouraged or promoted an abortion in Virginia. The case arose when a newspaper published an ad for legal abortions in New York.

The argument was that the ad was unprotected because it was commercial. However, the court held that the message that legal abortions were available in New York, "did more than simply propose a commercial transaction. It contained factual material of clear 'public interest.'" The court continued saying that the ad related to abortions, a service with which, generally the state couldn't interfere.

Because of the Supreme Court's 1973 decision in *Roe* v. *Wade*,[1] the Virginia court did not need to decide the "precise extent to which the First Amendment permits regulation of advertising that is related to activities the State may legitimately regulate or even prohibit." The goal of protecting commercial speech was to provide the consumer with the same access to information as his access to political and religious debate.

A year later, the Supreme Court clearly settled the issue of whether there is an exception to First Amendment protection for commercial speech in a case involving a woman who was required to take prescription drugs on a daily basis. The Court ruled that commercial speech is protected under the First Amendment.

A Virginia law stated that a pharmacist licensed in Virginia, would be guilty of unprofessional conduct if he "publishes, advertises or promotes, directly or indirectly, in any manner whatsoever, any amount, price, fee, premium, discount, rebate or credit terms . . . for any drugs which may be dispensed only by prescription."

The position was that prescription drug users would greatly benefit if advertising was allowed. The Virginia State Board of Pharmacy however, argued that advertising prescription drug prices was not protected by the First Amendment because it involved commercial speech.

The Supreme Court, in *Virginia State Board of Pharmacy* v. *Virginia Citizens Consumer Council, Inc.*[2] decided that advertising is valuable in that it provides information about who is producing and selling what product, why, and at what price. "So long as we preserve a predominantly free enterprise economy, the allocation of our resources in large measure will be made through numerous private economic decisions." The Court maintained that it was in the public's interest to promote those decisions by being knowledgeable and well informed. "To this end, the free flow of commercial information is indispensable."

The Court went on to say: "...that people will perceive their own best interests if only they are well enough informed, and that the best means to that end is to open the channels of communication rather than to close them." The end result was that Virginia could set whatever professional standards it wanted for its pharmacists, however "it may not do so by keeping the public in ignorance of the entirely lawful terms that competing pharmacists are offering."

Limiting Commercial Speech: The Central Hudson Case

While First Amendment protection now extends to commercial speech, it still earns less protection than other forms of expression. The government can still limit First Amendment protection of some forms of commercial speech. In 1980, the Supreme Court created a four-part test used to determine if a certain restriction on commercial speech is allowed.

The New York Public Service Commission ordered electric utilities in the state to cease all advertising that "promot[ed] the use of electricity." This was put into place because New York did not have a sufficient fuel supply to meet the demands of the 1973-1974 winter.

Three years later the fuel shortage eased, and the commission proposed to continue the ban on promotional advertising. The Central Hudson Gas & Electric Corporation opposed the ban on First Amendment grounds.

The court in *Central Hudson Gas & Electric Corp.* v. *Public Service Commission*[3] recognized that commercial speech was entitled to First Amendment protection in some cases. However, the U. S. Constitution, the Court reasoned, affords less protection to commercial speech than to other constitutionally guaranteed forms of expression.

The First Amendment's protection of commercial speech is intended to allow and encourage the forms of advertising that provide consumer information. On the other hand, the Court ruled that there is no constitutional reason to support commercial messages that do not accurately inform the public about lawful activities. As a result, the government may ban communications that are more likely to deceive the public than to inform it. Governments may also ban commercial speech regarding an illegal activity.

The Central Hudson Test

The Court in the *Central Hudson* case established a four part test for determining restrictions on commercial speech. This is known as the Central Hudson Test:

- Determine if the message qualifies for protection under the First Amendment. It must involve a legal activity and not be misleading;
- Determine whether the government's interest in restricting the commercial speech is substantial;
- If the first two points are met, the courts must then determine that regulation of the message directly supports the government's interest; and
- Lastly, the courts must determine whether regulating the message is more extensive than is necessary to further the government's interests.

The Court held that both the conservation of energy and

the state's desire to keep rates fair both represented valid governmental interests.

The Court also looked at whether the commission's complete suppression of speech, which would ordinarily be protected by the First Amendment, was too extensive and went further than necessary to justify the state's interest in energy conservation.

The commission's order covered all promotional advertising regardless of its impact on overall energy consumption. Yet, this rationale did not justify suppressing information about electric devices or services that would not increase total energy use. The commission could have limited the format and content of Central Hudson's advertising, and required ads to include information about the relative efficiency and expense of the service. The Court reasoned that a complete ban on advertising violated the First Amendment.

The Puerto Rico Casino Case

With the Puerto Rico casino case, protection for advertising took one step backward. This was the first time a court upheld a government's ban on truthful advertising of a legal product. The Games of Chance Act of 1948[4] was a law in Puerto Rico that legalized certain forms of casino gambling. The intent of the law was simply to promote tourism. In addition, the law prohibited casinos from advertising or promoting themselves to the public of Puerto Rico.

This law also banned casinos from using the word "casino" in matchbooks, inter-office and external correspondence, invoices, brochures, menus, elevator cards, lobby cards, flyers, telephone books, directories, lighters, envelopes, napkins, glasses, plates, banners, paper holders, pencils, bulletin boards, or any other hotel object that could be accessible to the public.

The Condado Holiday Inn Hotel and Sands Casino filed suit claiming that the law suppressed commercial speech by violating the First Amendment.

Using the *Central Hudson* test, the U. S. Supreme Court ruled in 1986 that the Puerto Rico law did not violate the First Amendment. The government of Puerto Rico had an important interest in restricting the ads because it would reduce the demand for casino gambling by the residents of Puerto Rico. This constituted a substantial governmental interest.

The Court also found that this view directly advanced the government's interest, saying, "In our view, the legislature's separate classification of casino gambling, for purposes of the advertising ban, satisfies the third step of the *Central Hudson* analysis."

The fourth step of the *Central Hudson* test was satisfied because the ban was no more extensive than necessary to further the government's interest.

But, what about cases in which the Supreme Court had struck down a ban on any "advertisement or display" of contraceptives and the one we just looked at in which it reversed a criminal conviction based on the advertisement of an abortion clinic? There is a difference between those cases and the casino case. In the two cases involving contraceptives and abortion the promoted activities were constitutionally protected and could not have been prohibited by the government. However, in the casino case, "the Puerto Rico Legislature surely could have prohibited casino gambling by the residents of Puerto Rico altogether." Gambling is not protected as a constitutional right. So, in the Court's opinion, "the greater power to completely ban casino gambling necessarily includes the lesser power to ban advertising of casino gambling."

The casino case, *Posadas de Puerto Rico Associates* v. *Tourism Company of Puerto Rico*,[5] has been heavily criticized, especially within the advertising community. This decision seems to permit virtually unlimited government regulation of commercial speech. The theory is that if the conduct the speech promotes can be banned, the commercial speech can be regulated as well.

On the other hand, one of the most recent Supreme Court commercial speech cases since the casino case, abolished a ban in Florida on in-person solicitation by certified public accountants. The case was *Edenfield* v. *Fane*.[6] Amazingly, this Court's decision focused on the *Central Hudson* analysis and never even mentioned the casino case. Possibly future restrictions on commercial speech will be limited to those few areas, such as gambling, where morality concerns overwhelm constitutional analysis.

It appears that if the business or product is protected under the U. S. Constitution, such as contraceptives or abortion, the advertising cannot be banned. However, if the business or product is not protected under the Constitution, such as access to gambling casinos, the advertising can be banned.

This is a very turbulent area of law (most constitutional issues are), which probably won't be uniformly resolved for some time. However, it affects all areas of advertising, especially those that we examine next.

U. S. CURRENCY RESTRICTIONS

One area of concern for advertisers is the use of certain elements in advertising. The use of U.S. currency in an ad has been a major issue for advertisers to deal with.

During the Civil War the first large issuance of paper money in the United States was made. As a result, a law[7] was enacted to protect the uncontrolled counterfeiting that went with the war time economy. At the time the law provided criminal liability for printing, photographing or making any impression "in the likeness of any obligation or other security, or any part thereof . . . ." In other words, you could not photograph or copy any money or part of it.

However, in 1958, Congress enacted another law[8] that allowed the "printing, publishing . . . of illustrations of . . . any . . . obligation or other security of the United States . . . for philatelic, numismatic, educational, historical, or newsworthy purposes in articles, books, journals, newspapers, or albums . . . ." Yet, this law limited how currency could be reproduced to avoid counterfeiting. The reproduction could only be in black and white, larger or smaller than actual size, and the negatives and plates had to be destroyed immediately after use.

The government, however, did not allow reproduction of currency for commercial advertising purposes to fall under this exception. In 1984, the U.S. Supreme Court made a decision in *Time, Inc. v. Donald T. Regan, Secretary of the Treasury, et al.*[9] that changed that. In that case, *Sports Illustrated* had used a color photograph of $100 bills pouring into a basketball hoop.

Time argued that Section 504 was unconstitutional in that it was a violation of free speech because the government could determine what was acceptable content or subject matter. The Court ruled in favor of Time in part.

In 1985, the Treasury Department formulated a policy statement regarding use of currency in ads.

The policy stated that the Department would:

[P]ermit the use of photographic or other likenesses of U.S. and foreign currency for any purpose, provided that the items were reproduced in black and white and were less than 3/4 of, or greater than 1-1/2 times the size, in linear dimension, of each part of the original item. further more, the negatives and plates used in making the likeness must be destroyed after their use. This decision will, for the first time, permit the use of currency reproduction in commercial advertisements, provided they conform to these size and color restrictions.

As a result, reproduction of currency is allowed in advertising under two conditions:

- It was not reproduced in full color; and
- It was reproduced less than 3/4 or more than
  1-1/2 the size of the original.
  Note: violating this law is a felony.

CONSIDERATIONS WHEN ADVERTISING PROFESSIONAL BUSINESSES

The first state to adopt an ethics code for attorneys was Alabama in the late nineteenth century. This specifically allowed newspaper ads to be used by members of the Alabama bar. However, in other states the practice was not allowed. In fact, a Denver, Colorado attorney was suspended for six months by the state Supreme Court in *People ex rel. Maupin* v. *MacCabe*,[10] for running a newspaper ad which claimed: "Divorces legally obtained very quietly, good everywhere." The Court noted in that case, "The ethics of the legal profession forbid that an attorney should advertise his talents or his skills as a shopkeeper advertises his wares."

In 1908, The American Bar Association published its Canons of Professional Ethics, which discussed attorney advertising. Cannon 27 (1908) stated, in part, "...solicitation of business by circulars or advertisements, or by personal communications, or interviews, not warranted by personal relations, is unprofessional."

It was not until 1977 that a major change occurred regarding attorney advertising. The landmark decision was the case of *Bates* v. *State Bar*.[11] Here, the U.S. Supreme Court upheld the First Amendment right of attorneys to advertise their services. However, the *Bates* case did not grant carte blanche to attorneys to advertise in any manner they wanted. The Court stressed that attorney advertising must not be false, deceptive or misleading. They noted: "As with other varieties of speech, it follows as well that there may be reasonable restrictions on the time, place and manner of advertising."

The state bar associations greeted *Bates* with little enthusiasm. In fact, they limited *Bates* to its facts, which essentially allowed price advertising of certain routine legal services.

Even though *Bates* dealt with advertising by attorneys, it lead the way for advertising by all professionals. Accountants, attorneys, doctors, dentists, pharmacists, and other professionals have been using advertising to attract clientele ever since.

In 1978, *Ohralik v. Ohio State Bar Association*,[12] decided the question of direct solicitation. The Court stated that truthful, restrained advertising of prices for routine legal services was not unprofessional conduct. However, the Court also indicated that states have a legitimate interest in protecting the public from attorney advertising involving fraud, undue influence, or intimidation.

The Court said:

> By discussing the origin and impact of the nonsolicitation rules, I do not mean to belittle those obviously substantial interests that the State has in regulating attorneys to protect the public from fraud, deceit, misrepresentation, overreaching, undue influence and invasions of privacy. But where honest, unpressed 'commercial' solicitation is involved—a situation not presented in either of these cases—I believe it is open to doubt whether the State's interests are sufficiently compelling to warrant the restriction on the free flow of information which results from a sweeping nonsolicitation rule and against which the First Amendment ordinarily protects.

The Supreme Court went further in another landmark attorney advertising case, *In re R.M.J.*[13] The Missouri Supreme Court's Advisory Committee tried to disbar an attorney for violating attorney advertising regulations by using direct mail and advertising his expertise in his area of practice ("personal injury") using wording that varied from that allowed by the code. The Missouri Supreme Court upheld the constitutional validity of these rules and reprimanded the lawyer. The U.S. Supreme Court, however, reversed this decision by saying:

> Truthful advertising related to lawful activities is entitled to the protection of the First Amendment. But when the particular content or method of the advertising suggests that it is inherently misleading or when experience has proved that in fact such advertising is subject to abuse, the States may impose appropriate restrictions. Misleading advertising may be prohibited entirely. But the States may not place an absolute prohibition on certain types of potentially misleading information, e.g., a listing of areas of practice, if the information also may be presented in a way that is not deceptive. Thus, the Court in Bates suggested that the remedy in the first instance is not necessarily a prohibition but preferably a requirement of disclaimers or explanation. . . . Although the potential for deception and confusion is particularly strong in the context of advertising professional services, restrictions upon such advertising may be no broader than reasonably necessary to prevent the deception.

The Court went on:

> Even when a communication is not misleading, the State retains some authority to regulate. But the state must assert a substantial interest and the interference with speech must be in proportion to the interest served. . . . Restrictions must be narrowly drawn, and the State lawfully may regulate

only to the extent regulation furthers the State's substantial interest.

In this case, the Court clearly stated the broad parameters of an attorney's—and by inference any professional's—right to advertise.

The U.S. Supreme Court continued to show little patience for state restrictions on an attorney's right to advertise truthfully as demonstrated in it's decision in *Zauderer* v. *Office of Disciplinary Counsel of the Supreme Court of Ohio*.[14] Because of this ruling, attorneys may use accurate illustrations in their ads, as well as nondeceptive claims in ads that openly solicit specific types of clients. However, the decision requires some attorney ads to contain certain disclosures.

In 1981, Philip Zauderer, an attorney in Columbus, Ohio, began placing ads in Ohio newspapers. One ad included a line drawing of the Dalkon Shield, along with the following copy.

● ● ● ● ● ● ● ● ● ● ● ● ● ● ● ● ●
DID YOU USE THIS IUD?
The Dalkon Shield Intrauterine Device is alleged
to have caused serious pelvic infections resulting
in hospitalizations, tubal damage,
infertility, and hysterectomies.

It is also alleged to have caused unplanned pregnancies
ending in abortions, miscarriages, septic abortions,
tubal or ectopic pregnancies and full term deliveries.
If you or a friend have had a similar experience
do not assume it is too late to take legal action
against the Shield's manufacturer.
Our law firm is presently representing
women on such cases.
The cases are handled on a
contingent fee basis of the amount recovered.

> If there is no recovery, no legal fees
> are owed by our clients.
> ● ● ● ● ● ● ● ● ● ● ● ● ● ● ● ●

The ad included Zauderer's firm name, address and phone number for "free information."

Zauderer received over 200 inquiries from the ad and ultimately initiated lawsuits on behalf of 106 women.

Another ad noted Zauderer's availability to represent people charged for drunk driving. That ad contained the phrase: "full legal fee refunded if convicted of drunk driving."

The Ohio Supreme Court publicly reprimanded Zauderer after ruling that the ads violated several rules in the state's Code of Professional Conduct. On July 29, 1982, Ohio's Office of Disciplinary Counsel (ODC) charged Zauderer with several disciplinary violations because of these ads. The case claimed that the drunk-driving ad violated Ohio Disciplinary Rule 2-101 (A), saying that it was "false, fraudulent, misleading, and deceptive to the public." The rational for this was that it offered representation on a contingent-fee basis in a criminal case, a violation under another disciplinary rule.

The complaint also charged that the line drawing in the Dalkon Shield ad violated Disciplinary Rule 2-101(B), which forbid use of illustrations in attorney ads, and limited the kind of information in such ads to an established list of 20 items. In addition, the ODC claimed that the ad violated another disciplinary rule forbidding a lawyer from "recommending employment, as a private practitioner, of himself, his partner, or associate to a non-lawyer who has not sought his advice regarding employment of a lawyer." Another rule stated that a "lawyer who has given unsolicited advice to a layman that he should obtain counsel or take legal action shall not accept employment resulting from that advice."

The case also dealt with another rule that required ads mentioning contingent-fee rates to "disclose whether percentages are computed before or after deduction of court costs and expenses." The failure to inform clients that they would be liable for costs (as opposed to legal fees) even if their claims were unsuccessful made the ad "deceptive."

It was never alleged that the Dalkon Shield ad was false or deceptive. In fact, the ODC stipulated that the information and advice in the ad relative to Dalkon Shield litigation was not false, fraudulent, misleading, or deceptive and that the line drawing accurately depicted the Dalkon Shield.

The Court said:

> Because all advertising is at least implicitly a plea for its audience's custom, a broad reading of the rules applied by the Ohio court (and particularly against self-recommendation) might suggest that they forbid all advertising by attorneys—a result obviously not in keeping with our decisions in *Bates* and *In re R.M.J.* Because appellant's statements regarding the Dalkon Shield were not false or deceptive, our decisions impose on the State the burden of establishing that prohibiting the use of such statements to solicit or obtain legal business directly advances a substantial governmental interest.

The Court concluded by saying the state did not meet that burden in this instance:

> An attorney may not be disciplined for soliciting legal business through printed advertising containing truthful and nondeceptive information and advice regarding the legal rights of potential clients.

Ohio's laws regarding the use of pictures or illustrations in an attorney's ad was invalid for similar reasons. The likely purpose behind the restrictions was to insure that attorney ads are "dignified." However, the court said it was "unsure that the State's desire that attorneys maintain their dignity in their communications with the public is an interest substantial enough to justify the abridgment of their First Amendment rights."

Zauderer was unsuccessful with the disclosure issue. The problem here involved a failure to include in the Dalkon Shield ad "information that clients might be liable for significant litigation costs even if their lawsuits were unsuccessful." The Court noted that Ohio's disclosure requirements do not prevent lawyers from advertising. Rather, lawyers are required by these rules to "provide somewhat more information than they might otherwise be inclined to present."

Specifically, the Dalkon Shield ad said that "if there is no recovery, no legal fees are owed by our clients." The drunk-driving ad said "full legal fee . . . refunded . . ." However, the ads failed to mention the subtle distinction between "legal fees" and "costs." The problem with this technical point was that a layman might not be aware of the distinction between "fees" and "costs." Therefore, the U.S. Supreme Court affirmed the Ohio court's reprimand of Zauderer to the extent that it was based on the omission of material information concerning his contingent-fee arrangements in the Dalkon Shield ads and his terms of representation in the drunk-driving ads.

The FTC's Role In Attorney Advertising

It's not surprising that the Federal Trade Commission has actively encouraged truthful attorney advertising, as well as truthful professional advertising in general. As we learned earlier in Chapters 2 and 3, the FTC is authorized to prevent unfair methods of competition and unfair or deceptive acts or practices in or affecting commerce. Under this mandate, the FTC encourages competition among professionals to a great extent. In recent years, the FTC has been looking into the competitive impact of restrictions on business arrangements that such state-licensed professionals as attorneys, doctors, and dentists can use. The commission's goal in that effort has been to urge the removal of those restrictions that restrain competition, raise prices, and hurt consumers without offering benefits.

In November 1984, for example, the FTC prepared a report, "Improving Consumer Access to Legal Services: The Case for Removing Restrictions on Truthful Advertising." Some 3,200 lawyers in seventeen states were surveyed to find out if restricting attorney advertising affected the availability of legal services and the prices that consumers paid for these services. One of the main conclusions of the report was that ". . . restrictions on the manner, content, and form of lawyer advertising have limited the flow of information to consumers about lawyers and their services." The report also found "convincing support for the proposition that greater flexibility to engage in nondeceptive advertising will be associated with lower prices for consumers of legal services."

The FTC also plays a significant part in the area of professional advertising by offering recommendations to the state licensing authorities.

For example, in 1984 two Iowa attorneys televised three commercials that contained:

- More than a single nondramatic voice;
- Background sound;
- Visual displays other than words and numbers; and
- A list of four fields of practice which they would handle on either a percentage basis or a contingent fee basis.

While not alleging or demonstrating that these ads were false, misleading, or deceptive, the Iowa State Bar Association's Committee on Professional Ethics and Conduct obtained a temporary injunction and sought to permanently stop the attorneys from using these commercials to advertise their legal services.

It was charged that the three spots violated Iowa's Code of

Professional Responsibility for Lawyers since they "contain more than a single non-dramatic voice, have background sound and visual displays of two or more people characterizing themselves as clients which make laudatory comment as to the defendants' services," and because they "list four areas of practice and contain no disclaimer."

As a result, the FTC urged the Iowa court not to restrict competition unnecessarily by limiting truthful, nondeceptive information. The commission listed three reasons why these ads were not deceptive:

- The ads did not make any misleading or deceptive statements or claims, nor was there any evidence on which the Iowa Supreme Court could base such a finding.
- A study submitted by the attorneys established that the public did not perceive the advertisements to be misleading or deceptive; and
- There was no evidence "in the record to support the premise generally that the technique of using dramatizations, background sounds or more than one nondramatic voice" in a television commercial is inherently misleading. The FTC noted that the plaintiff's witness "testified that in his professional opinion, the use of such format and techniques was not inherently misleading or deceptive."

The FTC also stated that the American Bar Association's Commission on Advertising found no support that the use of graphic dramatizations and music in lawyer advertising is inherently misleading, or potentially more misleading than advertisements which do not contain those elements.

Many state and local bar associations have used television commercials containing dramatizations, graphics, and music to advertise the availability of bar association-sponsored lawyer referral services. Therefore, the commission disagreed that a commercial featuring clients making laudatory comments about the attorney's services warranted an injunction. "All advertisements are, to some degree, self-laudatory," stated the commission.

As mentioned earlier, the FTC also offers advice to other professions. Generally, these comments also promote the FTC's strong opposition to restrictions on any truthful professional ad. For example, the New Jersey State Board of Dentistry proposed rules that would forbid "any statement offering gratuitous services or the substantial equivalent thereof." The FTC responded by stating that "a number of provisions in the proposed advertising rules would restrain truthful communication and thereby inhibit competition."

In fact, the FTC noted that this provision isn't needed to protect consumers: "To the contrary, truthful advertising of the availability of free services can be of great benefit to consumers and, in addition, such offers can be a valuable professional tool for new practitioners who are trying to establish themselves. While we are aware that there is a potential for deceptive schemes in the use of such advertising we believe that a total ban on the offering of free service is overly restrictive and unnecessary."

The ABA Code

Since the *Bates* decision, the American Bar Association (ABA) adopted its new Model Rules of Professional Conduct in 1983, which included rules dealing with attorney advertising. The FTC praised these new rules as promoting "a clearer and more objective standard for evaluating advertising content than appeared in previous ABA codes and in many state and local bar association codes. The proposed standard would allow truthful ads and prohibit only those that are false and deceptive."

Specifically, Rule 7.1 reads as follows:

A lawyer shall not make any false or misleading communication about the lawyer or the lawyer's services. A communication is false or misleading if it:

1. Contains a material misrepresentation of fact or law, or omits a fact necessary to make the statement considered as a whole not materially misleading;

2. Is likely to create an unjustified expectation about results the lawyer can achieve, or states or implies that the lawyer can achieve results by means that violate the rules of professional conduct or other law; or

3. Compares the lawyer's service with other lawyers' services, unless the comparison can be factually substantiated.

Other areas of the Code cover the media in which an attorney can advertise, and the use of trade names.

In fact, the FTC proposed its own "Model Code" (which follows) that would forbid "only false or deceptive advertising and false or deceptive trade names, and explicitly recognizes the legitimacy of using any media, including electronic broadcast or direct mail, to advertise legal services."

Model Code
COMMUNICATIONS CONCERNING A LAWYER'S SERVICES

A lawyer shall not make a false or deceptive communication about the lawyer or the lawyer's services.

Advertising

• A lawyer may advertise services through direct mail advertising or through public media, including but not limited to telephone directories, legal directories, newspapers or other periodicals, radio or television, provided the communication is not false or deceptive.

• A copy or recording of an advertisement or written communication shall be kept for (one year) after its dissemination along with a record of when and where it was used.

Direct Contact With Prospective Clients

A lawyer may initiate communications with a prospective client through personal contact, through individually directed written communication, or through telephonic communication for the purpose of obtaining professional employment, unless:

- The lawyer knows or reasonably should know that the physical, emotional or mental state of the person is such that the person could not exercise reasonable judgment in employing a lawyer;
- The person has made known to the lawyer a desire not to receive communications from the lawyer; or
- The lawyer knows or reasonably should know that the communication involves coercion, duress or harassment.

Communication Of Fields Of Practice

A lawyer may communicate the fact that the lawyer does or does not practice in particular fields of law. A lawyer shall not state or imply that the lawyer is an officially recognized or certified specialist except where the lawyer in fact has been certified in a particular field of practice.

Firm Names And Letterheads

A lawyer may use any firm name, letterhead or other professional designation provided it is not false or deceptive.

While the ABA code is clearly a key document, it is the various state bar associations—frequently acting in concert with state courts—that have direct authority over attorney conduct. So, it would be wise to check the specific state regulations for those states where ads will run.

It is important to understand that while *Bates*, *In re R.M. J.*, and *Ohralik* dealt with attorney advertising, the same principles are applicable to advertising by all professionals. Indeed, it was in the U.S. Supreme Court's ruling in *Virginia State Board of Pharmacy v. Virginia Citizens Consumer Council*,[15] where the court overturned a Virginia statute forbidding licensed pharmacists from advertising prescription drug prices. And, for example, in December 1978, the U.S. District Court for the Eastern District of Louisiana held that truthful newspaper advertising concerning the availability or cost of routine dental services was commercial speech protected by the First Amendment, finding a statute unconstitutional to the extent it restricted such advertising.

ISSUES WITH POLITICAL ADVERTISING

Certainly, under the First Amendment to the U. S. Constitution no other form of speech enjoys more protection than does political advertising. Political advertising items such as posters, leaflets, and buttons have long been staples of our political system. Beginning with the campaign of John F. Kennedy, television advertising has come into its own as the dominant form of political advertising. Today, political candidates spend tremendous sums of money on television ads. As a result, the use of television advertising brings up a variety of issues that must be understood by advertisers.

If you produce political advertising, you should be aware of an important federal statute —the Federal Election Campaign Act (FECA) of 1971.[16] Sections of this act, for example, discuss the disclosures a candidate should make in his or her ads, the time availability of the media, the contribution of services by an ad agency to a candidate, and many other relevant issues.

According to the FECA, ads involving a political candidate (or request for contributions to a campaign) must clearly name the candidate, authorized political committee, agent, or other person who paid for the ad. Campaign ads and other literature published by a political committee or person that are not authorized by a candidate to publish the material must also include notice that they are not authorized by the candidate.

The FECA requires broadcasters to allow reasonable access or allow candidates to buy reasonable amounts of time for federal elective office. On the other hand, newspapers and magazines aren't required to make space available to candidates.

The Federal Election Commission (FEC) was created by 1974 amendments to the FECA. The FEC regulations define "contribution" or "expenditure" as including any "direct or indirect payment distribution, loan, advance, deposit or gift of money, or any services. . . ." This includes any materials or services that ad agencies offer to a candidate without requesting payment.

Ad agencies should also be aware of one important financial pitfall. If a candidate fails to pay an advertising agency, the agency must try to collect the debt, or else it will be considered a political contribution.

The candidate, the candidate's ad agency, and the media should be aware of the American Association of Advertising Agencies' (4A's) guidelines for political advertising, which are reproduced below.

POLITICAL ADVERTISING—A SHARED RESPONSIBILITY

The Candidate

1. We regard the candidate as the advertiser. The candidate bears the same responsibility as any other advertiser for the content of any ad or commercial run in his behalf. This responsibility cannot be delegated to support groups.

2. We believe every candidate should sign and comply with the Code of Fair Campaign Practices administered by the Fair Campaign Practices Committee.

The Advertising Agency

1. We believe the advertising agency bears the same responsibility for the truth and accuracy of political advertising it prepares as it would for product advertising.

2. We believe the agency has a professional obligation to maintain standards of good taste and to avoid personal vilification and disparagement in the advertising it prepares for a candidate.

3. We see it as the agency's duty to use its communication skills to acquaint the electorate with the candidate, his character, programs and stands on issues. Techniques of communication should be used to inform, not to distract from the real issues.

4. Should the agency find that it no longer exercises sufficient control over the content or execution of the messages, we think it is the duty of the agency to make a public statement to that effect and to cease activity on that campaign. The 4 A's will make its public relations resources available to any member or non-member agency for such a statement.

The Media

1. We believe that all media should exercise the appropriate clearance standards and controls over the taste, content, truth and accuracy of political advertising as it would for product advertising. Media have the professional responsibility to reject any political messages which do not meet their standards of fairness and good taste.

2. We suggest that in addition to selling conventional time segments for political messages, broadcasters offer segments of at least five minutes for political announcements.

(Reprinted by permission of the American Association of Advertising Agencies).

In addition, the American Association of Advertising Agencies' Board of Directors has reapproved the following "Code of Ethics for Political Campaign Advertising:"

CODE OF ETHICS FOR POLITICAL CAMPAIGN ADVERTISING

The advertising agency has become an increasingly important factor in the conduct of American political campaigns.

Just as the political candidate must observe the highest standards of fairness and morality in his campaign, so must the advertising agency operate under a code that reflects the finest values of our political system rather than any unethical temptations that arise in the heat of the battle.

The advertising agency should not represent any candidate who has not signed or who does not observe the Code of Fair Campaign Practices of the Fair Campaign Practices Committee, endorsed by A.A.A.A.

The agency should not knowingly misrepresent the views or state record of any candidates nor quote them out of proper context.

The agency should not prepare any material which unfairly or prejudicially exploits the race, creed or national origin of any candidate.

The agency should take care to avoid unsubstantiated charges and accusations, especially those deliberately made too late in the campaign for opposing candidates to answer.

The agency should stand as an independent judge of fair campaign practices, rather than automatically yield to the wishes of the candidate or his authorized representatives.

The agency should not indulge in any practices which might be deceptive or misleading in word, photograph, film or sound.

(Reprinted by permission of the American Association of Advertising Agencies).

The 4A's Code of Fair Campaign Practices condemns the use of personal vilification, character defamation, whispering campaigns, libel, or misleading or falsified campaign material. Candidates that endorse the code agree to the following practices and constraints:

CODE OF FAIR CAMPAIGN PRACTICES

I SHALL CONDUCT my campaign in the best American

tradition, discussing the issues as I see them, presenting my record and policies with sincerity and frankness, and criticizing without fear or favor the record and policies of my opponent and his party which merit such criticism.

I SHALL DEFEND AND UPHOLD the right of every qualified American voter to full and equal participation in the electoral process.

I SHALL CONDEMN the use of personal vilification, character defamation, whispering campaigns, libel, slander, or scurrilous attacks on any candidate or his personal or family life.

I SHALL CONDEMN the use of campaign material of any sort which misrepresents, distorts, or otherwise falsifies the facts regarding any candidate, as well as the use of malicious or unfounded accusations against any candidate which aim at creating or exploiting doubts without justification, as to his loyalty and patriotism.

I SHALL CONDEMN any appeal to prejudice based on race, creed, or national origin.

I SHALL CONDEMN any dishonest or unethical practice which tends to corrupt or undermine our American system of free elections or which hampers or prevents the full and free expression of the will of the voters.

I SHALL IMMEDIATELY AND PUBLICLY REPUDIATE support deriving from any individual or group which resorts, on behalf of my candidacy or in opposition to that of my opponent, to the methods and tactics which I condemn.

(Reproduced by permission of the American Association of Advertising Agencies).

POLITICAL ADVERTISING AND THE FIRST AMENDMENT

Political advertising enjoys such an amazingly broad protection under the First Amendment that these ads are not reviewable by the Federal Trade Commission. For that matter, they are not reviewable by anyone else, either. Nevertheless, there are some limitations that can be placed on political advertising, specifically concerning where it is displayed. In 1984, for example, the United States Supreme Court ruled that a city's total ban on the posting of signs, including political signs, on public property did not violate the First Amendment. The case was *Members of City Council* v. *Taxpayers for Vincent*.[17]

In that case, Roland Vincent had run for the Los Angeles City Council. Some of his backers hired a political sign company to make and post signs with Vincent's name on them. The signs read: "Roland Vincent—City Council," and were attached to utility poles.

Acting under a town ordinance, city employees routinely removed all posters (including the political signs for Roland Vincent) attached to utility poles and similar objects.

On March 12, 1979, taxpayers and the political sign company, filed suit in U.S. district court, seeking an injunction against enforcement of the ordinance as well as compensatory and punitive damages. However, the district court concluded that the ordinance was constitutional.

The U.S. Supreme Court agreed with the district court's decision saying that: "The problem addressed by this ordinance —the visual assault on the citizens of Los Angeles presented by an accumulation of signs posted on public property— constitutes a significant substantive evil within the City's power to prohibit."

The Court continued:

As recognized in *Metromedia, Inc.* v. *San Diego*,[18] if the city has a sufficient basis for believing that billboards are traffic hazards and are unattractive, 'then obviously the most direct and perhaps the only effective approach to solving the problems they create is to prohibit them' . . . As is true of billboards, the esthetic interests that are implicated by temporary signs are presumptively at work in all parts of the city, including those where appellees posted their signs, and there is no basis in the record in this case upon which to rebut that presumption. These interests are both psychological and economic. The character of the environment affects the quality of life and the value of property in both residential and commercial areas. We hold that on this record these interests are sufficiently substantial to justify this content neutral, impartially administered prohibition against the posting of appellees' temporary signs on public property and that such an application of the ordinance does not create an unacceptable threat to the profound national commitment to the principle that debate on public issues should be uninhibited, robust, and wide-open.

BROADCAST ADVERTISING

FCC's Role In Broadcast Advertising Regulation

Most restrictions that apply to advertising in print media apply to broadcast advertising as well. However, there's one major difference between advertising on television or radio and advertising on any other medium: Broadcasters operate under a license issued by the Federal Communications Commission. Congress created the FCC in 1934 with the institution of the Communications Act. This act was designed to regulate "interstate and foreign commerce in communication by wire and radio so as to make available, so far as possible, to all the people of the United States a rapid, efficient, nation-wide, and world-wide wire and radio communications service . . ." (The word "radio" also applies to television.) The Act authorizes the FCC to "make such regulations not inconsistent with law as it may deem necessary to prevent interference between stations and to carry out the provisions of [the] Act."

There are over 10,000 licensed radio and full-service television stations in the United States. More than 9,000 of these operate commercially and are supported by advertising revenues, the remainder are nonprofit, noncommercial stations.

The FCC's main authority lies in the fact that it has the power to grant applications to construct broadcast stations and license stations. The requirements that need to be met, in the FCC's view, is whether these grants will serve the "public interest, convenience, and necessity."

Therefore, advertisers should be keenly aware of the following areas, as they directly affect advertising.

False Or Misleading Advertising—

The Federal Trade Commission (FTC) has the main responsibility for protecting viewers and listeners from false, deceptive, or misleading advertising (See Chapters 2 and 3). Yet, the FCC expects licensed stations to be diligent in seeing that such ads are not aired. Because of this the FCC and the FTC have an agreement whereby they exchange information on matters of common interest.

Commercial Volume—

The FCC has a policy statement which advises licensees that objectionably loud commercials are contrary to the public interest. According to the FCC, licensees are responsible for making sure that objectionably loud commercials are not aired.

Subliminal Ads—

The FCC strongly believes that the use of subliminal techniques in advertising is contrary to the public interest since, by their very existence, they're intended to be deceptive. This would also be a violation of the FTC Act.

Tobacco Ads—

Federal law prohibits the advertising of cigarettes and little cigars on any medium that falls under the FCC's jurisdiction. However, broadcast advertising for other tobacco products such as pipes, smoking accessories, or cigarette-making machines is not forbidden.

Sponsor Identification Of Advertising—

A station that broadcasts paid-for material must announce that it's paid for or sponsored, and by whom.

Despite its concerns with various aspects of broadcast advertising, the FCC is forbidden from censoring broadcast material including advertising. Accordingly, the FCC can't require its licensees to accept or reject ads for a particular product (unless Congress has passed a law forbidding its advertising, as in the case of cigarettes). In addition, the FCC cannot take actions against "offensive advertising," unless it's found to violate a specific law or regulation.

The End Of The NAB Code

On March 10, 1982, the National Association of Broadcasters (NAB) suspended enforcement of the advertising standards of its television and radio code. The NAB has never reinstated its code.

The NAB's action came in response to a decision on March 3, 1982 by a federal judge (*U.S.* v. *National Association of Broadcasters*[19]) finding that one of the code standards violated the Sherman Antitrust Act. Specifically, it was the NAB Television Code's multiple product standard forbidding the advertising of more than one product in a commercial lasting under sixty seconds.

The court found that:

It is apparent from the fact of this standard that

it has the effect of compelling some, perhaps many, advertisers to purchase more commercial time than their economic interest might dictate. In thus artificially increasing the demand for commercial time . . . the standard raises both the price of time and the revenues of the broadcasters, to the detriment of the users of the broadcast medium and the consumers of their products.

The NAB has argued that compliance with the Code is voluntary to each broadcaster and that it was not an agreement in restraint of trade. The court found that the Code "is not a mere set of advisory standards which subscribers may choose to ignore, but a contractual arrangement to which they are obligated to adhere." Essentially, the court reasoned that claiming that the code was voluntary was not a defense to a Sherman Act charge.

Following this case, the NAB agreed not to issue or enforce any rules that had been challenged by the government. After this decree was entered, NAB formally abandoned its Radio and Television Code Boards, and halted all Code activities.

Network Standards

The demise of the NAB Code has placed even more importance on the network's own policing activities, and their advertising guidelines and standards. This is why every advertiser must have a good working knowledge of these guidelines and standards. Copies can be obtained from the following addresses:

- American Broadcasting Company, Department of Broadcast Standards & Practices, 1330 Avenue of the Americas, New York, NY 10019;
- CBS/Broadcast Group, CBS Inc., 51 West 52 Street, New York, NY 10019; and
- National Broadcasting Company, Inc., Broadcast Standards Department, 30 Rockefeller Plaza, New York, NY 10020.

It must be understood that each of the networks is separate and the standards adopted individually are unrelated to the other networks' standards. In fact, each network maintains individual practices specifically to avoid a Sherman Act violation. The result is that a commercial acceptable to one network may not be acceptable to another network.

Nevertheless, there are many areas of similarity among the networks' standards. This chapter discusses areas of concern to advertisers, and how each of the networks' standards deals with then.

Any questions regarding the networks' guidelines, should be addressed to their clearance department for clarification.

Comparative Advertising Issues

All three networks accept comparative advertising.

CBS Guidelines

Comparative ads are acceptable, says CBS, if its claims are "truthful, fair and adequately substantiated."

NBC Guidelines

NBC will accept comparative ads if they meet the following guidelines:
- Competitors shall be fairly and properly identified.
- Advertisers shall refrain from disparaging or unfairly attacking competitors, competing products, services or other industries through the use of representations or claims, direct or implied, that are false, deceptive, misleading or have the tendency to mislead.
- The identification must be for comparison purposes and not simply to upgrade by association.
- The advertising should compare related or similar properties or ingredients of the product, dimension to dimension, feature to feature, or wherever possible by a

side-by-side demonstration.
- The property being compared must be significant in terms of value or usefulness of the product or service to the consumer.
- The difference in the properties being compared must be measurable and significant.
- Pricing comparisons may raise special problems that could mislead, rather than enlighten, viewers. For certain classifications of products, retail prices may be extremely volatile, may be fixed by the retailer rather than the product advertiser, and may not only differ from outlet to outlet but from week to week within the same outlet. Where these circumstances might apply, NBC will accept commercials containing price comparisons only on a clear showing that the comparative claims accurately, fairly and substantially reflect the actual price differentials at retail outlets throughout the broadcast area, and that these price differentials are not likely to change during the period the commercial is broadcast.
- When a commercial claim involves market relationships, other than price, which are also subject to fluctuation (such as but not limited to sales position or exclusivity), the substantiation for the claim will be considered valid only as long as the market conditions on which the claim is based continue to prevail.
- As with all other advertising, whenever necessary, NBC may require substantiation to be updated from time to time, and may re-examine substantiation, where the need to do so is indicated as the result of a challenge or other developments.

ABC Guidelines

ABC's comparative advertising guidelines are more specific. Like CBS, ABC demands that such ads be "truthful and fair." In addition, many of ABC's standards are quite similar to NBC's:

- Competitive products or services must be accurately and clearly identified.
- False or misleading disparagement of competitive products or services shall not be used. Falsely claiming that a competitive product or service has little or no value (i.e., 'ashcanning') is not permitted.
- Identification of a competitive product or service shall be for comparison purposes. Identification may not be used solely to upgrade the advertised product or service by associating it with a competitive product or service if such association creates a deceptive or misleading impression.
- Comparisons and demonstrations shall be based on specific differences between the products or services advertised, comparing similar or related properties or ingredients, dimension to dimension, feature to feature.
- When aspects of products or services are compared as to performance, they must be significant and meaningful to consumers.

ABC's standards provide specific guidance about commercials using superiority claims containing such words as "better" or "best." ABC also discusses subjective ("puffery") claims at length.

False, Misleading Or Deceptive Ad Claims

The three major networks, of course, agree that all advertising broadcast on their networks must not violate the definitions of false, misleading, and unfair advertising as specified in Federal Trade Commission cases and decisions, as well as the definitions of unfair and deceptive under the Federal Trade Commission Act. According to CBS, "False, misleading or deceptive advertising claims are unacceptable." NBC will not accept in its ads: "Claims or representations, direct or implied, which are false or have the tendency to deceive, mislead or misrepresent." And ABC notes that all material broadcast on it facilities must comply with governmental laws and regulations. Clearly, a thorough knowledge of FTC law, is important when working with the networks. See Chapters 2 and 3, for a discussion of FTC regulations.

Ads Directed At Children

Advertising to children poses sensitive compliance problems. Because of children's lower resistance to selling messages, it has long been recognized that more stringent safeguards are required for ads directed toward children.

Broadcasters also recognize their responsibility to protect children from certain kinds of child-directed advertising. Because of this, all three networks have fairly extensive guidelines for such advertising.

Before discussing these guidelines, however, it is first essential to define "child-directed ads."

NBC's Children's Advertising Guidelines, for example, apply to commercials:

- For products primarily used by children;
- Which are broadcast in or adjacent to children's programs; and
- Which are designed for or have the effect of primarily appealing to children.

ABC's guidelines apply to advertising that's "designed primarily for children 12 and under." CBS has a similar definition.

All three networks have similar concerns regarding ads directed to children. For example, they all find the following to be unacceptable:

- "Extortive language;"
- "Exaggeration and distortion" of product attributes;
- "Frightening" commercials;
- Ads that use peer pressure to sell;
- Use of the words "only" or "just" in reference to price;

- Commercials for nonprescription medications and vitamins; and
- Commercials using celebrities or authority figures as endorsers.

However, there exist different approaches among the networks in some major areas. For instance, ABC flatly considers competitive and superiority claims in child-directed ads to be unacceptable. Both CBS and NBC, however, will consider such claims on a case-by-case basis.

In addition, all three networks have additional guidelines applicable to advertising for toys and food. Similar concerns guide all three broadcasters. For example, they all require that any view of a toy or how it works is one that a child must be "reasonably capable of reproducing," when using the toy.

Regarding food advertising directed to children, all three networks require such ads to "be in accord with the commonly accepted principles of good eating." In addition, all three networks have similar guidelines requiring at least one audio and one video showing a balanced meal in breakfast commercials. In addition, they all have guidelines for such foods that, essentially, forbid suggestions of indiscriminate or immoderate use of such foods.

Both ABC and NBC have similar guidelines concerning children's premiums and offers:

- Forbid the use of fantasy, animation, stock footage or real-life counterparts with such ads.
- Require the inclusion of such disclosures as price, offer dates and separate purchase requirements in the audio portion of the ad.
- Require simultaneous audio and video disclosure of conditions attached to "free" offers.

Ads For Professional Services

All three networks accept advertising for professional services.

CBS will accept "lawful advertising for accountants, chiropractors, dentists, lawyers, physicians, psychologists and other recognized and established professionals."

ABC permits such ads for "members of the medical and legal professions."

NBC does not accept ads "for professional services which do not comply with applicable law or ethical codes," which implies that those that do comply would be acceptable.

What standards do the networks apply? CBS won't accept ads containing "professional advice of the kind that, under sound practice, would be given only within the context of an established practitioner-client relationship."

ABC's Professional Advertising Guidelines are in two sections: Medical and Legal. These sections require that ads:

- Comply with federal, state, and local rules and ABC policy;
- Comply with stringent standards of taste and copy documentation;
- Not be aired when there's a substantial youthful audience;
- Avoid "hard-sell" techniques;
- Not play on viewers' fears or insecurities; and
- Must be approved by the network's New York Broadcast Standards and Practices department.

In addition, under the medical ad guidelines, words such as "safe" or "harmless" may not be used. And the legal ad guidelines list the elements of permissible content of the ad, including basic factual data such as name, address, and telephone number.

Contests/Sweepstakes Guidelines

All three networks allow the advertising of contests by advertisers, but forbid the advertising of lotteries (federal law forbids the broadcast of ads concerning lotteries) —except those conducted by the state. The FTC defines a lottery[20] as the combination of chance, consideration and a prize. In addition, you should also be aware that the states have their own laws concerning sweepstakes and contests. See Chapter 9, for a detailed discussion of Contests and Lotteries.

However, before your proposed contest can air, you must submit detailed information to the network's Broadcast Standards and Practices Department for approval. CBS won't air such spots unless they've first been approved by their Commercial Clearance and Law Departments. It is highly recommended (and required by ABC) that you submit all such information before production of the commercial begins.

CBS has prepared a four-page "Contests/Sweepstakes Questionnaire" that seeks a wide variety of data about the proposed commercial, e.g., the final entry date, planned air dates for the spots, whether all prizes will be awarded, and any specific eligibility requirements. In addition to a completed contest questionnaire, CBS requires two copies of:
- Your contest's official rules;
- The actual entry blank and/or playing piece;
- A detailed statement of all prizes to be awarded; and
- Any applicable newspaper and magazine ads and point-of-sale displays.

A copy of the commercial itself must be submitted to CBS for review.

NBC also requires submission of a completed questionnaire, as well as a complete copy of the rules, an entry blank, promotional material and any published information about the contest, such as newspaper ads.

ABC needs to review all details of a proposed contest, an entry blank or game card, complete rules, and list of prizes.

The benchmark for all three networks is complete disclosure of all pertinent information. Each network has devised its own method and guidelines to achieve that end. Please note, if your want to advertise a contest or sweepstakes on a network, it is critical that you contact the network's Broadcast Standards and Practices or Commercial Clearance Department as early in the planning stages as possible.

Alcoholic Beverage Advertising

The advertising of beer and wine is acceptable to all three networks, subject to federal and local laws. We look specifically at alcohol advertising in Chapter 13. Commercials for hard liquor (distilled spirits such as whiskey, vodka and rum) are forbidden.

While wine and beer ads are acceptable, there are many network requirements advertisers must follow for such ads. For example, all three networks consider as unacceptable beer and wine commercials that:

- Encourage the use of such beverages by young people;
- Depict the use of such beverages in situations that may be hazardous or require a high level of alertness (e.g., driving); and
- Contain statements or implications concerning increased potency or alcoholic content (e.g., "extra strength").

Both NBC and ABC specifically forbid on-camera consumption of wine or beer. While CBS does not, apparently, specifically forbid such on-camera representations, it does forbid even implied references to excessive consumption and only accepts ads for beer and wine that are "presented tastefully." This means that ads featuring on-camera consumption will face a rigorous review by CBS's Clearance Department.

It should also be understood that alcoholic beverage advertising is undergoing much criticism. Groups such as Mothers Against Drunk Driving (MADD) have launched a highly effective campaign against the problem of drunk driving. There have been proposals to forbid the use of celebrities and sports figures in wine and beer ads, and even suggestions to ban televised wine and beer ads altogether. Accordingly, standards that have prevailed for years may become obsolete overnight.

Multiple Product Commercials

Multiple product announcements contain advertising for two or more products. The now-defunct NAB Code, which was followed by the networks, forbid the advertisement of more than one product in a commercial lasting less than sixty seconds.

Current network guidelines allow multiple product announcements. CBS and NBC allow as many as two products to be advertised in a sixty-second commercial. Moreover, CBS will allow ads for more than one product in a thirty-second spot so long as the announcement is "integrated." That is, if "the products or services are related and interwoven within the framework of the announcement, and the voice(s), setting, background and continuity are used consistently throughout so as to appear to a viewer as a single message."

NBC will also allow multiple product announcements in commercials that are shorter than sixty seconds if the ad "presents the products or services of a primary and secondary advertiser."

ABC allows the integrated advertising of two or more products or services in thirty-second ads.

Unacceptable Products or Services

There are certain products and services that the networks refuse to broadcast. NBC, for example, will not allow ads for the following products or services:
- Cigarettes;
- Hard liquor;
- Firearms, fireworks, ammunition and other weapons;
- Presentations promoting a belief in the efficacy of fortune telling, astrology, phrenology, palm reading, numerology, mind reading, character reading, or other occult pursuits;
- Tip sheets and race track publications seeking to advertise for the purpose of giving odds or promoting betting;
- The sale of franchises;

- Matrimonial, escort, or dating services;
- Contraceptives;
- Adult or Sex Magazines;
- X-rated Movies;
- Abortion Services;
- Ethical Drugs; and
- Anti-Law Enforcement Devices.

ABC and CBS as well do not allow ads for cigarettes[21] or astrology, fortune telling and similar services.

If you are aware that one network does not allow advertisements for your product, you should not assume that the other networks also follow suit. Pregnancy test kits are one example of this. CBS doesn't accept ads for such products. ABC, does allow ads for these products if they are "restrained and inoffensive," avoid "graphic representations," and do not play on people's "fears and insecurities."

Substantiation

All three networks require prior substantiation of all material claims prior to airing:

- CBS requires that all claims must be "fully substantiated" before approval is granted;
- NBC requires "substantiation for all material claims and authentication of all demonstrations and testimonial statements;" and
- ABC requires that "when affirmative claims are made for a product or service, the advertiser must submit substantiation or documentation providing a reasonable basis for the claims." ABC's guidelines give many specifics regarding the methodology of research done in substantiating claims.

It would be wise to contact the network's broadcast standards and practices or commercial clearance department before you conduct any claims research.

Other Areas Of Concern

There are many other areas covered in the various networks' guidelines. For instance, NBC has separate guidelines (in addition to those for advertising) that concern ads for children, health care products, personal products, alcohol products, products that control serum cholesterol, ads regarding weight reduction, gambling/lotteries and games of chance. As we've discussed, it's wise to contact the network(s) while a commercial is still in the planning stage.

Challenge Procedure For Commercials Aired On The Networks

Any commercial aired on ABC, CBS, or NBC can be challenged. And, the challenges are handled by each network's Broadcast Standards and Practices Department. This is the same department that reviews all commercials before they are aired. ABC and NBC have written challenge procedures; CBS also has procedures, but they are not written.

Who May Challenge The Networks

Most challenges are made by competing advertisers. Because of this, the majority of commercials that are challenged involve comparative claims and are made by a competitor whose product is unfavorably compared in some manner to the advertiser's product. Additionally, challenges are filed by public officials and organizations, trade associations, consumer groups, disgruntled customers, and individual viewers.

Typically, challenges involve a comparative ad that distorts or exaggerates differences between competitive products or services, lacks adequate substantiation for the claims being made, or creates a false impression. Another issue arises if the ad implies a claim and, if so, whether that claim has been supported by the advertiser.

How To Use The Challenge Procedures

The networks require that a challenge be made in writing for review by the network's Broadcast Standards Department. ABC and CBS will send the complaint to the challenged advertiser for a response, if they feel it has merit. NBC, on the other hand, will transmit the challenge under all circumstances. A challenge will not be pursued if it is considered to be without substance or involves advertising that has completed its scheduleand will not be aired in the future. On the other hand, if a challenge is made to advertising that has not yet been approved, the substantive matters raised will generally be considered during the clearance process.

When a challenge is received, ABC generally requests a response within fourteen days. CBS requests a shorter response time. Yet, all three networks will accelerate the process if a matter is urgent or relatively simple, but will grant reasonable requests for extensions of time.

The networks maintain the confidentiality of the substantiation originally submitted by the challenged advertiser to support the claims made in the advertising. Advertisers, though, are encouraged by the networks to submit a response with supporting information.

The networks will generally permit a challenged commercial to continue to run until a response is received and the challenge is fully resolved. In extraordinary circumstances, approval may be withdrawn or airing may be suspended immediately after receipt of a challenge. And, in fact, some commercials are accepted "subject to challenge," which implies borderline approval. Under these circumstances either withdrawal of approval upon receipt of a responsible complaint or a short deadline for response to a challenge is in order. If approval is withdrawn or suspended, the advertiser may still proceed with the challenge and try to persuade the network to change its mind and reinstate the advertising.

Once the advertiser's response is received, the procedure

used by each network is different. Later, after the challenge has been made each network may request a meeting with the challenger, advertiser or both. The networks may encourage the parties to obtain a resolution from an acceptable third party mediator if they believe that they do not have the expertise necessary to make a judgment.

After receiving the initial challenge, ABC will review it, and will only pass it on to the challenger if rebuttal would be useful, such as if more information is needed or new arguments have been made.

NBC will direct the advertiser to respond straight to the challenger. The network will then make a decision after enough information has been gathered.

CBS's procedure is more formal. Each side generally is given a chance to respond to and rebut the other.

The Role Of The Network's Broadcast Standards Department

At the end of the process, the networks' Broadcast Standards Department will make an independent decision as to how to resolve the challenge. The Broadcast Standards Department will generally allow a challenged commercial to run unless:

- It is voluntarily withdrawn by the challenged advertiser;
- The challenged advertiser refuses to cooperate with the challenge procedures; or
- A determination is made against the challenged advertiser by the network, by a third party to whom the matter has been referred, or by a government agency or an appropriate court.

Pros And Cons Of Network Challenge

In addition to filing a network challenge, the following actions are available:

- A complaint can be filed with the NAD or the FTC;

- Challenges can be made to individual stations or station groups that have aired a commercial;
- Suit can be filed against false comparative advertising under Section 43(a) of the Lanham Act; or
- Suit can be filed under state laws.

The following are some pros and cons of filing a network challenge:

- Network challenges are usually resolved more quickly than other types of complaints. They're less expensive to make and are more informal;
- A Lanham Act suit can produce the fastest result if the court is willing to grant a temporary restraining order or a preliminary injunction. However, there are difficult elements of proof. Discovery procedures are likely to be lengthy, time-consuming and expensive;
- Network challenges can be based on alleged violations of company policies, such as taste standards, as well as allegations of falsity or deceptiveness;
- The NAD will only consider complaints involving truth and accuracy;
- The National Advertising Review Board (NARB) will consider complaints involving the taste, morality, or social responsibility of advertising in general);
- FTC will only consider alleged violations of the FTC Act; and
- Lanham Act suits must contain allegations that the plaintiff has been or is likely to be injured as a result of the false advertising.

Filing a challenge with the networks has its limitations. The networks do not have subpoena power or other discovery procedures; they must rely on the information voluntarily submitted by the parties. There is no hearing at which both sides appear and present arguments. Further, no monetary damages are allowed in such a challenge.

NEW MEDIA CHALLENGES

Before the communications revolution, the choice of where to place an ad was limited to the broadcast, radio, and print media. Today, that choice is expanding to include such new electronic media as cable television, satellite television, low-power television, cabletext, videotex, teletext, and videodisc merchandise catalogs. It also includes media such as commercial messages run in movie theaters.

Advertisers and their ad agencies have learned how to use these new advertising resources. Now there is the chance to try brand-new types of advertising, such as "infomercials," to reach audiences. However, there is the great unknown factor of how regulatory bodies such as the Federal Trade Commission and the Federal Communications Commission will regulate advertising on these media. Be sure that advertising, regardless of the media utilized, is controlled by the FTC.

The FTC'S And FCC'S Roles

The starting point for examining the FTC's role in regulating advertising on the new media is Section 5 of the Federal Trade Commission Act, examined in Chapters 2 and 3. As we saw, Section 5 empowers the FTC to issue "cease-and-desist orders" requiring any "person, partnership or corporation" from "using any unfair method of competition or unfair or deceptive act or practice in commerce." In addition, other provisions of the act govern the FTC's advertising compliance role. If you plan to advertise on the new media, you should study the pertinent FTC cases that, so far, have largely dealt with advertising on the "old media."

In determining what is "deceptive" or "unfair" on cable television, look to previous cases that decided the same issues in relation to broadcast television. The message to viewers is the same, whether they get there via the airwaves or through a cable.

Therefore the regulation efforts will be similar.

Nevertheless, advertising regulatory differences will no doubt arise. This will mostly involve the FTC which is likely to confront advertising compliance issues involving cable TV that it probably will not face on broadcast television. The main reason for this we have discussed in the above sections. Each of the three networks have fairly extensive advertising guidelines that establish what is appropriate in a network commercial.

Cable television, on the other hand, does not have an analogous system to determine the acceptability of the commercial messages appearing in that medium. While there has been talk in the cable industry about establishing guidelines, they have not yet been adopted, if they ever will be. The advertising that appears on the cable stations is pretty much left to the discretion of the cable system operators.

Nevertheless, these systems are not operating on an entirely clean slate. In reality, the vast majority of commercials are from national and large regional advertisers that have already been cleared by one of the three networks. Moreover, the FTC's position is that commercials appearing on cable television are subject to the FTC authority.

While the FCC plays a role in the regulation of cable television, its involvement in advertising compliance issues is a minor one. The FCC rules affecting advertising include:

- Cablecasts for public office such as "political advertising;"
- The Fairness Doctrine (relative to "advocacy advertising");
- Sponsorship identification; and
- A ban on lotteries.

New Issues Involving Cable TV Ads

One of the major new forms of commercial to appear on cable is the "informercial." Essentially, these are longer-form commercials that generally run between ninety seconds and ten minutes. The marketing motivation behind this form of commercial is the recognition that the typical thirty- or sixty-second spot appearing on broadcast television is often not the best way to sell a product or service. It's usually too difficult, for example, to show consumers in these short spots how a product works or provide information on the safe usage of a product. In addition, this short format is clearly inferior in demonstrating the virtues, or the operation, of more complicated products. The longer-form "informercial," however, fits the bill for advertisers and marketers of these products.

There may be potential products liability or personal injury problems lurking in the ad.

You should also scrutinize infomercials for claims that give rise to any warranties under federal and applicable state laws. If the informercial specifically offers a warranty, you should make sure that warranty complies with the federal Magnuson-Moss Warranty Act.

Another important issue involving infomercials is whether the sponsor's name is disclosed in the commercial. A potential problem could arise if the informercial does not make it clear that it is a paid commercial and not a mini-program of some sort.

Another form of commercial that is growing in popularity on cable television is "adverprograms." An adverprogram is an ad that relates to a particular program. For example, a program on cooking might include one-minute "adverprograms" interlaced throughout the show describing how a particular company's food products might be used in certain recipes featured on the show. A potential problem with such ads is the resultant blurring of the lines between programming material and commercial messages.

[1] *Roe v. Wade,* 410 U.S. 113, 93 S.Ct. 705, 35 L.Ed. 2d 147 (1973).

[2] *Virginia State Board of Pharmacy v. Virginia Citizens Consumer Council,* Inc.
  425 U.S. 748, 96 S.Ct. 1817, 48 L.Ed. 2d 346 (1976).

[3] *Central Hudson Gas & Electric Corp. v. Public Service Commission,*
  447 U.S. 557, 100 S.Ct. 2343, 65 L.Ed. 2d 341 (1980).

[4] Games of Chance Act of 1948, Act No. 221, May 15, 1948, P.R. Laws Ann.,
  Tit. 15, §71 (1972).

[5] *Posadas de Puerto Rico Associates v. Tourism Company of Puerto Rico,*
  478 U.S. 328, 106 S.Ct. 2968, 92 L.Ed. 2d 266 (1986).

[6] *Edenfield v. Fane,* ____U.S.____, 113, S.Ct. 1792, 123 L.Ed. 2d 543 (1993).

[7] 18 U.S.C. §474.

[8] 18 U.S.C. §504.

[9] *Time, Inc. v. Donald T. Regan, Secretary of the Treasury,* et al, 468 U.S. 641,
  104 S.Ct. 3262, 82 L.Ed. 2d 487 (1981).

[10] *People ex rel. Maupin v. MacCabe,* 18 Colo. 186, 32 P. 280 (1893).

[11] *Bates v. State Bar of Arizona,* 433 U.S. 350, 97 S.Ct. 2691, 53 L.Ed. 2d 810 (1977).

[12] *Ohralik v. Ohio State Bar Association,* 436 U.S. 447, 98 S.Ct. 1912,
  56 L.Ed. 2d 444 (1978).

[13] *In re R.M.J.,* 455 U.S. 191, 102 S.Ct. 929, 71 L.Ed. 2d 64 (1982).

[14] *Zauderer v. Office of Disciplinary Counsel of the Supreme Court of Ohio.,* 471 U.S. 626,
  105 S.Ct. 2265, 85 L.Ed. 2d 652 (1985).

[15] *Virginia State Board of Pharmacy v. Virginia Citizens Consumer Council,* Inc.
  425 U.S. 748, 96 S.Ct. 1817, 48 L.Ed. 2d 346 (1976).

[16] Federal Election Campaign Act of 1971, 2 U.S.C. §431 (1982),
  P.L 92-225, 86 Stat. 3.

[17] Members of *City Council v. Taxpayers for Vincent,* 459 U.S. 1199, 105 S.Ct. 2265,
  85 L.Ed. 2d 652 (1984).

[18] *Metromedia, Inc. v. San Diego,* 453 U.S. 490, 101 S.Ct. 2882, 69 L.Ed. 2d 800
  (1981).

[19] *U.S. v. National Association of Broadcasters,* 395 U.S. 973, 89 S.Ct. 2126,
  23 L.Ed. 2d 762 (1982).

[20] 16 C.F.R. 15.57.

[21] 15 U.S.C. 1335.

CHAPTER 13

ADVERTISING CONCERNS WITH ALCOHOL AND TOBACCO

The most effective way of attacking vice is to
expose it to public ridicule.
—*Moliere*

A tall, powerful woman in a black dress marched into a
saloon in Medicine Lodge, Kansas one evening in 1890. For many
days prior, she had stayed outside the saloon reading the Bible —
intently praying for the close of the saloon. At the time, Kansas
was a "dry" (no alcohol) state, but the law was not effectively
enforced.

The woman had good reason for her vigil. Her drunkard
husband had died shortly after their marriage leaving her a lonely
and angry widow.

When her prayers did not work, she turned to violence.
The male patrons ran from the saloon, frantically stumbling, as she
smashed the place to pieces with her axe. The well placed blows
struck by Carry A. Nation echoed far beyond the small town in
Kansas. Around the beginning of the twentieth century there was
increasing government regulation in many areas. Congress had
begun to pass laws to protect the public from harmful foods and
drugs and to conserve the nation's natural resources. The
monopolies created by the Morgans and Rockefellers were
beginning to be broken up. All this allowed the prohibition
movement to catch fire as well.

It was not a new movement though. By the 1850's,
prohibition laws were in effect in thirteen states. The forces behind

the movement had roots in religious fundamentalism and support from the Women's Christian Temperance Union, founded in Ohio in 1874. In many states, local counties had the ability to vote themselves dry. And many did in West Virginia, Maryland, Illinois, Georgia, Missouri and Mississippi. But neighboring counties could still supply the product—and they did.

The temperance drive gained new momentum after 1900 however. Beer and whiskey sales had grown rapidly among the large numbers of Irish and German immigrants. And, as would be expected, this brought about an anti-foreign ring to the cries for prohibition. And as women gained the vote for the first time, the temperance drive grew also.

The Committee of Fifty, formed in 1893 to study the "liquor problem," led the battle. The committee investigated the nation's poverty, crime, mental disease and family decay, and traced them all to alcohol use. They believed that national prohibition was the only answer since temperance —a supposed result of education and self-control— had not worked.

Congressmen and even president William McKinley had started to listen to the prohibitionists and a nationwide law prohibiting alcohol sales went into effect. All this exasperated a man named Adolphus Busch, who personally took his argument to the president. Unfortunately the president was a Methodist who as early as 1867 had been identified with "total abstinence."

If any single person energized the prohibition movement it was Adolphus Busch. He had the most visible profile, and his kingly demeanor and pro-German sentiments offended many Americans. Closely identified with his company, Anheuser-Busch Brewery, he became a prime target of the prohibitionists. Leading the industry as he did, he also had the most to lose; a long string of his descendants depended on beer for their livelihood. Adolphus had no intention of permitting the empire he had built for his children to be legislated out of existence. And it wasn't.

The stage was set when, nine days after his inauguration,

president Roosevelt recommended that Congress officially sanction the return of beer. "I deem action at this time," he said, "to be of the highest importance." Congress, —they were thirsty too— quickly approved a law authorizing the sale of beer with a 3.2 percent alcohol content. Moments after Roosevelt signed the beer bill, Busch sent a telegram praising him for his "wisdom and foresight" and for restoring to the "American people an old and time-honored industry." Prohibition had survived for a little over thirteen years.

Prohibition ended on April 7, 1933, with a raucous, national street party. It was a coast-to-coast party unlike anything this country has ever seen. Not even the celebration that followed the armistice ending the Great War (now known as World War I) or Lindbergh's solo flight across the Atlantic compared. Beer was back and Anheuser-Busch screamed the fact in full-page advertisements.

True to form, the company tried to hit upon a good advertising gimmick to celebrate beer's return. They picked a masterpiece. One that would become one of the most famous corporate symbols in the world—a team of high-stepping, solemnly majestic, champing at the bit, Clydesdale horses pulling a beautifully detailed red and yellow beer wagon, assembled "for advertising purposes."

The first truck out of the Busch plant had headed for the airport, carrying cases of the new Budweiser for president Roosevelt and the governor of New York. When the beer arrived in New York City and in Washington, D.C., it was loaded onto wagons drawn by teams of Clydesdales. In New York the horses caused a sensation as they clamored down Fifth Avenue and stopped at the Empire State building. In Washington, the team pulled up to a White House already deluged with similar shipments from other brewers.

Within nine months, the required thirty-six states had ratified the twenty-first amendment, thereby repealing the eighteenth. But prohibition had taken a heavy toll on the nation's breweries. Of the 1,392 in operation in 1914, only 164 remained. For Anheuser-Busch the cost had been a staggering $34 million. But they had survived.

Today however, efforts are being made to restrict, or even ban, the advertising of alcoholic beverages. These efforts are the result of a growing national concern over the serious problems of drunk driving and alcoholism. In this chapter we examine current restrictions on the advertising of both alcoholic beverages and tobacco products (another hot issue). We'll examine both state and federal levels, as well as voluntary controls, warning labels, the Surgeon General's efforts, and products liability issues.

THE ADVERTISING OF ALCOHOL

In November 1983, the Center for Science in the Public Interest (CSPI), along with twenty-eight other organizations and three individuals, filed a petition with the Federal Trade Commission seeking commission regulation of alcoholic beverage advertising. The petition sought a number of remedies, including a ban on all alcoholic beverage advertising aimed at large numbers of youth or problem drinkers, and rotational warnings in otherwise permissible print ads.

In April 1985, the CSPI petition was denied by the FTC, which concluded that any action was unnecessary because there was no proved causal connection between alcohol advertising and alcohol abuse. Since 1985, there has been little FTC attention devoted to regulating alcoholic beverage advertising.

Significant Environmental Changes

There are three significant areas that have focused on alcohol abuse and its relation to advertising. State and federal governments may well look toward restrictions on the promotional practices used by alcoholic beverage marketers.

Alcohol Environment

There is America's new sobriety to consider, a reflection of the aging babyboomers' preoccupation with looking better and living longer. Babyboomers have stopped smoking. They exercise. They have begun to moderate or stop their use of alcohol.

We can see this trend in the annual increase in sales of seltzer and water products such as Perrier and Evian by 15 percent. There's an annual gain in sales of soft drinks, especially diet products and fruit juice by 5 percent.

These gains are being made at the expense of alcoholic beverage sales. Alcohol consumption has been declining steadily since 1982. In 1978, 71 percent of the American public was classified as drinkers. Today, that has dropped to 65 percent.

Marketing Environment

These societal changes in alcoholic beverage consumption have caused the development of new marketing strategies to cultivate the major market left to alcohol manufacturers— the twenty-one to twenty-five year old market.

The creation of wine coolers and Peach Schnapps have been specifically targeted to the younger market. We have seen Bruce Willis of *Moonlighting* and *Die Hard* fame advertise Seagram's coolers. We have seen the Coors Light "Silver Bullet" campaign featuring animated characters. We have seen a repositioning of several brands that now cater to the youth market. For instance, Bud Light was introduced with the theme "bring out your best," and featured spokesdog Spuds MacKenzie. Michelob produced a campaign a few years ago that appealed to the youth market by using rock music and by showing rock stars including Eric Clapton, Phil Collins, and Steve Winwood.

The assault on the youth market runs in conflict with the consumer movement that advocates reduced alcohol use, and abuse, by youth.

Consumer Movement

The consumer anti-alcohol movement, has been led by Mothers Against Drunk Driving and Students Against Drunk Driving, which have focused on better education about responsible drinking, training for servers in restaurants and bars, and stiffer penalties for drunk driving offenses.

Also, women's and medical groups are concerned that alcohol advertising may lead pregnant women to drink. Such drinking can lead to fetal alcohol syndrome in unborn children.

AREAS OF LAW CONCERNING ALCOHOL

Products Liability

Products liability lawsuits are coming to court in which alcohol is blamed for causing birth defects. The first such case, which was tried in a Seattle court in May 1980, involved Candace Thorp, a thirty-nine-year-old alcoholic, who sought $4 million in damages to support her four-year-old son. The child will require lifetime assistance for mental retardation and physical deformity, which were attributed to fetal alcohol syndrome. Thorp drank up to a half a fifth of Jim Beam bourbon a day while pregnant. She claimed in court that she would have quit if she had been warned about the risks that drinking posed for her baby.

Witnesses for Jim Beam Brands testified that Mrs. Thorp was repeatedly warned by relatives and friends about the dangers of drinking alcohol while pregnant, and that she and other alcoholics would not have heeded a label warning.

The jury reasoned that "there is overwhelming evidence that Candace Thorp would not have followed a label," even if there had been one on the bottle.

This case, of course, did not end the product's liability issue as it related to alcohol advertising.

Alcohol Warning Labels

Both public pressure and the fear of product's liability lawsuits caused the alcoholic beverage industry in 1988 to allow an alcohol warning label bill to pass Congress. Such warning labels have been required to appear in "a conspicuous and prominent place" on every container of beer, wine, and liquor sold in the United States since November, 1989. Congress prescribes the exact wording of the warning which must read:

GOVERNMENT WARNING: (1) According to the Surgeon General, women should not drink alcoholic beverages during pregnancy because of the risk of birth defects, (2) Consumption of alcoholic beverages impairs your ability to drive a car or operate machinery, and may cause health problems.

The warnings may be placed on the back of the bottle, may be printed vertically, or may appear in any manner that the industry chooses.

Surgeon General's Workshop

When the 100th Congress asked U.S. Surgeon General C. Everett Koop to declare drunk driving a national crisis, he responded by organizing a workshop on drunk driving in December, 1988. There were seven major advertising recommendations that emerged from the workshop's advertising and marketing panel. These recommendations can be divided into three categories: unreasonable, questionable, and reasonable.

The two unreasonable recommendations that generated the most debate dealt with removing the tax deductibility of alcohol advertising and with counteradvertising, including:

- Elimination of tax deductions for alcohol advertising and promotion other than price and product advertising; and
- A goal of equivalent exposure with the level of alcohol advertising for effective pro-health and safety messages.

The panel's other four major recommendations were directed at reducing the impact of alcohol beverage appeal to youth. Neither proposal would require government regulation, but would rely, instead, on voluntary cooperation through revision of broadcast and industry codes. These four recommendations are:

- Elimination of alcohol advertising and promotion on college campuses where a high proportion of the audience reached is under the legal drinking age;
- Elimination of alcohol advertising, promotion, and sponsorship of public events, such as musical concerts and athletic contests where the majority of the anticipated audience is under the legal drinking age;
- Elimination in alcohol advertising and promotion of the use of celebrities who have a strong appeal to youth; and
- Elimination of official sponsorship of athletic events, e.g., the Olympics, by the alcohol beverage industry.

Clearly, there are obstacles to implementing these recommendations. Yet, they should be strongly considered for action and could be enacted into voluntary industry and media guidelines.

Voluntary Efforts

In addition to organized action by government agencies and consumer groups, a number of individuals and organizations have taken steps to restrict alcoholic beverage advertising.

The Miller Brewing Company was forced to pull a March, 1989 ad entitled "Beachin' Times" that was a parody of spring break activities by college students. There were protests by students at several schools, including the University of Wisconsin and the University of Iowa. The University of Michigan's *Michigan Daily* and other college publications refused to run the ad. The University of Wisconsin at Madison passed a resolution calling for a boycott of Miller products unless the ad was withdrawn and the company apologized. Student groups criticized the ad as depicting women in an insulting way (they were shown as scantily-dressed "babes") and for including an account of a student vacationer's day: a twenty-four hour drinking marathon that included only two five-minute breaks for returning empties.

Even athletes have begun to speak out against the association between sports and alcohol beverage consumption. Houston Astros' first baseman Glenn Davis objected to the toast offered by local radio and television broadcasters for one of their sponsors after he, or one of his teammates, hits a home run: "Glenn Davis, this Bud's for you." Davis, who does not drink and is active in efforts to discourage youngsters from drinking, has objected to his implied endorsement of alcoholic beverages. As a result of his protest, Davis' name will no longer be used in the commercials.

Alcoholic beverage advertising is likely to be a point of controversy for many years. Not only will government officials and consumer advocates continue to press for restrictions, but private individuals and associations will seek changes as well.

FEDERAL REGULATION

As for the federal government, the Federal Communications Commission does not forbid the advertising of alcoholic beverages in broadcast media. On the other hand, the Federal Trade Commission and the Bureau of Alcohol, Tobacco and Firearms have joint authority over the advertising of alcoholic beverages.

FTC's Role In Alcohol Advertising

In April 1985, the FTC denied a petition seeking an industry-wide restriction on the advertising of alcoholic beverages. The FTC heard from the Center for Science in the Public Interest (CSPI), twenty-eight other organizations and three individuals, and reasoned that there was "no reliable basis on which to conclude that alcohol advertising significantly affects alcohol abuse. They concluded that rules banning or otherwise limiting alcohol advertising would offer no significant protection to the public."

In reaching its decision, the commission reviewed a large amount of marketing and research data on the consumption and abuse of alcoholic beverages. Their conclusion: "the (existing) literature sheds virtually no light on the relationship between alcohol advertising and abuse." The commission went on to say, "little, if any, evidence exists indicating that alcohol advertising or marketing practices deceptively or unfairly result in alcohol abuse or even increased consumption."

On the other hand, the FTC is keenly aware of the growing demand for alcoholic beverage restrictions, especially ones on advertising. Because of this, the FTC was quick to point out that it would keep looking into "how it can best apply its advertising and marketing expertise to the important issues raised by the petition."

In fact, one commissioner, Patricia P. Bailey, in her dissent in this case said that her disagreement was based on several "troubling promotional practices." Those included:

- A print advertisement depicting a beer bottle as part of a motorcycle and stating "when you do it, do it with Style. Old Style;"
- A print advertisement showing two young people waiting with a car at an intersection marked by a 'Beer XXing' sign and with several bottles and glasses of beer going by;
- A print advertisement depicting four glasses next to a bottle of the product and stating, after a hard day's work pour yourself some;
- A print ad depicting five brandy glasses and stating, the only thing better than [the advertised liquor] is another [of the advertised liquor];
- Various beer company promotions on college campuses involving chug-a-lug contests; and

• Various advertisements for alcoholic beverages placed in college publications in states where the drinking age is 21.

ATF's Role, Self-Regulation Issues

The other important federal agency having jurisdiction over the advertising of alcoholic beverages is the Bureau of Alcohol, Tobacco and Firearms. The ATF groups alcoholic beverages into three major beverage groupings: malt beverages, wine, and distilled spirits and, treats each group differently.

1. Malt beverages—

Under the Federal Alcohol Administration Act, a malt beverage is:

> A beverage made by the alcoholic fermentation of an infusion or decoction, or combination of both, in potable brewing water, of malted barley with hops, or their parts, or their products, and with or without the addition of [certain additional ingredients].[1]

Malt beverages are low in alcohol content as a percentage of volume and occasionally escape regulations aimed at alcoholic beverages in general.

2. Wine—

Includes grape wine, sparkling grape wine, citrus wine, aperitif wine, raisin wine, and sake.

3. Distilled spirits—

Includes vodka, whisky, gin, brandy, rum, tequila, cordials and liqueurs, flavored spirits as well as imitations of any of these.

According to the ATF, the following rules must be followed:

• All ads must include the name and city of the manufacturer and the designation of the type of product

involved;
- The ad may not make any false or misleading statements in any material respect or one that disparages a competitor's product;
- An ad may not make any statement that the manufacturer's beverage has intoxicating properties;
- Ads may not make any representation that the product has medicinal or therapeutic effects;
- Alcoholic beverage ads may not use any statement, design or representation regarding analysis, standards, or tests that may be considered misleading;
- An ad may not make a statement that's inconsistent with the product's label;
- An ad may not make any guaranty that is misleading; and
- An ad cannot use official flags, government insignia, or statements that can be construed as relating to the armed services.

In addition, there are other specific requirements regarding each type of alcoholic beverage.

Malt Beverages

The ATF does not allow advertising the alcoholic content of malt beverages and does not allow any product containing less than one-half of one percent alcohol by volume to be called "beer," "lager beer," "lager," "ale," "porter," or "stout."

The voluntary code that regulates beer advertising is controlled by the United States Brewers Association, Inc., 1750 K Street, N.W., Washington, D.C. 20006. The U.S.B.A. guidelines supplement the ATF regulations in several important areas. The full text of the U.S.B.A. guidelines follows:

BREWING INDUSTRY ADVERTISING GUIDELINES
DECEMBER 1984

INTRODUCTION

These Brewing Industry Advertising Guidelines have been developed as a service to those responsible for the advertising of beer. They are intended to provide guidance which will assist brewers in maintaining the highest ethical standards in their advertising. The brewing industry first developed voluntary Guidelines on advertising in the 1940's. Over the years, the industry has periodically revised and updated these Guidelines.

BASIC GUIDELINES FOR BEER ADVERTISING

Beer is a refreshing, wholesome beverage meant to be consumed in moderation. Its origins are ancient, and it has held a respected position in nearly every culture and society since the dawn of recorded history. Advertising is a legitimate effort by brewers to make consumers aware of the particular types, brands and prices of malt beverages that are available.

Three basic principles which have long been reflected in the policies of the brewing industry continue to underlie these Guidelines. First, beer advertising should not suggest directly or indirectly that any of the laws applicable to the sale and consumption of beer should not be scrupulously complied with. Second, brewers should adhere to standards of candor and good taste applicable to all commercial advertising. Third, brewers are responsible corporate citizens, sensitive to the problems of the society in which they exist, and their advertising should reflect that fact.

These Guidelines consist of more specific provisions describing the advertising policies of the brewing industry.

1. Beer advertisements should neither suggest nor encourage overindulgence. Because beer is a beverage of moderation, advertising should not portray or suggest its abuse,

even in a comical vein.

2. Beer advertising should neither portray nor encourage drinking by individuals below the legal age of purchase.

3. No beer advertisements should in any way suggest noncompliance with legal age of purchase limitations.

4. No beer advertisements should encourage or condone drunk driving.

5. Advertisements should not include scenes of inebriation, revelry, comical drunks, or any other depiction of beer drinkers who have in any way lost control of themselves. Beer advertisements should never directly or indirectly suggest misuse or abuse of the product.

6. Beer advertisements should make no scientifically unsubstantiated health claims. If there exists significant controversy in the medical or scientific community regarding the accuracy of a claim, the making of that claim without simultaneously revealing the existence of the controversy should be avoided.

7. Beer advertisements should not associate or portray beer drinking before or during activities in situations which require a high degree of alertness. Beer is for relaxation and is not compatible with driving or performing hazardous jobs.

8. Advertising should neither state nor carry any implication of alcohol strength. Advertisements should not refer to the "strength" of a beer or boast subtly of "kick," or otherwise promote its relative alcohol content Nor should advertisements include other subtle references to alcohol, such as puns on words like "spirit" or "proof," or any overt or implicit association with distilled spirits. Any claim of alcohol content permitted by applicable law or regulation shall be deemed to be in compliance with this Guideline.

9. Beer advertising should not portray sexual passion, promiscuity, or any other amorous activity as a consequence of drinking beer. Beer is not related to sexual stimulation, and should

not be portrayed in any fashion implying or suggesting that it is.

10. Advertisements should not contain suggestive double entendres or any other material that might be considered lewd or obscene.

11. Advertisements should not associate beer with crime, criminals, or any illegal activity. Advertisements should not associate beer with any illegal activity or disreputable circumstances. Men and women portrayed in beer advertisements should be law abiding and mannerly.

12. Taverns or other places portrayed in beer advertisements should always be depicted as well-kept and respectable gathering places.

13. Religion and religious themes should never be employed in the advertising of beer.

14. Advertisers of malt beverages should not improperly disparage competing beers.

Comparisons in advertising should be objective, truthful, and significant.

Advertising should address the merits of the products being offered. It should not characterize competing products falsely or inaccurately or in a misleading fashion.

Comparisons in advertising should be objective and truthful. Consistent with Federal regulatory policies, comparisons must be adequately substantiated. Moreover, such advertising should provide useful and significant information to the consumer.

15. Advertising should never suggest that competing beers contain objectionable additives or ingredients.

These include representations or implications that other beers contain "synthetic additives" or other "artificial ingredients." Because these words often have pejorative meanings, their use is inappropriate. No beer may contain ingredients not permitted or approved by the Food and Drug Administration and authorized by the Bureau of Alcohol, Tobacco, and Firearms.

16. Beer advertisements should not make exaggerated

product representations. Beer advertisements should restrict themselves to an honest and accurate statement of facts. This is desirable in all advertising. Unfulfilled and false claims about a product do not benefit consumers.

17. Advertising should not use scientific or pseudo-scientific terms to convey to convey the impression that a beer has special or unique qualities if in fact it does not.

18. No beer advertisements in college, campus, or other media should portray beer drinking as being important to education, nor should beer advertising directly or indirectly degrade study.

19. Beer advertising on television should make no representation of on-camera drinking, including sound effects of drinking.

20. Beer advertising should never show littering.
(Reprinted by permission of the United States Brewer's Association, Inc.)

Wines

The ATF will not allow ad claims that tend to create the impression that a wine contains distilled spirits, is comparable with a distilled spirit or has intoxicating qualities. The use of vintage and bottling dates and of the word, "old," is strictly controlled. So is the use of appellation of origin. Domestic products may not be described as imported.

The voluntary code governing wine producers is from the Wine Institute, 165 Post Street, San Francisco, California 94108. Since all the members of the Wine Institute are located in California, the code only governs wines produced in that state. The most distinctive feature of this code provides:

As stated in the Code of Advertising Standards, established by the Wine Institute, "[a] distinguishing and unique feature of wine is that it is traditionally served with meals or immediately before or following a meal." As a result, when wine advertising is produced it should visually depict a scene where wine is to be served.

The Code states that an ad should not suggest that wine is crucial for successful entertaining. Ads should not use models who appear to be under twenty-five years of age. Advertising should not use cartoon characters directed at those below the legal drinking age. Wine should not be presented in ads in association with "rites of passage" to adulthood. Finally, wine ads should not exploit the human form or show provocative or enticing poses.

The Wine Institute's Code of Advertising Standards applies to all advertising media, and follows:

CODE OF ADVERTISING STANDARDS
WINE INSTITUTE

April 1978

PREAMBLE

Informal principles of good advertising practice for the wine growing industry were first adopted in 1949. In recent years, it has become evident that more specific and significantly stronger standards are desired by wine advertisers to reflect the industry's concern with maximum social responsibility. This code is designed to encourage continued high standards so that wine advertising may increasingly be viewed as a positive contribution to society.

GUIDELINES

These guidelines shall apply only to the voluntary subscribers to this Code of Advertising Standards.

1. A distinguishing and unique feature of wine is that it is traditionally served with meals or immediately before or following a meal. Therefore, when subscribers to this code use wine advertising which visually depicts a scene or setting where wine is to be served, such advertising shall include foods and show that they are available and are being used or are intended to be used.

This guideline shall not apply to the depiction of a bottle of wine, vineyard, winery, label, professional tasting, etc., where emphasis is on the product.

2. Wine advertising should encourage the proper use of wine. Therefore, subscribers to this code shall not depict or describe in their advertising:

a. The consumption of wine for the effects its alcohol content may produce.

b. Direct or indirect reference to alcoholic content or extra strength, except as otherwise required by law or regulation.

c. Excessive drinking or persons who appear to have lost control or to be inappropriately uninhibited.

d. Any suggestion that excessive drinking or loss of control is amusing or a proper subject for amusement.

e. Any persons engaged in activities not normally associated with the moderate use of wine and a responsible life-style. Association of wine use in conjunction with feats of daring or activities requiring unusual skill is specifically prohibited.

f. Wine in quantities inappropriate to the situation or inappropriate for moderate and responsible use.

3. Advertising of wine has traditionally depicted wholesome persons enjoying their lives and illustrating the role of wine in a mature life-style. Any attempt to suggest that wine directly contributes to success or achievement is unacceptable. Therefore, the following restrictions shall apply to subscribers to this code:

a. Wine shall not be presented as being essential to personal performance, social attainment, achievement, success or wealth.

b. The use of wine shall not be directly associated with social, physical or personal problem solving.

c. Wine shall not be presented as vital to social acceptability and popularity or as the key factor in such popularity.

d. It shall not be suggested that wine is crucial for

successful entertaining.

4. Any advertisement which has particular appeal to persons below the legal drinking age is unacceptable. Therefore, wine advertising by code subscribers shall not:

a. Show models and personalities in advertisements who appear to be under 25 years of age.

b. Use music, language, gestures or cartoon characters specifically associated with or directed toward those below the legal drinking age.

c. Appear in children's or juveniles' magazines, newspapers, television programs, radio programs or other media specifically oriented to persons below the legal drinking age.

d. Be presented as being related to the attainment of adulthood or associated with "rites of passage" to adulthood.

e. Suggest that a wine product resembles or is similar to another type of beverage or product (milk, soda, candy) having particular appeal to persons below the legal drinking age.

f. Use traditional heroes of the young such as those engaged in pastimes and occupations having a particular appeal to persons below the legal drinking age. (For example, cowboys, race car drivers, rock stars, etc.).

g. Use amateur or professional sports celebrities, past or present.

5. Code subscribers shall not show motor vehicles in such a way as to suggest that they are to be operated in conjunction with wine use. Advertising should in no way suggest that wine be used in connection with driving.

6. Wine advertising by code subscribers shall not appear in or directly adjacent to television or radio programs or print media which dramatize or glamorize over-consumption or inappropriate use of alcoholic beverages.

7. Wine advertising by code subscribers shall make no reference to wine's medicinal values.

8. Wine advertising by code subscribers shall not degrade

the image or status of any ethnic, minority or other group.

9. Wine advertising by code subscribers shall not exploit the human form, feature provocative or enticing poses nor be demeaning to any individual.

All advertising—including, but not limited to direct mail, point-of-sale, outdoor, displays, radio, television and print media—should adhere to both the letter and the spirit of the above code.

The Wine Institute is the Trade Association of California Winegrowers, 165 Post Street, San Francisco, California 94018.

(Reproduced by permission of the Wine Institute, The Trade Association of California Winegrowers).

Distilled Spirits

Under the ATF rules alcoholic content by proof must be stated for all distilled spirits. It may be stated in terms of percentage by volume for cordials and liqueurs, cocktails, highballs, bitters and other specialties as approved by the ATF. The words "bond," "bonded," "bottled in bond," "aged in bond," or synonymous terms cannot be used unless they appear on the label pursuant to ATF regulations. "Pure" can only be used if part of the name of the permit holder or retailer for whom the distilled spirits is bonded. The words "double distilled" and "triple distilled" are strictly forbidden.

The Distilled Spirits Council of the United States (DISCUS), 1250 I St., N.W., Washington, D.C. 20005, is the voluntary authority that governs the advertising of distilled spirits.

The Code of Good Practice of the Distilled Spirits Council of the United States, forbids the advertising of distilled spirits by radio or television, which includes closed circuit TV. Ads may not appear on the comic pages, on theater screens, or in publications devoted primarily to religious topics. Ads may not be "in any manner directed or primarily intended to appeal to persons below the legal drinking age." Members may not seek endorsements on television. They cannot use advertising including Santa Claus or any biblical character. No ad should depict a child or suggest the presence of a child. Code subscribers may accept the public acknowledgment of charitable contributions. DISCUS members may accept the acknowledgment of public broadcasting support, but only when the "audience in the principle broadcast area is likely to be composed primarily of persons above the legal drinking age."

The full text of the Code of Good Practice of the Distilled Spirits Council of the United States, Inc., follows.

CODE OF GOOD PRACTICE OF THE DISTILLED SPIRITS COUNCIL OF THE UNITED STATES, INC.
Approved November 15, 1983

PREAMBLE

The members of the Distilled Spirits Council of the United States, Inc. (DISCUS), the trade association representing the distilled spirits industry, adopt this Code of Good Practice to restrict advertising of distilled spirits to responsible adult consumers, to avoid advertising and promotion of sale of distilled spirits to minors, and to provide guidelines to ensure that such advertising is presented in a tasteful and dignified manner.

Since repeal of the Eighteenth Amendment to the United States Constitution, which prohibited sale of beverage alcohol, the distilled spirits industry has openly acknowledged the problems inherent in abusive consumption of beverage alcohol and has joined with government and civic groups in efforts to encourage moderate and responsible use. The industry has both initiated and actively supported undertakings of many different kinds, i.e., informational, educational, research, and rehabilitative, in an effort to better understand, prevent, and combat misuse of its products. Included among such efforts is the adoption and voluntary adherence to this Code of Good Practice by the members of

DISCUS.

The members of DISCUS voluntarily adopt the provisions of this Code as guidelines to achieve the foregoing objectives. Since it is recognized that opinions may differ as to the interpretation of such guidelines, such questions will be addressed by the CODE REVIEW BOARD.

Therefore, the members of DISCUS voluntarily pledge to establish and maintain exemplary standards and practices by adhering to the following:

I. ADVERTISING

A. Distilled Spirits should not be advertised:

1. By means of radio or television, including both public and private closed circuit TV;

2. On the comic pages of newspapers, magazines, or other publications;

3. In publications devoted primarily to religious topics;

4. In any manner directed or primarily intended to appeal to persons below the legal drinking age;

5. On the screen of motion picture theaters or similar assemblies.

B. No advertisement of distilled spirits should contain advertising copy or an illustration unless it is dignified, modest, and in good taste. In addition, no advertisement should claim sexual or physical prowess as a result of the consumption of distilled spirits.

C. Members should not, directly or indirectly, provide any compensation for advertising "plugs" on radio or television.

D. No advertisement of distilled spirits should contain the name of or depict Santa Claus or any Biblical character.

E. No advertisement of distilled spirits should depict a child or immature person, portray objects (such as toys) suggestive of the presence of a child, or in any manner be designed to be especially appealing to children or immature persons.

F. All advertisements of distilled spirits should be modest, dignified, and in good taste.

II. GOOD FAITH COMPLIANCE

The provisions of this Code should not be violated or evaded through subterfuge or indirection, such as through institutional advertising and/or program sponsorship.

Financial support of or contributions to charitable organizations or events and to public broadcasting and public telecommunications entities as defined in Title 47 of the United States Code are approved where the contribution is publicly acknowledged by the recipient by reference only to the name of the grantor making the contribution. The name of the grantor may include a brand name but should not include a class or type or other product description (e.g. The XYZ Whiskey Distilling Company or XYZ Whiskey). In the case of contributions to public broadcasting and public telecommunications entities the contributor should specify that the acknowledgment is to be made when the audience in the principal broadcast area is likely to be composed primarily of persons above the legal drinking age.

III. MEMBERS SUBSCRIBE

The members of DISCUS voluntarily subscribe to this Code.

IV. JURISDICTION

This Code is applicable to the states of the United States only.

V. CODE REVIEW BOARD

There shall be established and maintained a CODE REVIEW BOARD, which shall meet when necessary to consider complaints lodged by DISCUS members or other interested parties.

The CODE REVIEW BOARD shall be comprised of no less than five (5) members in good standing of the Board of Directors of DISCUS. Each member shall serve for a term of not more than three (3) years and shall, upon the vote of a majority of the members of the Board of Directors, be succeeded by another member of the Board of Directors who has not served as a member of the CODE REVIEW BOARD for a period of at least two (2) years.

Findings of the majority of the members of the CODE REVIEW BOARD shall be communicated promptly to the responsible advertiser and in appropriate circumstances to all members of the Board of Directors of DISCUS.

(Reproduced by permission of the Distilled Spirits Council of the United States, Inc.)

NETWORK GUIDELINES

Wine and beer ads (but not those for distilled spirits) may appear on the three major television networks. NBC forbids the advertisement of alcoholic beverages as "necessary to maintain social status, obtain personal achievements, relieve stress or as a solution to personal problems."

On-camera consumption of alcohol is strictly forbidden. Ads for liquor outlets are acceptable to NBC if there is no reference to unacceptable wine or distilled spirits. Ads on NBC for airlines and restaurants may make incidental reference to cocktails, but advertising of mixed drinks is not acceptable, nor is the use of terms like "Martini" or "Bloody Mary." Glassware associated with distilled spirits is not an acceptable prop to NBC, except in relation to the "incidental reference" mentioned above. NBC will review advertisements alerting the public to the dangers of alcohol abuse on a "case-by-case" basis.

ABC has a very similar set of guidelines; one minor difference is that ABC prohibits even the incidental display of cocktail props.

CBS has a policy against direct or implied references to

excessive consumption of beer and wine.

RECENT STEPS BY THE BUREAU OF ALCOHOL, TOBACCO AND FIREARMS

In 1984 the ATF published regulations controlling the advertising and labeling of alcoholic beverages. The agency delayed decision, however, on such controversial issues as the use of the terms, "natural" and "light."

A significant part of the regulations deals with comparative advertising of alcoholic beverages requiring that comparative ads shall "not be disparaging of a competitive product." The regulations also require advertisers to follow "any scientifically accepted procedure" in so-called taste tests. Advertisers must also include the name and address of the testing administrator in taste-test ads. Both broadcast and print ads must comply with these rules.

The regulations state unequivocally that "subliminal or similar techniques are prohibited." Subliminal messages are defined as the "use of any device or technique that is used to convey or attempts to convey a message to a person by means of images or sounds of a very brief nature that cannot be perceived at a normal level of awareness."

The ATF is undecided about the issue of athlete endorsement of alcoholic beverages. Ads by currently active athletes have long been precluded.

References to the illustrations of prominent athletes consuming or preparing to consume the advertised malt beverages are considered likely to mislead the public and therefore are subject to provisions (concerning misleading alcohol advertising).[2]

Likewise, the use of illustrations of athletic activities in connection with distilled spirits is forbidden.[3]

STATE CONTROLS

The most extensive control over advertising of alcohol comes from the individual states. They have restricted advertising on billboards, in circulars, and on radio and television. Displays on retail premises, newspaper and magazine advertising, retailer novelties, consumer novelties, premium offers, cents-off offers, samples, contests, and refunds are also considered state issues. It is important for any advertiser to investigate the specific regulations in any state in which he advertises. The detailed regulations of each state are too overwhelming for discussion in this chapter.

The Twenty-first Amendment to the Constitution gives the states some special powers. In *Capital Cities Cable, Inc.* v. *Crisp,*[4] the U.S. Supreme Court ruled against Oklahoma's advertising ban requiring cable television operators to screen out alcoholic beverage advertising that was part of the out-of-state signals they retransmitted by cable to their subscribers. The main reasoning behind the Court's ruling was that since cable television operates under FCC regulations, Oklahoma must follow federal law. In addition, Oklahoma's ban ran against established FCC regulations and their goal of making the benefits of cable television available nationally.

Two other important cases have upheld state control of liquor ads. In *Queensgate Inv. Co.* v. *Liquor Control Comm'n,*[5] the United States Supreme Court dismissed an appeal from an Ohio state court's ruling upholding an Ohio regulation prohibiting retail liquor permittees from advertising the price of alcoholic beverages off their premises. The Fifth Federal Circuit then followed that precedent and upheld Mississippi statutes and regulations banning liquor ads on billboards, in print, and over the air within the state in *Dunagin* v. *City of Oxford, Mississippi.*[6]

CIGARETTE ADVERTISING

Each year, heroin and cocaine together cause the death of

approximately 5,000 Americans. Yet, this tragedy is dwarfed by the Surgeon General's conclusion that cigarette smoking is responsible for over 390,000 unnecessary deaths each year in this country alone. According to these numbers, almost 1 out of 6 deaths in the United States can be traced back to cigarette smoking. Although smoking among adults dropped from 40 percent in 1965 to 29 percent in 1987, approximately 55 million Americans still smoke.

Surgeon General's Findings: Consequences Of Cigarette Smoking

1. Responsible for 85-90 percent of the 120,000 annual lung cancer deaths and is a major cause of cancer of the larynx, oral cavity, and esophagus and a contributing factor in cancer of the urinary tract, bladder, kidney, and pancreas.

2. The major cause of chronic bronchitis and emphysema and responsible for over 80 percent of deaths from chronic obstructive pulmonary diseases.

3. A prime contributor to 21 percent of coronary heart disease deaths and 18 percent of stroke deaths.

4. Leads to a significantly elevated risk of miscarriage, stillbirth, premature births, and birth-weight deficiencies.

5. Resulted, in 1985, in the United States health care system spending an estimated $22 billion to treat smoking-related diseases (of which the government paid about $4.2 billion), while lost productivity costs due to smoking-related illnesses and premature deaths were estimated to be upwards of $43 billion.

6. Leads to the ingestion of hazardous tobacco additives, gases, and other chemical constituents whose identity continues to go undisclosed. (Report of the Surgeon General 1989).

The Controversy Over Cigarette Marketing And Advertising

The controversy over cigarette advertising continues to

grow. Critics condemn all types of advertising and promotion used to market cigarettes. On the other hand, many industry voices claim advertising is highly overrated as a factor in causing people to smoke. They cite peer pressure and parental role-modeling as more relevant causes.

Here we'll take a look at some of the concerns about cigarette marketing and advertising in more depth. First, there is the concern over the scope of cigarette advertising. In 1988 the tobacco industry spent close to $2.5 billion (that's about $6.5 million a day) for advertising and promotion.

The vast majority of new smokers are teenagers or younger. By one estimate, 60 percent are under the age of fourteen. This statistic is a cause for particular concern over the effects of cigarette advertising on children and teenagers.

In addition, there has been a dramatic shift in the allocation of overall marketing budgets. The result of this is that promotional expenditures today account for over 60 percent of marketing expenditures, compared to only 25 percent in 1975. Increasingly, cigarette companies are promoting their brands through sponsorship of sporting events and concerts, which reach a youthful segment of the market.

The industry also uses logos on non-tobacco products having special appeal to teenagers and pays to have cigarettes displayed in youth-oriented movies, including a recent James Bond film (for which Philip Morris paid $350,000), *Superman II*, and *Supergirl* (Luken 1989), to mention a few.

The tobacco industry, on the other hand, has argued that advertising informs consumers about brand differences and leads to brand switching rather than to smoking initiation. Critics emphasize advertising's role in the glamorization of smoking, attracting new smokers, and impeding the efforts of smokers to quit. There simply is no way to determine which view is provable.

Since most merely switch among brands of Philip Morris and R.J. Reynolds, who control approximately two-thirds of the

U.S. cigarette market, this seems to validate the critics' charges that the goals of advertising and promotion are somewhat broader than would be guessed.

Policy Alternatives

Some of the more noteworthy public policy developments of the past thirty years affecting the sale and use of cigarettes are listed in the table below.

Actions Affecting Cigarette Sales and Use

YEAR *ACTION*

1965   Congress approved legislation requiring warning labels for cigarette packages.

1970   Congress approved legislation prohibiting cigarette advertising on radio and television and strengthened the cigarette package warning label.

1973   Congress approved legislation to include little cigars in the radio and television broadcast advertising ban.

1973-88 Beginning with Arizona and supported by the 1975 Minnesota Clean Indoor Air Act, by 1987, 84 percent of the states and many governmental agencies and communities had enacted regulations to safeguard workers and occupants of public places from exposure to cigarette smoke.

1982   Congress approved legislation to double the federal excise tax on cigarettes and cigars.

1984   Congress approved legislation requiring that stronger warning statements appear on labels and in advertisements for cigarettes on a rotating basis.

1986   Congress approved legislation banning smokeless tobacco advertising from radio and television and requiting warning labels on smokeless tobacco product packages and in smokeless tobacco print ads.

1987 Congress approved legislation banning smoking on airplane flights of two hours or less.

1988 A jury hearing the Cipollone case found that smoking was the cause of death of a woman who had begun smoking in 1941 and died in 1984 from lung cancer. It awarded her husband $400,000 in damages. Further, the jury found that advertising had made express warranties about health aspects of cigarettes.

Restrictions On Cigarette Sales

The suggestion of an outright ban on the sale of cigarettes often invokes the response that Prohibition didn't work and further, that making the sale of cigarettes illegal and thereby branding many millions of people criminals is not in the public interest. Sentiment over freedom of choice runs very deep, especially on matters that appear to involve personal consequences rather than broad societal concerns. However, several types of lesser restrictions are receiving consideration, though the regulatory setting is a stumbling block to action.

As an example, under the Federal Food, Drug, and Cosmetic Act,[7] a drug is misbranded and can be removed from sale if it is falsely labeled. One might argue that failing to reveal the fact that the product contains nicotine (an addictive drug), the fact that forty-three known carcinogenic agents are contained in tobacco smoke, and the types of additives employed to make low tar cigarettes each constitute mislabeling.[8] The Food and Drug Administration has, however, taken the position that it does not have authority over tobacco products.

Further, Congress has apparently exempted tobacco from regulation under the Consumer Products Safety Act,[9] the Toxic Substances Control Act,[10] the Fair Packaging and Labeling Act,[11] the Controlled Substances Act,[12] and the Federal Hazardous Substances Labeling Act.[13] Thus, new legislation seems necessary for any restrictions on the sale of mislabeled cigarettes.

Restrictions On Cigarette Advertising And Promotion

Though legislation to ban all advertising and promotion of tobacco products has been attempted, it has run into strong opposition on three issues:
- The claim that an advertising ban is unconstitutional;
- The claim that such a ban would be ineffective; and
- The claim that a ban would lead to similar restrictions on other consumer products (the "slippery-slope" theory).

The constitutional issue posed by cigarette advertising involves the regulation of commercial speech, the substantiality of the public interest, and whether the remedy is not more extensive than is necessary.

Experts differ in their assessment of the precise effects of an ad ban, and point out that the effect would depend on how extensive the ban was and how long it was in effect. For example, since many of the important brand and product symbolic associations are now well established, different types of promotional activities (e.g., event sponsorship, signs, the use of brand logos on nontobacco products), if unregulated, may be quite effective by themselves, at least in the short run.

The Canadian Initiative

The Tobacco Products Control Act became enforceable in Canada in January, 1989.[14] All Canadian magazine and newspaper advertising of tobacco products ceased, and the voluntary ban on broadcast ads became mandatory. The dollar value of billboard and poster advertising were reduced by one-third each year until termination in January, 1991. All on-premise retail signs was prohibited after January, 1993. In addition, the use of tobacco brand names on nontobacco items (racing cars, T-shirts, etc.) was banned, although brand name sponsorships in place on January, 1988, may continue, but only at 1987 levels of support. Free distribution of tobacco products, as well as the use of rebates, contests, and prizes were also prohibited. The law contains other provisions that will not be discussed here (e.g., companies must provide information on toxic constituents and have an obligation to warn consumers fully). One interesting provision gives the government the ability to exempt a tobacco product when it is likely to be used as a substitute for other tobacco products and poses less risk to the health of users than the products it substitutes.

A series of legal challenges to this act have been initiated. The courts must now consider other important issues raised by the government's decision to restrict freedom of expression in order to protect the health of its citizens, as well as to consider factual evidence regarding the role of advertising and promotion as an inducement to purchase.

Restrictions On Image Advertising

Many in the U.S. consider the Canadian-style ban to be politically unrealistic. As a result, they have focused on those aspects of advertising that may play the most significant role in smoking initiation. Among generally similar bills, the Children's Television Act of 1990[15] prohibits the use in tobacco advertising of human figures and facsimiles, brand logos and symbols, and pictures other than that of a single package (no larger than actual size) against a neutral white background. Further, the product package must comply with similar restrictions.

No tobacco ads would be permitted in stadiums or sports facilities or on sports-related equipment, such as racing cars and boats. It would be unlawful to distribute tobacco products as free samples or at reduced cost, or to sponsor any athletic, musical, or similar events in the name of a registered brand name or so that a tobacco product is associated with the event (unless the brand name was also the corporate name prior to January, 1986). Non-tobacco products (clothing, toys, etc.) or services could not use a tobacco product brand name or symbol (except as above), nor could a tobacco company pay to have the product or its name and symbol appear in any movie, television show, or other form of entertainment (except as above). Tobacco products advertised or promoted in violation of the above provisions would be a misbranded drug under the Federal Food, Drug, and Cosmetic Act.

Proposed advertising restrictions have come under attack such as "tombstone advertising." Opponents also invoke both First Amendment and "slippery slope" arguments. Proponents argue that such bills would allow tobacco companies to communicate product information, hence the bills do not restrict commercial speech more than necessary to prohibit the images, depictions, and symbolic associations most likely to entice children to begin smoking.

Strengthening Consumer Knowledge And Defenses

There is concern over the visibility and impact of the existing warnings—moving them to the front of cigarette packages and using eyecatching symbols would certainly increase the attention they receive. By itself, however, strengthening the warnings is unlikely to have a huge effect on cigarette smoking. Warnings are helpful and signal some level of government concern however, the dire consequences they present are long-term in nature. Thus a smoker may overweight the absence of short-term symptoms, particularly since the certainty of consequences does not extend to the individual. The contradiction between the healthy and vigorous people appearing in the ads, and the product warnings may lead people to believe that the warnings are overstated or that that smoking in moderation may be okay.

Products Liability Lawsuits

A final economic disincentive is the threat of product liability suits. We looked at this subject in detail in Chapter 4. A recent jury verdict went against tobacco interests in *Cipollone* v. *Liggett Group, Inc.*,[16] producing three major results:

- The monetary award of $400,000;
- The release of extensive and previously confidential strategy and research documents from company and Tobacco Institute files, paving the way for future cases; and
- The willingness of a jury to determine that cigarette advertising has made express warranties about health aspects of cigarettes and that these contributed to the person's smoking and death.

In several cases, including *Cipollone*, courts did not allow the introduction of evidence of company failure to warn and negligence after 1966 (when the Cigarette Labeling and Advertising Act took effect). Both the likelihood and magnitude of awards in the future will depend on judicial clarification of;

- Underlying liability theories (risk-utility concepts, implied warranties); and
- Admissibility and weight given to the conduct of both the smoker and the cigarette company after 1966.

A number of jurists and legislators have subsequently expressed the conviction that Congress, by mandating a particular warning could not possibly have intended to shield tobacco companies from all responsibility to warn consumers or to give companies license to fail intentionally to disclose important health information by mandating a particular warning.

The ultimate irony is: the cigarette companies can now escape liability for their deceptive ads because the federal courts have misinterpreted a law which was intended to impede the use of this death-dealing product by giving consumers more, not less, information.[17]

However, until Congress acts or the Supreme Court overturns lower court decisions, consumers' injuries resulting primarily from smoking in the period after 1966, may be immune from recovery under products liability theories.

Increased Regulatory Control

We have already discussed the regulatory problems associated with a lack of oversight by any agency specifically charged with protecting the health and safety of the public. There is substantial interest in possible congressional action to declare tobacco products an addictive drug (to be regulated by the Food and Drug Administration). Thus, there is at least the potential for the Food and Drug Administration to acquire broad power to examine tobacco additives and constituents, require appropriate disclosures of potential harm, require reductions or deletion of certain additives, and insure that the information provided in advertising is not in conflict with these determinations.

[1] Federal Alcohol Administration Act, 27 CFR 7.20.

[2] Rev. Rul. 54-513.

[3] Rev. Rul. 54-326.

[4] *Capital Cities Cable, Inc.* v. *Crisp*, 467 U.S. 691, 104 S.Ct. 2694, 81 L.Ed. 2d 580
(1984), reversing *Oklahoma Telecasters* v. *Crisp*, 699 F.2d. 490
(10th Cir. 1983).

[5] *Queensgate Inv. Co.* v. *Liquor Control Comm'n*, 459 U.S. 807, 103 S. Ct. 31,
74 L.Ed. 2d 45 dismissing appeal from 69 Ohio St. 2d 361,
433 N.E. 2d. 138 (1982) (per curiam).

[6] *Dunagin* v. *City of Oxford, Mississippi*, 718 F.2d. 738 (5th Cir. 1983).

[7] Federal Food, Drug, and Cosmetic Act, 21 U.S.C. §301.

[8] Report of the Surgeon General 1989, 79-94.

[9] Consumer Products Safety Act, 15 U.S.C. §1193 (1988).

[10] Toxic Substances Control Act, 15 U.S.C. §2601 (1988).

[11] Fair Packaging and Labeling Act, 15 U.S.C. §1451 (1988).

[12] Controlled Substances Act, 21 U.S.C. §801 (1988).

[13] Federal Hazardous Substances Act, 15 U.S.C. §1261 (1988).

[14] The Tobacco Products Control Act, R.S. 1985, c. 14 (4th Supp.).

[15] Children's Television Act of 1990, P.L. 101-437, 104 Stat. 996 (Oct. 18, 1990).

[16] *Cipollone* v. *Liggett Group, Inc.*, 789 F.2d 181 (3d Cir. 1986), <u>cert. denied</u>,
479 U.S. 1043, 107 S.Ct. 907, 93 L.Ed. 2d 857 (1987).

[17] Excerpt from a letter from Representatives Whittaker and Luken urging
co-sponsorship of the Cigarette Testing and Liability Act, May 11, 1988.

APPENDIX A

NBC BROADCAST STANDARDS FOR TELEVISION

ADVERTISING STANDARDS

Clearance Procedures

While the ultimate responsibility for advertising rests with the advertiser, advertising agencies preparing commercial messages intended for broadcast on NBC facilities should consult the Broadcast Standards Department in advance of production. Such advance discussion enables the Broadcast Standards Department to provide initial guidance on questions that might arise under NBC standards.

For each commercial, advertising agencies are asked to submit shooting script or storyboard, a new product sample and label/package insert, substantiation for all material claims and authentication of all demonstrations and testimonial statements.

When the pre-production discussions have concluded, the agency produces the commercial and must submit the finished version for screening and final clearance.

NBC accepts advertising only after securing satisfactory evidence of the integrity of the advertiser, the availability of the product or service, the existence of support for the claims and the authentication of demonstrations, compliance with applicable laws and the acceptable taste of the presentation. Advertisers should deal affirmatively with the results expected from the use of the product or service, not dwell excessively on the results of failure to use the product or service.

I

Billboards

Billboards may be used as stipulated by NBC, provided they include no more than the identity of the program and the sponsor's name, product or service and a brief factual description of the general nature thereof. Only products, services or companies being advertised in the program may be billboarded. Any claims allowed must be supported. Billboards may not mention contests, offers, promotional teasers or cross-references to other programs.

Charitable Appeals

An advertiser may surrender commercial time to schedule an approved public service announcement or theme. Appeals within a commercial announcement will be considered on a case-by-case basis and will require submission of complete details of how the contributions will be handled. Clear sponsorship identification is required in these instances.

Comparative Advertising Guidelines

NBC will accept comparative advertising which identifies, directly or by implication, a competing product or service. As with all other advertising, each substantive claim, direct or implied, must be substantiated to NBC's satisfaction and the commercial must satisfy the following guidelines and standards for comparative advertising established by NBC:

1. Competitors shall be fairly and properly identified.

2. Advertisers shall refrain from disparaging or unfairly attacking competitors, competing products, services or other industries through the use of representations or claims, direct or implied, that are false, deceptive, misleading or have the tendency to mislead.

3. The identification must be for comparison purposes and not simply to upgrade by association.

4. The advertising should compare related or similar properties or ingredients of the product, dimension to dimension,

feature to feature, or wherever possible by a side-by-side demonstration.

5. The property being compared must be significant in terms of value or usefulness of the product or service to the consumer.

6. The difference in the properties being compared must be measurable and significant.

7. Pricing comparisons may raise special problems that could mislead, rather than enlighten, viewers. For certain classifications of products, retail prices may be extremely volatile, may be fixed by the retailer rather than the product advertiser, and may not only differ from outlet to outlet but from week to week within the same outlet. Where these circumstances might apply, NBC will accept commercials containing price comparisons only on a clear showing that the comparative claims accurately, fairly and substantially reflect the actual price differentials at retail outlets throughout the broadcast area, and that these price differentials are not likely to change during the period the commercial is broadcast.

8. When a commercial claim involves market relationships, other than price, which are also subject to fluctuation (such as, but not limited to, sales position or exclusivity), the substantiation for the claim will be considered valid only as long as the market conditions on which the claim is based continue to prevail.

9. As with all other advertising, whenever necessary, NBC may require substantiation to be updated from time to time, and may reexamine substantiation, where the need to do so is indicated as the result of a challenge or other developments.

Challenge Procedure

Where appropriate, NBC will implement the following procedures in the event a commercial is challenged by another advertiser.

1. If an advertiser elects to challenge the advertising of

another advertiser, he shall present his challenge and supporting data to NBC in a form available for transmittal to the challenged advertiser.

2. The challenged advertiser will then have an opportunity to respond directly to the challenger. NBC will maintain the confidentiality of the advertiser's original supporting data which was submitted for substantiation of the claims made in the commercial. However, NBC will ask the challenged advertiser to provide it with a copy of its response to the challenger and, where the response is submitted directly to NBC, the challenged advertiser will be requested to forward a copy of its response to the challenger.

3. Where NBC personnel do not have the expertise to make a judgment on technical issues raised by a challenge, NBC will take appropriate measures in its discretion to assist the advertiser and challenger to resolve their differences, including encouraging them to obtain a determination from an acceptable third party.

4. NBC will not withdraw a challenged advertisement from the broadcast schedule unless:

a. It is directed to do so by the incumbent advertiser.

b. The incumbent advertiser refuses to submit the controversy for review by some appropriate agency when deemed necessary by NBC.

c. A decision is rendered by NBC against the incumbent advertiser.

d. The challenged advertiser, when requested, refuses to cooperate in some other substantive area.

e. NBC, prior to final disposition of the challenge, determines that the substantiation for the advertising has been so seriously brought into question that the advertising can no longer be considered substantiated to NBC's satisfaction.

5. NBC may take additional measures in its discretion to resolve questions raised by advertising claims.

Dramatizations and Reenactments

Dramatized or reenacted events must be clearly disclosed as such and may be utilized only when based on an actual occurrence.

Government Action Regarding a Product or Service Being Advertised

In the event government action is proposed with respect to a product or service or claims being made for it (as for example, the issuance of a complaint or proposed rules by the FTC or the FDA), Broadcast Standards will determine whether the subject questioned is part of a current schedule on NBC's facilities. If so, the substantiation and the authentication originally furnished by the advertising agency in support of the commercial message will be reevaluated in light of the matter being questioned by such proposed government action.

The schedule will be maintained, if NBC is satisfied that either the advertising is acceptable under existing standards or that it presents a matter about which it would be inappropriate for NBC to make a judgment. This is done so that NBC action will not have the effect of adjudicating the question being considered by the governmental agency. A similar evaluation will be made of any proposed commercial message which involves subjects questioned by government action initiated prior to acceptance of the commercial for broadcast by NBC. If the governmental agency finally resolves the issue against the advertiser, NBC will withdraw its schedule.

Cross References in Advertising

References by advertisers within their commercial time to another program they are sponsoring are permitted provided that the references do not identify a competing facility, the day, or hour of the program. Statements urging the viewer to check television listings for such information are permissible.

Advertisers may not refer to other programs scheduled at a

later hour on the same day on a competing facility.

Guarantee and Warranty Offers

Whenever the terms "guarantee," "warranty" or similar words that constitute a promise or representation in the nature of a guarantee or warranty appear in a television advertisement, certain additional information concerning material terms and conditions of such a guarantee or warranty offer must be clearly and unambiguously disclosed to the viewer.

In general, any commercial announcement in which a guarantee/warranty is mentioned should also disclose:

a. The nature and extent of the guarantee.

b. The identity of the guarantor.

c. The manner in which the guarantor intends to perform.

d. Information concerning what a purchaser wishing to claim under the guarantee need do before the guarantor will perform pursuant to its obligations under the guarantee.

e. Where applicable, whether a warranty is full or limited.

This disclosure must be made so it will not be misunderstood by the typical viewer. Simultaneous disclosure in both the audio and video often proves to be the best and most certain method of achieving full, clear and effective disclosure. However, a commercial announcement using only audio may constitute clear and conspicuous disclosure because of the clarity and completeness of the representation and the non-distracting manner of presentation. Video disclosure alone may not necessarily satisfy the above criteria.

Placement and Scheduling

NBC reserves the right to determine the scheduling, format and length of commercial breaks during and adjacent to programs carried over its facilities and the acceptability, number and placement of commercials, promotions and other announcements within such breaks, including those involving cast or celebrities.

In-program advertisements must be placed within the

framework of the sponsored program. The program must be announced and clearly identified before the first commercial placement and terminated after the last commercial placement.

Research or Surveys

Reference may be made to the results of bona fide surveys or research relating to the product advertised, provided the results do not create an impression the research does not support.

Sound Level

The sound level of commercials should not appear to exceed that of the surrounding program.

Sponsor Identification

Identification of sponsorship shall be made in all commercials and programs in accordance with the requirements of the Communications Act, the rules and policies of the Federal Communications Commission and with the NBC Compliance and Practices Manual.

Time Standards for Advertising

In order to maintain the quality, audience appeal and integrity of programs presented on the NBC Television Network, NBC shall apply the following Standards to the amount, format and scheduling of non-program material.

1. Definition of Non-Program Material

Non-program material includes commercials; station breaks; promotional announcements; sponsor billboards; announcements that must be logged as commercial matter pursuant to FCC regulations and the NBC Compliance and Practices Manual; and show credits which exceed the allocations specified on pages 10 of the General Entertainment Program Standards.

The following shall not be considered non-program material:

a. Public service announcements.

b. Paid political announcements not in excess of four minutes per hour during a limited number of broadcast hours.

c. Credits for theatrical films, opening program titles, episode titles, starring and co-starring credits.

d. Audio or "voice over" promotional announcements which are presented simultaneously over show credits and do not exceed 30 seconds in length.

e. Announcements regarding the scheduling of special news programs.

f. Scheduling information contained in programs of indeterminate length regarding an immediately upcoming program whose regular broadcast time has been affected.

g. Certain prize-related announcements broadcast as part of a game, contest or award program or program element.

1. Station call letter and network identification.

2. Time Limitations for Non-Program Material

a. Prime time:

For purposes of these Non-Program Material Time Limitation standards, Prime Time is defined as a consecutive three hour period designated by NBC between the hours of 6:00 p.m. and 11:00 p.m.

Non-program material in Prime Time entertainment programs will not exceed 10 minutes per hour.

Non-program material in Prime Time sports programs shall not exceed 16 minutes per hour.

b. All other time periods:

Non-program material in programs not scheduled during Prime Time shall not exceed 16 minutes per hour.

c. Special promotional material:

NBC may, in its discretion, from time to time vary the Prime Time and Other Time Periods Standards to accommodate promotional material for special programming.

d. Children's programs:

For purposes of these Standards, children's programming is defined as those programs initially designed primarily for children 12 years of age and under.

Notwithstanding the Non-Program Material Time Limitations set forth in a and b above, in no event shall the "commercial matter" (any advertising message or announcement for which a charge is made or consideration reached) in children's programs exceed:

(1) 9½ minutes per hour during weekend and Prime Time children's programs and

(2) 12 minutes per hour during weekday, non-Prime Time children's programs.

Fractional periods of less than one hour will be pro-rated on the basis of one hour.

3. Unit of Sale

The NBC Television Network makes sponsorship opportunities available in units of not less than 30 seconds in length for the advertising of a sponsor's product or service (except for advertisements placed in "news capsules").

4. Multiple Product Advertisements

The NBC Television Network will not accept a single commercial which advertises more than one product or service unless:

a. The participation purchased is at least 60 seconds in length and contains no more than two announcements.

b. The commercial presents the products or services of a single advertiser which have a related or common purpose and use, and such products or services are portrayed in a unified and integrated manner and setting.

c. The commercial is less than 60 seconds in length, but presents the products or services of a primary and secondary advertiser. The time devoted to the product or service of the secondary advertiser may not exceed one-sixth of the total time of the commercial.

Visual Supers

When superimposed copy is essential to qualify claims, it must be presented so it can be read easily against a plain, contrasting background, held sufficiently long and be large enough to meet NBC technical specifications (available on request).

Unacceptable Commercial Presentations, Approaches and Techniques

NBC does not accept in advertising:

1. Claims or representations, direct or implied, which are false or have the tendency to deceive, mislead or misrepresent.

2. Unqualified references to the safety of a product, if package, label or insert contains a caution or the normal use of the product presents a possible hazard.

3. Appeals to help fictitious characters in supposed distress by purchasing a product or service or sending for a premium.

4. "Bait and switch" tactics which feature goods or services not intended for sale but designed to lure the public into purchasing higher priced substitutes.

5. The use of "subliminal perception" or other techniques attempting to convey information to viewer by transmitting messages below the threshold of normal awareness.

6. Unacceptable products or services promoted through advertising devoted to an acceptable product.

7. The misuse of distress signals.

8. Disrespectful use of the flag, national emblems, anthems and monuments.

9. Direct or implied use of the office of the President of the United States or any governmental body without official approval.

10. Newsroom settings and techniques.

11. Sensational headline announcements in advertising of publications prior to the identification of sponsor.

12. Scare approaches and presentations with the capacity to induce fear.

13. Interpersonal acts of violence and antisocial behavior or

other dramatic devices inconsistent with prevailing standards of taste and propriety.

14. Damaging stereotyping.

15. Unsupported or exaggerated promises of employment or earnings.

16. Presentations for professional services which do not comply with applicable law or ethical codes.

Unacceptable Commercial Classifications

1. Cigarettes.

2. Hard liquor.

3. Firearms, fireworks, ammunition and other weapons.

4. Presentations promoting a belief in the efficacy of fortune telling, astrology, phrenology, palm reading, numerology, mind reading, character reading or other occult pursuits.

5. Tip sheets and race track publications seeking to advertise for the purpose of promoting illegal betting. (See Lotteries.)

6. The sale of franchises.

7. Matrimonial, escort or dating services.

8. Contraceptives.

9. "Adult" or sex magazines.

10. X-rated movies.

11. Abortion services.

12. Ethical drugs.

13. Anti-law-enforcement devices.

Advertising Contests

Any advertiser-supplied contest furnished to NBC for proposed broadcast must be initially reviewed to insure that it is not a lottery, that the material terms are clearly stated, and that it is being conducted fairly, honestly and according to its rules.

1. Contest information is further reviewed to make certain that:

a. The security arrangements are adequate to prevent

"rigging."

b. The terms, conditions and requirements under which contestants compete for prizes are clearly stated in the "Rules" so that there is no reasonable opportunity for any misunderstanding.

c. The value, nature and extent of the prizes are clear.

d. The public interest will not be adversely affected.

e. The contest meets with federal, state and local laws.

2. Complete details and continuity must be submitted to the Broadcast Standards Department at least ten business days prior to the first public announcement of the contest.

3. All broadcast copy regarding contests must contain clear and complete information regarding:

a. Complete contest rules or when and how they may be obtained by the public.

b. The availability of entry forms and how to enter, including alternate means of entry where appropriate.

c. The termination date of the contest.

d. Any restrictions or eligibility requirements.

e. The prize suppliers, when applicable.

f. For chance contests, the necessary language: No Purchase Necessary Void Where Prohibited

g. For skill contests, judging criteria must be stated.

4. A complete copy of the rules, the entry blank, a completed NBC Compliance and Practices Questionnaire, promotional material and/or any published information (e.g., newspaper advertisements) about the contest should be included with the broadcast copy.

5. All contest rules must be complete and contain:

a. Eligibility requirements.

b. Restrictions as to the number of entries made by an individual.

c. The nature, extent and value of the prizes.

d. Where, when and how entries are submitted.

e. The basis on which prizes will be awarded.

f. The termination date of the contest.

g. When and how winners will be selected, including tie breaking procedures, when necessary.

h. How winners will be notified.

i. Time limits to claim or use prizes, if any.

j. Restrictions as to the number of times an individual can win.

k. Reference to "participating dealers" if not all outlets are involved.

Beer and Wine

Advertising of beer and wine is acceptable subject to federal, state and local laws and the requirements of the NBC Alcohol Products Advertising Guidelines.

Children

1. Commercial messages placed within children's programs or in station breaks between consecutive programs designed specifically for children, advertising of products designed primarily for children and advertising or other messages designed primarily for children are subject to all applicable provisions of NBC'S Children's Advertising Guidelines.

2. Within programs designed primarily for children 12 years of age or under, appropriate separator devices shall be used to clearly delineate the program material from commercial material.

3. Advertising concerning health and related matters which are more appropriately the responsibility of physicians and other adults shall not be primarily directed to children.

4. Commercial messages shall not be presented by a children's program personality, host or character, whether live or animated, within or adjacent to the programs in which such personality, host or character regularly appears.

5. Taking into account the age of the actors appearing within a commercial as well as the composition of the audience it

is likely to reach, advertising approaches and techniques shall not disregard accepted safety precautions.

Door-to-Door Sales Representatives and In-Home Selling

All such advertising must be in accordance with applicable federal, state and local laws and shall be reviewed with special care. The reputation and reliability of the sponsor and the supervision exercised by the advertiser over its sales representatives, are important considerations. Each proposed commercial is evaluated on a case-by-case basis to insure its acceptability.

In general, advertising recruiting door-to-door representatives primarily for the sale of medical products and services having direct health considerations is not acceptable.

Employment Agencies

Reputable concerns are considered on a case-by-case basis and subject to exercise of care in order to avoid over-promising results.

Funeral Homes

The advertising of funeral services and mortuaries requires restrained presentation.

Health-Related Product Advertising

All advertisements for health-related products shall comply with the NBC Health Care Products Advertising Guidelines.

1. Ethical Drugs

NBC does not accept advertising for ethical drugs. Institutional advertising for pharmaceutical manufacturers, industry associations, and other responsible sponsors is considered on a case-by-case basis.

2. Proprietary Products (Over-the-Counter Medications)

The advertising of proprietary products presents important

considerations to the health of consumers. The following principles and procedures govern the acceptability of such advertising on NBC facilities:

a. The advertiser must give assurance that the advertising for the proprietary product complies with all applicable governmental rules and regulations.

b. Advertising for proprietary products is accepted only after relevant data, including adequate substantiation regarding both product efficacy and any particular claims asserted, have been submitted to Broadcast Standards for examination and appraisal.

c. NBC does not accept advertising for products used in the treatment of conditions known to be chronic or irremediable or for conditions in which self-diagnosis or self-medication might present an element of danger unless:

(1) They can be self-administered without the order and supervision of a physician.

(2) They carry on their labels the cautions required by the Federal Food, Drug and Cosmetic Act of 1939.

(3) Appropriate cautionary references are included in the advertising proposed for broadcast.

d. No claims must be made or implied that the product is a panacea or alone will effect a cure.

e. Words such as "safe," "without risk," "harmless," or terms of similar meaning may not be used in an unqualified manner.

f. Advertising appeals may not be made to children for such products.

3. Statements from the Medical Profession

Physicians, dentists or nurses, or actors representing them, may not be employed directly or by implication in any commercial for proprietary products or other products involving health considerations. Advertisements of an institutional nature which are not intended to sell specific products or services to the consumer, public service announcements by non-profit organizations, as well as presentations for professional services, may be presented by physicians, dentists or nurses, subject to prior approval by Broadcast Standards.

Investments

Advertising of the services of financial institutions must be consistent with all applicable federal, state and local laws and regulations. The mention of specific securities in commercials requires the prior approval of the Law as well as Broadcast Standards Department.

Legalized Lotteries and Gambling

The lawful advertising of government organizations that conduct legalized lotteries is acceptable provided such advertising does not unduly exhort the public to bet.

The advertising of private or governmental organizations that conduct legalized betting on sporting contests is acceptable provided it does not unduly exhort the audience to bet.

Acceptable advertisements for legalized lotteries or betting shall comply with the NBC Guidelines on Gambling, Betting, Lotteries and Games of Chance.

"Personal" Products

Advertising for "personal" products, when accepted, must be presented in a restrained and tasteful manner and comply with the NBC Personal Products Advertising Guidelines.

Premiums and Offers

1. Full details and continuity including "build-up copy," and a sample of the premium or offer, must be submitted to Broadcast Standards well in advance of commitment.

2. The termination date of any offer should be announced as far in advance as possible. Such announcement will include the statement that responses postmarked not later than midnight of the business day following withdrawal of the offer shall be

honored.

3. All audience responses to premiums, offers or contests made by advertisers must be sent to a stated Post Office box or to an outside address arranged for by the advertiser.

4. As to the premium merchandise offered:

a. A premium or offer may not be harmful to person or property.

b. The lesser of one half the total time or 20 seconds in a self-contained portion of any commercial message may deal with the premium scheduled in a children's program. Such premiums and offers will be subject to all other applicable premium and toy advertising requirements of the NBC Children's Advertising Guidelines.

c. Descriptions or visual representations of premiums or offers may not enlarge their value or otherwise be misleading.

d. The advertiser must provide NBC with written assurance that it will honor any request for return of money based on dissatisfaction with premiums or offers and that a sufficient supply of the premium or offer is readily available so as to avoid audience ill-will caused by delivery delay or impossibility of delivery.

5. The advertiser will hold NBC and its affiliated stations harmless from any liability which may arise in connection with any premium or offer.

6. The premium or offer may not appeal to superstition on the basis of "luck-bearing" powers or otherwise.

7. Mail order offers should indicate any additional postage/handling charges, as well as expected delivery time.

Testimonials

The following seven point provision constitutes NBC policy relating to testimonials included in advertising of products, services or organizations.

1. Testimonials used, in whole or in part, must honestly reflect in spirit and content the sentiments of the individuals

represented.

2. All claims and statements in a testimonial, including subjective evaluations of testifiers, must be supportable by facts and free of misleading implication. They shall contain no statement that cannot be supported if presented in the advertiser's own words.

3. Advertisers are required to disclose any connection between the advertiser and the endorser that might materially affect the weight or credibility of the endorsement.

4. In the event a consumer endorsement does not fairly reflect what a substantial proportion of other consumers are likely to experience, the advertising must clearly disclose this fact.

5. Expert endorsements are permitted only as long as the endorser continues to hold those views.

6. The laws of certain states require written consent of individuals for the use of their names. The advertiser must submit to NBC, in writing, confirmation of such consent or a blanket release assuming full responsibility for obtaining such consent for each testimonial covering its period of use on NBC facilities.

7. NBC staff employees may not give personal testimonials.

Public Service Announcements

The following guidelines are designed to assure that public service announcement time on NBC is used as effectively as possible.

1. All public service announcements proposed for network use apply to a nationwide audience.

2. The sponsoring organization must be national and devoted to public service or charitable activities. Announcements must pertain solely to public service or charitable causes and may not promote directly or indirectly the sale of commercial products or services or deal with sectarian, politically partisan or controversial subjects or issues, nor be designed to influence legislation or other government action.

3. Public service time for fund or membership solicitation is given only to demonstrably responsible organizations. In assessing the qualifications of sponsoring organizations, NBC may consult the Advertising Council, the National Information Bureau or comparable agencies for their evaluations and recommendations.

4. Public service announcements must deal affirmatively with the causes they advocate. Announcements that attack or demean other persons, organizations or causes are not acceptable.

5. The final judgment concerning acceptability and scheduling of public service messages rests solely with NBC.

6. All appeals and solicitations for charities and other non-profit organizations on NBC television facilities must have prior approval of the Broadcast Standards Department.

GLOSSARY

Advertising Terms

Body copy: The text copy in an advertisement other that the headline.

Comparative advertising: An advertisement or campaign that compares the advertiser's product or service to that of a competitor either by name, implication, or reputation.

Comprehensive layout: A rough depiction of an advertisement to show basic placement of elements. Used to represent what the final advertisement will look before it is produced.

Deceptive advertising: Advertising that, in any way, creates a false, misleading, or deceptive message within the mind of the average consumer to which the ad was directed.

Endorsement: A claim, either implied or express, by a person or entity of significant standing, image or reputation in support of an advertiser, his product or service.

Freelancer: An independent contractor. A person who is not an employee of either the principal or agency, but sells his work or services to various parties on a project basis.

Genericide: The term used to describe a situation where a trademark is allowed to be used improperly so that the mark looses its status as an mark (which is owned) and therefore becomes a generic item.

Good will: The value of a business in patronage and reputation above and beyond its tangible assets.

Look-alikes: One person who bears a strong resemblance to another. Usually used in the context of a person who looks very much like a specific celebrity. The look-alike is used (as if he were the actual celebrity) in advertising to enhance the advertiser's image and promote a product or service.

Marks: A trade mark or service mark. The physical combination of symbols and words which make up the trademark.

Palming-off: The practice of creating the false impression that the advertiser's product is actually made by a manufacturer of greater reputation, thereby trading on another's image and status.

Puffery: Exaggerated sales talk or boasting by an advertiser about the quality of his product or service. Puffery claims have no material way of being proven or disproven.

Qualifying language: Language used in an advertisement to clarify or offset another claim in the same ad which would otherwise be deceptive if taken on its own merit. Qualifying language must have the same weight and visibility as the otherwise deceptive statement.

Royalties: The share of the proceeds from his work, usually a specified percentage, paid to an author or artist.

Service marks: A trademark used in connection with a business that sells a service, as opposed to a product to which a trademark can be affixed. See also: trademark.

Small print: Also called a disclaimer: Small type used to clarify a previously mentioned point within an advertisement.

Storyboard: A depiction, in drawn form, of what a final television commercial will look like. Usually drawn scene-by-scene to depict the sequence of the final commercial.

Testimonial: A statement testifying to a person's or company's qualifications, abilities, and character or to the value of some product or service.

Trade secret: A proprietary fact, process or item of knowledge gained through a working relationship with a company that would not be commonly know to the public.

Trademark: A mark used in connection with a product or service to which value attaches, and which is owned by the company as a property right.

Voice-Over: The narrated voice portion of a television or radio commercial.

Legal Terms

Actual damages: Compensation for actual injury or loss suffered by the plaintiff.

Bailment: A delivery of goods or personal property for the execution of a contract, usually for the benefit of both the bailor (one who delivers) and the bailee (one who receives). Example: Bailor parks her car in a parking garage. Bailee provides parking space.

Basis of bargain: That on which any affirmation of fact or promise relating to goods sold is based, creating an express warranty.

Breach of contract: Failure without legal excuse to perform a promise which forms the whole of part of a contract.

Breach of warranty: Failure without legal excuse to meet the obligations created by the representations or promises made contemporaneously with a sale.

Cease and desist order: An order of an administrative agency or court prohibiting a course of conduct from continuing.

Class actions: A legal action by or on behalf of a large group of persons who are similarly interested in the matter. Available in federal and most state courts. Usually, the number of plaintiffs must be so numerous that it would not be practical or possible to bring separate suits. Also called "representative action."

Common law: The body of law that comes from the decrees of courts and hence the customs of the people, as opposed to laws created by state legislatures or the Congress in the form of a statute.

Compensatory damages: An award in an amount sufficient to compensate for the injury sustained and no more.

Consent: Voluntary agreement by a person with sufficient mental and legal capacity who is not acting on the basis of fraud or under duress.

Consideration: A giving over of a sum, right, interest, or benefit in return for the promise of another in creating a contract. Consideration may also be a promise or forbearance, detriment, or loss again given up as part of the contractual agreement.

Contract: An agreement by which the parties promise to do or not to do that which is the basis of the contract.
Lit. I promise to do this if you promise to do that.

Damages: Financial compensation which may be recovered through the courts by a plaintiff who has suffered loss, detriment or injury as a result of the unlawful act, omission, or negligence of the defendant.

Foreseeability: Reasonable anticipation that an act or failure to act may result in injury or harm.

Fraudulent concealment: The deliberate failure to reveal a material fact with the intent to defraud.

Injunction: A court order issued at the request of one party to an action against another party in that action to refrain from an act. May be temporary pending the outcome of the action, or may be made permanent as a part of the decision of the court.

Jurisdiction: The legal right by which courts exercise their authority over parties and subject matter. May also literally refer to the physical location or boundaries where the courts or law enforcement agencies may exercise their authority.

Liability: Legal responsibility for the consequences of an action or inaction which may give rise to the award of damages to an injured party.

Merchantability (fitness for a particular purpose): In sales context that the article sold is fit for the purpose it is sold when used in the ordinary way normally to be expected.

Monetary damages: Also can be called pecuniary damages. Those damages that can be calculated and compensated by an award of the court in the form of the payment of money.

Prior restraint: The concept that under the First Amendment to the United States Constitution a publication cannot be prohibited unless extreme circumstances require. The corollary concept is that if anyone is harmed or defamed by the publication, that party is free to pursue damages in a libel action after the fact.

Products liability: The concept that manufacturers are responsible for the goods they produce when defects in those products cause injury to the purchaser or user.

Public domain: The status of publications, products or processes that are not protected under patent or copyright and hence belong to the public rather than the creator, writer, inventor, or developer.

Punitive damages: Also called exemplary damages. An amount awarded by the court over and above the damages required to make an injured party whole where the injury was caused by particular malice, fraud, or deliberate conduct on the part of the party at fault. These damages are intended to punish the party at fault, comfort the injured party, and set an example to society as a whole in an effort to deter future similar acts.

Quantum meruit: The concept that no one should benefit unjustly from the labor of others under which a court will award a reasonable amount under an implied contract.

Reasonable man: An imaginary individual used by the court to determine if an injured party's conduct or expectations were that of the average person in similar circumstances. The standard one must have in mind to avoid liability for negligence.

Recision: In contract law the right to cancel a contract when a certain kind of default by the other party occurs. Note: Not every default creates a right to rescind the contract.

Regulation: A set of rules set out by an agency of either a state or the federal government, i.e. a department, at the direction of the legislative body in the form of a statute.

Remedies: The recourse available an injured party either by contract or by order of a court to rectify a wrong or injury whether by an award of money or an order to do or not to do something.

Restrictive covenants: Agreements to refrain from doing something specified in the agreement. May be used in deeds, but for purposes of this book refers to employment contracts where an employee promises not to compete with the employer, in the event the employment is terminated, for a certain period of time within a certain geographic area. A restrictive covenant will only be enforced by the courts if it is reasonable.

Sole liability clauses: In a principal/agency relationship, a provision in a contract with a third party where the agent assumes full liability for any breach of the contract. Specifically, in advertising, sole liability clauses are commonly found in media contracts entered into between the media and the agent whereby the agent agrees to be fully liable for the debts incurred on behalf of the principal.

Specific performance: A provision in a contract or an order by a court that money damages will not suffice to compensate an individual for losses incurred as a result of the breach of a contract. In these cases, the breaching party must actually perform the promise made in the contract.

Standing: The concept that a party has sufficient stake in a matter to take it to court. Lit. Standing to sue.

Statutes: An act of a state legislature or the federal Congress that creates a law requiring or prohibiting certain actions by citizens.

Strict liability in tort: The concept that everyone involved in the manufacture and sale of a product is liable for any injury received by a consumer as a result of a defective product that is expected to and does reach the user without substantial change after manufacture or assembly.

Warranty: A statement or representation made by a seller of goods, contemporaneously with and as a part of the contract of sale having reference to the character, quality, or title of goods and by which the seller promises to insure that certain facts are or shall be as they are represented.

BIBLIOGRAPHY

Cone, Fairfax M. *With All Its Faults.* Boston: Little, Brown & Company, 1969.

Cooke, Alistair. *America.* New York: Alfred A. Knopf, 1973.

Della Femina, Jerry. *From Those Wonderful Folks Who Gave You Pearl Harbor.* New York: Simon & Schuster, 1970.

Fox, Stephen. *The Mirror Makers.* New York: Vintage Books, Random House, 1984.

Hernon, Peter, and Terry Ganey. *Under The Influence.* New York: Avon Books, 1991.

Kotler, Philip. *Principles of Marketing.* Englewood Cliffs, N.J.: Prentice-Hall, 1980.

Nash, Jay Robert. *Hustlers and Con Men.* New York: M. Evans & Co., 1976.

Nayak, P Ranganath, and John Ketteringham. *Breakthroughs!* New York: Rawson Associates, 1986.

Preston, Ivan L. *The Great American Blow-Up: Puffery in Advertising and Selling.* University of Wisconsin Press, 1975.

Pritikin, Robert C. *Christ Was an Adman.* San Francisco: Harbor Publishing, 1980.

Rembar, Charles. *The Law of the Land.* New York: Touchstone, 1980.

Ries, Al, and Jack Trout. *Positioning: The Battle for Your Mind.* New York: McGraw-Hill, 1986.

Rosden, George, and Peter Rosden. *The Law of Advertising.* New York: Mathew Bender, 1978.

Wakeman, Frederic. *The Hucksters.* New York: Buccaneer Books, 1993.

INDEX OF CASES

A

B

Z

INDEX

A

B

D

G

L

N

O

P

S

T

U